Lecture Notes in Computer Science 11226

Commenced Publication in 1973
Founding and Former Series Editors:
Gerhard Goos, Juris Hartmanis, and Jan van Leeuwen

More information about this series at http://www.springer.com/series/7409

Yang Xiang · Jingtao Sun
Giancarlo Fortino · Antonio Guerrieri
Jason J. Jung (Eds.)

Internet and Distributed Computing Systems

11th International Conference, IDCS 2018
Tokyo, Japan, October 11–13, 2018
Proceedings

 Springer

Editors
Yang Xiang
Swinburne University of Technology
Hawthorn, VIC, Australia

Antonio Guerrieri
ICAR-CNR
Rende (CS), Italy

Jingtao Sun
National Institute of Informatics
Tokyo, Japan

Jason J. Jung
Chung-Ang University
Seoul, Republic of Korea

Giancarlo Fortino
University of Calabria
Rende (CS), Italy

ISSN 0302-9743 ISSN 1611-3349 (electronic)
Lecture Notes in Computer Science
ISBN 978-3-030-02737-7 ISBN 978-3-030-02738-4 (eBook)
https://doi.org/10.1007/978-3-030-02738-4

Library of Congress Control Number: 2018950190

LNCS Sublibrary: SL3 – Information Systems and Applications, incl. Internet/Web, and HCI

This Springer imprint is published by the registered company Springer Nature Switzerland AG
The registered company address is: Gewerbestrasse 11, 6330 Cham, Switzerland

Preface

Following the previous ten successful editions of IDCS – IDCS 2008 in Khulna, Bangladesh, IDCS 2009 in Jeju Island, Korea, IDCS 2010 and IDCS 2011 in Melbourne, Australia, IDCS 2012 in Wu Yi Shan, China, IDCS 2013 in Hangzhou, China, IDCS 2014 in Calabria, Italy, IDCS 2015 in Windsor, UK, IDCS 2016 in Wuhan, China, IDCS 2017 in Fiji — IDCS 2018 was the 11th in the series to promote research in diverse fields related to the Internet and distributed computing systems.

Modern systems such as distributed systems, cloud computing, mobile computing, edge computing, fog computing, and cyber-physical systems have a tendency toward complexity, elasticity, dependability, and security especially when dealing with dynamic events or actions in their environments and/or Internet applications. We not only need to keep those systems running normally, but also need them to be self-adaptive to many changes. On the other hand, the development of the Internet is very rapid, and it has already entered the 5G era. The Internet as a society infrastructure and the widespread use of mobile edge, wireless wearable devices, or IoT sensors have laid the foundation for the emergence of innovative network applications and transportation and logistics. Under the influence of these most advanced technologies, human production and life are gradually changing. The academic and industrial worlds are constantly developing and innovating in areas such as mechanical learning, artificial intelligence, and media stream processing. These technologies enrich and improve not only the quality of life of modern people, but also the process of integration in many fields, the huge amount of data processing, and the integration of the digital world with the physical environment; they also contribute toward constructive development in biological, agricultural, and policy.

IDCS 2018 received papers on emerging models, paradigms, technologies, and novel applications related to cloud computing, distributed systems, Internet of Things, cyber-physical systems, wireless sensor networks, next-generation collaborative systems, extreme-scale networked systems, and self-adaptive systems.

The audience included researchers and industry practitioners who were interested in different aspects of the Internet and distributed systems, with a particular focus on practical experiences with the design and implementation of related technologies as well as their theoretical perspectives.

IDCS 2018 received a large number of submissions from which 23 regular papers were accepted after a careful review and selection process. This year's conference also featured four invited talks: (1) "Inter-Cloud Computing over Academic and Public Clouds" from Associate Professor Atsuko Takefusa, National Institute of Informatics and The Graduate University for Advanced Studies, Tokyo, Japan; (2) "Interconnecting the Edge with Software-Defined Overlay Virtual Private Networks" from Professor Renato J. Figueiredo, University of Florida, USA; (3) "Towards Opportunistic IoT Services: A Novel Paradigm for Engineering the Next-Generation IoT Systems" from Professor Giancarlo Fortino, University of Calabria, Italy; and (4) "Simultaneous

Scheduling of Routes for On-Demand Bus and Walking Passengers" from Associate Professor Naoki Shibata, Nara Institute of Science and Technology, Japan.

IDCS 2018 was held in the wonderful Hitotsubashi Hall, National Center of Sciences Building, in the center of Tokyo, Japan. The conference organization was supported by the National Institute of Informatics (Japan), Swinburne University of Technology (Australia), Western Sydney University (Australia), and the University of Calabria (Italy).

The successful organization of IDCS 2018 was possible thanks to the dedication and hard work of a number of individuals.

Specifically, we would like to thank our program chairs, Bahman Javadi (Western Sydney University, Australia), Giuseppe Di Fatta (University of Reading, UK), Lei Zhong (Toyota InfoTechnology Center, Japan), Sisi Duan (University of Maryland, Baltimore County, USA), and Markus Ullrich (University of Applied Sciences Zittau/Görlitz, Germany), our publicity and industry chairs, Antonio Guerrieri (ICAR-CNR, Italy), Mukaddim Pathan (Telstra, Australia), and Qiang Wang (Wuhan University of Technology, China), and our Web chair, Mingkang Chen (Central China Normal University, China), for their commendable work with the conference organization. We also express our gratitude to the general chair, Yang Xiang (Swinburne University of Technology, Australia), and the conference co-chairs, Jingtao Sun (National Institute of Informatics, Japan), Giancarlo Fortino (University of Calabria, Italy), and Jason J. Jung (Chung-Ang University, South Korea), for their supports of the conference.

October 2018

Yang Xiang
Jingtao Sun
Giancarlo Fortino
Antonio Guerrieri
Jason J. Jung

Organization

General Chair

Yang Xiang   Swinburne University of Technology, Australia

Co-chairs

Jingtao Sun   National Institute of Informatics, Japan
Giancarlo Fortino   University of Calabria, Italy
Jason J. Jung   Chung-Ang University, South Korea

Program Chairs

Bahman Javadi   Western Sydney University, Australia
Giuseppe Di Fatta   University of Reading, UK
Lei Zhong   Toyota InfoTechnology Center, Japan
Sisi Duan   University of Maryland, Baltimore County, USA
Markus Ullrich   University of Applied Sciences Zittau/Görlitz, Germany

PhD Workshop Chair

Kazushige Saga   National Institute of Informatics, Japan

Publicity and Industry Chairs

Antonio Guerrieri   ICAR-CNR, Italy
Mukaddim Pathan   Telstra, Australia
Qiang Wang   Wuhan University of Technology, China

Web Chair

Mingkang Chen   Central China Normal University, China

Steering Committee - IDCS Series

Jemal Abawajy   Deakin University, Australia
Rajkumar Buyya   University of Melbourne, Australia
Giancarlo Fortino   University of Calabria, Italy
Dimitrios   RMIT University, Australia
   Georgakopolous
Mukaddim Pathan   Telstra, Australia
Yang Xiang   Swinburne University, Australia

Program Committee

Abdelkarim Erradi	Qatar University, Qatar
Andrea Omicini	Università di Bologna, Italy
Andrea Vinci	ICAR-CNR, Italy
Antonio Guerrieri	ICAR-CNR, Italy
Antonio Liotta	University of Derby, UK
Bahman Javadi	Western Sydney University, Australia
Bin Guo	Institut Telecom SudParis, France
Carlo Mastroianni	ICAR-CNR, Italy
Claudio De Farias	PPGI-IM/NCE-UFRJ, Brazil
Claudio Savaglio	University of Calabria, Italy
Dimitrios Katsaros	University of Thessaly, Greece
George Pallis	University of Cyprus, Cyprus
Giancarlo Fortino	University of Calabria, Italy
Gianluca Aloi	University of Calabria, Italy
Giorgio Terracina	University of Calabria, Italy
Giuseppe Di Fatta	University of Reading, UK
Hu Xiaoya	Huazhong University of Science and Technology, China
Jason Jung	Chung-Ang University, South Korea
Jie Mei	Wuhan University of Technology, China
Lei Zhong	Toyota InfoTechnology Center, Japan
Marcin Paprzycki	IBS PAN and WSM, Poland
Markus Ullrich	University of Applied Sciences Zittau/Görlitz, Germany
Mengchu Zhou	New Jersey Institute of Technology, USA
Mukaddim Pathan	Telstra Corporation Limited, Australia
Norihiko Yoshida	Saitama University, Japan
Paolo Trunfio	University of Calabria, Italy
Pasquale Pace	University of Calabria, Italy
Raffaele Gravina	University of Calabria, Italy
Ragib Hasan	University of Alabama at Birmingham, USA
Riaz Ahmed Shaikh	King Abdul Aziz University, Saudi Arabia
Ruppa Thulasiram	University of Manitoba, Canada
Sergio Ochoa	University of Chile, Chile
Sisi Duan	University of Maryland Baltimore County, USA
Sun Jingtao	National Institute of Informatics, Japan
Valeria Loscri	Inria, France
Wenfeng Li	Wuhan University of Technology, China
Xinqing Yan	NCWU, China
Xiuwen Fu	Shanghai Maritime University, China
Yang Xiang	Swinburne University of Technology, Australia
Jingjing Cao	Wuhan Technology University, China
Bui Khac Hoai Nam	Chung-Ang University, South Korea
Zhengxue Cheng	Waseda University, Japan

Contents

Implementation of Self-adaptive Middleware for Mobile Vehicle Tracking
Applications on Edge Computing 1
   Jingtao Sun, Cheng Yang, Tomoya Tanjo, Kazushige Sage,
   and Kento Aida

Towards the Succinct Representation of m Out of n 16
   Victor Parque and Tomoyuki Miyashita

Extending the Advisor Concept to Deal with Known-Ahead
Transportation Tasks 27
   Nick Nygren and Jörg Denzinger

A Framework for Task-Guided Virtual Machine Live Migration 40
   Cho-Chin Lin and Yuan-Han Kuo

Verifiable Privacy-Preserving Payment Mechanism for Smart Grids......... 52
   Chun-I Fan, Yi-Fan Tseng, Jheng-Jia Huang, Yen-Hao Chen,
   and Hsin-Nan Kuo

Increasing Interoperability Between Heterogeneous Smart
City Applications 64
   Alexander Rech, Markus Pistauer, and Christian Steger

Reduced Transmission in Multi-server Coded Caching................. 75
   Minquan Cheng, Qiaoling Zhang, Jing Jiang, and Ruizhong Wei

Distributed Sensor Fusion for Activity Detection in Smart Buildings....... 87
   C. Papatsimpa and J. P. M. G. Linnartz

Climbing Ranking Position via Long-Distance Backlinks 100
   V. Carchiolo, M. Grassia, A. Longheu, M. Malgeri, and G. Mangioni

Financial Application on an Openstack Based Private Cloud............. 109
   Deepak Bajpai, Muskan Vinayak, Ruppa K. Thulasiram,
   and Parimala Thulasiraman

Towards Island Networks: SDN-Enabled Virtual Private Networks
with Peer-to-Peer Overlay Links for Edge Computing 122
   Kensworth Subratie and Renato Figueiredo

Almost-Fully Secured Fully Dynamic Group Signatures with Efficient
Verifier-Local Revocation and Time-Bound Keys 134
   Maharage Nisansala Sevwandi Perera and Takeshi Koshiba

Path Planning for Multi-robot Systems in Intelligent Warehouse   148
  Hailong Chen, Qiang Wang, Meng Yu, Jingjing Cao, and Jingtao Sun

Dynamic Framework for Reconfiguring Computing Resources
in the Inter-cloud and Its Application to Genome Analysis Workflows.   160
  *Tomoya Tanjo, Jingtao Sun, Kazushige Saga, Atsuko Takefusa,
  and Kento Aida*

Game-Theoretic Approach to Self-stabilizing Minimal Independent
Dominating Sets   173
  Li-Hsing Yen and Guang-Hong Sun

Towards Social Signal Separation Based on Reconstruction Independent
Component Analysis   185
  *Hoang Long Nguyen, Khac-Hoai Nam Bui, Nayoung Jo, Jason J. Jung,
  and David Camacho*

Performance, Resilience, and Security in Moving Data from the Fog
to the Cloud: The DYNAMO Transfer Framework Approach   197
  *Raffaele Montella, Diana Di Luccio, Sokol Kosta, Giulio Giunta,
  and Ian Foster*

Development of a Support System to Resolve Network Troubles
by Mobile Robots   209
  Kohichi Ogawa and Noriaki Yoshiura

A Benchmark Model for the Creation of Compute Instance
Performance Footprints   221
  *Markus Ullrich, Jörg Lässig, Jingtao Sun, Martin Gaedke,
  and Kento Aida*

Developing Agent-Based Smart Objects for IoT Edge Computing:
Mobile Crowdsensing Use Case   235
  *Teemu Leppänen, Claudio Savaglio, Lauri Lovén, Wilma Russo,
  Giuseppe Di Fatta, Jukka Riekki, and Giancarlo Fortino*

Path Planning of Robotic Fish in Unknown Environment with Improved
Reinforcement Learning Algorithm   248
  Jingbo Hu, Jie Mei, Dingfang Chen, Lijie Li, and Zhengshu Cheng

Review of Swarm Intelligence Algorithms for Multi-objective
Flowshop Scheduling.   258
  Lijun He, Wenfeng Li, Yu Zhang, and Jingjing Cao

Exploiting Long Distance Connections to Strengthen Network Robustness . . .   270
  V. Carchiolo, M. Grassia, A. Longheu, M. Malgeri, and G. Mangioni

An Online Adaptive Sampling Rate Learning Framework for Sensor-Based
Human Activity Recognition   278
    Zeyi Jin, Jingjing Cao, Jingtao Sun, Wenfeng Li, and Qiang Wang

A Secure Video-Based Robust and Aesthetic 2D Barcode   282
    Changsheng Chen, Fengbo Lan, and Wai Ho Mow

A Migratable Container-Based Replication Management for Inter-cloud   288
    Mingkang Chen and Jingtao Sun

Dilated Deep Residual Network for Post-processing in TPG Based
Image Coding.   293
    Yuan Yuan, Jingtao Sun, and Miaohui Wang

Underground Intelligent Logistic System Integrated with Internet
of Things.   298
    Qiang Yang, Guohao Li, Ting Cai, and Qiang Wang

Author Index   303

Implementation of Self-adaptive Middleware for Mobile Vehicle Tracking Applications on Edge Computing

Jingtao Sun[1]([✉]), Cheng Yang[1,2], Tomoya Tanjo[1], Kazushige Sage[1], and Kento Aida[1]

[1] National Institute of Informatics, Tokyo 101-8430, Japan
{sun,cheng,tanjo,saga,aida}@nii.ac.jp
[2] Zhejiang University of Technology, Hangzhou 310023, China

Abstract. Unstructured data gathered from various IoT sensors is rapidly increasing due to inexpensive electronic devices and high-speed networks. On the other hand, mobile edge computing (MEC) is an attractive data processing method that can shorten the communication distance and reduce the latency of computation-intensive tasks by distributing data to the edge servers close to the users, unlike processing data on clouds that are located far from users. In the present paper, we propose a specialized self-adaptive middleware for reconfiguration of image/video contents for adaptation to changes with the movement of a vehicle. The key concept behind this approach is to introduce the rule-based relocation of objects among sensor devices, edge servers, and existing clouds as a basic adaptation mechanism to recognize and track mobile vehicles. Experimental results show that tracking precision with a state-of-the-art tracker is up to 89% for MEC.

Keywords: Internet of Things · Mobile edge computing
Self-adaptive middleware · Object recognition · Object tracking

1 Introduction

Due to the low cost of electronic devices and the high speed and large capacity of mobile networks, data collection from various Internet of Things (IoT) sensors is rapidly increasing [15–17]. In general, most of the collected large amounts of unstructured data are transferred to the cloud and processed by cloud computing [14]. However, cloud computing is suitable for high-speed processing, not for scenarios of a real-time nature of that require low latency or high quality of service (QoS). On the other hand, mobile edge computing (MEC) is a novel paradigm that extends cloud-computing capabilities and services to the edge of the network. Mobile edge computing has high mobility and can not only support applications and services with reduced latency and improved QoS on open platforms but also process highly regional or privacy data and improve the real-time nature of applications.

© Springer Nature Switzerland AG 2018
Y. Xiang et al. (Eds.): IDCS 2018, LNCS 11226, pp. 1–15, 2018.
https://doi.org/10.1007/978-3-030-02738-4_1

A vehicle tracking system not only requires a strong real-time nature but must also consider the mobility of the target vehicle. Although various vehicle tracking systems have been developed, most studies are based on data collected from a stationary camera for tracking [11,12]. With the vehicle movement, it is necessary not only to consume a large amount computing resources and time but also to adapt to various changes. For instance, when the target vehicle enters a tunnel, the data collected by camera sensors cannot autonomously adapt to surrounding light changes. Moreover, when it is raining, camera sensors cannot automatically adapt to video blurring, or, when traffic is congested, camera sensors cannot optimize a partially blocked moving vehicle.

In order to achieve real-time mobile vehicle tracking and adapt to the different changes that occur during the movement of the vehicles, the present paper proposes a specialized self-adaptive middleware for reconfiguration of image/video contents for adaptive mobile edge computing. The key concept behind the approach is to introduce the rule-based relocation of objects among sensor devices, edge servers, and existing clouds as a basic adaptation mechanism. The object described herein refers to a series of functional functions designed by the proposed middleware for vehicle tracking, such as brightening the acquired image by a night vision camera sensor, converting a regularly collected image into a video, image deblurring, or using an open-source license plate library for recognition. Since the environment may change during tracking, we not only use stationary camera sensors but also use mobile camera sensors for high-vision and real-time vehicle tracking through continuously captured images for recognition. Using the proposed middleware, the collected images were then converted into short videos, which were difficult to resolve using traditional methods, and a replica of this video was distributed to cloud instances for wide-range tracking [11,12].

The following are key contributions of the present paper.

- We designed and implemented a specialized self-adaptive middleware. During the movement of vehicles, many changes may occur that make recognition and tracking difficult, whereas the proposed middleware system can self-adaptively manage the topology.
- We designed and implemented a rule format for engineers to define their requirements. This rule format separates the concerns of users, so that the users can obtain more reliable results and can facilitate the programming problem by automating much of the administration.
- We not only used the image data captured by the camera sensors and stored for up to two days[1] for recognition and tracking but also implemented a parallel replication mechanism for regular data storage collected by the camera sensors and performed a wide range of decentralized recognition and tracking through replicas.

---

[1] In our research, we use two types of sensor cameras, namely, day and night cameras, which work alternately. We captured an image every five seconds, and the memory capacity of these sensor devices allows data to be collected for up to two days.

– Our evaluation results showed a tracking precision of 100% in two video sequences under sunny conditions and a tracking precision of 89% in another video sequence under rainy conditions at a threshold distance of 36 pixels[2].

The remainder of the present paper is organized as follows. We review related research on existing adaptation methods of mobile edge computing and mobile vehicle recognition and tracking in Sect. 2. We describe the proposed approach in detail in Sect. 3. We then present the design and implementation of the proposed middleware in Sect. 4. Next, we implement a mobile vehicle tracking system, which is a potential application of the proposed middleware. Finally, we conclude the paper in Sect. 6.

2   Related Work

The notion of adaptation has rapidly influenced the area of MEC. There are some challenges [15–18] to implementing adaptations of MEC, most of which have aimed at dynamically cooperating with cloud providers [16] or providing programming models for defining the event handlers instead of defining adaptation conditions [17]. However, it is difficult for MEC to implement real-time monitoring applications with complex situations such as mobile vehicle tracking because, with changes in the positions of moving targets, not only the network and computer resources may change but also monitoring of moving targets, ambient light, weather, traffic jams, sensor device storage, and computation also change frequently.

There has been substantial work on building vehicle tracking systems [11–14,18]. Some systems [11] recognize and track vehicles in a frame-by-frame manner by using video streams, which are often generated by high-performance computers or cloud instances. Due to long distances between users, the delay time is slightly longer than in the case of real-time processing [12]. On the other hand, recent research has started to focus on the use of mobile camera sensors [13] or to use GPS sensors [18] for vehicle tracking. The former is very close to our research target; however, unlike [13], we can dynamically adapt these changes by relocating the execution position of the object according to the user-defined rules to the many complex changes in the movement of a mobile vehicle. Although the latter can be tracked to the latitude and longitude of a moving vehicle, the cost is high and real-time monitoring is not possible, unlike our research.

The use of mobile camera sensors is very close to our research target; however, unlike [13], we can dynamically adapt these changes by relocating the execution position of the object according to the user-defined rules to the many complex changes in the movement of a mobile vehicle. Although the latter can be tracked to the latitude and longitude of a moving vehicle, the cost is high and real-time monitoring is not possible, unlike in the present study.

In addition, object tracking is a widely studied *computer vision* problem [1] that returns the locations of an object of interest frame by frame in a given video

---

[2] The processing speed for all sequences is above 60 fps.

sequence. In general, automated vehicle tracking consists of two phases: vehicle recognition and vehicle object tracking. For vehicle recognition, there has been substantial work focusing on license plate recognition [3], which is among the best ways of identifying one or multiple vehicles in the first frame of a given video sequence. An object tracker [1] can then be adopted to compute the location of the vehicle of interest in subsequent video frames. These acquired locations in the video sequence can be used for localization of the targeted mobile vehicle(s) in the real world.

However, the following image effects are generally inevitable in a realistic scenario: (1) *motion blur* due to a relatively short camera exposure period and sudden vehicle acceleration or direction change, (2) *low light* due to a lack of street light sources, and (3) *partial occlusion* due to multiple vehicles being present in the camera scene at the same time, each of which may lead to instability or failure of vehicle recognition and tracking. Under mild conditions, blur- and occlusion-robust object trackers [6–8] can be incorporated into the vehicle tracking module. However, in the presence of severe motion blur and extremely low light, specific *image processing* techniques, namely, image deblurring algorithms [4] and low-light enhancement algorithms [5], are required to remove serious motion blur and improve the ambient lighting condition, respectively, in the video sequences before the vehicle recognition and tracking stages.

3   Approach

In this section, we first present the proposed scenario for mobile vehicle tracking. We then present our basic concepts through the data acquired from Raspberry PI.

3.1   Scenario

The camera sensors used in our research can be divided into two categories having the following two configurations:

– Fixed camera sensors placed on the roads.
– Mobile camera sensors incorporated in patrol cars.

Assume that a car owner realizes that his/her car was stolen (Fig. 1) and immediately reports the vehicle's information, *e.g.*, the car manufacturer, color, license plate, report time, estimated time stolen, and location, to the police. In this case, the police will recognize and track the license plate of the stolen car by invoking images captured by road sensor cameras during the incident.[3] When the location of the stolen car is determined, the police attempt to capture the

---

[3] Note that these images are periodically captured by camera sensors scattered around the city; although these sensors have low-level computing power, their computational capabilities are sufficient for general low-level image processing and license plate recognition.

car by sending instructions to nearby patrol cars, which track and surround the stolen car at a specific location according to predictive conditions, such as the speed and acceleration of the stolen car and the location of the stolen vehicle. In addition, patrol cars are positioned at different intersections to further surround and induce the stolen car into the capture zone.

The proposed approach can be efficiently and reasonably distributed sensor deployment, and be used in different computation resources without reducing the recognition accuracy. In Sect. 5, we present our experimental license plate recognition and mobile vehicle tracking results.

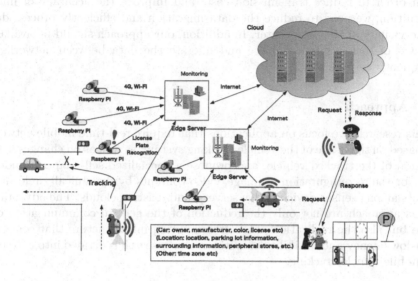

Fig. 1. Mobile vehicle tracking scenario

3.2 Requirements

The proposed system must satisfy the following requirements according to the features of MEC.

Mobility. In the proposed scenario, the entire process of vehicle tracking has a variety of changes due to mobility. We thus consider *Mobility* to be one of the essential indicators in the proposed system. Geographical distribution is another key characteristic of IoT deployment, where users can benefit from edge computing, which is another essential indicator considered herein.

Adaptability and Fault Tolerance. In order to provide stable services that are capable of operating 24 h a day, both the internal and external environments of the system must be updated when necessary. Thus, the proposed system must be able to dynamically adapt to these changes so that the data can be processed more efficiently in the optimal location and return results to the user with low latency. In addition, the adaptability that we provide does not allow interruption of the system operation, so that a constructed system with strong fault tolerance is required.

Privacy Protection and Security. With the development of the IoT, issues of privacy protection and security must be considered. The proposed system must not only consider how to easily acquire and use data but also preserve data as securely as possible and protect the data content as necessary.

In order to reduce transmission costs and improve the accuracy of image recognition, we need to reduce the data migration and efficiently process data in the vicinity of the data center. In addition, our approach should be available in cases of such limited resource and migrate the data between networks as infrequently as possible.

3.3 Approach

In this research, we focus on applications that require real-time mobile networking based on the usage of the vehicle tracking system, as well as on changes in the location of the tracked vehicle, and propose a specialized self-adaptive middleware for the reconfiguration of image/video contents by dynamically relocating objects among sensor devices, edge servers, and existing clouds. The advantages of this approach are not only the reduction of the general communication distance but also the realization of a soft computing infrastructure that combines ultra-low latency and flexibility of systems. Our research is divided into two steps for mobile vehicle tracking.

Data Collection

- In our research, we deployed our data collection environment using Raspberry Pi 3 and Zero W in combination with the following two types of camera sensors during the day and night when we called sensor devices.
- We regularly collected image data from sensor devices and then compressed and transferred these data to the edge servers via a mobile network instead of a Wi-Fi environment.
- The collected image data are customized as short video streams according to the user's needs, and we then deploy these short video streams through parallel replication protocol between edge servers and clouds via the Internet. In addition, the video streams are periodically synchronized (every two days) on the proposed middleware system.

Data Processing

- *Recognition phase.* Many changes occur both inside and outside the mobile vehicle recognition phase. For instance, for the case in which the sensors have difficulty capturing sharp video frames or can only capture blurred images due to changes in the movement speed/acceleration of the stolen vehicle, the proposed middleware system can dynamically change the execution position of objects from edge servers to sensor devices by user-defined rules to pre-process the video streams, and then send the pre-processed video streams to the edge server for license plate recognition (Fig. 2). Another example, in accordance with the change in the ambient light condition in tunnels where thefts often occur, the execution location of the low-luminance correction object is migrated from the edge servers to the sensor devices in order to improve the license plate recognition rate by changing the original image type to another type, such as a sketch, blur, or other type of image[4] on the edge servers.

– *Tracking phase.* In the tracking process, the sensor devices may provide unsatisfactory video streams because of the undesirable position of the targeted vehicle. For instance, when a vehicle is at a high speed, we often can only capture blurred video streams, or, in the case of traffic congestion, the tracking vehicle and the general vehicle are mixed, and a part of the tracking vehicle is shielded, or we need to protect some of the scenes in the video streams with a video mosaic. In the above cases, we need to change the execution location of the objects between the edge servers and clouds (Fig. 2). In our research, we adopt a kernelized correlation filter (KCF object) [8], which is a state-of-the-art computationally efficient and accurate tracker [2], as the mobile vehicle tracking module. When changes occur, the middleware system can migrate the KCF object from the edge devices to the clouds. Since the computing power and computing resources of clouds are larger than those of edge servers and can be distributed to handle many videos at the same time, we use such cloud features to improve the accuracy of mobile vehicle tracking.

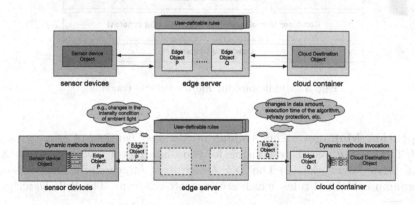

Fig. 2. Migration of smart objects

---

[4] Raspberry PI camera document. https://projects.raspberrypi.org.

4   Design and Implementation

In order to realize the above scenario, we designed and implemented specialized self-adaptive middleware for dynamically adapting to several changes among sensor devices, edge servers, and cloud resources by reconfiguration of images and video.

4.1   Design of Self-adaptive Middleware

As shown in Fig. 3, our proposed middleware system consists of two parts: an adaptation manager and a runtime system, where each of the middleware systems is implemented on a base docker environment running on the edge servers. Moreover, we adopted Kubernetes[5] on AWS EC2 to manage these containers.

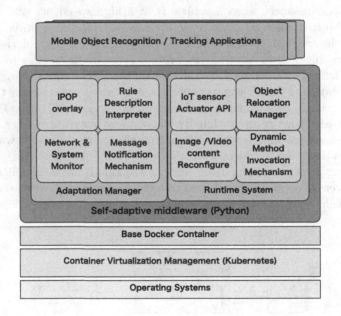

Fig. 3. Middleware for mobile vehicle tracking

Adaptation Manager. The *Adaptation Manager* consists of four parts. (1) The *IPOP overlay*[6] part is responsible for coordinating the mobile networks with virtual private networks. (2) The *Rule Description Interpreter* is responsible for managing user-defined rules, which are separate concerns. The Rule Description

---

[5] Kubernetes is an open-source system for automating deployment, scaling, and management of containerized applications. https://kubernetes.io/.
[6] IPOP (IP-Over-P2P) is an open-source user-centric software virtual network allowing end users to define and create their own virtual private networks (VPNs). http://ipop-project.org/.

Interpreter contains a pair of a condition and an action, such as a period of time or a location, and relocating objects and duplicating and migrating objects. (3) The *Network and System monitor* is responsible for monitoring changes, such as user-defined conditions, the network configuration, and the system's properties and permissions between the inside and outside of the vehicle tracking systems. (4) Finally, the *Message Notification Mechanism* is responsible for notifying users of the results.

Runtime System. The *Runtime System* also contains four parts. (1) The IoT sensor API is responsible for providing a sensor actuator API for developers to control their IoT-based camera sensors. (2) The *Image/Video Content Reconfiguration* is responsible for changing contents from regularly captured images to a short video and sending duplicate videos as replicas to cloud instances for large-scale tracking. (3) The *Object Relocation Manager* is responsible for relocating and duplicating objects among sensor devices, edge servers, and cloud resources based on user-defined rules. (4) The *Dynamic Methods Invocation Mechanism* is responsible for invoking methods from relocated objects and communicates with the destination's object.

4.2 Implementation

Currently, parts other than IoT sensor Actuator APIs of the runtime system and rule description in the proposed middleware are implemented. In addition, the proposed self-adaptive middleware system is based on Python v3.6 on various operating systems.

Dynamic Methods Invocation Mechanism. In the proposed middleware system, each object is a general-purpose programmable entity defined as a collection of Python objects. The system can migrate and duplicate itself among sensor devices, edge servers and clouds after serialization. In Python, users can serialize various objects by using the *pickle* package, despite the fact that in the realization of serialization, users can choose the "json" form or "pkl" form. However, since the latter is saved as a text form, the internal content of which is easy to view, we adopt the latter to achieve our object serialization mechanism.

After the objects have been deployed via implemented by TCP socket through network, the relocated objects can be deserialized, and the pre-created instance in the destination can dynamically communicate between the relocated objects and the destination objects by invoking the previous method name.

Currently, our implementation only supports specified destinations, and the objects are not within the *Thread*. In the future, we intend to improve our implementation to enable dynamic selection of destinations and thread migration.

User-Definable Rules. Each rule is specified as a pair of *conditions and actions*. The former is written in a first-order logic and its predicates reflect tracking camera sensors and network properties, e.g., changes in day and night alternation, changes in location networks, changes in speed and acceleration of mobile vehicles, gamma correction of images, changes in pixels and resolution of videos, and application-specific conditions. The latter is specified as the relocation, duplication and destroy of objects. Our adaptation was intended to be specified in a rule-style notation (Fig. 4). However, existing general-purpose rule-based systems tend to be unwieldy because they cannot express necessary adaptation expertise or subtleties of adaptation.

```
rule name:
        condition:
                when conditions
                location conditions
        action:
                migration object id to destination ip ||
                duplication number of object, and object id to destination ips
                then:
                invoke methods
                last:
                object self-extinction || *migration
```

Fig. 4. User-definable rules

There are three built-in functions in the proposed rule formats.

- *relocation...to* is a function that is responsible for migrating the objects from their executing location to their destination in order to adapt to changes among sensor devices, edge servers, and clouds.
- *duplication...to* is a function that is responsible for making multiple copies of objects and then migrating the objects from their execution location to destinations.
- *self-extinction* is a function that is responsible for destroying the executed tasks according to the needs of users.

Currently, our implementation only supports the above three built-in functions, and repeated migration is not supported in the proposed middleware system. In the future, we intend to improve the implementation in order to enable adaptation to more typical changes.

5   Mobile Vehicle Tracking Application

In order to verify the performance of the proposed and implemented middleware, we implemented the application scenario of the license plate recognition and tracking of a mobile vehicle.

The mobile vehicle tracking application can be divided into two steps. The first step is to identify the license plate of the car as a whole based on images captured by fixed sensors on the road. The second step is first based on a video replica generated by continuous images for *large-scale* search and is then based on mobile sensors that are embedded in patrol cars to chase the target car through real-time video for *precise-scale* search until the vehicle is intercepted.

5.1   Vehicle Recognition

As mentioned in Sect. 3.1, when a request is received from the local police, an engineer will first define a *large-scale* search request based on the *Rule format* proposed in Sect. 4.2 and will then retrieve regularly captured images of the stolen vehicle within a specified time and location by stationary sensor cameras placed on the road. In order to automatically recognize the information of the stolen vehicle, we imported the OpenALPR[7] library in the proposed middleware.

There are two types of license plate recognition considered herein.

– If a vehicle was confirmed to have been stolen within two days[8], we can dynamically invoke images captured by the camera sensor devices for license plate recognition according to the user-defined rules given the time and location at which the theft occurred. For example, if a vehicle on the opposite side of the road turns on high-beam headlights when the target vehicle is moving at night or is blocked by buildings or other vehicles in the captured images, it is difficult for camera sensors to capture sharp images for license plate information. In such cases, the proposed middleware can migrate low-illumination correction objects from edge servers to camera sensor devices in order to pre-process images prior to license plate recognition. In addition, if a stolen vehicle moves at a very high speed on a road or moves on a rainy day, the camera sensors can only capture blurred images. In such cases, the proposed middleware can migrate the blurred object from edge servers to camera sensors for image pre-processing.
– If a theft is confirmed to have occurred more than two days ago, short replica videos that were saved in the cloud instances must be used for *large-scale* search. Due to the limited storage capacity of camera sensor devices, the data are stored as video replicas in cloud instances. However, as the above changes (*e.g.*, reflected light, partially blocked objects, high speed, and inclement weather) occur, we migrate objects from edge servers to cloud instances for replica video pre-processing prior to license plate recognition.

Based on our setup of the 4G mobile network environment (the Internet speed is approximately 790 Kbps), we (1) tested the latency of transmitting objects[9] between the edge server and camera sensor devices and three types of Amazon EC2 cloud instances (e.g., t2.small, t2.medium, and t2.large) and Asia Pacific (Tokyo) region in Ubuntu 16.04 for evaluation, and (2) evaluated the performance of the license plate recognition through OpenALPR. The results are shown in Tables 1 and 2). Both tables show that a sunny day has more

---

[7] OpenALPR is an open-source automatic license plate recognition library that analyzes images and video streams to identify license plates.

[8] Due to the limited storage of the sensor camera, we can save data for up to two days then regularly free its space. In addition, the image sequence data in the sensor are periodically sent to the edge server every five minutes, and in which converted into a video stream.

[9] We used a low-luminance object and a vehicle recognition object for evaluation, the object size of the low-luminance object is 915 bytes, and the vehicle recognition object is 10 KB.

vehicles and a higher image pixel intensity than a rainy day. On the other hand, the detection accuracy on a sunny day is higher and has a longer processing time as compared to that on a rainy day.

Table 1. Latency of object transmission

Devices/objects	Raspberry PI 3	Small instance	Middle instance	Large instance
Low luminance object	0.476878 ms	0.719185 ms	0.441196 ms	0.432655 ms
Vehicle recognition object	0.415435 ms	0.408388 ms	0.485288 ms	0.444157 ms

Table 2. License plate recognition rate

Image files/confidence	Max_confidence	Min_confidence	Total processing time
Test_sunny_Image	94.97	83.1	2.067 s
Test_rainy_Image	94.97	67.85	0.627 s

5.2 Mobile Vehicle Tracking

The choice of either *large-scale* or *precise-scale* search criterion follows the license plate recognition method described in Sect. 5.1. (1) Under the *large-scale* mode, we migrate the tracker objects from the edge servers to the clouds and perform mobile vehicle tracking on the cloud side in the video replica given the location of the recognized license plate. (2) Likewise, under the *precise-scale* mode, the tracker object in the edge servers is deployed for mobile vehicle tracking in (i) the most recently uploaded videos from the road-cameras and (ii) the most recently uploaded videos from patrol car cameras. In addition, we collected three video sequences sunny1, sunny2, and rainy with different combinations of the video conditions shown in Table 3.

Given the pixel coordinates of the recognized license plate in the first video frame, we adopt a Kernelized Correlation Filter (KCF) [8] as the vehicle tracking module. The example video frames are shown in Fig. 5, where the tracker results are indicated by yellow rectangles and ground truth locations (*i.e.*, the location that is manually observed) are indicated by red rectangles. Note that in sunny2 and rainy, we designate the region of interest (ROI) to be the mobile vehicle region instead of the license plate region when the license plate region is too small and it is impractical for video tracking. Given the data of the recognized license plate, the tracking region can be automatically updated for optimal trade-off between stability and efficiency of the tracking stage, which is part of our on-going research. Specifically, when there is a significant scale change of the ROI, the ROI will be updated from the license plate region to the majority or full part of the vehicle when the scale becomes significantly smaller than in previous frames, and vice versa. As shown in Table 3, the processing speed for all sequences is above 60 fps, which is sufficient for real-time processing.

The tracking precision results are shown in Fig. 6, where the `Precision`-axis denotes the division of the number of frames that are *accurately tracked* over the total number of tracked frames. The `Precision`, denoted as **acc.**, is formulated as:

$$\mathbf{acc.} = \frac{1}{N} \sum_{i=1}^{N} \mathbb{1}_{D_i}(t), \quad D_i = \|c_T - c_G\|, \quad i \in \{1, \dots, N\}, \tag{1}$$

where N denotes the total number of tracked frames, c_T and c_G denote the center coordinates of the tracker region and the ground truth region, respectively, t denotes the threshold (as the `Threshold`-axis in Fig. 6) in pixels, and $\mathbb{1}_{D_i}(t)$ is an Boolean indicator function that returns 1 if the Euclidean distance D_i is smaller than t and 0 otherwise. Both `sunny1` and `sunny2` achieve 100% tracking precision with a threshold of $t \geq 36$, while `rainy` achieves 89% tracking precision with the same threshold. The loss of tracking precision for sequence `rainy` is mainly due to severe motion blur and partial occlusion. In the future, we intend to evaluate the performance of the overall proposed approach, in addition to the effectiveness of the proposed approach in terms of the mobile vehicle license plate recognition and tracking shown in Sects. 5.1 and 5.2.

Table 3. Video sequence profiles of `sunny1`, `sunny2`, and `rainy` with tracking precision. Here, $[\cdot, \cdot]$ denotes the tested frame range, and $\mathbb{1}_b, \mathbb{1}_l$, and $\mathbb{1}_o$ denote the Boolean indicators of the motion blur, low light, and partial/full occlusion conditions, respectively, and return 1 if the condition is true ($\checkmark$) and 0 otherwise. α, β, and γ are heuristically set parameters, where α denotes the extra area surrounding the ROI, β denotes the interpolation factor, and γ denotes the Gaussian kernel scaling factor. In addition, v denotes the processing speed in frames per second (fps), and **acc.** denotes the tracking precision of the KCF tracker at a threshold of 50 pixels (see Fig. 6), ranging between 0 and 1.

Video profile	Parameter settings						v	**acc.**
	$\mathbb{1}_b$	$\mathbb{1}_l$	$\mathbb{1}_o$	α	β	γ		
sunny1 @29.97 fps 1080 p [90, 360]				1.5	0.5	0.01	83.64	1.00
sunny2 @29.97 fps 1080 p [899, 1049]	$\checkmark$	$\checkmark$		1	0.9	0.5	87.36	1.00
rainy @29.97 fps 1080 p [0, 210]	$\checkmark$		$\checkmark$	3	0.01	1	60.15	0.89

Fig. 5. Example video frames used in the mobile vehicle tracking in the test video sequences `sunny1`, `sunny2`, and `rainy`. An enlarged version of the tracked region is shown at the top-left/bottom-right corners of the frames. The ground truth is highlighted by red rectangles and the tracker results are shown in yellow. (Color figure online)

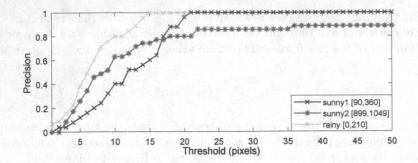

Fig. 6. Precision plots for all of the tested video sequences. The `Precision`—axis denotes the division of the number of frames that are *accurately tracked* over the total number of tracked frames. The `Threshold`—axis denotes t in Eq. 1, and $[\cdot, \cdot]$ denotes the tested frame range.

6   Conclusion

In the present paper, we propose a specialized self-adaptive middleware for dynamic adaptation to changes in a mobile vehicle tracking application. We introduce the reconfiguration of image/video contents by dynamically relocating objects among sensor devices, edge servers, and existing clouds as a base mechanism for adaptation. In particular, the proposed middleware is capable of adapting to changes in the ambient light condition, the vehicle displacement, the weather conditions, and the mobile network coverage. The mobile vehicle is recognized and then tracked through the vehicle movement in the vicinity of the data source. Moreover, we separate the user-defined rules and the traditional adaptation functions. The proposed middleware has a simple structure while providing various adaptations to support vehicle tracking without any centralized management. In the future, we intend to improve the proposed method and evaluate the performance of the proposed system on real data in terms of both precision and latency.

Acknowledgement. This work was supported by the Japan Science Technology under CREST Grant JPMJCR1501.

References

1. Yilmaz, A., Javed, O., Shah, M.: Object tracking: a survey. ACM Comput. Surv. (CSUR) **38**(4), 1–45 (2006)
2. Wu, Y., Lim, J., Yang, M.H.: Object tracking benchmark. IEEE Trans. Pattern Anal. Mach. Intell. **37**(9), 1834–1848 (2015)
3. Hu, L., Ni, Q.: IoT-driven automated object detection algorithm for urban surveillance systems in smart cities. IEEE IoT J. **5**(2), 747–754 (2018)
4. Bai, Y., Cheung, G., Liu, X., Gao, W.: Graph-based blind image deblurring from a single photograph. In: arXiv

5. Li, M., Liu, J., Yang, W., Sun, X., Guo, Z.: Structure-revealing low-light image enhancement via robust retinex model. IEEE Trans. Image Process. **27**(6), 2828–2841 (2018)
6. Zhao, S., Zhang, S., Zhang, L.: Towards occlusion handling: object tracking with background estimation. IEEE Trans. Cybern. (in press)
7. Wu, Y., Ling, H., Yu, Y., Li, F., Mei, X., Cheng, E.: Blurred target tracking by blur-driven tracker. In: IEEE International Conference on Computer Vision, Barcelona, Spain, pp. 1100–1107 (2011)
8. Henriques, J.F., Caseiro, R., Martins, P., Batista, J.: High-speed tracking with kernelized correlation filters. IEEE Trans. Pattern Anal. Mach. Intell. **37**(3), 583–596 (2015)
9. National Center for Biotechnology Information. http://www.ncbi.nlm.nih.gov
10. Lamport, L., Malkhi, D., Zhou, L.: Vertical paxos and primary-backup replication. In: Proceedings of the 28th ACM Symposium on Principles of Distributed Computing. ACM, pp. 312–313 (2009)
11. Thome, N., Vacavant, A., Robinault, L., Miguet, S.: A cognitive and video-based approach for multinational license plate recognition. Mach. Vis. Appl. **22**(2), 389–407 (2011)
12. Arth, C., Limberger, F., Bischof, H.: Real-time license plate recognition on an embedded DSP-platform. In: IEEE Conference on Computer Vision and Pattern Recognition, pp. 1–8. IEEE (2007)
13. Yilmaz, A., Li, X., Shah, M.: Contour-based object tracking with occlusion handling in video acquired using mobile cameras. IEEE Trans. Pattern Anal. Mach. Intell. **26**(11), 1531–1536 (2004)
14. Du, S., Ibrahim, M., Shehata, M., Badawy, W.: Automatic license plate recognition (ALPR): a state-of-the-art review. IEEE Trans. Circuits Syst. Video Technol. **23**(2), 311–325 (2013)
15. Abbas, N., Zhang, Y., Taherkordi, A., Skeie, T.: Mobile edge computing: a survey. IEEE IoT J. **5**(1), 450–465 (2018)
16. Farris, I., Militano, L., Nitti, M., Atzori, L., Iera, A.: MIFaaS: a mobile-IoT-federation-as-a-service model for dynamic cooperation of IoT cloud providers. Futur. Gener. Comput. Syst. **70**, 126–137 (2017)
17. Hong, K., Lillethun, D., Ramachandran, U., Ottenwälder, B., Koldehofe, B.: Mobile fog: a programming model for large-scale applications on the Internet of Things. In: Proceedings of the Second ACM SIGCOMM Workshop on Mobile Cloud Computing, pp. 15–20. ACM (2013)
18. Bajaj, D., Gupta, N.: GPS based automatic vehicle tracking using RFID. Int. J. Eng. Innov. Technol. (IJEIT) **1**(1), 31–35 (2012)

Towards the Succinct Representation
of m Out of n

Victor Parque[1,2(✉)] and Tomoyuki Miyashita[1]

[1] Waseda University, 3-4-1 Okubo, Shinjuku-ku, Tokyo 169-8555, Japan
parque@aoni.waseda.jp
[2] Egypt - Japan University of Science and Technology,
Borg El Arab, Alexandria 21934, Egypt

Abstract. Combinations of n objects taken m at the time are ubiquitous in a wide range of combinatorial problems. In this paper, we introduce a novel approach to generate combinations from given integer numbers by using a gradient-based algorithm through plural number of CPU and GPU processors. The time complexity is bounded by $O(m^2)$ when using a single processor, and bounded by $O(m \log m)$ when using at most $O(m/\log m)$ processors. Relevant computational experiments confirmed the practical efficiency within computationally allowable limits. Our approach offers the building blocks to represent combinations with succinct encoding and complexity being independent of n, which is meritorious when n is very large, or when n is time-varying.

Keywords: Combinations · Unranking · Optimization
Parallel computing · Complexity · Representation

1 Introduction

Combinations of n objects taken m at the time, or well-known as m out of n, are relevant mechanisms which allow to tackle optimization problems ubiquitously. To mention a few of the most representative fields: Reliability Engineering [1], Machine Learning [2], Chemistry [3], Cryptography [4], Data Science [5], Mathematics [6], Material Science [7], and Cognitive Science [8]. In this paper, we focus on the unranking of m out of n, which consists in generating combination objects of the form $(x_1, x_2, ..., x_m)$ given an integer number $g \in [0, \binom{n}{m} - 1]$. Generating combinations given numbers is advantageous:

- when the integer $g \in [0, N-1]$ can be used as a succinct representation achieving the information-theoretic tight bound,
- when parallelization is able to speed up the sampling and evaluation of a subset of combination objects from the complete combinatorial space,
- when the evaluation of duplicated combinations is expensive and irrelevant, and the integer number g identifies and relates to $(x_1, x_2, ..., x_m)$.
- when generating all combinations is computationally expensive, specially for large $\binom{n}{m}$, and generating a small subset is rather preferable.

© Springer Nature Switzerland AG 2018
Y. Xiang et al. (Eds.): IDCS 2018, LNCS 11226, pp. 16–26, 2018.
https://doi.org/10.1007/978-3-030-02738-4_2

1.1 Related Works

The related works have proposed approaches to generate combinations completely [9–15], sequentially [16,17] or arbitrarily [16,18,19]. On the other hand, and having a different scope, the unranking of combinations are able to generate combinations either arbitrarily, completely or sequentially, which is only guided by the integer number g.

Thus, researchers have studied the unranking problem in combinations since the late seventies, in which the first unranking algorithm was proposed by Buckles and Lybanon [20], and a correction was proposed thirty years later by Crouse [21]. And, inspired by the applicability in the above mentioned problem scenarios, the first hardware realization was implemented in the earliest of this decade by Butler and Sasao [22].

A well-known and basic unranking algorithm finds the maximal element x_m subject to $\binom{x_m}{m} \leqslant g$; then, finds the maximal x_{m-1} subject to $\binom{x_{m-1}}{m-1} \leqslant g - \binom{x_m}{m}$, and so on. Yet, since evaluating binomial constrains are computationally inefficient, a number of surrogate approaches were proposed [16,23–32].

For practical realizations, the unranking efficiency of the above mentioned approaches depend on the value of n, which is restrictive in application scenarios considering very large n. Yet, in a different perspective, n-independent unranking is of special interest since they allow scalability as a function of m only, which is meritorious in cases of very large n and in cases in which m is much smaller than n. Here, Kokosinskiński proposed UNRANKCOMB-E as the first algorithm running in $O(m)$ time [26] and, more recently, Shimizu et. al. proposed the SFN algorithm running in $O(m^{3m+3})$ time [33]. Whereas both approaches use structurally different sampling mechanisms to generate combinations, the UNRANKCOMB-E algorithm requires n^2 processors and $O(n^2)$ space, which is restrictive in contexts of large n and of limited computing memory; and the SFN algorithm is restricted to sampling through Dynamic Programming.

1.2 Contributions

We present a novel approach for unranking m out of n by capitalizing the benefits of parallelism and optimization to render n-independent unranking. Basically, we generate each element x_i of the tuple $(x_1, x_2, ..., x_m)$ ordered with the *revolving door*[16] by solving m minimization problems. As a result, the expected complexity is $O(m^2)$-like time, in case of using a single processor, and is $O(m \log m)$-like time, in case of using at most $O(m/\log m)$ processors[1]. To the best of our knowledge, n-independent unranking of combinations capitalizing the benefits of parallel computing has received little attention in the literature; in which the conventional schemes require quadratic number of processors (being detrimental for standard computing environments) and conjectured polynomial space[2].

---

[1] unless otherwise stated, log() refers to $\log_2()$.

[2] personal communication with Ref. [33].

2 Proposed Approach

2.1 Preliminaries

Given positive integers n and m, and $[n] = \{1, 2, 3, ..., n\}$, a combination object is defined as the tuple $(x_1, x_2, x_3, ..., x_m)$ in which $x_i \in [n], i \in [m]$ and $n \geq m$.

For integer number g, the unranking algorithm consists in generating the combination object uniquely associated with the number g, with respect to some ordering, as follows:

$$\text{unranking} : g \rightarrow (x_1, x_2, x_3, ..., x_m), \tag{1}$$

where $0 \leq g \leq \binom{n}{m} - 1$.

To encode combinations, we use the *revolving* door order starting with $(1, ..., m)$, and ending with $(1, ..., m - 1, n)$; wherein combinations are recursively divided either including or avoiding the element n, and holding the condition $x_1 < x_2 < ... < x_m$.

The key motivation of using the revolving door order is due to the minimal change order and the *ordered cyclic sequence* since the Hamiltonian path in a polytope formed with $\binom{n}{m}$ vertices minimizes the distance between neighbor (close) combinations [29]. Thus, the above facts make the *revolving door* relevant to build sampling-based learning algorithms with *canonical* concepts [34].

2.2 Unranking Using Optimization

The basic idea in our proposed unranking algorithm is shown by Algorithm 1, in which the element x_i is generated by minimizing the cost function $|J(x, i, g)|$ for variable x and constraint $x \geq i$. Here,

$$J(x, i, g) = \left[\sum_{p=1}^{i} \log_b \left(\frac{x - i}{p} + 1 \right) \right] - \log_b(g), \tag{2}$$

where i denotes the index in the *for* loop of Algorithm 1 ($i = m$ at initial iteration), g denotes the integer number representing the combination, and the base b in $\log_b(.)$ is a user-defined constant (the larger the coefficient $\binom{n}{m}$ is, larger the b to handle very large numbers accurately). For standard computing environments, we use $b = 10$ since it allows to compute $\log_b(g)$ in known range.

To find the minimal of $|J|$ in $x \in [i, +\infty]$, we used the term of the Taylor Series up to the first order, as follows:

$$x_i^{k+1} = \begin{cases} x_i^k - \frac{J}{J'}, & \text{if } x_i^{k+1} \geq i \\ i, & \text{otherwise,} \end{cases} \tag{3}$$

where $i \in [m]$, k denotes the iteration number, and the subscript J' denotes the first derivative of the function J with respect to x_i^k.

$$J'(x, i) = \frac{1}{\ln(b)} \sum_{p=0}^{i-1} \frac{1}{(x - p)} \tag{4}$$

Algorithm 1. Unranking Algorithm

1: **procedure** UNRANK(g, m)

2:    **Input** g ▷ Rank Number

3:    **Output** $(x_1, x_2, ..., x_m)$ ▷ Combination Object

4:      $x_m^o \leftarrow m$ ▷ Initial approximate solution

5:    **for** $i \leftarrow m$ **downto** 1 **do**

6:        $x_i \leftarrow 1 + \left\lfloor \text{Minimize } |J(x, i, g)| \text{ with } x \geqslant i \right\rfloor$

7:        $g \leftarrow \binom{x_i}{i} - g - 1$

8:    **end for**

9:    **return** $(x_1, x_2, ..., x_m)$ ▷ Combination object

10: **end procedure**

Due to the concavity of the function J in $x \in [i, +\infty]$, the initial solutions $x_i^o \in [i, +\infty]$ ensure convergence to the root of J, and are initialized as follows:

$$x_i^o = \begin{cases} m, & \text{if } i = m \\ x_{i+1}, & \text{otherwise} \end{cases} \tag{5}$$

The above is based on the revolving door ordering principle: $x_1 < x_2 < ... < x_m$, and the closeness of x_i to x_{i+1}, which ensures efficient convergence to the global optima.

As for termination criterion, we use $|J'| < \delta$ and $|x^{k+1} - x^k|/|x^k| < \varepsilon$; in which δ and ε are threshold tolerances to avoid division and sampling with very small numbers. Without loss of generality within the context of standard desktop environments, we use $\delta = \varepsilon = 10^{-8}$.

2.3   Parallelization

Both functions J and J' are computable in $O(i)$ time by using a single processor, and in $O(\log i)$ time by using at most $O(i/\log i)$ processors (to ensure work-efficiency in parallel cores according to the Brent's Theorem[3]).

For parallelization of the cost function J and J', we used Algorithm 2 which reduces i sums in multiple elements per thread in a CUDA-enabled Graphics Processing Unit. Here, *gdata* is the array with i elements, each of which corresponds to the computed value of $\frac{x-i}{p} + 1$ for $p \in [i]$. The number of blocks B is set to 64 to ensure 1024 elements per thread [35].

---

[3] assuming algebraic operations with numbers in $O(1)$.

Algorithm 2. Reduction Algorithm

1: **procedure** REDUCE($gdata, n, B$, nIsPow2)
2:     **Input** $gdata$ ▷ Array
3:     **Input** n ▷ Length of $gdata$
4:     **Input** B ▷ Block size
5:     **Input** nIsPow2   ▷ Boolean, if n is Power of 2
6:     **Output** $gdata$ ▷ Array
7:     $*D \leftarrow SharedMemory()$
8:     $t \leftarrow threadIdx.x$
9:     $i \leftarrow (2B)blockIdx.x + threadIdx.x$
10:     $G \leftarrow (2B)gridDim.x$
11:     $S \leftarrow 0$
12:     $S \leftarrow INITIALIZE(B, n, gdata, i, S, nIsPow2)$
13:     $i \leftarrow i + G$
14:     **while** $i < n$ **do**
15:         $S \leftarrow S + gdata[i]$
16:         **if** nIsPow2 $\lor$ $(i + B < n)$ **then**
17:             $S \leftarrow S + gdata[i + B]$
18:         **end if**
19:         $i \leftarrow i + G$
20:     **end while**
21:     $D[t] = S; \; syncthreads()$
22:     $D[t] \leftarrow S \leftarrow REDUCE1(B, 512, D, t, S)$
23:     $D[t] \leftarrow S \leftarrow REDUCE1(B, 256, D, t, S)$
24:     $D[t] \leftarrow S \leftarrow REDUCE1(B, 128, D, t, S)$
25:     **if** $t < 32$ **then**
26:         $volatile double * M = D$
27:         $M[t] \leftarrow S \leftarrow REDUCE2(B, 64, M, t, S)$
28:         $M[t] \leftarrow S \leftarrow REDUCE2(B, 32, M, t, S)$
29:         $M[t] \leftarrow S \leftarrow REDUCE2(B, 16, M, t, S)$
30:         $M[t] \leftarrow S \leftarrow REDUCE2(B, 8, M, t, S)$
31:         $M[t] \leftarrow S \leftarrow REDUCE2(B, 4, M, t, S)$
32:         $M[t] \leftarrow S \leftarrow REDUCE2(B, 2, M, t, S)$
33:         **if** $t = 0$ **then**
34:             $gdata[blockIdx.x] = D[0]$
35:         **end if**
36:     **end if**
37:     **return** $gdata$ ▷ Array
38: **end procedure**

Algorithm 3. Initialize

1: **procedure** INITIALIZE($B, n, gdata, i, S$, nIsPow2)
2:    **if** $i < n$ **then**
3:        $S \leftarrow gdata[i]$
4:        **if** $n > 1$ **then**
5:            **if** nIsPow2 $\lor$ $(i + B < n)$ **then**
6:                $S \leftarrow S + gdata[i + B]$
7:            **end if**
8:        **end if**
9:    **end if**
10:    **return** S
11: **end procedure**

Algorithm 4. Reduction Algorithm, Type 1 and Type 2

1: **procedure** REDUCE1(B, β, D, t, S)
2:    **if** $B > \beta$ **then**
3:        **if** $t < \beta/2$ **then**
4:            $S \leftarrow S + D[t + \beta/2]$;
5:        **end if**
6:        $syncthreads()$;
7:    **end if**
8:    **return** S
9: **end procedure**
10:
11:
12: **procedure** REDUCE2(B, β, M, t, S)
13:    **if** $B \geq \beta$ **then**
14:        $S \leftarrow S + M[t + \beta/2]$;
15:    **end if**
16:    **return** S
17: **end procedure**

---

3   Computational Experiments

In order to evaluate the computational efficiency of the proposed unranking algorithm by using parallel realizations, we used diverse scenarios which reflect our foci for future potential applications, as well the applicability in standard computing environments.

3.1 Basic Settings

We implemented Algorithm 1 in MATLAB, Intel i7 4930K @ 3.4 GHz, Windows 8.1, 64 bit, wherein the computation of the subscript $\frac{J}{J'}$ in Eq. 3 is realized through a Graphics Processing Unit, GPU, GeForce GTX TITAN, ensuring the rigourous evaluations of our proposed approach for unranking.

3.2 Experiment Instances

We used relevant values of numbers n and m within computable float numbers for binomial coefficients in a standard desktop environment, which in our case is represented as $1.7977 * 10^{308}$. Thus, we used n up to 1000, and m up to 100. Also, with the aim of evaluating the proposed approach exhaustively, we generated combination objects associated with numbers *uniformly distributed* on a fixed range. For simplicity and without loss of generality, we generated combinations from numbers g in the domain $[0, 10^9]$ for each $n = \{100, 200, 300, ..., 1000\}$, and $m = \{10, 20, 30, ..., 100\}$, with 30 independent runs per each case.

We believe the above experimental instance is representative and useful to evaluate a wide-range of problems involving the generation of combinations within standard computing environments. Thus, the applicability to other contexts becomes straightforward.

3.3 Complexity Function

In order to evaluate the computational efficiency of our proposed algorithm, we argue that the time complexity mainly depends on the following elements:

- the number of iterations which are used to solve Eq. 5,
- the asymptotic behaviour of J/J' and
- the asymptotic behaviour of evaluating the binomial coefficients at line 7 of Algorithm 1.

Thus, we define the asymptotic behaviour as the function:

$$T(m) \approx F(m) + G(m) \tag{6}$$

$$F(m) \approx \sum_{l=1}^{m} \sum_{j=1}^{t_l} \alpha(l) \tag{7}$$

$$G(m) \approx \sum_{l=1}^{m} \beta(l) \tag{8}$$

where l denotes the order of the loop in Algorithm 1, in which $l = 1$ when $i = m$, and $l = m$ when $i = 1$; t_l represents the number of iterations which are used to solve the root finding problem by Eq. 5 during the l-th loop of Algorithm 1; $\alpha(l)$ denotes the complexity of evaluating the objective function J and its gradient J' during the l-th loop of Algorithm 1; and $\beta(l)$ denotes the time complexity of evaluating the binomial coefficient of line 7 of Algorithm 1.

Basically, $T(m)$ aims at computing the expected complexity to solve the m root-finding problems, denoted by the function $F(m)$, as well as to compute the m binomial coefficients, denoted by the function $G(m)$.

In order to evaluate the performance when using single and multiple computing cores, we considered the following when analyzing the expected behaviour of functions F and G:

- c_1: When using a single processor, the time complexity of both $\alpha(l)$ and $\beta(l)$ is $O(i)$. Then, the expected behaviour of the functions F and G are as follows:

$$F(m) \approx mt_1 + (m-1)t_2 + (m-2)t_3 + \ldots + t_m \tag{9}$$
$$G(m) \approx m^2 \tag{10}$$

- c_m: When using at most $O(m/\log m)$ processors in parallel, the time complexity of both $\alpha(l)$ and $\beta(l)$ is $O(\log i)$. Then, the expected behaviours become:

$$F(m) \approx \log(m)t_1 + \log(m-1)t_2 + \ldots + \log(1)t_m \tag{11}$$
$$G(m) \approx m\log(m) \tag{12}$$

The gradient-based algorithm of Eq. 5 uses a sequential, non-parallel, approach; that is, using a single processor, wherein x_i^{k+1} is sampled and evaluated after x_i^k. Using parallel algorithms in the root finding problem has interesting implications to improve the asymptotic behaviour of our algorithm even further. Exploring parallel approaches in gradient-based algorithm is a natural extension to this paper and is left for future work.

Note that if the number of iterations t_l throughout all the loops is constant in the worst case, that is $t_1 = t_2 = \ldots = t_l = \ldots = t_m = t$, then the time complexity is bounded by $O(m^2)$, when using a single processor, and bounded by $O(m\log m)$, when using at most $O(m/\log m)$ processors.

To portray the complexity function experimentally, Fig. 1 shows the asymptotic behaviour of the function $F(m)$ over all the independent unranking instances. In Fig. 1, we depicted the following elements:

- Alpha transparency is used to visualize the frequency of occurrence; thus, darker lines imply higher frequency.
- The expected behaviour of function $F(m)$ when using both single and multiple processors are compared.
- In line of the above, c_1 denotes the complexity function F when using *a single processor*.
- c_m denotes the complexity function F when using *at most $O(m/\log m)$ processors in parallel*, through the Graphics Processing Unit.
- The symbols "$+$" and "$\circ$" denote the upper bounds on the computed plots c_1 and c_m, denoting the experimental worst case scenarios.

We also evaluated the main differences among the asymptotic behaviours of the studied experimental instances. By observing the achieved results in Fig. 1, we can note the following facts:

– It is faster to generate combinations when m is close to n, while it is harder to generate combinations when m is close to $\lfloor \frac{n}{2} \rfloor$.
– Using multiple cores enables to realize the computationally efficient unranking combinations; in which for all studied cases, using a single computing core renders in quadratic-like complexity as shown by c_1 curves in Fig. 1, whereas using multiple processors renders in linear-like complexity as shown by c_m curves in Fig. 1. We argue that when using a single processor (c_1) our algorithm is expected to be bounded by $O(m^2)$, and when using at most $O(m/\log m)$ processors in parallel (c_m), our algorithm is expected to be bounded by $O(m \log m)$.

Our results suggest that the use of parallelism is beneficial to improve the efficiency frontiers of our proposed unranking algorithm. We believe our results provide useful and foundational tools to realize the smart sampling, evaluation and generation of combinatorial objects with running performance being independent of n, which is meritorious in applications when n is large or time-varying.

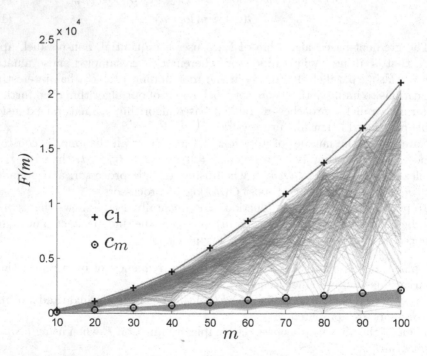

Fig. 1. Asymptotic behaviour of the complexity function F as a function of m. Here c_1 represents the complexity function F when using a single processor, and c_m represents the complexity function F when using at most $O(m/\log m)$ processors in parallel (hardware executing parallel instructions is GeForce GTX TITAN).

4   Concluding Remarks

In this paper, we have proposed an approach for generating combinations from given integer numbers by solving minimization problems of a tailored cost function being evaluated by reductions in a CUDA-enabled Graphics Processing Hardware. Relevant experiments within computationally allowable limits have shown the practical efficiency, achieving the $O(m^2)$ in case of using a single processor, and $O(m \log m)$ in case of using at most $O(m/\log m)$ processors, and offering the generation of m out of n with n-independency, which is meritorious when n is large or time-varying. We believe our results provide useful and foundational tools to allow the succinct representation of combinatorial problems.

Acknowledgement. We acknowledge the support from Kakenhi No. 15K18095 to fund this work.

References

1. Myers, A.F.: k-out-of-n: G system reliability with imperfect fault coverage. IEEE Trans. Reliab. **56**(3), 464–473 (2007)
2. Tamada, Y., Imoto, S., Miyano, S.: Parallel algorithm for learning optimal bayesian network structure. J. Mach. Learn. Res. **12**, 2437–2459 (2011)
3. Imada, T., Ota, S., Nagamochi, H., Akutsu, T.: Enumerating stereoisomers of tree structured molecules using dynamic programming. J. Math. Chem. **49**, 910–970 (2010)
4. Suzuki, K., Yokoo, M.: Secure combinatorial auctions by dynamic programming with polynomial secret sharing. In: Blaze, M. (ed.) FC 2002. LNCS, vol. 2357, pp. 44–56. Springer, Heidelberg (2003). https://doi.org/10.1007/3-540-36504-4_4
5. Agrawal, R., Mannila, H., Srikant, R., Toivonen, H., Verkamo, A.I.: Fast discovery of association rules. In: Advances in Knowledge Discovery and Data Mining, pp. 307–328 (1996)
6. Khachiyan, L., Boros, E., Borys, K., Elbassioni, K., Gurvich, V., Makino, K.: Enumerating spanning and connected subsets in graphs and matroids. J. Oper. Res. Soc. Jpn. **50**, 325–338 (2007)
7. Chisholm, B.J., Webster, D.C.: The development of coatings using combinatorial/high throughput methods: a review of the current status. J. Coat. Technol. Res. **4**(1), 1–12 (2007)
8. Scott-Phillips, T.C., Blythe, R.A.: Why is combinatorial communication rare in the natural world, and why is language an exception to this trend? J. R. Soc. Interface **10**(88) (2013)
9. Knuth, D.E.: Generating All Combinations and Partitions: The Art of Computer Programming, Fascicle 3. Addison Wesley, Reading (1968)
10. Mifsud, C.J.: Algorithm 154: combination in lexicographical order. Commun. ACM **6**(3), 103 (1963)
11. Chase, P.J.: Algorithm 382: combinations of m out of n objects. Commun. ACM **13**(6), 368 (1970)
12. Akl, S.G.: A comparison of combination generation methods. ACM Trans. Mathe. Softw. **7**(1), 42–45 (1981)

13. Martínez, C., Molinero, X.: An experimental study of unranking algorithms. In: Ribeiro, C.C., Martins, S.L. (eds.) WEA 2004. LNCS, vol. 3059, pp. 326–340. Springer, Heidelberg (2004). https://doi.org/10.1007/978-3-540-24838-5_25
14. Ruskey, F., Williams, A.: The coolest way to generate combinations. Discret. Math. **309**, 5305–5320 (2009)
15. Xiang, L., Ushijima, K.: On o(1) time algorithms for combinatorial generation. Comput. J. **44**(4), 292–302 (2001)
16. Nihenjuis, A., Wilf, H.S.: Combinatorial Algorithms for Computers and Calculators. Academic Press, New York (1978)
17. Kurtzberg, J.: Algorithm 94: combination. Commun. ACM **5**(6), 344 (1962)
18. Flajolet, P., Zimmerman, P., Van Cutsem, B.: A calculus for the random generation of combinatorial structures. Theor. Comput. Sci. **132**(1), 1–35 (1994)
19. Knuth, D.E.: The Art of Computing Programming: Volume 2 Seminumerical Algorithms. Addison Wesley, Reading (1968)
20. Buckles, B.P., Lybanon, M.: Algorithm 515: generation of a vector from the lexicographical index. ACM Trans. Math. Softw. **3**(2), 180–182 (1977)
21. Crouse, D.F.: Remark on algorithm 515: generation of a vector from the lexicographical index combinations. ACM Trans. Math. Softw. **33**(2), 15 (2007)
22. Butler, J.T., Sasao, T.: Index to constant weight codeword converter. In: Koch, A., Krishnamurthy, R., McAllister, J., Woods, R., El-Ghazawi, T. (eds.) ARC 2011. LNCS, vol. 6578, pp. 193–205. Springer, Heidelberg (2011). https://doi.org/10.1007/978-3-642-19475-7_21
23. Er, M.C.: Lexicographic ordering, ranking and unranking of combinations. Int. J. Comput. Mathe. **17**, 277–283 (1985)
24. Tang, C., Du, M., Lee, R.: Unranking combinations in parallel. In: Proceedings of International Computer Symposium, pp. 1006–1010 (1984)
25. Akl, S.: Design and Analysis of Parallel Algorithms. Prentice Hall, Upper Saddle River (1989)
26. Kokosinskiński, Z.: Unranking combinations in parallel. In: Second International Conference Parallel and Distributed Processing Techniques and Applications, pp. 79–82 (1996)
27. Kapralski, A.: New methods for generation permutations, combinations and other combinatorial objects in parallel. J. Parallel Distrib. Comput. **17**, 315–326 (1993)
28. Kokosinskiński, Z.: Algorithms for unranking combinations and other related choice functions. Report 95-1-006, The University of Aizu (1995)
29. Kreher, D., Stinson, D.: Combinatorial Algorithms: Generation Enumeration and Search. CRC Press, Boca Raton (1998)
30. Nayak, A., Stojmenovic, I.: Handbook of Applied Algorithms: Solving Scientific, Engineering and Practical Problems. Wiley-Blackwell, Hoboken (2008)
31. Savage, C.: A survey of combinatorial gray codes. SIAM Rev. **39**, 605–629 (1997)
32. Liu, C.N., Tang, D.T.: Distance-2 cyclic chaining of constant-weight codes. IEEE Trans. Comput. **C–22**(2), 176–180 (1973)
33. Shimizu, T., Fukunaga, T., Nagamochi, H.: Unranking of small combinations from large sets. J. Discret. Algorithms **29**(5), 8–20 (2014)
34. Woodward, J.R., Bai, R.: Canonical representation genetic programming. In: Proceedings of the First ACM/SIGEVO Summit on Genetic and Evolutionary Computation. GEC 2009, New York, NY, USA, pp. 585–592. ACM (2009)
35. Harris, M.: Optimizing parallel reduction in CUDA. NVIDIA Developer Technology. Accessed 20 June 20 2018

Extending the Advisor Concept to Deal with Known-Ahead Transportation Tasks

Nick Nygren and Jörg Denzinger(✉) ⓘ

Department of Computer Science, University of Calgary, Calgary, Canada
{ndnygren,denzinge}@ucalgary.ca

Abstract. The efficiency improvement advisor can improve the quality of the emergent solutions created by self-organizing emergent multi-agent systems by identifying recurring tasks. In particular, those recurring tasks that the agents in the self-organizing system do not solve well become valuable knowledge because this knowledge is used to create exception rules for the appropriate agents that improve their task-fulfilling behavior. In this paper, we present an extension to the advisor that allows it to use certain knowledge about future tasks in addition to the (somewhat uncertain) knowledge gained from the system history. By now creating groups of exception rules for each expected task, the self-organizing emergent system can achieve near optimal solutions for static problem instances and good solutions for a range of expected tasks, while still being able to deal with dynamic (and unpredicted) tasks, as shown by experiments in a pickup and delivery transportation scenario.

Keywords: Efficiency improvement advisor · Analytics
Dynamic optimization · Known-ahead tasks
Pickup and delivery problems

1 Introduction

Transportation is a multi-faceted industry highly influenced by the particular tasks it fulfills and how dynamic these tasks are. If all tasks are known well in advance, static optimization methods are sufficient to achieve efficient if not totally optimal fulfillment of these tasks. The more it is possible for tasks to pop up at any time and to need immediate attention, the more difficult it becomes to use these static optimizers to plan task fulfillment, since often there is not enough time to do replanning. Alternatively, task fulfillment can be performed by several agents as a self-organizing system, where the agents on their own react to dynamically appearing tasks. Static optimizers and self-organizing systems are the two extremes of a spectrum of approaches to task fulfillment. Often some additional coordination tries to avoid having all or many agents flock to one task while other tasks are ignored for a long time. Examples for such self-organizing systems are [1] or [2]. While methods for these two ends of the spectrum are well established, many kinds of transportation problems require solutions that

© Springer Nature Switzerland AG 2018
Y. Xiang et al. (Eds.): IDCS 2018, LNCS 11226, pp. 27–39, 2018.
https://doi.org/10.1007/978-3-030-02738-4_3

are somewhere between those extremes, able to cover parts of the spectrum or even the whole spectrum and able to use various kinds of knowledge to improve or guarantee efficiency.

In this paper, we present an improvement to the so-called efficiency improvement advisor (EIA, see [3] and [4]) that allows it to use knowledge about known-ahead tasks to provide a coverage of the whole spectrum. The EIA was designed to improve methods for the purely dynamic end of the spectrum by performing analytics of the past work of the agents, identifying recurring tasks and using knowledge about these tasks to provide advice to the agents (in form of exception rules) to improve the performance of the whole system. If there are enough recurring tasks in the problem instance, the EIA has proven to improve efficiency compared to the non-advised system, although from time to time an instance might be performed worse.

Our improvement, the extended efficiency improvement advisor (EEIA), additionally allows to use knowledge about known-ahead tasks to be converted into exception rules for an upcoming problem instance. Since the EEIA can naturally also be applied to a problem instance where none of the tasks are dynamic, an EEIA-based system covers the whole spectrum between purely dynamic and completely static problem instances.

We evaluated the EEIA for the application area of pickup and delivery problems. Our experiments show that the EEIA keeps the EIA's abilities to deal with dynamically appearing tasks and to use knowledge about recurring tasks. It is additionally able to make use of knowledge about known-ahead tasks substantially outperforming the EIA and it gets near-optimal performance when dealing with purely static problem instances.

This paper is organized as follows: after this introduction, in Sect. 2 we present the EIA, the base system it improves upon and their instantiation to pickup and delivery problems. In Sect. 3, we introduce the EEIA. Section 4 reports on our various experimental series that we performed to proof our claims around the EEIA. Section 5 provides short references to related work and Sect. 6 provides concluding remarks and some possible future work.

2   The EIA for Pickup and Delivery Problems

In this section, we first formally describe pickup and delivery problems (PDPs), then present digital infochemical coordination (DIC, see [1]) which is the basic self-organizing system method we improve on with the EIA and EEIA and then describe the EIA for DIC and PDP.

2.1   Pickup and Delivery Problems

In pickup and delivery problems a set A of vehicles (agents) acting in a world (the environment $\mathcal{E}nv$) are performing transportation requests that consist of picking up some good or person at a particular location in the world and delivering it to another location (a task ta). There are many instantiations of PDP. In a dynamic PDP, a task is formally described by $ta = (l_{pickup}, l_{delivery}, ncap)$, where l_{pickup} is the coordinates of the pickup location, $l_{delivery}$ the coordinates of the delivery location and $ncap$ is the capacity needed for fulfilling this task, and is announced at a time t (at which it can also be started). Task plus announcement time is called an event. Each agent Ag in A also has a capacity cap_{Ag}. We look at sequences of events, so-called *run instances* that have to be fulfilled in a given time interval $Time$, for example a day: $((ta_1, t_1), (ta_2, t_2), \ldots, (ta_m, t_m))$. To allow for analytics, we consider a sequence of such run sequences (called a *run*), which formally is

$$(((ta_{11}, t_{11}), (ta_{21}, t_{21}), \ldots, (ta_{m_1 1}, t_{m_1 1})), \ldots, ((ta_{1k}, t_{1k}), (ta_{2k}, t_{2k}), \ldots,$$
$$(ta_{m_k k}, t_{m_k k}))).$$

Usually, the agents start and end a run instance in a depot.

After the agents in A have fulfilled all the tasks in a run instance they have created an emergent solution sol for that run instance, formally $sol = ((ta'_1, Ag'_1, t'_1), (ta'_2, Ag'_2, t'_2), \ldots, (ta'_m, Ag'_m, t'_m))$, where $ta'_m \in \{ta_1, \ldots, ta_m\}$, $ta'_i \neq ta'_j$ for all $i \neq j$, $Ag'_i \in A$, $t'_i \leq t'_{i+1}$, $t'_i \in Time$. A tuple (ta'_1, Ag'_1, t'_1) means task ta'_i was started by Ag'_i at time t'_i.

For some applications of pickup and delivery just fulfilling all tasks is the goal. But for many other applications the vehicles in A are supposed to create good, if not optimal solutions, which requires some kind of quality measure $qual(sol)$ for a solution sol. In this paper, we use two such quality measures, namely $qual^{time}$, the final completion time for a run instance, and $qual^{dist}$, the sum of the distances travelled by each vehicle during the run instance. The later was already used in [3] and [4].

2.2 Digital Infochemical Coordination

As already mentioned, we use as a base approach for the coordination of the agents digital infochemical coordination (DIC), a generalization of pheromone-based coordination. The basic idea is to use various kinds of so-called infochemicals that are propagated through $\mathcal{E}nv$ and provide information to the agents that perceive them at their current location creating a local view of the environment for decision making. In addition to vehicles, also other entities can emit such infochemicals, like, for example locations in $\mathcal{E}nv$.

In the base system for PDP, tasks are announced to the agents by having the pickup location l_{pickup} and the delivery location $l_{delivery}$ emit one kind of infochemical called synomones. They are propagated through $\mathcal{E}nv$ and a location receiving them stores their existence and intensity. A synomone on a location evaporates after a certain time so that the two locations for the task have to repeat the synomone emission until the pickup, respectively the delivery have happened. The synomone emitted from l_{pickup} provides a vehicle with the emitter's location as well as $ncap$ and the synomone from $l_{delivery}$ provides just information on that location.

The decision making of an Ag_i computes a utility for each task with infochemicals at its current location and then goes for the task with the highest current utility. The task utility combines the intensity of the perceived infochemical with the agent's current state. This way, it is possible to focus on delivering the goods of a task if the pickup has already happened. Among the infochemicals considered by a vehicle are not only the synomones mentioned above, but also so-called allelochemicals that the pickup location emits as soon as a vehicle has picked up the goods of the task. If an agent perceives such an allelochemicals it will ignore all synomones related to this task. A third infochemical, a pheromone, is used by the vehicles themselves to indicate to other agents which task they currently intend to fulfill. Since such pheromones are only propagated in a small area thus creating a trail and agents that can perceive such a trail are behind another agent and will also ignore the synomones related to the task. For more details on DIC and the instantiation to PDP, please see [1].

2.3   The Efficiency Improvement Advisor for DIC for PDP

The efficiency improvement advisor (EIA) concept for improving self-organizing groups of agents that solve dynamic task fulfillment problems was first presented in [3]. It is based on the observation that in many dynamic applications, like pickup and delivery, there are tasks that appear in most of the run instances in a run. And using the knowledge of such recurring tasks can allow improvements of the efficiency of the system, if the agents in A do not already handle these recurring tasks well. The general idea is to add to A an additional agent Ag_{EIA} that is an analytics and advice component (not in any way a central control). Between run instances, Ag_{EIA} gets information from the other agents in A about the tasks they fulfilled in a run instance whenever communication with these agents is possible. This allows to identify recurring tasks, to compare the emergent solutions for these recurring tasks with optimal (or at least very good) solutions (which naturally can be computed a posteriori by Ag_{EIA}) and to create so called exception rules for the agents in A if the emergent solutions are substantially worse than the optimal ones. The later is done using both the emergent behavior and what the optimal behavior would be.

More precisely, Ag_{EIA} goes through the following steps after each run instance (but, before the next begins):

1. **receive** collects the local history H_i for each $Ag_i \in A$, when Ag_i is able to communicate during the run instance. H_i contains all observations, internal states and decisions of Ag_i since the sequence of run instances started.
2. **transform** takes the local histories $H_1, \ldots, H_n$ of all agents and creates the global history $GHist$, which essentially is the sequence of run instances $(ri_1, \ldots, ri_k) = ((ta_{11}, t_{11}), \ldots, (ta_{m_11}, t_{m_11})), \ldots, ((ta_{1k}, t_{1k}), \ldots, (ta_{m_kk}, t_{m_kk}))$ the agents have fulfilled so far and the emergent solution sol_j for each run instance ri_j that the agents achieved.
3. **extract** extracts from $GHist$ a sequence of recurring tasks/events $((ta_1^{rec}, t_1^{rec}), \ldots, (ta_p^{rec}, t_p^{rec}))$.

4. **optimize** computes the optimal solution $opt^{rec} = ((ta_1^{rec}, Ag_1'^{rec}, t_1'^{rec}), \ldots, (ta_p^{rec}, Ag_p'^{rec}, t_p'^{rec})), Ag_j'^{rec} \in A, t_j'^{rec} \in Time$, for just having to do the tasks $ta_1^{rec}, \ldots, ta_p^{rec}$ if they are already known at the beginning of $Time$. This step also includes comparing $qual(opt^{rec})$ with the quality $qual(last)$ of the last emergent solution $last$ for the tasks $ta_1^{rec}, \ldots, ta_p^{rec}$ that was created by the agents. If $qual(last)/qual(opt^{rec}) > qualthresh$ then the agents in A performed well and Ag_{EIA}'s work is done until new information arrives.
5. **derive** creates for each agent Ag_i a set R_i of exception rules, if the agents did not perform well. Note that an R_i can also be empty.
6. **send** communicates the set R_i to Ag_i for each agent the next time communication with it is possible.

Since the EIA and its application to DIC and PDP has been discussed already in [3] and [4], we will focus in the following discussion on the step that has to be modified to deal with the knowledge of known-ahead tasks to show the difference between the original step and the modifications that we will discuss in the next section. This step is **derive**.

There are different kinds of exception rules and due to this different ways how **derive** can be realized. [3] introduced ignore rules of the form $cond_{ig} \rightarrow \neg a_{ta}$. For PDP, the condition $cond_{ig}$ was realized by requiring that a task announced by a synomone is within a similarity threshold of ta (based on Euclidean distance between their respective locations). The action, $\neg a_{ta}$, means that any synomones of that task are being ignored by the agent. An ignore rule does not tell an agent what to do, it tells it what not to do, which is much less restrictive than what pro-active rules do. A pro-active rule, introduced in [4], has the form $cond_{proa} \rightarrow prep(ta)$, which for PDP was realized by $cond_{proa}$ requiring that a certain time before the usual occurrence time of ta is reached and $prep(ta)$ overriding the normal infochemical decision making of the agent and sending it to the pickup location of ta.

Both types of exception rules are created by Ag_{EIA} by comparing the optimal solution $opt^{rec} = ((ta_1^1, Ag_1^1, t_1^1), \ldots, (ta_p^1, Ag_p^1, t_p^1))$ for the recurring tasks with the emergent solution $last = ((ta_1^2, Ag_1^2, t_1^2), \ldots, (ta_p^2, Ag_p^2, t_p^2))$ for these recurring tasks extracted and computed from the global history. Ag_{EIA} targets the first j with either $ta_j^1 \neq ta_j^2$ or $Ag_j^1 \neq Ag_j^2$ which is the first task taken by an agent that deviates from the optimal solution.

In order to use an ignore rule to deal with this situation, Ag_{EIA} creates a rule for Ag_j^2 as described above. If Ag_{EIA} deals with the deviation of emergent solution from optimal solution using a pro-active rule, then a rule for Ag_j^1 is created, which has as its action $prep(ta_j^1)$.

3 The EEIA for Pickup and Delivery

There is more knowledge around pickup and delivery problems than recurring tasks. An obvious additional type of knowledge are guaranteed known-ahead tasks that customers have communicated to the system before the interval $Time$.

In contrast to the recurring tasks identified by analyzing the sequence of previous run instances, which come still with some (small) possibility that they will not occur again in the next run instance, such known-ahead tasks represent certain knowledge (by, for example, having the customers pay in advance for them). Since the advisor as described in the previous section treats the recurring tasks as if they are certain in its planning, it should be rather straightforward to add to the recurring tasks the known-ahead tasks, but, as we will see in the following, the integration of this kind of knowledge is, while possible, not as straightforward as it seems.

More precisely, in the following $(ta_1^{know}, t_1^{know}), \ldots, (ta_q^{know}, t_q^{know})$ is a set of known-ahead tasks with the times the system can start fulfilling them that are given to the advisor before the next run instance starts and while the communication with the other agents is possible. Then the EEIA performs the steps **receive** and **extract** as described for the EIA. It then adds a step **merge**, which combines the recurring tasks $ta_1^{rec}, \ldots, ta_p^{rec}$ with the known-ahead tasks $ta_1^{know}, \ldots, ta_q^{know}$ to create the complete knowledge set for the next run instance (including the times when all these tasks are available to be fulfilled). It then uses the step **optimize** to compute the optimal solution $opt^{r+k} = ((ta_1^{r+k}, Ag_1^{'r+k}, t_1^{'r+k}), \ldots, (ta_{p+q}^{r+k}, Ag_{p+q}^{'r+k}, t_{p+q}^{'r+k})), Ag_j^{'r+k} \in A, t_j^{'r+k} \in Time$ for the complete knowledge set of tasks. Then a new version of the step **derive** is always performed creating exception rule sets R_i for all agents in A reflecting opt^{r+k}. This step will be described in more detail below. Like the EIA, the EEIA finishes with the step **send** as described before.

The step **merge** is an additional step that we added to make sure that there are no tasks that have been detected as recurring that now are given as a known-ahead task (perhaps because the customer with this task realized that he has this task every day). Naturally, such "duplicates" need to be eliminated.

Since we have to assume that some of the known-ahead tasks will be one-off tasks, there is no emergent solution to which the produced solution opt^{r+k} can be compared and therefore the EEIA always performs **derive**. And **derive** produces exception rules for all the tasks in opt^{r+k}. In fact, it creates several rules for each task in opt^{r+k}. And, due to the increase in rules and consequent possibilities for additional unintended emergent behavior, the trigger conditions of the rules need to be more precise than what we used before.

More precisely, for each $(ta_i^{r+k}, Ag_i^{'r+k}, t_i^{'r+k})$ in opt^{r+k} we create the following exception rules:

– For $Ag_i^{'r+k}$, we create
  • a pro-active rule that has as trigger condition $cond_{proa}$
    * having reached the time $t_i^{'r+k} - preptime(ta_i^{r+k}) - clustervar(ta_i^{r+k})$ and
    * having not reached the time $t_i^{'r+k} + timeout$ and
    * $Ag_i^{'r+k}$ has not already performed $prep(ta_i^{r+k})$ after the time $t_i^{'r+k} - preptime(ta_i^{r+k}) - clustervar(ta_i^{r+k})$ and,

* in case that ta_i^{r+k} is not the first task assigned to $Ag_i'^{r+k}$ in this run instance and that ta' is the task $Ag_i'^{r+k}$ has to fulfill directly before ta_i^{r+k} in opt^{r+k}, having fulfilled ta'

and as action $prep(ta_i^{r+k})$.

- an ignore rule that has as trigger condition $cond_{ig}$ that time $t_i'^{r+k} - preptime(ta_i^{r+k}) - clustervar(ta_i^{r+k})$ has not been reached and as action $\neg a_{ta_i^{r+k}}$.

– For every $Ag_j'^{r+k}$ with $i \neq j$ we create

- an ignore rule that has as trigger condition $cond_{ig}$ that
  * fulfillment of task ta_i^{r+k} can be started and
  * time $t_i'^{r+k} + timeout$ has not been reached

and as action $\neg a_{ta_i^{r+k}}$.

In the above, $preptime(ta)$ is a function that provides for a task ta the time that the agent needs to prepare for performing the first action a_{ta} of the task ta. The function $clustervar(ta)$ returns for a given recurring task ta the variance in starting times of the tasks within the occurrences of ta in the past. If ta is not a recurring task, then $clustervar(ta) = 0$. And $timeout$ is a system variable that determines how long an agent waits for a task that it was assigned by a pro-active rule to be performable before looking for other tasks to do.

All the exceptions rule created for an agent Ag_i form R_i. Note that the trigger conditions are chosen to avoid any conflicts between the rules for one agent (if $timeout$ is well chosen). Overall, with so many exception rules we restrict the autonomy of the individual agents more than the original advisor concept does. As a consequence, the tasks in the knowledge set are treated better than dynamically occuring tasks, which reflects an acknowledgement of customers that are providing their tasks early.

4   Experimental Evaluation

We have performed several different experimental series to evaluate our different claims around the EEIA. We will first present the general setup for all experiments and then look into how the EEIA deals with purely static run instances, runs with recurring, dynamic and kown-ahead tasks, and runs using different numbers of vehicles.

4.1   Setup

All experiments were performed in a world $\mathcal{E}nv$ that is a 11 by 11 grid with one depot at $5, 5$. This $\mathcal{E}nv$ is represented as a directed weighted graph, including diagonals, where the edge weight represents distance. Vertical and horizontal edges have distance 1, while diagonal edges have distance $\sqrt{2}$, effectively Euclidean distance. All vehicles are limited to a speed of 1 per time step, so they may have locations on edges rather than vertices.

The first two experimental series use exactly two vehicles, while the third series evaluates different numbers of vehicles. We use $qual^{time}$ for the first two series and $qual^{dist}$ for the third (see the explanation for why there). The tasks have $ncap = 20$ and all vehicles have $cap_{Ag} = 20$, making the experiments unit-weight.

On the EIA/EEIA side, in the conditions of the exception rules we used $clustervar = 0$ (due to the way we created run instances), $timeout = 50$ and the function $preptime$ returns always 10. For the EIA, we use the same way to create exception rules as for the EEIA, except that naturally known-ahead tasks are not part of the solution created by the optimization step. As optimizer we used a genetic algorithm (for both $qual$-functions).

4.2 The EEIA for Static Run Instances

Our first experimental series is concerned with how well the EEIA enhanced the system dealing with run instances that are purely static, without any dynamically occuring tasks. As some properties related to performance scale differently with run instance size, these trials have been run for different values of m (number of tasks in a run instance). Random tasks are generated by selecting a pair of locations, $(l_{pickup}, l_{delivery})$ in $\mathcal{E}nv$, such that $l_{pickup} \neq l_{delivery}$. Random run instances are generated as a sequence of random tasks, with uniqueness enforced. To make the run instances purely static, all tasks are announced outside of $Time$.

Table 1. Average efficiency of executing plans for purely static run instances

m	Efficiency	m	Efficiency	m	Efficiency	m	Efficiency	m	Efficiency
4	0.24 ± 1.16	10	0.29 ± 0.70	16	0.66 ± 1.57	22	0.85 ± 1.14	28	1.33 ± 1.68
5	0.10 ± 0.47	11	0.52 ± 1.41	17	0.85 ± 1.24	23	1.02 ± 1.42	29	1.35 ± 1.65
6	0.29 ± 0.92	12	0.55 ± 1.07	18	0.67 ± 0.98	24	0.84 ± 1.17	30	1.22 ± 1.69
7	0.10 ± 0.38	13	0.87 ± 1.50	19	1.38 ± 1.76	25	1.05 ± 1.41	31	1.02 ± 1.48
8	0.39 ± 1.05	14	0.79 ± 1.26	20	1.16 ± 1.55	26	1.47 ± 1.47	32	1.44 ± 1.65
9	0.48 ± 0.95	15	0.94 ± 1.61	21	0.74 ± 1.09	27	0.99 ± 1.17	33	0.69 ± 0.92

For each value of m, 50 random run instances were generated. The entire run instance was included in the knowledge set, and rules were generated based upon it. The efficiency ($qual^{time}$) of each was measured and normalized for comparison as percent worse than optimal, which is the $qual^{time}$-value of the solution that was used by the EEIA to generate the rules.

As Table 1 shows, the system using the EEIA is producing results within 1% point standard deviation of 0 (the "optimal") for every level of m. Not achieving the exact optimal solution can be accounted for by the simulator's enforcement of strict vehicle dead-lock (i.e. multiple vehicles are not permitted simultaneously on the same pathway). While the simulator enforces this, the static optimizer does not plan for it, occasionally causing vehicles to fall behind schedule due to a "traffic jam".

4.3   Comparison of the Systems for Two Vehicles

In the second series of experiments, we evaluate the gains that can be made by combining knowledge of known-ahead tasks with knowledge of recurring tasks. This required to both create runs that allowed EIA and EEIA to be applicable and randomness to evaluate the generality of the concepts within the boundaries of their applicability. In order to be realistic, we also need the recurring tasks to not occur in every run instance (just in enough to make them recurring), to explore the dangers advice (using then misleading knowledge) can produce.

To achive the above, we used the following procedure to create runs, centered around a parameter δ. We first created a base instance $\{(ta_1, t_1), \ldots, (ta_m, t_m)\}$ of random events. Then each event (ta_i, t_i) is assigned a probability p_i from the range $[\delta, 1.0]$, to be used in a weighted coin toss to determine if (ta_i, t_i) will be in a run instance or not. More precisely, any run instance within the run is created as $\{(ta'_1, t'_1), \ldots, (ta'_k, t'_k)\} \cup \{(ta_1^{know}, t_1^{know}), \ldots, (ta_q^{know}, t_q^{know})\}$, where $(ta'_i, t'_i) = (ta_i, t_i)$ if a random number created between 0 and 1 is smaller or equal to p_i and (ta'_i, t'_i) is a new randomly created event else. $\{(ta_1^{know}, t_1^{know}), \ldots, (ta_q^{know}, t_q^{know})\}$ is the set of known-ahead events for the run instance and tasks and times in it are created randomly, again.

For all experiments, we used $q = 5$ and a run consisted of 55 run instances (5 to establish some recurring tasks and 50 to observe the differences) constructed in the above manner. The **extract** step considered a task as recurring, if it occurred 4 times in the last 5 run instances the system encountered. This means that depending on δ we have that events from the base instance might from time to time not even be considered a recurring task and if it is considered recurring it might still not occur in a particular run instance. The later means that EIA or EEIA will have a vehicle preparing for that event, but it will never appear, which means that that part of the knowledge the advisor used was then misleading (and perhaps resulting in a worse performance than the basic strategy for this run instance). Naturally, this is always the danger when we use analytics of the past to predict the future.

Table 2. Comparison of $qual^{time}$ for base system vs EIA vs EEIA: average over 5 runs with $\delta = 0.75$

m	base	EIA	$EEIA$
10	7673.0	8128.4	7546.6
20	11038.8	11031.6	10342.8
25	12747.6	12501.8	11954.2
30	14267.6	13777.4	13432.8
35	14969.0	14497.2	14084.2

We did some initial experiments with different values of δ and for $\delta = 0.75$ we got mixed results for the EIA, while for all higher δ-values the EIA was always improving on the base system substantially. Therefore we performed the experiments for Table 2 with the somewhat challenging δ-value of 0.75. Each entry of Table 2 represents the average of 5 runs. As the table shows, the size of a run instance has quite some influence on what the EIA and EEIA can accomplish. Especially the EIA should have problems with smaller values of m compared to the base system, since for it all known-ahead tasks are dynamically appearing tasks[1]. And this is exactly what happened, although for $m = 20$ the EIA is already slightly better than the base system. But what is really interesting is that the EEIA outperforms both the EIA and the base system, being hundreds of time units faster.

Naturally, if the number of known-ahead tasks and the number of identified recurring tasks is small compared to the number of tasks in a run instance, then the EEIA (or the EIA) will not produce any exception rules, letting the base system do what it is supposed to do, namely dealing with highly dynamic run instance. And this, together with the experiments of the previous subsection and this subsection shows that the EEIA indeed covers the whole spectrum of dynamism.

4.4   EEIA vs EIA vs Base System for Two and More Vehicles

So far, all experimental series we have presented used only two vehicles, which made the work for the optimizer in step **optimize** easier. But, naturally, this could also mean that the EEIA only works for two vehicles. In this subsection we therefore provide an experimental series that compares the three systems over runs using more than two vehicles, namely additionally 3 and 4.

Using as solution evaluation criteria the time until the last vehicle is back in the depot is not a good evaluation method, since it does not measure, for example, unnecessary driving around by vehicles as long as this happens before the last task is fulfilled. In fact, as already mentioned before, multiple vehicles flocking to a particular task is a possible problem for self-organizing systems. In order to measure this potential waste of resources, we therefore decided to perform this experimental series using the $qual^{dist}$ measure (which naturally also serves to show that the EEIA is an improvement for both measures).

We created run instances as discribed in the last subsection using as δ-value 0.75 (again) and also 0.85 and we then performed each created run with all 3 system variants and with the 3 different numbers of vehicles. We used $m = 30$ for which we know that both EIA and EEIA are successful for 2 vehicles. And we report on the average over 5 runs.

As Table 3 shows, for every value of δ and every number of vehicles, the EIA improved the performance of the base system and the EEIA improved on the performance of the EIA. Unsurprisingly, the improvements are better for $\delta = 0.85$ compared to a value of 0.75. As explained above, having more resources leads to

---

[1] For $m = 10$, for example, we can expect on average the knowledge set used by EIA to contain 8 accurate tasks and 1 misleading task, with the 6 remaining tasks having to be handled as dynamically occuring.

Table 3. Comparison of $qual^{dist}$ for base system vs EIA vs EEIA for different numbers of vehicles: average over 5 runs for $m = 30$

δ	Nr. of Vehicles	base	EIA	EEIA
0.75	2	14169.0	14014.4	13604.2
	3	14439.2	14149.8	13754.8
	4	14688.2	14347.8	13837.0
0.85	2	14782.4	14088.6	13431.6
	3	14959.4	13906.0	13380.8
	4	15240.8	14246.4	13639.0

being able to waste some of these resources, as the numbers especially for the base system show (nearly 300 more distance units used when having 3 instead of 2 vehicles and over 500 more when using 4 instead of 2 for $\delta = 0.75$ and nearly 200 units more for 3 and nearly 500 more for 4 than for 2 for $\delta = 0.85$. And this was on the same run instances and runs!). When using EIA and EEIA the waste is reduced compared to the base system and for 3 vehicles and a δ of 0.85 we even have less waste than for 2 vehicles. Naturally, as long as there are purely dynamic tasks dealing with them is based on the strategies of the base system and therefore still allows for wasting resources. And, due to using a genetic algorithm for planning, we are not guaranteed to find an optimum, which also contributes to more vehicles creating more wasted resources (the real optimum for a static problem is naturally not worse distance-wise if more vehicles are available).

5   Related Works

Due to the importance of transportation in general and pickup and delivery in particular, there are quite a number of works dealing with them. [5] and [6] are surveys of the state-of-the-art. On the purely dynamic side of the dynamism spectrum, there are also several works, see [7] for a specialized survey.

An approach that tries to include information about known-ahead tasks is [2] (with several follow-up works), using an auction based approach with a central auctioneer, but no analytics. [8] also uses an auction based approach, but has the good to transport (its container, in fact) acting as auctioneer. Again, there is no use of analytics.

If we only look at works that try to improve on purely dynamic task fulfillment, [9] presents the so-called Observer/Controller architecture. But this approach requires the ability of the controller to intervene at any point in time which requires to be able to observe all agents at all the time. The approach in [10] has the same requirements and problems.

6 Conclusion and Future Work

In this paper, we presented the extended efficiency improvement advisor (EEIA) that extends the efficiency improvement advisor (EIA) concept to cover the whole spectrum of dynamism a distributed transportation system might encounter. In addition to using knowledge gained from analyzing the history of a self-organizing transportation system as the EIA does, the EEIA uses knowledge about known-ahead tasks to create a plan for all these tasks and transforms this plan into exception rules for the vehicles that still allow these vehicles to deal with dynamically appearing tasks.

Our experiments with a variant of pickup and delivery problems showed that the EEIA indeed covers the whole spectrum of dynamism: for purely static problem instances the EEIA comes very near to the planned solution (failing to produce the planned solution only in case of traffic jams), for limited dynamic tasks (i.e. a small number compared to the number of tasks with knowledge about them) it produces substantially better results than the base system, even if some of the knowledge is from time to time misleading amd everything else is covered by the self-organizing ability of the base system.

Future work will be towards finding additional knowledge sources that might be useful for the efficiency of an advised system. We also will instantiate and evaluate the EEIA for other problems than pickup and delivery.

References

1. Kasinger, H., Bauer, B., Denzinger, J.: Design pattern for self-organizing emergent systems based on digital infochemicals. In: Proceedings of EASe 2009, San Francisco, pp. 45–55 (2009)
2. Fischer, K., Müller, J.P., Pischel, M.: Cooperative transportation scheduling: an application domain for DAI. Appl. Artif. Intell. **10**(1), 1–34 (1996)
3. Steghöfer, J.-P., Denzinger, J., Kasinger, H., Bauer, B.: Improving the efficiency of self-organizing emergent systems by an advisor. In: 2010 Seventh IEEE International Conference and Workshops on Engineering of Autonomic and Autonomous Systems, pp. 63–72 (2010)
4. Steiner, T., Denzinger, J., Kasinger, H., Bauer, B.: Pro-active advice to improve the efficiency of self-organizing emergent systems. In: Proceedings of EASe 2011, Las Vegas, pp. 97–106 (2011)
5. Berbeglia, G., Cordeau, J.-F., Gribkovskaia, I., Laporte, G.: Static pickup and delivery problems: a classification scheme and survey. TOP **15**, 1–31 (2007)
6. Parragh, S.N., Doerner, K., Hartl, R.F.: A survey on pickup and delivery models part I: transportation between customers and depot. J. für Betriebswirtschaft **58**, 21–51 (2008)
7. Berbeglia, G., Cordeau, J.-F., Laporte, G.: Dynamic pickup and delivery problems. Eur. J. Oper. Res. **202**(1), 8–15 (2010)
8. Mes, M., Van Der Heijden, M., Van Harten, A.: Comparison of agent-based scheduling to look-ahead heuristics for real-time transportation problems. Eur. J. Oper. Res. **181**(1), 59–75 (2007)

9. Tomforde, S., et al.: Observation and control of organic systems. In: Müller-Schloer, C., Schmeck, H., Ungerer, T. (eds.) Organic Computing - A Paradigm Shift for Complex Systems, pp. 325–338. Springer, Basel (2011). https://doi.org/10.1007/978-3-0348-0130-0_21
10. Schumann, R., Lattner, A.D., Timm, I.J.: Management-by-exception-a modern approach to managing self-organizing systems. Commun. SIWN **4**, 168–172 (2008)

A Framework for Task-Guided Virtual Machine Live Migration

Cho-Chin Lin[✉] and Yuan-Han Kuo

Department of Electronic Engineering, National Ilan University,
Yilan City 26047, Taiwan
cclin@niu.edu.tw

Abstract. Virtual machine is an emulation environment developed for dependable computing. Live migration mechanism provides the functionality that moves an ongoing virtual machine across hosts seamlessly so as to provide non-stop services. However, service quality cannot be satisfied if excessive pages are synchronized at the stop-and-copy phase. In this paper, a task-guided framework is proposed for live migration to start at an opportune time such that a short service downtime can be guaranteed. In our framework, a code entity which updates pages within a small range or in a low frequency is tagged. Once a tag has been detected, the coordinator either approves a pending live migration request or withdraws the permission to an ongoing live migration depending on the tag types. The prototype which is capable of task-guided live migration has been implemented. Our experiments show that both the service downtime and the task execution time have been improved by our task-guided approach regardless of the possibly existing suspension overhead.

Keywords: Virtual machine · Live migration · Cloud computing

1 Introduction

Virtualization enables system performance consolidated as well as resource utilization flexible [1]. From the view of operating system (OS), the virtualization technique is classified into two categories: the modified guest OS and unmodified guest OS [2]. Virtual machines (VM's) and their hypervisor are important components of a virtualization platform. In general, VM's are deployed above the layer where the hypervisor sits for managing resource sharing. Recently, the concept of virtualization has attracted many research interests due to its advantages in deploying the architectures for cloud computing. One of the advantages is that it is easy to maintain efficient resource utilization by balancing the loads among the components of cloud computing platform. This advantage is achieved by migration mechanism which moves the VM running on an overloaded host

This research is supported by Ministry of Science and Technology under the grant MOST 106-2221-E-197-004.

to another. VM migration duplicates operating system, state and service applications from the source host to the target host. According to the definition of migrations in [3], VM live migration can be an instance of strong migration. The suspended VM on the source will restart on the target after the migration has successfully done.

The customers purchasing services on potentially migrating VM's may experience a long service downtime. For some service applications, a long service downtime results in violating the service level agreement cosigned by the service provider and the customer. Thus, a VM hypervisor should minimize the downtime whenever a migration is needed. To achieve this goal, the live migration mechanism has been developed to migrate an ongoing VM across hosts seamlessly. The mechanism synchronizes pages across hosts iteratively and tries to find an opportune time for temporarily stopping the VM. The interval of temporarily stopping the VM is called stop-and-copy (SaC) phase. The time is given by a set of terminating conditions. Some of the terminating conditions may indicate that the number of recently updated pages falling below a threshold. In this case, a short SaC phase can be expected. The other conditions are designed to avoid endless iterations of page synchronizations. Once one of the terminating conditions is satisfied, the live migration enters the SaC phase and the VM will restart on the target later on.

Bounded downtime computation is an important issue for migrating applications with critical response time demand. Compared with the traditional migration, migrating VM experiences a short service downtime if the live migration enters the SaC phase due to the number of recently updated pages falling below a threshold. However, it is possible that a live migration cannot but enter the SaC phase to avoid endless iterations. In this case, a long service downtime may be experienced. It implies that an approach for suggesting an opportune time of starting live migration is necessary. In this paper, a framework for task-guided (TAG) live migration is proposed for suggesting the opportune time. It is achieved by inserting tags at the boundaries of a code entity which updates pages either within a small range or in a low frequency. Once a tag has been detected, the coordinator either approves a pending live migration request or withdraws the permission to an ongoing live migration depending on the tag types. The prototype which is capable of task-guided live migration has been implemented. Our experiments have shown that both the service downtime and the task execution time have been improved by our TAG live migration regardless of the possible overhead of temporarily withdrawing migration.

The paper is organized as follows. The background and related works are discussed in Sect. 2. In Sect. 3, the framework of our TAG live migration is developed and a state diagram which models an essential component is described. In Sect. 4, based on the proposed framework, two suits of experiments are conducted to demonstrate the effectiveness of our TAG approach. Finally, concluding remarks and future research directions are provided in Sect. 5.

2   Background and Related Works

Live migration synchronizes pages across hosts before it enters the SaC phase. Page synchronization activity may continue for several iterations without severely affecting service computations. In an iteration, the page statuses are checked and those which satisfy the live migration protocol are selected for page synchronization. In general, a live migration can be divided into three phases: the push phase, the SaC phase and the pull phase [4]. The push and pull phases synchronize pages without severely affecting service quality. Although a live migration scheme can incorporate all the phases, most practical approaches only select two phases in their implementations. If a live migration incorporates the SaC and pull phases, it is considered as a live migration with the post-copy scheme. If a live migration incorporates the push and SaC phases, it is considered as a live migration with the pre-copy scheme.

Xen is an open source virtualization platform at which live migration employs the iterative pre-copy scheme [1]. In each iteration, computation activity at the source may write values to pages and a subset of pages are selected for sending to the target for synchronization purpose. Three bitmaps are used in Xen to implement its synchronization protocol: to_skip, to_send and to_fix [5]. Once the live migration starts an iteration, to_send is updated immediately. In contrast with to_send, to_skip is updated several times in an iteration to respond the most recent memory access pattern. Bitmap $to\_send[j] = 1$ if a value has been written to the page j in the most recent iteration; $to\_send[j] = 0$, otherwise. Bitmap $to\_skip[j] = 1$ if a value has been written to the page j some time in this iteration; $to\_skip[j] = 0$, otherwise. The entries of to_send and to_skip are scanned and compared one by one. Page j is synchronized if $to\_skip[j] = 0$ and $to\_send[j] = 1$. Those selected pages are copied to a buffer and sent to the target in several rounds. Four terminating conditions are defined to avoid an endless pre-copy process [6]. The live migration terminates iterative pre-copy phase and enters the SaC phase if one of the following conditions is satisfied. Condition C1: the number of updated pages after an iteration is less than fifty; condition C2: twenty-nine iterations have been reached; condition C3: the number of total pages sent to the target exceeds threefold of the VM memory space; Condition C4: the number of synchronized pages in this iteration is larger than that in the previous iteration and the measured network bandwidth reaches its maximal value. Condition C1 guarantees a short downtime because only few pages need to be synchronized. Conditions C2 and C3 force the iterative pre-copy phase to terminate and enter the SaC phase in case of condition C1 never occurs. Condition C4 implies the number of pages to be synchronized tends to increase.

The performance of live migration can be measured using total migration time and service downtime. The total migration time is expressed using the equation [6]: $T_{total} = T_a + \sum_{i=1}^{n} t_{copy}(i) + T_b$, where T_a and T_b are the constant overheads ahead and behind the phase of iterative copy, respectively. T_a includes the time for initialization and resource reservation. T_b includes the time for commitment and VM activation. $t_{copy}(i)$ is the time of the ith iteration. Note that, for the pre-copy scheme, the nth iteration is the SaC phase. The sum of T_b

and $t_{copy}(n)$ is also referred as service downtime. In general, most of the total migration time is spent at processing page synchronization. Nevertheless, the value of $t_{copy}(n)$ can affect the service downtime experienced by the virtual VM customers. In [7], the post-copy scheme which synchronizes pages on the event of page faults was proposed to further reduce service downtime. Although the downtime can be small, page-faults slow down the VM performance. Compared with the pre-copy scheme, it has the risk of recovering the broken VM's running at a source host. The authors also employ balloon mechanism to further reduce the total migration time.

In [8], a two-phase strategy was proposed to reduce the number of synchronized pages by giving a second chance to an updated page Compared with the original live migration, the strategy synchronizes less pages in each iteration without increasing the number of pages to be synchronized at the SaC phase. In [9], a method which analyses memory access pattern vertically and horizontally is developed for bounded-downtime applications. The method predicts and resizes memory space available to an application such that the computation can proceed in accord with its response time limit. In [10], a technique was proposed to avoid the transmission of frequently updated pages. It is achieved by adding an additional bitmap to mark the frequently updated pages and those pages can only be synchronized in the last iteration. In [11], agile live migration based on a hybrid pre/post-copy technique with active push and demand-paging was developed for quick response to resource pressure. A virtualized memory device was also employed to maintain the desired performance. In [12], theoretical work was conducted to determine the bandwidth needed for guaranteeing the total migration time and service downtime. Based on their analysis, the authors proposed a transport control mechanism rSAB to maintain the expected bandwidth during live migration.

3   Task Guided Live Migration

In this section, the motivation of TAG approach is explained first. Then, the interactions among the functional units for achieving TAG live migration are described. In addition, a state diagram is given to model the coordinator which is the essential unit of the platform.

A program consists of code entities and data segments which are partitioned into pages of a fixed size. To accommodating the pages, the host memory space is partitioned into frames of the same size as well. Code entities conduct tasks to perform computations on data segments. Denote e_i as the ith code entity. A page is an associated page of an entity if it can be updated by the entity. The jth associated page of e_i is denoted as p_{ij}. Its corresponding page at the target is denoted as p'_{ij}. Page p_{ij} is inconsistent if it is updated after the page pair (p_{ij}, p'_{ij}) has been synchronized. Denote P_i as the set of pages associated with entity e_i. Note that $P_i \cap P_j$ may not be an empty set.

The live migration with the pre-copy scheme is considered in this paper. The hypervisor selects inconsistent pages to synchronize across hosts at the pre-copy

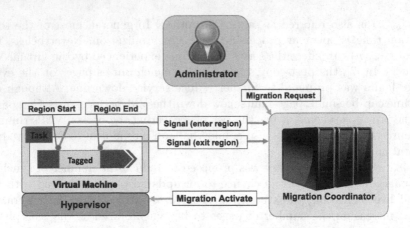

Fig. 1. Framework of TAG live migration

phase. Since synchronization and computation proceed concurrently, a synchronized page may become inconsistent again. Thus, one more synchronization is needed to restore the consistency. In a live migration with the pre-copy scheme, a page may become inconsistent for several times until the SaC phase starts. It is worth to mention that the number of inconsistent pages is no more than $|P_i|$ soon after entity e_i has been executed. It implies that the SaC phase takes no more than $|P_i|/B$ seconds if it has started before the task has exited entity e_i, where B is the network bandwidth in pages per second.

By analyzing the pattern that an entity accesses data segments, the maximum number of inconsistent pages could be known in advance. Based on the analysis, the head and tail tags are inserted at the boundary of a feasible code entity. The framework for achieving TAG live migration is illustrated in Fig. 1. Based on the figure, our TAG live migration is explained as follows. Once the administrator decides a live migration is necessary, it issues a live migration request to the coordinator. From the time being, the coordinator waits for a running task to execute a feasible entity. After a head tag has been detected, the task informs the coordinator to check if there is any pending live migration. The coordinator asks the hypervisor to activate the pending live migration if any. A task may have completed a feasible entity before an approved live migration enters the SaC phase. In this case, a tail tag will be detected and the coordinator is informed to withdraw the ongoing live migration if any. Then, the ongoing live migration is suspended by the hypervisor and it becomes pending again. Once another head tag is detected later on, the pending live migration will be approved.

The coordinator can be modelled using the state diagram which consists of two states S_0 and S_1 as shown in Fig. 2. In the figure, notations X and $-$ mean don't care and no-action, respectively. Initial state S_0 indicates no migration has been started yet or an ongoing live migration has been suspended. State S_1 indicates a live migration is in progress. The next state S_j and output are determined by the two-variable input $x_a x_t$ and the current state S_i. The first

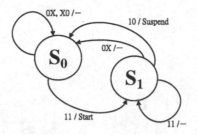

Fig. 2. State diagram of the coordinator for TAG live migration

Table 1. The specifications of the hosts and VM's

	Processor	Main memory	Resource manager
Source (target) host	i7-4790	8 GBytes	Xen 4.0.1
Coordinator host	i7-6700	32 GBytes	Xen 4.5.5
Source (target) Dom U	1 core	768 MBytes	CentOS 5.9
Coordinator Dom 0	8 core	32 GBytes	Ubuntu server 14.04

variable $x_a = 1$ if a live migration request has been issued by the administrator. It is reset by the hypervisor after a live migration has successfully completed. The second variable $x_t = 1$ if a task has detected a head tag; $x_t = 0$, otherwise. It is set or reset by the task. The output can be no-action or a signal which is sent to the hypervisor for starting an approved live migration or suspending an ongoing live migration. According to the diagram, the coordinator informs the hypervisor to start a live migration if $x_a x_t = 11$ and to suspend an ongoing live migration by if $x_a x_t = 10$. Both of these cases, the coordinator will transfer from the current state to the other. When a live migration has successfully completed, the hypervisor resets $x_a = 0$. Then, the input to the coordinator becomes $x_a x_t = 0X$ and its state returns to the initial state S_0. For the other input cases, the coordinator stays at the same state with no-action.

4   Experiments and Analysis

Two experiments are conducted to demonstrate the TAG approach is useful for reducing downtime. In contrast to the TAG live migration, we call the live migration without tagging any entity as normal live migration. The first experiment shows that our approach is applicable by implementing the platform with tagging capability. The second experiment shows that the benefit from the TAG live migration overwhelms the overhead of temporarily suspending a live migration and restarting at the next tagged entity. The specifications of the hosts and VM's are given in Table 1. Our experiments are conducted in LAN environment and the hosts are connected by 100 Mbps Ethernet. The source host is used as the NFS server.

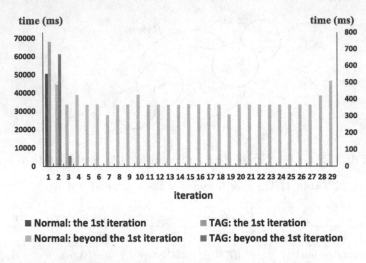

Fig. 3. Iteration times under normal and TAG.

In the first experiment, a program consisting of two code entities is employed. The first entity (e_{b50}) sorts a sequence of about 50 million numbers using a revised bubble sort which stops computation as soon as the sequence is sorted. The sequence is formed by 51200 subsequences; each of which consists of 1024 numbers in decreasing order. In addition, the smallest number in a subsequence is greater than the largest number in its preceding subsequence. The pattern of the sequence guarantees the entity e_{b50} updates all the pages in P_{b50} repetitively, where $|P_{b50}| \approx 200$ MBs. The second entity (e_{m3700}) multiplies a pair of 3700 × 3700 matrices. The multiplication algorithm computes the entries of the result matrix row by row from left to right. $|P_{m3700}| \approx 52$ MBs which is one third of the data segments reserved for the multiplication. Compared to entity e_{m3700}, entity e_{b50} updates pages on a broader range with a higher frequency. It leads to a long downtime and a large number of pages to be synchronized at the pre-copy stage. Thus, entity e_{m3700} is tagged in the program for TAG live migration. The first experiment is conducted as follow: the administrator issues a live migration request to the coordinator as soon as the task starts. The times to synchronize pages across hosts for each iteration under the normal and TAG live migrations are illustrated in Fig. 3. The y axis at the left side is scaled for the first iteration. The y axis at the right side is scaled for the other iterations. For normal live migration, many pages are synchronized at the pre-copy phase. It leads to that the condition C1 is never satisfied. The live migration has gone through the maximum number of iterations set up by condition C2 before the task exits entity e_{b50}. However, for the TAG approach, the live migration starts immediately after the task detects the head tag of entity e_{m3700}. The condition C1 is satisfied after three iterations and the TAG live migration immediately enters the SaC phase. The comparisons on the numbers of synchronized pages at the SaC phase and the task execution times under the normal and TAG live migrations

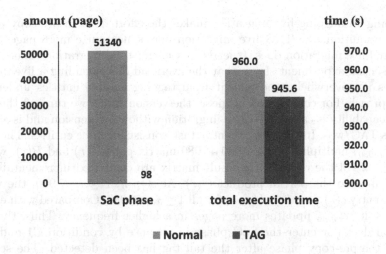

Fig. 4. Numbers of synchronized pages and execution times under normal and TAG.

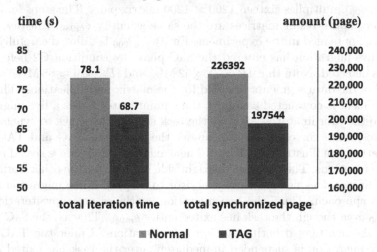

Fig. 5. Iteration times and numbers of synchronized pages under normal and TAG.

are illustrated in Fig. 4. The figure shows that TAG live migration outperforms normal live migration with respect to the downtime and total execution time by appropriately tagging the entities. The total iteration times and total numbers of synchronized pages under the normal and TAG live migrations are given in Fig. 5. The improvements on the total iteration times and the numbers of total synchronized pages are about 13%.

A task may have exited a tagged entity before the live migration starts the SaC phase. In this case, the task may suffer from a long downtime if the SaC phase starts in another entity which is infeasible. Thus, suspending an ongoing live migration is necessary when a tail tag is detected. The suspended live migration will be restarted only after the next tagged entity has been detected.

Suspending an ongoing live migration makes the effort done in pre-copy phase vainly. In addition, the TAG live migration may synchronize more pages than the normal live migration does. It leads to a longer total migration time.

The second experiment shows that the overhead of suspending a live migration does not overwhelm the benefit from tagging feasible entities under the TAG approach. For comparison purpose, the version which we turn off the suspension capability is called TAG live migration without suspension and is abbreviated as TAG/wos. In the experiment, a task consists of three entities. The first entity (e_{m980}) multiplies sixteen 980×980 matrix pairs $A(r)$ and $B(r)$, where $1 \leq r \leq 16$. All the entries of a result matrix are computed incrementally by adding values to the partial product $C(r)$. At step k, $1 \leq k \leq 980$, the value added to entry $c(r)_{ij}$ is $a(r)_{ik}b(r)_{kj}$, for all $1 \leq i, j \leq 980$. Compared with entity e_{m3700}, entity e_{m980} updates more pages in a higher frequency. Thus, the live migration does not enter the SaC phase in advance by condition C1 and still stays in the pre-copy phase after the tail tag has been detected. The second entity is the same as the entity e_{b50} used in the first experiment. The third entity (e_{m1200}) multiplies sixteen 1200×1200 matrix pairs. The steps for entity e_{m1200} to compute result matrices are the same as entity e_{m980}. Entities e_{m980} and e_{m1200} are tagged in the experiment. Entity e_{m1200} is tailored carefully such that the live migration has entered the SaC phase by condition C2 before the tail tag is detected. Note that $|P_{m980}| \approx 52$ MBs and $|P_{m1200}| \approx 88$ MBs; all are one third of the data segments reserved for the matrix multiplications. The second experiment is conducted as follow: the administrator issues a live migration request to the coordinator as soon as the task starts. The times to synchronize pages across hosts for each iteration under the successful TAG and TAG/wos live migrations are illustrated in Fig. 6. The y axis at the left side is scaled for the first three iterations. The y axis at the right side is scaled for the other iterations. The coordinator does not ask the hypervisor to suspend a live migration under TAG/wos approach. Thus, the live migration continues pre-copy iterations in entity e_{b50} even though the task has exited entity e_{m980}. That is, the SaC phase starts in the non-tagged entity e_{b50} after 29 iterations. Under the TAG approach, live migration is suspended immediately after the task has exited entity e_{m980} and will be resumed as soon as the head tag of entity e_{m1200} is detected. Since entity e_{m1200} updates pages in a higher frequency than entity e_{m3700}, the pre-copy phase does not terminate by condition C1 and it enters the SaC phase after 29 iterations.

The execution times of the three entities taken by the TAG/wos and TAG live migrations are illustrated in Fig. 7. Denote $\Delta(e_i) = \Psi_{\text{TAG}}(e_i) - \Psi_{\text{TAG/wos}}(e_i)$, where $\Psi_{\text{TAG}}(e_i)$ and $\Psi_{\text{TAG/wos}}(e_i)$ are the execution times of entity e_i on VM's with TAG and TAG/wos settings, respectively. The figure shows that $\Delta(e_{b50}) \approx -17.5$ s and $\Delta(e_{m1200}) \approx 2.2$ s. The experimental result is in accordance with our settings such that the SaC phases start in entity e_{b50} and entity e_{m1200} under TAG/wos and TAG approaches, respectively. The number of synchronized pages at the SaC stage and the total execution time of the task are given in Fig. 8. Compared with TAG/wos, TAG live migration synchronizes less

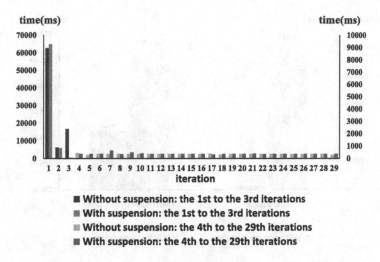

Fig. 6. Iteration times under TAG/wos and TAG.

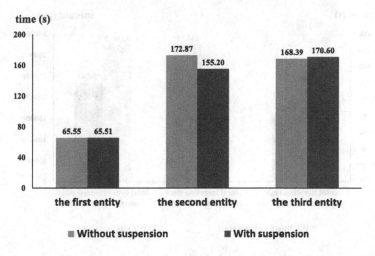

Fig. 7. Execution times of the three entities under TAG/wos and TAG.

pages at the SaC phase. It also leads to a shorter total execution time. The left column of Fig. 9 shows the total iteration times of the successful live migrations under the TAG and TAG/wos approaches. The numbers of total synchronized pages for both live migrations are also plotted in the right column of the figure. The improvements on the times and page numbers are about 27%. If the times include the successful and suspended pre-copy phase, the TAG live migration takes 55.5 s more than TAG/wos as shown in the middle column of Fig. 9. Thus, the suspension is considered as the overhead of a live migration. However, the overhead of suspending an ongoing live migration does not overwhelms the benefit from tagging feasible entities using the TAG approach.

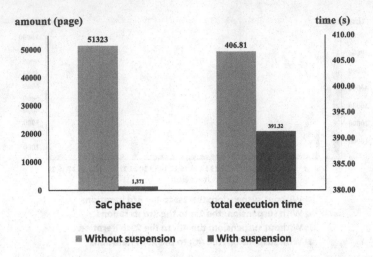

Fig. 8. Numbers of synchronized pages and execution times under TAG/wos and TAG.

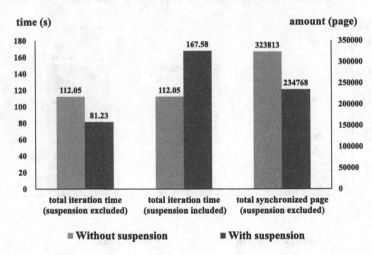

Fig. 9. Iteration times and numbers of synchronized pages under TAG/wos and TAG.

5   Concluding Remarks and Future Directions

In this paper, a TAG framework is developed to guarantee a live migration
starts at an opportune time. Service quality can be guaranteed by tagging the
code entities which produces small numbers of inconsistent pages in performing
computations. In our framework, feasible code entities are selected for tagging
such that a pending live migration request can be activated while the head tag is
detected. Our experiments have shown that the TAG live migration outperforms
the normal live migration regarding to the downtime, even though the overhead

of live migration suspension does exist. In the future, the memory access patterns which lead to short downtimes will be studied and characterized. Based on this, more practical applications will be extensively benchmarked using our TAG approach.

References

1. Barham, P., Dragovic, B., Fraser, K., et al.: Xen and the art of virtualization. In: Proceedings of 19th ACM Symposium on Operating Systems Principles, pp. 164–177 (2003)
2. Rodríguez-Haro, F., Freitag, F., Navarro, L., et al.: A summary of virtualization techniques. Proc. Technol. **3**, 267–272 (2012)
3. Rothermel, K., Schwehm, M.: Mobile agents. In: Encyclopedia for Computer Science and Technology, vol. 40, pp. 155–176, May 1999
4. Clark, C., Fraser, K., Hand, S., et al.: Live migration of virtual machines. In: Proceedings of 2nd Symposium on Networked Systems Design and Implementation, pp. 273–286 (2005)
5. Liu, Z., Qu, W., Yan, T., et al.: Hierarchical copy algorithm for Xen live migration. In: Proceedings of International Conference on Cyber-Enabled Distributed Computing and Knowledge Discovery, October 2010, pp. 361–364 (2010)
6. Akoush, S., Sohan, R., Rice, A., et al.: Predicting the performance of virtual machine migration. In: Proceedings of IEEE International Symposium on Modeling, Analysis and Simulation of Computer and Telecommunication Systems, August 2010, pp. 37–46 (2010)
7. Hines, M.-R., Gopalan, K.: Post-copy based live virtual machine migration using adaptive pre-paging and dynamic self-ballooning. In: Proceedings of ACM SIGPLAN/SIGOPS International Conference on Virtual Execution Environments, pp. 51–60 (2009)
8. Lin, C.-C., Huang, Y.-C., Jian, Z.-D.: A two-phase iterative pre-copy strategy for live migration of virtual machines. In: Proceedings of 8th International Conference on Computing Technology and Information Management, April 2012, pp. 29–34 (2012)
9. Lin, C.-C., Jian, Z.-D., Xie, D.-Y., et al.: Bounded-downtime computation for virtual machine live migration based on memory alternation cross reference. In: International Conference on Platform Technology and Service, February 2017, pp. 28–33 (2017)
10. Ma, F., Liu, F., Liu, Z.: Live virtual machine migration based on improved pre-copy approach. In: Proceedings of IEEE International Conference on Software Engineering and Service Sciences, July 2010, pp. 230–233 (2010)
11. Deshpande, U., Chan, D., Guh, T.-Y., et al.: Agile live migration of virtual machines. In: Proceeding of Cluster Computing, IEEE International Parallel and Distributed Processing Symposium, pp. 1061–1070 (2016)
12. Zhang, J., Ren, F., Shu, R., et al.: Guaranteeing delay of live virtual machine migration by determining and provisioning appropriate bandwidth. IEEE Trans. Comput. **65**(9), 2910–2917 (2016)

Verifiable Privacy-Preserving Payment Mechanism for Smart Grids

Chun-I Fan$^{(\boxtimes)}$ iD, Yi-Fan Tseng iD, Jheng-Jia Huang iD, Yen-Hao Chen,
and Hsin-Nan Kuo

Department of Computer Science and Engineering, National Sun Yat-sen University,
Kaohsiung 80424, Taiwan
cifan@mail.cse.nsysu.edu.tw

Abstract. Smart grids have become a future trend due to the development of technology and increased energy demand and consumption. In smart grids, a user's electricity consumption is recorded by their smart meters, and the smart meters submit the data to the operation center in each time unit for monitoring. The operation center analyzes the data it receives to estimate user's electricity usage in the next time unit and to ensure dynamic energy distribution. Compared to traditional grids, the electricity can be flexibly controlled, and waste is decreased in smart grids. However, details of user's daily lives may be leaked out through the frequent monitoring of user's electricity usage, which causes the problem of privacy preserving. To solve the problem, data aggregation mechanisms are adopted in this environment. The power usage data in the same units are aggregated before being sent to the operation center. This aggregation prevents personal electricity usage data from being shared with the operation center. Thus, a user's privacy is protected. Along with the increase in the number of research studies on smart grids, many studies on the privacy-preserving issues of power usage have been published. However, both power usage data and electricity payment data may jeopardize user's privacy. The operation center is able to obtain user's private information by analyzing a user's electricity payments. Therefore, we propose a verifiable privacy-preserving payment mechanism for smart grids. In our scheme, users can submit electricity payments without revealing any private information and the operation center can verify the correctness of the payment.

Keywords: Smart grid · Data aggregation · Blind signature
Electronic cash · Privacy-preserving

1 Introduction

Smart grid [13] has prospered in many countries, making it the future trend of energy grids and there have been several related developments and researches studies [10–14, 19, 23, 25, 27, 29–31]. There are three main categories [3] ofresearch

Y. Xiang et al. (Eds.): IDCS 2018, LNCS 11226, pp. 52–63, 2018.
https://doi.org/10.1007/978-3-030-02738-4_5

in the smart grid environment. First, energy management [16,20,22] mainly relates to the power distribution and consumption. Second, information management [4,5,28,32] focuses on data transmission. Last, security [15,21,24] is about the protection of users' power usage data and privacy.

In traditional electricity grids, the electricity usage data of each user is recorded by her/his meter. Then the generator is mainly responsible for the energy distribution and electricity payment. Unlike the traditional way, in a smart grid, users' electricity consumption is recorded by smart meters, which submit the data to the operation center in each time unit for monitoring. The operation center analyzes the data and helps the generator dynamically distribute the energy. Through the flexible control of electricity consumption, wasted energy can be reduced. However, the frequent monitoring of users' electricity usage may lead to the leakage of the details of users' daily lives, which causes the problem of privacy-preserving in smart grids. To preserve privacy, data aggregation mechanisms [1,6,9,11,18,19,23] are adopted in smart grids. The electricity usage data in same units are aggregated before being sent to the operation center by an aggregator. This aggregation prevents personal electricity usage data from being leaked to the operation center.

A survey of different kinds of privacy preservation mechanisms of smart grid revealed that there are few studies on the issue of possible privacy leaking in payment mechanisms. For instance, adversaries may eavesdrop and analyze users' electricity payment data to obtain their power usage data. A straightforward solution is to keep the electricity payment data secret and ensure only users know how much they pay for the electricity. However, this would mean the operation center would not know if users cheat on their electricity payment, which would be another issue for the operation center. To address the issues mentioned above and due to the e-cash(s) cannot be aggregated like that of electricity consumption data, we propose a verifiable payment mechanism with privacy-preserving for smart grids. Our scheme is inspired from Fan et al.'s rewarding scheme [8]. In the proposed scheme, the power consumption data of each user are encrypted by using an additive homomorphic encryption under the operation center's public key, so that those encrypted data can be aggregated. However, the e-cash(s) for the payment cannot be aggregated owing to e-cash unforgeability. If one can aggregate some e-cash(s) into a new one, it means that he can forge an e-cash and the e-cash scheme is not secure.

The proposed scheme preserves users' privacy in the smart grid environment when the users submit their electricity payments to the operation center. Moreover, our scheme ensures that the operation center receives correct electricity payment. In our mechanism, the blind messages of e-cash(s) are generated by the smart meter, so the users are not able to spend the e-cash(s) they withdraw.

2 Preliminaries

2.1 System Model

In our scheme, we mainly focus on how residential users' send their electricity payment to the aggregator privately, without being intercepted or eavesdropped by the operation center. There are four entities in the system model.

- **Residential Users:** Smart meters help residential users to generate electricity consumption data and corresponding electricity payment. After users withdraw the e-cash, smart meters help the users to submit their e-cash to the aggregator.
- **Aggregator:** The aggregator is mainly responsible for collecting the e-cash sent from the smart meters of the residential users.
- **Operation Center:** The operation center receives the e-cash of the residential users from the aggregator, then submit the e-cash to the bank for changing money. For the issue of privacy-preserving, the operation center and the aggregator are assumed not to collude with each other.
- **Bank:** The bank is mainly responsible for the electronic cash issuing in our payment mechanism.

2.2 Security Requirement

Security is the most important issue for our verifiable payment mechanism in smart grid. The operation center and the aggregator both are regarded as honest but curious parties in our mechanism. However, users' electricity payment data and electronic cash may be eavesdropped or even steal by adversaries through hiding in the residential area to pretend residential users or intruding into the database of the operation center. In addition, adversaries could also invading the data transmission to tamper the data. Therefore, to prevent privacy of users from being known or modifying by adversaries, several security requirements must be achieved in our mechanism are shown as follows.

- **Unlinkability:** The user who pays the electricity payment should be prevented from being known by the operation center or the bank.
- **Unforgeability:** The proposed mechanism should prevent users' electricity payment data from being forged or modified by attackers.
- **Confidentiality:** No matter the adversaries hiding in the residential area to eavesdrop or intercepting the communications between each party, the encrypted electricity payment data and blind electronic cash cannot be derived in polynomial time. Moreover, the aggregator and the operation center should not know the detailed electricity payment data of users.

2.3 Partially Blind Signature Scheme

In a partially blind signature scheme [2], a common information can be embedded into blind signatures by the signer under some agreement with the users in advance. A generic partially blind signature scheme is defined in this section. Let M be a set of messages and W is a finite set of predefined strings which are defined by the signer and the users beforehand. There are five polynomial-time computable functions in a generic partially blind signature scheme P. The five functions B_P, H, S_P, U_P, and V_P are shown as follows.

- $H : M \rightarrow M$ H is a public one-way hash function.
- $S_P : M \times W \rightarrow M^K$ S_P is the signing function where K is a positive integer, and the signer keeps S_P secret. For a message m in M and a information w in W, it is intractable to compute $S_P(H(m), w)$ without S_P.
- $V_P : M^K \times M \times W \rightarrow \{\text{true, false}\}$ V_P is the public verification function. For every m in M and w in W, $V_P(t, H(m), w) = \text{true}$, t is the signer's signature on m. For $V_P(t, H(m), w) = \text{true}$, it is intractable to derive a triple (t, m, w) without S_P.
- $B_P : M \times R \rightarrow M$ B_P is the blinding function of P. For every m in M and r in R, it is basically impossible to find m from $B_P(m, r)$ without r, where r is known as m's blinding factor.
- $U_P : M^K \times R \rightarrow M^K$ U_P is the unblinding function of P where K is a positive integer. For every m in M, r in R and w in W, $U_P(S_P(B_P(m, r), w), r) = S_P(m, w)$. Without r, it is basically impossible to find $S_P(m, w)$ from $S_P(B_P(m, r), w)$.

The detailed steps of partially blind signature scheme are described as follows.

- Blinding: A user chooses a message m in M, a information w in W and keeps blinding factor r secret which is randomly selected in R. The user generates the blind message of $H(m)$ by computing $B_P(H(m), r)$. Then the user submits $(B_P(H(m), r), w)$ to the signer to request the signer's signature on m and w.
- Signing: The signer applies the signing function S_P to computes $S_P(B_P(H(m), r), w)$, which is the blind signature. Then the signer sends the blind signature to the user. Besides, the signer performs the verification function $V_P(S_P(B_P(H(m), r), w), B_P(H(m), r), w) = \text{true}$.
- Unblinding: After receiving the blind signature, the user obtains $S_P(H(m), w)$ by applying the unblinding function $U_P(S_P(B_P(H(m), r), w), r)$. The signature-message triple is $(S_P(H(m), w), m, w)$. Besides, the user performs the verification function $V_P(S_P(H(m), w), H(m), w) = \text{true}$.

2.4 Online Electronic Cash Protocol

An untraceable electronic cash protocol [7] based on the generic blind signature scheme will be introduced in this section. In the electronic cash protocol, the signer and the users are respectively acted by the bank and the customers in the blind signature scheme.

In the protocol, every e-cash issued by the bank is worth n dollars, and the customers open their own accounts in the bank. The electronic cash protocol based on the blind signature scheme X is shown as follows.

- **Withdrawing:** A customer respectively randomly selects a message m in M and a blinding factor r in R. The customer first computes $\alpha = B_X(H(m), r)$, then submits α to the bank. After receiving α from the customer, the bank computes $t = S_X(\alpha)$ to generate the signature and sends t to the customer. Then the bank deducts c dollars from the account of customer in the bank.
- **Unblinding:** After receiving t from the bank, the customer applying the unblinding operation $U_X(t, r) = S_X(H(m))$ to obtain the bank's signature on m. In the electronic cash protocol, the signature-message pair $(S_X(H(m)), m)$ is an e-cash.
- **Paying:** The customer sends $(S_X(H(m)), m)$ to a payee if the customer wants to pay the e-cash to the payee. After receiving $(S_X(H(m)), m)$ from the customer, the payee performs the verification function $V_X(S_X(H(m)), H(m)) =$ true to verify the e-cash, then the payee requests the bank to check whether the e-cash $(S_X(H(m)), m)$ is double-spent or not by searching spent e-cash which are stored in the bank's database. The payee accepts and deposits the e-cash $(S_X(H(m)), m)$ into the bank if the e-cash is not double-spent. Then the amount of the payee's account will be increased n dollars by the bank, and the bank records $(S_X(H(m)), m)$ in its database for future double-spending checking.

In the electronic cash protocol, the bank cannot link the customer who withdrawing the e-cash to the e-cash it receives from the payee due to the unlinkability property of blind signatures. That is, given the e-cash $(S_X(H(m)), m)$, it is basically impossible for the bank to determine the instance of the withdrawing protocol that produced $(S_X(H(m)), m)$. This is the property of unlinkability or untraceability.

3   The Proposed Scheme

The notations used in the proposed scheme are defined in Table 1 and our proposed scheme contains the following phases which are performed continuously.

3.1   System Initialization

- **Bank:**
  - Let $\pi = \{\pi_1, \ldots, \pi_n\}$ be the set of all possible denominations.
  - Generate a key pair (PK_B, SK_B). Publish PK_B and keep SK_B secretly.
- **Operation Center:**
  - Generate a key pair (PK_{OC}, SK_{OC}). Publish PK_{OC} and keep SK_{OC} secretly.
- **Aggregaator:**
  - Generate a key pair (PK_A, SK_A). Publish PK_A and keep SK_A secretly.
- **User i:**
  - Generate a key pair (PK_i, SK_i). Publish PK_i and keep SK_i secretly.
- **Smart meter SM_i:**
  - Generate the electricity fee d_i and inform U_i.

Table 1. The notations

Notation	Meaning
U_i	Residential user i
SM_i	Smart meter i
d_i	U_i's electricity fee
(PK_i, SK_i)	Public/secret key pair of residential user i
(PK_B, SK_B)	Public/secret key pair of the bank
(PK_A, SK_A)	Public/secret key pair of the aggregator
(PK_{OC}, SK_{OC})	Public/secret key pair of the operation center
π	The set of denominations
RA	Residential area tag
P	The generic partially blind signature scheme
Y	The generic digital signature scheme
E_K	Secure encryption algorithm with key K
M	A finite set of messages
R	A finite set of random strings

3.2 User Payment Generation

After receiving the electricity fee d_i, the user i withdraws the e-cash(s) from the bank and sends e-cash(s) to the aggregator through the smart meter. The steps and flowcharts are as follows (Fig. 1).

1. U_i picks $w_{i,1}, \cdots, w_{i,t_i}$ in π such that $w_{i,1} + \cdots + w_{i,t_i} = d_i$, where $t_i \in \mathbb{N}$ and $1 \le t_i \le d_i$, and then sends the picked denominations $w_{i,1}, \ldots, w_{i,t_i}$ to SM_i.
2. For $k = 1, \ldots, t_i$, SM_i randomly selects message $m_{i,k}$ in M and blinding factors $r_{i,k}$ in R, and then computes $\alpha_{i,k} = B_P(H(m_{i,k}), r_{i,k})$.
3. SM_i sends $\{\alpha_{i,k}\}_{1 \le k \le t_i}$ to U_i.
4. U_i computes and sends $E_{PK_B}(\{(\alpha_{i,k}, w_{i,k})\}_{1 \le k \le t_i})$ to the bank.
5. The bank decrypts $E_{PK_B}(\{(\alpha_{i,k}, w_{i,k})\}_{1 \le k \le t_i})$ and computes $\{S_P(\alpha_{i,k}, w_{i,k})\}_{1 \le k \le t_i}$.
6. The bank computes and sends $E_{PK_i}(\{(S_P(\alpha_{i,k}, w_{i,k}))\}_{1 \le k \le t_i})$ to U_i, and then deducts $(w_{i,1} + \cdots + w_{i,k})$ dollars from U_i's account.
7. U_i decrypts $E_{PK_i}(\{(S_P(\alpha_{i,k}, w_{i,k}))\}_{1 \le k \le t_i})$ and sends $\{S_P(\alpha_{i,k}, w_{i,k})\}_{1 \le k \le t_i}$ to SM_i.
8. SM_i verifies the total value of e-cash(s) if equal to the denominations it receives previous and computes $\{V_P(S_P(\alpha_{i,k}, w_{i,k}), \alpha_{i,k}, w_{i,k}) = \text{true}\}_{1 \le k \le t_i}$. Then, it computes $\{(C_{OC})_{i,k}\}_{1 \le k \le t_i} = \{E_{PK_{OC}}(S_P(\alpha_{i,k}, w_{i,k}) \parallel m_{i,k} \parallel r_{i,k} \parallel w_{i,k})\}_{1 \le k \le t_i}$.
9. SM_i computes and sends $(C_A)_i = E_{PK_A}(\{(C_{OC})_{i,k}\}_{1 \le k \le t_i})$ to the aggregator.

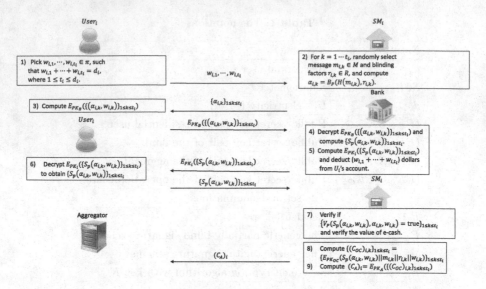

Fig. 1. User payment generation

3.3 Collecting Blinded E-Cash

After receiving the encrypted data $(C_A)_i$ from each user i in the residential area RA, the aggregator performs and flowcharts as follows (Fig. 2).

1. Decrypt $\{(C_A)_i\}_{\forall i \in RA}$ to obtain $\{\{(C_{OC})_{i,k}\}_{1 \leq k \leq t_i}\}_{\forall i \in RA}$.
2. Scramble the elements in $\{\{(C_{OC})_{i,k}\}_{1 \leq k \leq t_i}\}_{\forall i \in RA}$ to form a set $T = \{(C_{OC})_j\}_{1 \leq j \leq \sum_{i \in RA} t_i}$, and send T to the operation center.

3.4 Obtaining Electricity Payment

After receiving T, the operation center performs the following steps and flowcharts (Fig. 2).

1. Decrypt T to obtain $\{(S_P(\alpha_j, w_j) \parallel m_j \parallel r_j \parallel w_j)\}_{1 \leq j \leq \sum_{i \in RA} t_i}$.
2. Perform the unblinding operations $\{U_P(S_P(\alpha_j, w_j), r_j)\}_{1 \leq j \leq \sum_{i \in RA} t_i} = \{S_P(H(m_j), w_j)\}_{1 \leq j \leq \sum_{i \in RA} t_i}$. Thus, the operation center obtains the electricity fee, the e-cash(s) $\{(S_P(H(m_j), w_j), m_j, w_j)\}_{1 \leq j \leq \sum_{i \in RA} t_i}$.
3. Perform the verifying operations $\{V_P(S_P(H(m_j), w_j), H(m_j), w_j)\}_{1 \leq j \leq \sum_{i \in RA} t_i}$.
4. Compute $E_{PK_B}(\{(S_P(H(m_j), w_j), m_j, w_j)\}_{1 \leq j \leq \sum_{i \in RA} t_i})$.
5. Compute and send $S_Y(E_{PK_B}(\{(S_P(H(m_j), w_j), m_j, w_j)\}_{1 \leq j \leq \sum_{i \in RA} t_i}))$ to deposit the e-cash(s) into the bank.

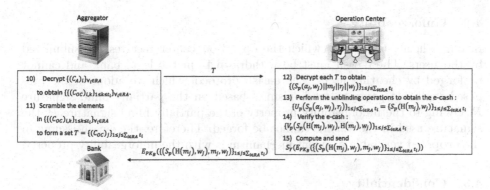

Fig. 2. Collecting blinded e-cash & obtaining electricity payment

4 Security

4.1 Unlinkability

First, we will prove that the bank cannot link the e-cash submitted by the operation center to the user who withdrew the e-cash from the bank in the proposed scheme. Second, we will prove that the operation center cannot link the e-cash received from the aggregator to the user who sent the e-cash to the aggregator in the proposed scheme. The underlying partially blind signature scheme used for e-cash issuing in the proposed payment mechanism is unlinkable.

In our mechanism, the bank, the operation center, and two users are involved in the unlinkability game. Two messages, m_u and m_v, which are used in the game are output by the bank. Let $(S_P(\alpha_0), \alpha_0)$ and $(S_P(\alpha_1), \alpha_1)$ be the views of the bank when the two users respectively perform the data exchanged during the protocol. Finally the two signatures $(S_X(H(m_u)), m_u)$ and $(S_P(H(m_v)), m_v)$ are unblinded and sent to the bank by the operation center. Given a pair $(S_P(H(m)), m) \in \{(S_P(H(m_u)), m_u), (S_P(H(m_v)), m_v)\}$ and for any view $(S_P(\alpha), \alpha) \in \{(S_P(\alpha_0), \alpha_0), (S_P(\alpha_1), \alpha_1)\}$, the bank can always derive a blinding factor r such that $B_P(H(m), r) = \alpha$. Thus, from the bank's point of view, $(S_P(H(m_u)), m_u)$ and $(S_P(H(m_v)), m_v)$ are perfectly indistinguishable. The bank will only make a correct guess with advantage 0 in the game. Therefore, the underlying partially blind signature scheme used for e-cash issuing that between the e-cash and users are with the unlinkability property to the bank in the proposed verifiable payment mechanism. For the situation between the e-cash and users to the operation center, that is different from the situation between the e-cash and users to the bank since the operation center knows the blinding factor r. From the view of the operation center, it is not able to know the signatures (which are e-cash in our proposed scheme) it received from the aggregator are respectively belong to which user. Thus, to the operation center, the users and the e-cash are unlinkable. Besides, based on the basic assumption of general smart meter scheme, the operation center and the aggregator are not conspiracy in the proposed verifiable payment mechanism.

4.2   Unforgeability

In our scheme, the e-cash which the operation center receives are submitted by the users. The e-cash must be withdrawn from the legal bank and cannot be forged by cheating users. The e-cash protocol which we adopt in the proposed verifiable payment mechanism is based on the partially blind signature P. Owing to the unforgeability property of the partially blind signature P, the signature used in the scheme cannot be forged. Therefore, the e-cash issuing in the proposed verifiable payment mechanism is with the unforgeability property.

4.3   Confidentiality

The proposed verifiable payment scheme can prevent the users' electricity payment from being known by the aggregator. All the electricity payment given to the aggregator for collecting are encrypted with the public key of the operation center, without the private key of the operation center, the aggregator is not able to decrypt the encrypted data to obtain the electricity payment. Besides, each party in the proposed verifiable payment scheme is not conspiracy to others.

5   Comparison

To the best of our knowledge, there is no specific payment mechanism designed for smart grid. Therefore, we compare our verifiable payment mechanism with typical payment protocol in smart grids based on [7] in this chapter. The comparisons of two schemes are summarized in Table 2. Both our scheme and typical payment protocol can achieve the properties of unlinkability to the bank and unforgeability. However, for the second situation of unlinkability, the operation center cannot link to users by e-cash it received which is different from typical payment protocol. In typical payment protocol, the operation center receives electricity fee from the users directly. However, in our mechanism, the users in the residential area submit electricity fee via the aggregator. Through this way, the operation center would not know the electricity fee of each other and the privacy of users can be protected. Besides, in typical payment protocol, the operation center need to immediately deposit the e-cash(s) into the bank to check if the e-cash is double-spent by searching its database. Different from basic typical payment protocol, the e-cash submitted to the operation center is blinded.

Table 2. Feature comparison

	Ours	Typical*
Unlinkability to the bank	Yes	Yes
Unforgeability	Yes	Yes
Privacy-preserving of users	Yes	No
Offline payment based on online e-cash	Yes	No

Typical*: a typical payment protocol based on an online e-cash protocol

Therefore, the operation center receives the fresh e-cashes and it is unnecessary to deposit the e-cash(s) into the bank immediately for double-spent checking.

6   Conclusion

In the smart grid environment, many works on the topic of data aggregation have been proposed. However, few research studies on payment mechanism in the smart grid environment have been discussed and developed. In this manuscript, we have proposed a verifiable payment mechanism with privacy-preserving in smart grid. The proposed generic construction of the payment mechanism consists of a secure partially blind signature scheme and a secure public key encryption scheme. Both verifiability and preservation of user's privacy can be achieved in our payment mechanism. The mechanism realizes that every residential user can submit his/her electricity payment with blinded e-cash to the operation center via his/her own smart meter without revealing his/her identity to the operation center. The users are not able to spend the e-cash(s) they withdraw due to the blind messages of each e-cash are generated by the users' smart meters and the users cannot unblind the e-cash(s). And then the smart meters can verify the blinded e-cash(s) from the users. Moreover, the operation center can receive the correct electricity payment of each user. In the future, we will attempt to apply time-of-use billing [17,26], which may be real-time-based or tariff-based. According to the different ways of billing, there will be different kinds of electricity payment. In our method, each degree of electricity fee is the same. However, in real situation, the electricity fee of each degree may be dynamic along with the different kind of billing. Hence, it is necessary to apply time-of-use billing in our mechanism. Besides, we aim at proposing a generic framework of billing for smart grids. The efficiency and feasibility is also based on that of the underlying encryption and partially blind signatures. In the future, we will try to implement our framework based on some efficient primitives.

Acknowledgement. This work won the 2016 Thesis Award from Taiwan Institute of Electrical and Electronic Engineering. This work was supported in part by the Ministry of Science and Technology of Taiwan under grants MOST 105-2923-E-110-001-MY3 and MOST 107-2218-E-110-014, and in part by the Information Security Research Center at National Sun Yat-sen University and the Intelligent Electronic Commerce Research Center from The Featured Areas Research Center Program within the framework of the Higher Education Sprout Project by the Ministry of Education (MOE) in Taiwan.

References

1. Abdallah, A.R., Shen, X.S.: Lightweight lattice-based homomorphic privacy-preserving aggregation scheme for home area networks. In: 2014 Sixth International Conference on Wireless Communications and Signal Processing (WCSP), pp. 1–6. IEEE (2014)
2. Abe, M., Okamoto, T.: Provably secure partially blind signatures. In: Bellare, M. (ed.) CRYPTO 2000. LNCS, vol. 1880, pp. 271–286. Springer, Heidelberg (2000). https://doi.org/10.1007/3-540-44598-6_17

3. Bera, S., Misra, S., Rodrigues, J.J.P.C.: Cloud computing applications for smart grid: a survey. IEEE Trans. Parallel Distrib. Syst. **26**(5), 1477–1494 (2015)
4. Bu, S., Yu, F.R., Liu, P.X.: Dynamic pricing for demand-side management in the smart grid. In: 2011 IEEE Online Conference on Green Communications (Green-Com), pp. 47–51. IEEE (2011)
5. Bu, S., Yu, F.R., Liu, P.X.: Stochastic unit commitment in smart grid communications. In: 2011 IEEE Conference on Computer Communications Workshops (INFOCOM WKSHPS), pp. 307–312. IEEE (2011)
6. Castelluccia, C., Mykletun, E., Tsudik, G.: Efficient aggregation of encrypted data in wireless sensor networks. In: Second Annual International Conference on Mobile and Ubiquitous Systems: Networking and Services, pp. 109–117. IEEE (2005)
7. Chaum, D., Fiat, A., Naor, M.: Untraceable electronic cash. In: Goldwasser, S. (ed.) CRYPTO 1988. LNCS, vol. 403, pp. 319–327. Springer, New York (1990). https://doi.org/10.1007/0-387-34799-2_25
8. Fan, C.I., Huang, S.Y., Ho, P.H., Lei, C.L.: Fair anonymous rewarding based on electronic cash. J. Syst. Softw. **82**(7), 1168–1176 (2009)
9. Fan, C.I., Huang, S.Y., Lai, Y.L.: Privacy-enhanced data aggregation scheme against internal attackers in smart grid. IEEE Trans. Ind. Inform. **10**(1), 666–675 (2014)
10. Fouda, M.M., Fadlullah, Z.M., Kato, N., Lu, R., Shen, X.: A lightweight message authentication scheme for smart grid communications. IEEE Trans. Smart Grid **2**(4), 675–685 (2011)
11. Fu, S., Ma, J., Li, H., Jiang, Q.: A robust and privacy-preserving aggregation scheme for secure smart grid communications in digital communities. Secur. Commun. Netw. **9**(15), 2779–2788 (2015)
12. Galli, S., Scaglione, A., Wang, Z.: For the grid and through the grid: the role of power line communications in the smart grid. Proc. IEEE **99**(6), 998–1027 (2011)
13. Gungor, V.C., et al.: Smart grid technologies: communication technologies and standards. IEEE Trans. Ind. Inform. **7**(4), 529–539 (2011)
14. Hashmi, M., Hanninen, S., Maki, K.: Survey of smart grid concepts, architectures, and technological demonstrations worldwide. In: 2011 IEEE PES Conference on Innovative Smart Grid Technologies (ISGT Latin America), pp. 1–7. IEEE (2011)
15. Khurana, H., Hadley, M., Lu, N., Frincke, D.A.: Smart-grid security issues. IEEE Secur. Priv. **1**(8), 81–85 (2010)
16. Koutitas, G., Tassiulas, L.: A delay based optimization scheme for peak load reduction in the smart grid. In: Proceedings of the 3rd International Conference on Future Energy Systems: where Energy, Computing and Communication Meet, p. 7. ACM (2012)
17. Lee, A., Brewer, T.: Smart grid cyber security strategy and requirements. Draft Interagency Report NISTIR 7628 (2009)
18. Li, C., Lu, R., Li, H., Chen, L., Chen, J.: PDA: a privacy-preserving dual-functional aggregation scheme for smart grid communications. Secur. Commun. Netw. **8**, 2494–2506 (2015). https://doi.org/10.1002/sec.1191
19. Li, F., Luo, B., Liu, P.: Secure information aggregation for smart grids using homomorphic encryption. In: 2010 First IEEE International Conference on Smart Grid Communications (SmartGridComm), pp. 327–332. IEEE (2010)
20. Li, Q., Zhou, M.: The future-oriented grid-smart grid. J. Comput. **6**(1), 98–105 (2011)
21. Liu, J., Xiao, Y., Li, S., Liang, W., Chen, C.: Cyber security and privacy issues in smart grids. IEEE Commun. Surv. Tutor. **14**(4), 981–997 (2012)

22. Logenthiran, T., Srinivasan, D., Shun, T.Z.: Demand side management in smart grid using heuristic optimization. IEEE Trans. Smart Grid **3**(3), 1244–1252 (2012)
23. Lu, R., Liang, X., Li, X., Lin, X., Shen, X.: EPPA: an efficient and privacy-preserving aggregation scheme for secure smart grid communications. IEEE Trans. Parallel Distrib. Syst. **23**(9), 1621–1631 (2012)
24. Metke, A.R., Ekl, R.L.: Security technology for smart grid networks. IEEE Trans. Smart Grid **1**(1), 99–107 (2010)
25. Petrlic, R.: A privacy-preserving concept for smart grids. Sicherh. Vernetzten Systemen **18**, B1–B14 (2010)
26. Rial, A., Danezis, G.: Privacy-preserving smart metering. In: Proceedings of the 10th Annual ACM Workshop on Privacy in the Electronic Society, pp. 49–60. ACM (2011)
27. Son, H., Kang, T.Y., Kim, H., Roh, J.H.: A secure framework for protecting customer collaboration in intelligent power grids. IEEE Trans. Smart Grid **2**(4), 759–769 (2011)
28. Vytelingum, P., Voice, T.D., Ramchurn, S.D., Rogers, A., Jennings, N.R.: Agent-based micro-storage management for the smart grid. In: Proceedings of the 9th International Conference on Autonomous Agents and Multiagent Systems, vol. 1, pp. 39–46. International Foundation for Autonomous Agents and Multiagent Systems (2010)
29. Wang, W., Xu, Y., Khanna, M.: A survey on the communication architectures in smart grid. Comput. Netw. **55**(15), 3604–3629 (2011)
30. Yang, L., Xue, H., Li, F.: Privacy-preserving data sharing in smart grid systems. In: 2014 IEEE International Conference on Smart Grid Communications (SmartGridComm), pp. 878–883. IEEE (2014)
31. Yang, Z., Yu, S., Lou, W., Liu, C.: Privacy-preserving communication and precise reward architecture for V2G networks in smart grid. IEEE Trans. Smart Grid **2**(4), 697–706 (2011)
32. Yu, F.R., Zhang, P., Xiao, W., Choudhury, P.: Communication systems for grid integration of renewable energy resources. IEEE Netw. **25**(5), 22–29 (2011)

Increasing Interoperability Between Heterogeneous Smart City Applications

Alexander Rech[1]([✉]), Markus Pistauer[1], and Christian Steger[2]

[1] CISC Semiconductor GmbH, 9020 Klagenfurt, Austria
{a.rech,m.pistauer}@cisc.at
[2] Graz University of Technology, 8010 Graz, Austria
steger@tugraz.at

Abstract. Due to the increasing need for networked systems we can observe a rapid advance of IT-solutions in various sectors. However, most of the developed systems are custom-tailored solutions for specific problems and application areas, leaving us with a set of diverse frameworks. The resulting jungle of heterogeneous systems makes it difficult to find common interfaces for interconnecting the underlying businesses with each other, especially in regard to Smart City concepts. We envision a new paradigm shift towards "Smart City as a service" fueled by increased interoperability between different services with an additional emphasis on privacy-preserving data processing. This would contribute to a new level of connectivity between the environment, service providers, and people, facilitating our daily activities and enhancing the level of trust of the users. In order to achieve interoperability in the context of smart, connected cities, we propose the design of a generic, platform-independent novel architecture for interconnecting heterogeneous systems, their services, and user pools.

Keywords: Interoperability · Connected services · Data privacy
Smart City

1 Introduction

The need for stronger interrelationships between different services is constantly increasing. However, when interoperability between independent systems has to be established, we face several issues. One major problem is that systems tend to be tailored to a specific application area, so boundaries are often rigid and inflexible and only users of one specific application are addressed. Second, combining two or more systems can be a considerable challenge and, if integration is indeed attempted, integration methodologies can be very time- and cost-consuming which in turn results in longer time-to-market cycles. Third, when different parties have to share user-related datasets, special attention has to be paid to the correct use and processing of the data, especially in view of the increasingly stringent data protection laws.

© Springer Nature Switzerland AG 2018
Y. Xiang et al. (Eds.): IDCS 2018, LNCS 11226, pp. 64–74, 2018.
https://doi.org/10.1007/978-3-030-02738-4_6

A Smart City is a place where many different information systems come together. At first glance, some of these systems are already embedded into our daily lives. Smart services such as managing parking facilities, renting e-bikes or placing orders via mobile applications are already feasible in many cities. However, closely examined there is poor or almost no interaction between services of different kinds, as for the above mentioned, for instance. Therefore, in order to cope with the increasing amount of heterogeneous services in a Smart City, pervasive computing technologies should offer collaboration methodologies among businesses and their users to enable benefits for all participants involved. This, in further consequence, would contribute to a new level of connected services within cities, enabling businesses to collaborate more easily with each other. Due to this cooperation, more users could be addressed, resulting in additional advantages in terms of higher revenue. In contrast, users are provided with easier access to different, independent services. More specifically, users may save time and profit from additional offers, which in the end facilitates their daily activities.

We call into question the current situation where businesses are limited to a predefined scope regarding their services and users. We want to increase collaboration between independent entities through a federated solution, so that multiple parties do not have to completely adapt to each other's requirements in order to achieve mutual benefits. In further consequence, to accomplish a paradigm shift towards "Smart City as a service" we are working on a generic, platform-independent architecture that gives businesses and their applications access to a predefined set of services of other participating service providers. To avoid high integration costs, the functionality to enable this federated solution shall be offered as additional software layer to pre-existing systems. Additionally, since data needs to be shared across multiple parties, the privacy of the users shall be protected by abstracting their real identity.

This paper is organized as follows. Section 2 describes related work while Sect. 3 discusses design choices of our architecture and gives an overview on its components. Last but not least, Sect. 4 summarizes our ideas and offers suggestions regarding future work.

2   Related Work

Everyday life is becoming evermore connected to the digital world. Information services and applications run on an extensive set of different systems and are in constant interaction with people and their environment. Federated concepts are essential for increased system and business relationships. In order for these systems to communicate seamlessly with each other and to overcome the heterogeneity between them, interoperability is becoming increasingly important. Especially due to the increasing need for networked services from different businesses, interoperability is required ever more. According to IEEE the term interoperability is the "ability of two or more systems or components to exchange information and to use the information that has been exchanged" [1]. A more generic definition of interoperability is given by [2]. It is the "ability of things to interact for a specific purpose, once their differences have been overcome". This definition tries to expand the concept where a system is simply composed of single components, by saying that a system may also consist of multiple diverse autonomous subsystems. Only if cooperation between all systems is ensured and solutions are made to eliminate discrepancy between all components, can interoperability be achieved within the resulting system of systems [3].

In this context, a Smart City can be viewed as a larger system overarching diverse subsystems, which on their own act as autonomous components that should work together seamlessly. New concepts for information sharing among different services as well as for enhancing collaboration between Smart City services are being analyzed and elaborated [4,5].

The connection of different services is also a topic that is being elaborated by the Horizon 2020 STEVE project. The focus of the project is to implement and test a human-centric approach to electro-Mobility-as-a-Service (eMaaS), by connecting different e-vehicle solutions and "gamified" services for enhancing users' awareness, engagement and vehicle energy efficiency [6].

The idea of encapsulating an organization's functionality within an appropriate interface, advertising it as services, and trying to connect it with other similar services is not new [7]. In this sense, semantic web service-paradigms have been trying to enhance automated discovery, access, combination, and management of web services for years. Both academia and industry are researching ways to provide machine understandable representations of services, their properties, capabilities, and behavior [8,9].

Furthermore, interoperable networking is becoming increasingly important to concatenate different backends. There already exist a few approaches on how to combine heterogeneous cloud systems for sharing different datasets across geographically distributed resources and for better cooperation between different services [10–12].

Especially in the electronic marketplace area, the notion of interoperability is often closely associated with the term integration. From the perspective of service providers, pure integration methodologies may be advantageous: If businesses merge into clusters they often have a decreased management overhead with less setup and maintenance costs for instance. However, the downside is that such integration technologies and frameworks are often associated with high adaption costs, especially for businesses with rigid standards [13].

In our opinion, we do not only need new concepts for merging multiple systems and their services, which often proves to be difficult, costly or time consuming. More importantly, we need to emphasize on technologies that give multiple independent businesses the possibility and freedom to interconnect each others' services with negligible adaption costs for maximized mutual benefit. A collaboration of different service providers also means that each company may address more users. In this context, the more companies work together and exchange data, the more important data privacy protection rules become, especially in light of increasingly stringent data protection rules like the European General Data Protection Regulation (GDPR) [14]. Therefore, increased interoperability should not only offer advantages such as easier cooperation between multiple independent businesses, but also adequate data protection for end users.

3   Design of Architecture

This section is about the design of our proposed architecture. First, requirements are discussed and an overview on our architecture is given in 3.1. Afterwards, the architecture's business layer components and the core layer components will be described more detailed in Sects. 3.2 and 3.3.

3.1   Architectural Overview

Our proposed architectures addresses the following topics:

- *Interoperability.* Collaboration between different independent businesses and service providers shall be improved. Nowadays we do not have much cooperation between independent businesses, e.g. parking provider with a restaurant, or a museum with a car-rental service. No matter which product or which service a company offers, it would be beneficial if companies were able to utilize services from other businesses for increased collaboration between them as well as for addressing more users, and for offering more services to them. An example use case would be the following: A user authenticates himself at a parking gate using his smartphone for getting access to the shopping mall. As soon as he enters the garage, he receives a new service in form of a digital restaurant voucher, pushed onto his phone. In this example, two independent businesses, a garage provider and a restaurant, collaborate by sharing their users and services. The reverse case is also possible: a user getting a parking voucher as reward for eating in a restaurant.
- *Integration cost.* It is time consuming to define agreements between companies and to elaborate common interfaces. Therefore, the platform shall provide ways to facilitate this agreement process. Pre-defined interfaces shall be provided for faster integration and shorter time to market cycles.
- *Data Privacy.* When data, especially user-related data needs to be passed between different parties for enabling collaboration, privacy aspects become more important. In this context, only anonymized user data shall be passed between companies and the link between real and anonymized data shall be revocable at any time in order to be compliant with data protection rules.

With these requirements in mind we now present and discuss the structure of our architecture, which will be described more precisely in 3.2 and 3.3. Figure 1 provides a high-level overview. The overall architecture consists of at least one business layer as well as a core layer, both of which are further subdivided into several components.

Each business layer is managed by a company and contains service and user related datasets. Generally speaking, it consists of client and vendor applications as well as of a corresponding server unit that offers application specific functionality. While the client application is adapted to the user's needs, such as giving an overview on current services, the purpose of the vendor application is to provide and manage these services. Both applications operate in constant interaction with the business layer which provides them with application specific functionality and keeps the data synchronized across all devices.

Regarding the core layer's position in the proposed architecture, it is placed on top of a business layer. It can be reached by the components of the business layer via a RESTful interface. The idea behind the concept of the core layer is to provide a common trusted layer responsible for abstracting products and services from various business layers in order to establish an interrelationship between multiple heterogeneous businesses. Even if a company already utilizes its own business layer and corresponding applications, it should be feasible to communicate to the core layer in order to create new means for interacting with other service providers or rather other business layers. As interrelationships between different businesses involve a lot of time and effort for all participating businesses, we see the need for enhancing this integration and cooperation process in regard to speed and costs. Therefore, the entities of the business layer shall be extended by dedicated software libraries defining how to interact with the core and its subcomponents: the Tokenization and the Federation layer.

In order to interconnect different platforms and to anonymize datasets coming from different business applications, we introduce the Tokenization layer. Its task is to abstract application specific data of the business layer such as product and user data for bringing down all datasets to a common denominator, and increasing the level of privacy of the end users. After this abstraction process a mapping between the anonymized and the real data is created and stored at business side. This means that only the business layer which triggered the tokenization process of the data in the first place, may access the derived data from the core layer. Last but not least, there is an additional module called Federation layer. It is responsible for creating and managing services between different vendors. Furthermore, it is able to arrange trusted agreements between independent parties. This makes it possible to automate the issuing process of services as soon as predefined conditions are met.

3.2 Business Layer Components

The business layer provides users with features based on the respective application area of the system and the corresponding service provider. In summary, it consists of the three key components described below. Companies who already utilize their own business layer, may establish a link to the core via the RESTful interface.

Client Application. The mobile client app is used by customers of a specific vendor, shop or company. Together with application specific features it offers a user interface for acquiring services, e.g. parking app for booking parking tickets, restaurant app for ordering food. Regarding the redemption process of

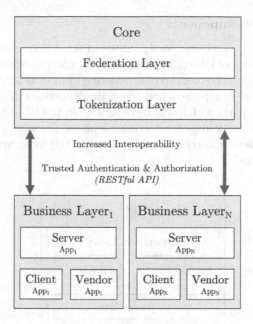

Fig. 1. Architectural overview

the acquired service we distinguish between two cases, depending on the specific application area and the service type in question. On one hand, the client application may redeem the service by directly communicating to the vendor application. In a parking use case, the drivers may redeem their parking voucher directly at the embedded vendor application of the parking gate. On the other hand, services can also be redeemed directly via an online interface without additional interaction of other devices (online food delivery).

Vendor Application. The vendor-side application functions as front-end for service providers to manage both their user pools as well as their services. Depending on the use case, the vendor application decides on how the services should be redeemed, e.g. online via server requests or by first communicating locally to a specific device. Just as with the client application, the vendor application works closely with the application server.

Application Server. The application server communicates with client and vendor devices and keeps them synchronized. On one hand, it is responsible for managing the users of the client application. On the other hand, it offers the possibility to manage shop- and service-relevant data on vendor side. If a business decides to cooperate with other service providers, interaction with the core layer, which is explained in the following, is required.

3.3   Core Layer Components

The goal of this layer is to seamlessly interconnect different services, thus contributing to a new level of interrelationships in the context of Smart City applications. The idea is to attach it on top of an existing system as an additional trusted ubiquitous layer that can be reached via a predefined set of REST calls. It is subdivided into two parts which will be described in the following. Figure 2 gives an overview on the most important components of the core layer, while Fig. 3 describes the high-level-interrelationship between the most important datasets of the different layers.

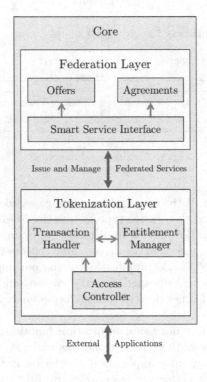

Fig. 2. Overview of core layer subdivided into Tokenization and Federation layer

Tokenization Layer. This layer provides the entry point for external applications. In the first place, the business layer of a system may use it for enabling cooperation with other applications. Since each company usually has its own implementation, this layer is mainly there to abstract the datasets coming from different businesses. This abstraction process converts the information received from the application layer into a mapping of several IDs that uniquely identify businesses, their services and users. Additionally, the Tokenization layer keeps log of transactions via the *Transaction Handler*. Each transaction refers to the participating users on client and vendor side and the acquired or redeemed services in question. According to the specified use case, the Tokenization layer may also communicate with the Federation layer to issue new services in form of entitlements or goods. The Tokenization layer distinguishes between two different token types:

- *Access Token.* The user- and device related AccessTokens are managed by the *Access Controller.* They are issued in the course of a distributed Kerberos-based authentication procedure and signed by the core layer. Furthermore, they are responsible for providing user devices with authentication when communicating with the core layer and for countering eavesdropping and replay attacks.
  The real user data stored on the business layer is never forwarded to the core layer, but converted into anonymous IDs which are linked with the AccessTokens. Only the business in charge of the creation of the user account knows the user data, thus anonymizing the user's identity for all other participating businesses.
- *Service Token.* All business and service relevant data is transformed into a signed ServiceToken by the *Entitlement Manager.* Just as for the user data, also in case of service data, unique IDs are derived, identifying the service and the company. Each ServiceToken belongs to one AccessToken, authorizing a specific user to utilize a certain service. Furthermore, it can be determined which entity purchased or redeemed which services, and how many of them, via the *Transaction Handler.*

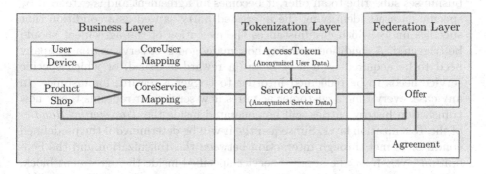

Fig. 3. Overview of interrelationship between datasets of business, Tokenization and Federation layers

Federation Layer. The Federation layer is an interface for interconnecting services from different businesses. It can be considered as federated service market place where businesses can place their products and services for special conditions or purchase services from other participants. Consequently, this cooperation enables companies to offer a wider range of services. Combined with gamification methodologies, goods and services of other companies can be forwarded as rewards to customers, enhancing both user satisfaction as well as revenue for the participating service providers. The Federation layer operates in interaction with the Tokenization layer and utilizes the tokenized data, including AccessTokens and ServiceTokens, to address services and users. In contrast to the actual user data which is only stored on business layer side, some product and company relevant data has to be forwarded from the Business layer to the Federation layer to be utilized by other interested businesses. In this sense, obligatory fields such as the name of the company and its address, have to be submitted together with optional key value pairs identifying the corresponding company's products and services. In summary, the Federation layer handles the services under discussion in two different ways:

- *Offer.* A service provider utilizing the Federated layer is authorized to publish specific services in this domain, stored as offers. Other providers are able to search for offers and acquire them. This layer functions as a market place where products and services can be found according to specific key words such as name, price, or category, for instance. Providers may acquire them and a new ServiceToken would be generated inside the Tokenization Layer. In further consequence, the link between the ServiceToken and the user's AccessToken will be established, enabling the user to utilize the service. In this sense, loyal customers can be rewarded with goods and services of other companies, e.g. a user who rented an e-bike gets an additional voucher for visiting a museum.
- *Agreement.* The idea behind agreements is that there should be the possibility to issue entitlements, aka ServiceTokens in an automated way. As soon as businesses subscribe to an offer, it becomes an agreement and is extended by specific datasets identifying the interested party as well as a condition that specifies under which circumstances the execution of the agreement should be triggered. A condition specifies how many goods or services of a company need to be acquired by a user before a reward is issued, or which specific service needs to be redeemed in order to trigger a reward, for instance. In any case, every time a customer acquires new services or redeems them, new transaction history entries will be generated inside the *Transaction Handler* of the Tokenization layer. Subsequently, it will be determined if the predefined condition is met through interaction between the Tokenization and the Federation layer. If so, the good or service specified inside the agreement block, will be acquired by the subscribed vendor and forwarded to the customer who triggered the current transaction. Furthermore, customers and vendors can keep track of the service-completion-state by utilizing the entries of the *Transaction Handler* as reference. An additional advantage for customers is that, even if they do not actively track the completion state, they can still receive rewards in an automated way.

4 Conclusion and Future Work

On account of poor integration methodologies, high integration costs, and rigid system interfaces, the widespread use of ubiquitous Smart City applications is still in its inception. In order to overcome these problems we are currently working on a generic software platform for increasing the cooperation between participating heterogeneous systems, service providers and user pools. In this paper we gave an overview on our proposed architecture, mainly subdivided into a business and a core layer. The core layer can be seen as additional layer that can be put on top of existing networked systems and enables them to exchange their services. Furthermore, in regard to user-data privacy, especially in view of strict data protection laws, we introduced a Tokenization Layer which task it is to reconcile user- and business-related datasets coming from arbitrary application servers. The user data itself is masqueraded and saved in a privacy-preserving way. In contrast, the Federation Layer provides means for service-based collaboration between independent companies.

The design of the architecture presented in this article is a starting point for us. Parts of the framework discussed in this paper will be evaluated within the European Union's Horizon 2020 project STEVE. Future work will concentrate on a research on semantic service oriented architectures to extend the interfaces between the business and core layer in a more dynamic way. Additionally, we are currently investigating on how to increase the level of trust between different entities. Blockchain in combination with smart contracts could therefore be suitable for our plans.

Acknowledgments. This work is supported by CISC Semiconductor and Graz University of Technology. A part of this work has been performed in the European Union's Horizon 2020 STEVE project under grant agreement No. 769944.

References

1. IEEE standard glossary of software engineering terminology. IEEE Std 610.12-1990, pp. 1–84 (1990)
2. Motta, R.C., De Oliveira, K.M., Travassos, G.H.: Rethinking interoperability in contemporary software systems. In: IEEE/ACM Joint 5th International Workshop on Software Engineering for Systems-of-Systems and 11th Workshop on Distributed Software Development, Software Ecosystems and Systems-of-Systems (JSOS), pp. 9–15 (2017)
3. Boardman, J., Sauser, B.: System of systems - the meaning of of. In: IEEE/SMC International Conference on System of Systems Engineering, pp. 6–11 (2006)
4. Cledou, G.: A virtual factory for smart city service integration. In: Proceedings of the 8th International Conference on Theory and Practice of Electronic Governance, pp. 536–539 (2014)
5. Antonić, A., Marjanović, M., Žarko, I.P.: Modeling aggregate input load of interoperable smart city services. In: Proceedings of the 11th ACM International Conference on Distributed and Event-Based Systems, pp. 34–43 (2017)
6. The European Commission: Smart-taylored L-category electric vehicle demonstration in hetherogeneous urban use-cases (2017). http://www.steve-project.eu
7. Cardoso, J., Sheth, A.: Introduction to semantic web services and web process composition. In: Cardoso, J., Sheth, A. (eds.) SWSWPC 2004. LNCS, vol. 3387, pp. 1–13. Springer, Heidelberg (2005). https://doi.org/10.1007/978-3-540-30581-1_1

8. Benatallah, B., Nezhad, H.R.M.: Interoperability in semantic web services. In: Cardoso, J., Sheth, A. (eds.) SWSWPC 2004. LNCS, vol. 3387, pp. 22–25. Springer, Heidelberg (2005). https://doi.org/10.1007/978-3-540-30581-1_3

9. Cardoso, J., Miller, J., Su, J., Pollock, J.: Academic and industrial research: do their approaches differ in adding semantics to web services? In: Cardoso, J., Sheth, A. (eds.) SWSWPC 2004. LNCS, vol. 3387, pp. 14–21. Springer, Heidelberg (2005). https://doi.org/10.1007/978-3-540-30581-1_2

10. Bavier, A., et al.: GENIcloud and transcloud: towards a standard interface for cloud federates. In: Proceedings of the 2012 Workshop on Cloud Services, Federation, and the 8th Open Cirrus Summit, pp. 13–18 (2012)

11. Zou, M., et al.: Collaborative marketplaces for eScience: a medical imaging use case. In: International Conference on Collaboration Technologies and Systems (CTS), pp. 500–506 (2014)

12. Akolkar, R., et al.: Towards cloud services marketplaces. In: 8th International Conference on Network and Service Management (CNSM) and Workshop on Systems Virtualiztion Management (SVM), pp. 179–183 (2012)

13. Guo, J.: Business interoperability on E-marketplace. In: Xu, L.D., Tjoa, A.M., Chaudhry, S.S. (eds.) Research and Practical Issues of Enterprise Information Systems II. ITIFIP, vol. 254, pp. 257–267. Springer, Boston, MA (2007). https://doi.org/10.1007/978-0-387-75902-9_26

14. European Parliament and European Council: Regulation 2016/679 on the protection of natural persons with regard to the processing of personal data. Official J. Eur. Union (L119) **1**, 1–88 (2016)

Reduced Transmission in Multi-server Coded Caching

Minquan Cheng[1]($\boxtimes$), Qiaoling Zhang[1]($\boxtimes$), Jing Jiang[1], and Ruizhong Wei[2]

[1] Guangxi Key Lab of Multi-source Information Mining and Security,
Guangxi Normal University, Guilin, China
chengqinshi@hotmail.com, qlzhang2017@hotmail.com,
jjiang2008@hotmail.com
[2] Department of Computer Science, Lakehead University,
Thunder Bay, ON P7B 5E1, Canada
rwei@lakeheadu.ca

Abstract. Coded caching has been widely used in computer networks for shifting some transmissions from the peak traffic time to the off-peak traffic time. Multi-server coded caching, which can share responsibility for the total amount of transmission by means of the collaboration among these servers, can be seen everywhere in our life. In this paper we consider the centralized caching system with three servers setting (two data servers and one parity check server) and propose a modified caching scheme which has performance better than the previously known schemes.

Keywords: Coded caching scheme · Multi-server · Bipartite graph
Saturating matching · Rate

1 Introduction

Predominantly driven by video content demand, there is a dramatic increase in network traffic now. The high temporal variability of network traffic results in communication systems that are congested during peak-traffic times and under-utilized during off-peak times. Caching is a natural strategy to cope with this high temporal variability by shifting some transmissions from peak to off-peak times with the help of cache memories at the network edge.

Maddah-Ali and Niesen in [7] proved that coded caching does not only shift some transmissions from peak to off-peak times, but also further reduces the amount of transmission during the peak traffic times by exploiting caches to create multicast opportunities. They focused on the following scenario [7]: A single server containing N files with the same length connects to K users over a shared, error-free link and each user has a cache memory of size to store M files. During the off-peak traffic time the server places some contents to each user's cache. In this phase the server does not know what file each user will require next. During the peak traffic times, each user requires a file from server randomly.

© Springer Nature Switzerland AG 2018
Y. Xiang et al. (Eds.): IDCS 2018, LNCS 11226, pp. 75–86, 2018.
https://doi.org/10.1007/978-3-030-02738-4_7

Then according to the distribution of files in users cache, the server sends a coded signal (XOR of some required packets) to the users such that various user demands are satisfied. In this system, each user equally shared link with the central server, and we call it a *centralized caching system*. The well known coded caching scheme, which is called MN scheme in this paper, was proposed in [7]. In this paper, we will follow [7] and use the same settings of networks as used in [7]. It is worth to mention that the transmitting amount of MN scheme for the worst request, where all the requirements are different from each other, is at most four times larger than the lower bound when $K \leq N$ [3]. We denote such amount by $R_{MN}(K, \frac{M}{N})$. So far MN scheme has been extensively employed in practical scenarios and theoretical studies, see, for examples, [3–6,8–16].

The coded caching used in multi-server setting now are widely used. In this paper we focus on the centralized caching system with three servers, which is also widely used (e.g. redundant array of independent disks-4) in real life, i.e., two data servers A, B stored $N/2$ disjoint files respectively and a parity server P stored the bitwise XOR of the information in A and B in the centralized caching system. The servers connect to users and operate on independent error free channels. This implies that these servers can transmit messages simultaneously and without interference to the same or different users. In practice servers are aware of the content cached by each user and of the content stored in other servers. So even any two files sorted on different servers can not be combined into a single message, the servers can still coordinate the messages of these two files. Similar to the single server setting, assume that each user request one file from N files and sends to the three servers. Then each server combines multiple segments from its own files into a single message, and transmit them to users such that each user can be satisfied by means of its cache and the received signal messages from servers. We prefer that the amount of transmission in each channel is as small as possible. Denote the maximum amount transmitted from the three servers by R files for all the requests. Clearly it is desired to have a scheme such that R is as small as possible. R is referred to the rate of a scheme.

Luo et al., in [6] constructed the first determined coded caching scheme by using MN scheme and some results on saturating matching in bipartite graph. They first considered the symmetric request, i.e., both data servers receive the same number of requests. Then a scheme and the related rate for the other requests can be obtained directly by means of several classes of schemes in symmetric requests. So it is meaningful to study the case of symmetric requests in the coded caching scheme.

In this paper we investigate the schemes in [6] more carefully and further use combinatorial methods to reduce the rate of the scheme when $\frac{KM}{N}$ is an odd integer.

The rest of this paper is organized as follows. We first summarize the results of [6] and our contributions, and list corresponding comparisons in Sect. 2. Section 3 briefly reviews MN scheme, the scheme proposed in [6] and the related concepts. In Sect. 4, an improved scheme is proposed. Then we discussed briefly the more refined methods in Sect. 5. Conclusion is drawn in Sect. 6.

2 Known Result and Our Main Results

First let us introduce the result in [6]. In the following we denote the files in server A and B by $\{A_1, \ldots, A_{N/2}\}$ and $\{B_1, \ldots, B_{N/2}\}$ respectively. So the files in parity server P are $\{A_1 \oplus B_1, \ldots, A_{N/2} \oplus B_{N/2}\}$. Denote the set of users requesting files from server A by $\mathcal{K}_A$, and the set of users requesting files from server B by $\mathcal{K}_B$. Let $K_A = |\mathcal{K}_A|$ and $K_B = |\mathcal{K}_B|$. Clearly $K = K_A + K_B$ since the set of all the users is $\mathcal{K} = \mathcal{K}_A \bigcup \mathcal{K}_B$. Let $\lambda = \frac{M}{N}$.

Theorem 1 ([6]). Based on MN scheme, when $K_A = K_B$, there exits a scheme for three servers caching system with rate

$$R_T(K, \tfrac{M}{N}) = \begin{cases} \frac{1}{2} R_{MN}(K, \frac{M}{N}) & \text{if } \frac{KM}{N} \text{ is even} \\ (\frac{1}{2} + \frac{1}{6}\Delta) R_{MN}(K, \frac{M}{N}) & \text{if } \frac{KM}{N} \text{ is odd} \end{cases} \tag{1}$$

where $\Delta \approx \frac{1}{3}$ when K is large.

In this paper by modifying the schemes in [6] we improve the following rate when $\frac{KM}{N}$ is odd.

Theorem 2. Based on MN scheme, when $K_A = K_B$, there exits a scheme for three servers caching system with rate

$$R_T(K, \tfrac{M}{N}) = \begin{cases} \frac{1}{2} R_{MN}(K, \frac{M}{N}) & \text{if } \frac{KM}{N} \text{ is even} \\ (\frac{1}{2} + \frac{1}{6}\Delta') R_{MN}(K, \frac{M}{N}) & \text{if } \frac{KM}{N} \text{ is odd} \end{cases} \tag{2}$$

where

$$\Delta' \approx \begin{cases} \frac{|1-3\lambda|(1-\lambda)+\lambda^2}{3} & \text{If } 0 < \lambda \leq \frac{3-\sqrt{5}}{2} \\ \frac{1}{3}|2\lambda - 1| & \text{If } \frac{3-\sqrt{5}}{2} < \lambda \leq \frac{\sqrt{5}-1}{2} \\ \frac{(1-\lambda)^2 + \lambda|3\lambda-2|}{3} & \text{If } \frac{\sqrt{5}-1}{2} < \lambda < 1 \end{cases} \tag{3}$$

when K is large.

Clearly $\Delta' \approx \frac{1}{27}$ if λ towards $\frac{1}{3}$ and $\frac{2}{3}$, and $\Delta' \approx 0$ if λ towards $\frac{1}{2}$. By comparison between Δ and Δ' in Theorems 1 and 2, when K is large we have

$$\frac{\Delta'}{\Delta} \approx \begin{cases} |1 - 3\lambda|(1-\lambda) + \lambda^2 & \text{If } 0 < \lambda \leq \frac{3-\sqrt{5}}{2} \\ |2\lambda - 1| & \text{If } \frac{3-\sqrt{5}}{2} < \lambda \leq \frac{\sqrt{5}-1}{2} \\ (1-\lambda)^2 + \lambda|3\lambda - 2| & \text{If } \frac{\sqrt{5}-1}{2} < \lambda < 1 \end{cases} \tag{4}$$

This is draw in Fig. 1. Clearly Δ' is obviously smaller than Δ in most cases. In particular when K is large, $\frac{\Delta'}{\Delta} \approx 0$ if $\frac{M}{N} = \frac{1}{2}$, and $\frac{\Delta'}{\Delta} \approx \frac{1}{9}$ if $\frac{M}{N} = \frac{1}{3}$ and $\frac{2}{3}$.

Using the method in [6], we can also obtain a scheme and the related rate for the other requests directly based on a symmetric requests. Without loss of generality, we assume that $K_A > K_B$ and $K_A - K_B = l$. Then we divide $\mathcal{K}_A$ into two parts, one part is of the size K_B and other part is of size l. For the first part with $\mathcal{K}_B$, we can use the previous method by pairing the effective $t + 1 - l$ subsets. The remaining request is just like a request for the one server system. Now consider the all possible values of l, we obtain the peak rate as

$$\sum_{l=0}^{t+1} \binom{K_A - K_B}{l} R_T(2K_B, t - l),$$

where $R_T(2K_B, t - l)$ is as in (2).

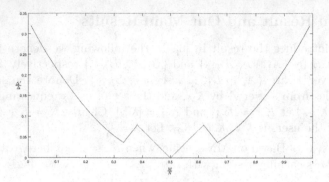

Fig. 1. The value of $\frac{\Delta'}{\Delta}$

3   Preliminaries

3.1   MN Scheme

We consider a network of K users and N files, denote by $W_1, W_2, \ldots, W_N$, such that each user has a cache with capacity for M files. We denote that network as a (K, M, N) caching system. In the single server setting, when $t = \frac{KM}{N}$ is an integer, an MN scheme can be described as follows [7].

- During the off-peak traffic times, file W_i is divided into $F = \binom{K}{t}$ equal packets, so that $W_i = \{W_{i,\mathcal{T}} \mid \mathcal{T} \subseteq [1, K], |\mathcal{T}| = t\}$. User k caches $\mathcal{Z}_k = \{W_{i,\mathcal{T}} \mid k \in \mathcal{T}, i = 1, 2, \ldots, N\}$.
- During the peak traffic times, each user requires a file randomly. Denote the K file numbers requested by $\mathbf{d} = (d_1, d_2, \ldots, d_K)$. Then for each $t + 1$ subset of users $\mathcal{S}$, the server sends the following coded signal to each user of $\mathcal{S}$.

$$\bigoplus_{k \in \mathcal{S}} W_{d_k, \mathcal{S} \setminus \{k\}} \tag{5}$$

Clearly the server transmits $\binom{K}{t+1}$ times. So the amount of transmission by server is $R_{MN}(K, \frac{M}{N}) = \binom{K}{t+1} / \binom{K}{t} = \frac{K-t}{t+1}$. Then each user uses the cached segments to recover the designed segment and then the requested file.

3.2   Bipartite Graph and the Scheme in [6]

First the concept of a bipartite graph and its a related result are useful. A graph is denoted by $\mathbf{G} = (\mathcal{V}, \mathcal{E})$, where $\mathcal{V}$ is the set of vertices and $\mathcal{E}$ is the set of edges. A subset of edges $\mathcal{M} \subseteq \mathcal{E}$ is a matching if no two edges have a common vertex. A bipartite graph, denoted by $\mathbf{G} = (\mathcal{X}, \mathcal{Y}; \mathcal{E})$, is a graph whose vertices are divided into two disjoint parts $\mathcal{X}$ and $\mathcal{Y}$ such that every edge in $\mathcal{E}$ connects a vertex in $\mathcal{X}$ to one in $\mathcal{Y}$. The degree of a vertex is the number of vertices adjacent to it. If every vertex of $\mathcal{X}$ has the same degree, we also call such a degree the degree of $\mathcal{X}$ and denote $d(\mathcal{X})$.

Lemma 1 ([1]). Given a bipartite graph $\mathbf{G} = (\mathcal{X}, \mathcal{Y}; \mathcal{E})$, if there exist two positive integers m and n such that $d(\mathcal{X}) = m$ and $d(\mathcal{Y}) = n$, then there is a saturating matching, i.e., there exists a matching with $|\mathcal{X}|$ or $|\mathcal{Y}|$ edges.

Assume that the kth user of $\mathcal{K}_A$ requests the d_k-th file in server A, and the kth user of $\mathcal{K}_B$ requests the d_k-th file in server B. Following [6], we only consider the case that $t = \frac{KM}{N}$ is an integer for the simplicity. Luo et al., in [6] used the same caching strategy as MN scheme during the off-peak traffic times for each server, but modified the coded signals in (5) during the peak traffic times as follows. Given a subset of users $\mathcal{S}_1$ of size $t + 1$, it can be divided into three parts, say $\mathcal{Q}_A$, $\mathcal{Q}_B$ and $\mathcal{Q}'_A$ where $\mathcal{Q}_A, \mathcal{Q}'_A \subseteq \mathcal{K}_A$ and $\mathcal{Q}_B \subseteq \mathcal{K}_B$. If there exists another subset $\mathcal{S}_2$ of size $t+1$ which can be divided into $\mathcal{Q}_A$, $\mathcal{Q}_B$ and $\mathcal{Q}'_B$ where $\mathcal{Q}'_B \subseteq \mathcal{K}_B$, then the pair $(\mathcal{S}_1, \mathcal{S}_2)$ is called an effective pair. Servers A, B and P transmit the following messages respectively

$$m_{\mathcal{S}_1}^A = \left(\bigoplus_{k \in \mathcal{Q}_A} A_{d_k, \mathcal{S}_1 \setminus \{k\}} \right) \oplus \left(\bigoplus_{k \in \mathcal{Q}_B} A_{d_k, \mathcal{S}_1 \setminus \{k\}} \right) \oplus \left(\bigoplus_{k \in \mathcal{Q}'_A} A_{d_k, \mathcal{S}_1 \setminus \{k\}} \right)$$

$$m_{\mathcal{S}_2}^B = \left(\bigoplus_{k \in \mathcal{Q}_A} B_{d_k, \mathcal{S}_2 \setminus \{k\}} \right) \oplus \left(\bigoplus_{k \in \mathcal{Q}_B} B_{d_k, \mathcal{S}_2 \setminus \{k\}} \right) \oplus \left(\bigoplus_{k \in \mathcal{Q}'_B} B_{d_k, \mathcal{S}_2 \setminus \{k\}} \right)$$

$$m_{\mathcal{S}_1 \cap \mathcal{S}_2}^P = \left[\bigoplus_{k \in \mathcal{Q}_B} \left(A_{d_k, \mathcal{S}_1 \setminus \{k\}} \oplus B_{d_k, \mathcal{S}_1 \setminus \{k\}} \right) \right] \oplus \left[\bigoplus_{k \in \mathcal{Q}_A} \left(B_{d_k, \mathcal{S}_2 \setminus \{k\}} \oplus A_{d_k, \mathcal{S}_2 \setminus \{k\}} \right) \right]$$

$$= \left[\left(\bigoplus_{k \in \mathcal{Q}_B} A_{d_k, \mathcal{S}_1 \setminus \{k\}} \right) \oplus \left(\bigoplus_{k \in \mathcal{Q}_B} B_{d_k, \mathcal{S}_1 \setminus \{k\}} \right) \right]$$
$$\oplus \left[\left(\bigoplus_{k \in \mathcal{Q}_A} B_{d_k, \mathcal{S}_2 \setminus \{k\}} \right) \oplus \left(\bigoplus_{k \in \mathcal{Q}_A} A_{d_k, \mathcal{S}_2 \setminus \{k\}} \right) \right]$$

Then each user in $\mathcal{S}_1$ and $\mathcal{S}_2$ can obtain the requested segments from $m_{\mathcal{S}_1}^A$, $m_{\mathcal{S}_2}^B$ and $m_{\mathcal{S}_1 \cap \mathcal{S}_2}^P$. So if the sets $\mathcal{S}_1$ and $\mathcal{S}_2$ form an effective pair, then the messages indexed by $\mathcal{S}_1$ and $\mathcal{S}_2$ can be replaced by three messages.

In the following we will focus on the symmetric request. [6] investigated the value of Δ by the following settings.

Remark 1. Each vertex of a graph is always represented a subset $\mathcal{S} \subseteq \mathcal{K}$ with size $t + 1$. And for any bipartite graph $\mathbf{G} = (\mathcal{X}, \mathcal{Y}; \mathcal{E})$ where a vertex $\mathcal{S} \in \mathcal{X}$ is adjacent to $\mathcal{S}' \in \mathcal{Y}$ if and only if they can form an effective pair.

3.3 Research Motivation

A brief review of the proof of Theorem 1 is useful to understand our proofs. Here we take the case that $t = \frac{KM}{N}$ is odd as an example. For each $w = 0, 1, \ldots, t+1$, define

$$\mathcal{V}_w = \{\mathcal{S} \subseteq \mathcal{K} \mid |\mathcal{S}| = t + 1, |\mathcal{S} \cap \mathcal{K}_A| = w\} \tag{6}$$

Clearly $\binom{K}{t+1} = \sum_{w=0}^{t+1} \binom{K_A}{w}\binom{K_B}{t+1-w}$. When $K_A < t+1$, $\mathcal{S} \cap \mathcal{K}_A \neq \emptyset$ always holds for each subset $\mathcal{S} \subseteq \mathcal{K}$ with cardinality $t + 1$. So they did not need to consider the case $w = 0$. When $K_A \geq t + 1$ and $w = 0$, assume that server A (and B) transmit the messages $m_{\mathcal{S}}^A$ (and $m_{\mathcal{S}}^B$), $\mathcal{S} \subseteq \mathcal{K}_A$ (and $\mathcal{S} \subseteq \mathcal{K}_B$) independently. When $w > 0$, Luo et al. [6] constructed several classes of bipartite graphes in the following two steps and showed that these graphes satisfy Lemma 1.

- Define $\mathbf{G}_w = (\mathcal{V}_w, \mathcal{V}_{t+1-w}; \mathcal{E}_w)$ for each $w \in [1, \frac{t-1}{2})$.
- Define $\mathbf{G} = (\mathcal{X}, \mathcal{Y}; \mathcal{E})$ where $\mathcal{X} = \mathcal{V}_{\frac{t-1}{2}} \bigcup \mathcal{V}_{\frac{t+3}{2}}$ and $\mathcal{Y} = \mathcal{V}_{\frac{t+1}{2}}$.

Now let us consider the amount of the unpaired messages in these above steps respectively.

- The first step. The unpaired messages is zero since $|\mathcal{V}_w| = |\mathcal{V}_{t+1-w}| = \binom{K_A}{w}\binom{K_B}{t+1-w} = \binom{K_A}{t+1-w}\binom{K_B}{w}$ by the hypothesis that $K_A = K_B$.
- The second step. We have that the number of unpaired messages is

$$n = \left| \binom{K_A}{(t+1)/2}\binom{K_B}{(t+1)/2} - \binom{K_A}{(t-1)/2}\binom{K_B}{(t+3)/2} - \binom{K_B}{(t-1)/2}\binom{K_A}{(t+3)/2} \right|$$

and the ratio of unpaired messages is $\Delta = \frac{n}{\binom{K}{t+1}}$. Since each unpaired message can be transmitted by any two servers, each server could transmit $\frac{2}{3}n$ unpaired messages. So the rate is

$$R_T(K, \tfrac{M}{N}) = \frac{((1-\Delta+\frac{2}{3}\Delta)\binom{K}{t+1})}{\binom{K}{t}} = (\tfrac{1}{2} + \tfrac{1}{6}\Delta) R_{MN}(K, \tfrac{M}{N}). \tag{7}$$

This is the result in Theorem 1.

Clearly we can improve the value of Δ to reduce the rate $R_T(K, \frac{M}{N})$. This is the main purpose of this paper.

4   Improved Scheme for Three Servers

In this section, we focus on the case of symmetric request for the case that $t = \frac{KM}{N}$ is odd. Clearly an intuitive approach to reduce the ratio of unpaired messages is finding the maximal matching of graph $\mathbf{G} = (\mathcal{V}_{\frac{t-1}{2}} \bigcup \mathcal{V}_{\frac{t+1}{2}} \bigcup \mathcal{V}_{\frac{t+3}{2}}, \mathcal{E})$. It is well known that this maximal problem is an NP-hard and its complexity is very high since there are $\binom{K/2}{(t+1)/2}\binom{K/2}{(t+1)/2} + \binom{K/2}{(t-1)/2}\binom{K/2}{(t+3)/2} + \binom{K/2}{(t+3)/2}\binom{K/2}{(t-1)/2}$ vertices. We will propose a local maximal matching method to reduce the complexity.

4.1   Refined Methods

Denote $\mathcal{K}_A = \{a_1, a_2, \ldots, a_{K_A}\}$ and $\mathcal{K}_B = \{b_1, b_2, \ldots, b_{K_B}\}$. We divide sets $\mathcal{V}_{\frac{t-1}{2}}$, $\mathcal{V}_{\frac{t+1}{2}}$ and $\mathcal{V}_{\frac{t+3}{2}}$ into four subsets respectively in the following way:

$$\mathcal{V}_{w;a_1,b_1} = \{\mathcal{S} \in \mathcal{V}_w \mid a_1 \in \mathcal{S}, b_1 \in \mathcal{S}\}, \mathcal{V}_{w;a_1,\bar{b}_1} = \{\mathcal{S} \in \mathcal{V}_w \mid a_1 \in \mathcal{S}, b_1 \notin \mathcal{S}\},$$
$$\mathcal{V}_{w;\bar{a}_1,b_1} = \{\mathcal{S} \in \mathcal{V}_w \mid a_1 \notin \mathcal{S}, b_1 \in \mathcal{S}\}, \mathcal{V}_{w;\bar{a}_1,\bar{b}_1} = \{\mathcal{S} \in \mathcal{V}_w \mid a_1 \notin \mathcal{S}, b_1 \notin \mathcal{S}\}, \tag{8}$$

where $w = \frac{t-1}{2}, \frac{t+1}{2}, \frac{t+3}{2}$. It is easy to check that

$$
\begin{aligned}
|\mathcal{V}_{w;a_1,b_1}| = \binom{K/2-1}{w-1}\binom{K/2-1}{t-w}, & \qquad |\mathcal{V}_{w;a_1,\bar{b}_1}| = \binom{K/2-1}{w-1}\binom{K/2-1}{t+1-w}, \\
|\mathcal{V}_{w;\bar{a}_1,b_1}| = \binom{K/2-1}{w}\binom{K/2-1}{t-w}, & \qquad |\mathcal{V}_{w;\bar{a}_1,\bar{b}_1}| = \binom{K/2-1}{w}\binom{K/2-1}{t+1-w}.
\end{aligned}
\tag{9}
$$

Given a fixed number $\lambda = \frac{M}{N}$, Table 1 can be obtained by (9) when K is large.

Table 1. The cardinality of subsets in (8)

Subsets	Cardinality	$|\mathcal{V}_{w;,}|/|\mathcal{V}_{\frac{t+1}{2};\bar{a}_1,\bar{b}_1}|$	$|\mathcal{V}_{w;,}|/|\mathcal{V}_{\frac{t+1}{2};\bar{a}_1,\bar{b}_1}| \approx$
$\mathcal{V}_{\frac{t-1}{2};a_1,b_1}$	$\binom{K/2-1}{(t-3)/2}\binom{K/2-1}{(t+1)/2}$	$\frac{(t+1)(t-1)}{(K-t+1)(K-t-1)}$	$\frac{\lambda^2}{(1-\lambda)^2}$
$\mathcal{V}_{\frac{t-1}{2};a_1,\bar{b}_1}$	$\binom{K/2-1}{(t-3)/2}\binom{K/2-1}{(t+3)/2}$	$\frac{(t+1)(t-1)(K-t-3)}{(t+3)(K-t+1)(K-t-1)}$	$\frac{\lambda}{1-\lambda}$
$\mathcal{V}_{\frac{t-1}{2};\bar{a}_1,b_1}$	$\binom{K/2-1}{(t-1)/2}\binom{K/2-1}{(t+1)/2}$	$\frac{t+1}{K-t-1}$	$\frac{\lambda}{1-\lambda}$
$\mathcal{V}_{\frac{t-1}{2};\bar{a}_1,\bar{b}_1}$	$\binom{K/2-1}{(t-1)/2}\binom{K/2-1}{(t+3)/2}$	$\frac{(t+1)(K-t-3)}{(t+3)(K-t-1)}$	1
$\mathcal{V}_{\frac{t+1}{2};a_1,b_1}$	$\binom{K/2-1}{(t-1)/2}\binom{K/2-1}{(t-1)/2}$	$\frac{(t+1)(t+1)}{(K-t-1)(K-t-1)}$	$\frac{\lambda^2}{(1-\lambda)^2}$
$\mathcal{V}_{\frac{t+1}{2};a_1,\bar{b}_1}$	$\binom{K/2-1}{(t-1)/2}\binom{K/2-1}{(t+1)/2}$	$\frac{t+1}{K-t-1}$	$\frac{\lambda}{1-\lambda}$
$\mathcal{V}_{\frac{t+1}{2};\bar{a}_1,b_1}$	$\binom{K/2-1}{(t+1)/2}\binom{K/2-1}{(t-1)/2}$	$\frac{t+1}{K-t-1}$	$\frac{\lambda}{1-\lambda}$
$\mathcal{V}_{\frac{t+1}{2};\bar{a}_1,\bar{b}_1}$	$\binom{K/2-1}{(t+1)/2}\binom{K/2-1}{(t+1)/2}$	1	1
$\mathcal{V}_{\frac{t+3}{2};a_1,b_1}$	$\binom{K/2-1}{(t+1)/2}\binom{K/2-1}{(t-3)/2}$	$\frac{(t+1)(t-1)}{(K-t+1)(K-t-1)}$	$\frac{\lambda^2}{(1-\lambda)^2}$
$\mathcal{V}_{\frac{t+3}{2};a_1,\bar{b}_1}$	$\binom{K/2-1}{(t+1)/2}\binom{K/2-1}{(t-1)/2}$	$\frac{t+1}{K-t-1}$	$\frac{\lambda}{1-\lambda}$
$\mathcal{V}_{\frac{t+3}{2};\bar{a}_1,b_1}$	$\binom{K/2-1}{(t+3)/2}\binom{K/2-1}{(t-3)/2}$	$\frac{(t+1)(t-1)(K-t-3)}{(t+3)(K-t+1)(K-t-1)}$	$\frac{\lambda}{1-\lambda}$
$\mathcal{V}_{\frac{t+3}{2};\bar{a}_1,\bar{b}_1}$	$\binom{K/2-1}{(t+3)/2}\binom{K/2-1}{(t-1)/2}$	$\frac{(t+1)(K-t-3)}{(t+3)(K-t-1)}$	1

Now let us consider the sets in (6) and their subsets in (8). We can obtain a bipartite graph for any two different subsets. However we only interested in the bipartite graph which has at least one edge. It is not difficult to check that any two elements of a set can not form an effective pair since they have the same number of users requiring from server A(and sever B). So we only need to consider any two subsets from distinct sets.

Example 1. Let us consider the degrees of bipartite graph $\mathbf{G} = (\mathcal{V}_{\frac{t+1}{2};\bar{a}_1,\bar{b}_1}, \mathcal{V}_{\frac{t-1}{2};\bar{a}_1,b_1}; \mathcal{E})$.

– Given a vertex

$$
\mathcal{S} = \{a_{i_1}, \ldots, a_{i_{(t+1)/2}}, b_{i'_1}, \ldots, b_{i'_{(t+1)/2}}\} \in \mathcal{V}_{\frac{t+1}{2};\bar{a}_1,\bar{b}_1},
$$

$a_1 \notin \{i_1, \ldots, i_{(t+1)/2}, i'_1, \ldots, i'_{(t+1)/2}\}$, it is adjacent to $(t+1)/2$ vertices $\mathcal{S}_j = \mathcal{S} \bigcup\{b_1\} \setminus \{a_{i_j}\} \in \mathcal{V}_{\frac{t-1}{2};\bar{a}_1,b_1}$. Hence $d(\mathcal{V}_{\frac{t+1}{2};\bar{a}_1,\bar{b}_1}) = (t+1)/2$.

– Given a vertex

$$\mathcal{S} = \{a_{i_1,}, \ldots, a_{i_{(t-1)/2}}, b_{i'_1}, \ldots, b_{i'_{(t+1)/2}}, b_1\} \in \mathcal{V}_{\frac{t-1}{2};\overline{a}_1,b_1},$$

$a_1 \notin \{i_1, \ldots, i_{(t-1)/2}, i'_1, \ldots, i'_{(t+1)/2}\}$, it is adjacent to $\frac{K}{2} - \frac{t+1}{2} = \frac{K-t-1}{2}$ vertices, i.e., $\mathcal{S} \bigcup \{a\} \setminus \{b_1\} \in \mathcal{V}_{\frac{t+1}{2};\overline{a}_1,\overline{b}_1}$ for each $a \in \mathcal{K}_A \setminus (\{a_1\} \bigcup \mathcal{S})$. That is $d(\mathcal{V}_{\frac{t-1}{2};\overline{a}_1,b_1}) = \frac{K-t-1}{2}$.

Similarly we can compute the degree of each vertex in the bipartite graph $\mathbf{G} = (\mathcal{X}, \mathcal{Y}; \mathcal{E})$ generated by any two subsets from distinct sets and list them in Table 2 where $d(\mathcal{X})$ and $d(\mathcal{Y})$ are respectively on the top and bottom of the diagonal in the entry indexed by $\mathcal{X}$ and $\mathcal{Y}$. It is easy to check that the elements on the top and bottom of the diagonal in the entry indexed by $(\mathcal{V}_{\frac{t-1}{2};\overline{a}_1,b_1}, \mathcal{V}_{\frac{t+1}{2};\overline{a}_1,\overline{b}_1})$ are $\frac{t+1}{2}$ and $\frac{K-t-1}{2}$ respectively. Here the entry is defined by empty when there is no edges in the related bipartite graph.

Table 2. The degrees for each bipartite graph

$\mathcal{Y}$ \ $d(\mathcal{V}_{\frac{t+1}{2}})$ / $\mathcal{V}$ \ $d(\mathcal{V})$	$\mathcal{V}_{\frac{t+1}{2},a_1,b_1}$	$\mathcal{V}_{\frac{t+1}{2},a_1,\overline{b}_1}$	$\mathcal{V}_{\frac{t+1}{2},\overline{a}_1,b_1}$	$\mathcal{V}_{\frac{t+1}{2},\overline{a}_1,\overline{b}_1}$
$\mathcal{V}_{\frac{t-1}{2},a_1,b_1}$	$\frac{(t-1)(K-t-1)}{4}$ / $\frac{(K-t+1)(t+1)}{4}$	$\frac{(t-1)(K-t-3)}{4}$ / $\frac{(K-t+1)(t+3)}{4}$		
$\mathcal{V}_{\frac{t-1}{2},a_1,\overline{b}_1}$		$\frac{(t-1)(K-t-3)}{4}$ / $\frac{(K-t+1)(t+3)}{4}$		
$\mathcal{V}_{\frac{t-1}{2},\overline{a}_1,b_1}$	$\frac{K-t-1}{2}$ / $\frac{t+1}{2}$	1 / 1	$\frac{(K-t-1)(t+1)}{4}$ / $\frac{(K-t-1)(t+1)}{4}$	$\frac{t+1}{2}$ / $\frac{K-t-1}{2}$
$\mathcal{V}_{\frac{t-1}{2},\overline{a}_1,\overline{b}_1}$		$\frac{K-t-3}{2}$ / $\frac{t+3}{2}$		$\frac{(t+1)(K-t-3)}{4}$ / $\frac{(K-t-3)(t+3)}{4}$
$\mathcal{V}_{\frac{t+3}{2},a_1,b_1}$	$\frac{(t-1)(K-t-1)}{4}$ / $\frac{(t+1)(K-t+1)}{4}$		$\frac{t-1}{2}$ / $\frac{K-t+1}{2}$	
$\mathcal{V}_{\frac{t+3}{2},a_1,\overline{b}_1}$	$\frac{K-t-1}{2}$ / $\frac{t+1}{2}$	$\frac{(K-t-1)(t+1)}{4}$ / $\frac{(t+1)(K-t-1)}{4}$	1 / 1	$\frac{t+1}{2}$ / $\frac{K-t-1}{2}$
$\mathcal{V}_{\frac{t+3}{2},\overline{a}_1,b_1}$			$\frac{(K-t-3)(t-1)}{4}$ / $\frac{(t+3)(K-t+1)}{4}$	
$\mathcal{V}_{\frac{t+3}{2},\overline{a}_1,\overline{b}_1}$			$\frac{K-t-3}{2}$ / $\frac{t+3}{2}$	$\frac{(K-t-3)(t+1)}{4}$ / $\frac{(t+3)(K-t-1)}{4}$

$\mathcal{V}_{\frac{t+3}{2}}$ / $d(\mathcal{V}_{\frac{t+3}{2}})$; $\mathcal{V}_{\frac{t-1}{2}}$ \ $d(\mathcal{V}_{\frac{t-1}{2}})$	$\mathcal{V}_{\frac{t+3}{2},a_1,b_1}$	$\mathcal{V}_{\frac{t+3}{2},a_1,\overline{b}_1}$	$\mathcal{V}_{\frac{t+3}{2},\overline{a}_1,b_1}$	$\mathcal{V}_{\frac{t+3}{2},\overline{a}_1,\overline{b}_1}$
$\mathcal{V}_{\frac{t-1}{2},a_1,b_1}$	$\left(\frac{K-t+1}{2}\right)\left(\frac{t+1}{2}\right)$ / $\left(\frac{t+1}{2}\right)\left(\frac{K-t+1}{2}\right)$	$\frac{K-t-1}{2}\left(\frac{t+1}{2}\right)$ / $\frac{t+1}{2}\left(\frac{K-t+1}{2}\right)$		
$\mathcal{V}_{\frac{t-1}{2},a_1,\overline{b}_1}$		$\left(\frac{K-t+1}{2}\right)\left(\frac{t+3}{2}\right)$ / $\left(\frac{t+1}{2}\right)\left(\frac{K-t-1}{2}\right)$		
$\mathcal{V}_{\frac{t-1}{2},\overline{a}_1,b_1}$	$\frac{K-t-1}{2}\left(\frac{t+1}{2}\right)$ / $\frac{t+1}{2}\left(\frac{K-t+1}{2}\right)$	$\frac{(t+1)(K-t+1)}{4}$ / $\frac{(K-t+1)(t+1)}{4}$	$\left(\frac{K-t-1}{2}\right)\left(\frac{t+1}{2}\right)$ / $\left(\frac{t+1}{2}\right)\left(\frac{K-t-1}{2}\right)$	$\frac{K-t-1}{2}\left(\frac{t+3}{2}\right)$ / $\frac{t+1}{2}\left(\frac{K-t-1}{2}\right)$
$\mathcal{V}_{\frac{t-1}{2},\overline{a}_1,\overline{b}_1}$		$\frac{K-t-1}{2}\left(\frac{t+3}{2}\right)$ / $\frac{t+1}{2}\left(\frac{K-t-1}{2}\right)$		$\left(\frac{K-t-1}{2}\right)\left(\frac{t+3}{2}\right)$ / $\left(\frac{t+1}{2}\right)\left(\frac{K-t-3}{2}\right)$

In order to make the cardinality of a maximal matching as large as possible, we can also use several subsets to generate a bipartite graph.

Example 2. A bipartite graph $\mathbf{G} = (\mathcal{X}, \mathcal{Y}_2; \mathcal{E})$ where

$$\mathcal{X} = \mathcal{V}_{\frac{t+1}{2};\overline{a}_1,\overline{b}_1}, \qquad \mathcal{Y} = \mathcal{V}_{\frac{t-1}{2};\overline{a}_1,b_1} \bigcup \mathcal{V}_{\frac{t+3}{2};a_1,\overline{b}_1}, \tag{10}$$

can be obtained. From Table 2, we have $d(\mathcal{V}_{\frac{t+1}{2};\bar{a}_1,\bar{b}_1}) = \frac{t+1}{2} + \frac{t+1}{2} = t + 1$ and $d(\mathcal{V}_{\frac{t-1}{2};\bar{a}_1,b_1} \bigcup \mathcal{V}_{\frac{t+3}{2};a_1,\bar{b}_1}) = \frac{K-t+1}{2}$. From Lemma 1 there is a saturating matching. So there are $|\mathcal{V}_{\frac{t-1}{2};\bar{a}_1,b_1} \bigcup \mathcal{V}_{\frac{t+3}{2};a_1,\bar{b}_1}|$ or $|\mathcal{V}_{\frac{t+1}{2};\bar{a}_1,\bar{b}_1}|$ vertices in the maximal matching of $\mathbf{G}$ generated by (10). Of course we can also assume that

$$\mathcal{X} = \mathcal{V}_{\frac{t+1}{2};\bar{a}_1,\bar{b}_1}, \quad \mathcal{Y} = \mathcal{V}_{\frac{t-1}{2};\bar{a}_1,b_1} \quad \text{or} \quad \mathcal{X} = \mathcal{V}_{\frac{t+1}{2};\bar{a}_1,\bar{b}_1}, \quad \mathcal{Y} = \mathcal{V}_{\frac{t+3}{2};a_1,\bar{b}_1}.$$

Similarly we can also show that they have saturating matchings respectively. It is easy to check that cardinality of the maximal matching by the first assumption is maximal.

4.2 Modified Scheme

With the aid of a computer, we have the following bipartite graphes such that the number of the unpair of messages is minimal according to the value of λ.

- When $0 < \lambda \leq \frac{3-\sqrt{5}}{2}$, we use bipartite graphs

$$\mathbf{G}_1 = (\mathcal{V}_{\frac{t+1}{2};\bar{a}_1,\bar{b}_1}, \mathcal{V}_{\frac{t-1}{2};\bar{a}_1,b_1} \bigcup \mathcal{V}_{\frac{t+3}{2};a_1,\bar{b}_1}; \mathcal{E}_1)$$

$$\mathbf{G}_2 = (\mathcal{V}_{\frac{t+1}{2};\bar{a}_1,b_1}, \mathcal{V}_{\frac{t+3}{2};\bar{a}_1,b_1}; \mathcal{E}_2) \quad \mathbf{G}_3 = (\mathcal{V}_{\frac{t+1}{2};a_1,\bar{b}_1}, \mathcal{V}_{\frac{t-1}{2};a_1,\bar{b}_1}; \mathcal{E}_3) \quad (11)$$

$$\mathbf{G}_4 = (\mathcal{V}_{\frac{t-1}{2};\bar{a}_1,\bar{b}_1}, \mathcal{V}_{\frac{t+3}{2};\bar{a}_1,\bar{b}_1}; \mathcal{E}_4) \quad \mathbf{G}_5 = (\mathcal{V}_{\frac{t-1}{2};a_1,b_1}, \mathcal{V}_{\frac{t+3}{2};a_1,b_1}; \mathcal{E}_5)$$

- When $\lambda \in (\frac{3-\sqrt{5}}{2}, \frac{\sqrt{5}-1}{2}]$, we use bipartite graphs

$$\mathbf{G}_1 = (\mathcal{V}_{\frac{t+1}{2};a_1,b_1}, \mathcal{V}_{\frac{t-1}{2};\bar{a}_1,b_1}; \mathcal{E}_1) \quad \mathbf{G}_2 = (\mathcal{V}_{\frac{t+1}{2};a_1,\bar{b}_1}, \mathcal{V}_{\frac{t-1}{2};a_1,\bar{b}_1}; \mathcal{E}_2)$$

$$\mathbf{G}_3 = (\mathcal{V}_{\frac{t+1}{2};\bar{a}_1,b_1}, \mathcal{V}_{\frac{t+3}{2};\bar{a}_1,b_1}; \mathcal{E}_3) \quad \mathbf{G}_4 = (\mathcal{V}_{\frac{t+1}{2};\bar{a}_1,\bar{b}_1}, \mathcal{V}_{\frac{t+3}{2};a_1,\bar{b}_1}; \mathcal{E}_4) \quad (12)$$

$$\mathbf{G}_5 = (\mathcal{V}_{\frac{t-1}{2};a_1,b_1}, \mathcal{V}_{\frac{t+3}{2};a_1,b_1}; \mathcal{E}_5) \quad \mathbf{G}_6 = (\mathcal{V}_{\frac{t-1}{2};\bar{a}_1,\bar{b}_1}, \mathcal{V}_{\frac{t+3}{2};\bar{a}_1,\bar{b}_1}; \mathcal{E}_6)$$

- When $\lambda \in (\frac{\sqrt{5}-1}{2}, 1)$, we use bipartite graphs

$$\mathbf{G}_1 = (\mathcal{V}_{\frac{t+1}{2};a_1,b_1}, \mathcal{V}_{\frac{t-1}{2};\bar{a}_1,b_1} \bigcup \mathcal{V}_{\frac{t+3}{2};a_1,\bar{b}_1}; \mathcal{E}_1)$$

$$\mathbf{G}_2 = (\mathcal{V}_{\frac{t+1}{2};a_1,\bar{b}_1}, \mathcal{V}_{\frac{t-1}{2};a_1,\bar{b}_1}; \mathcal{E}_2) \quad \mathbf{G}_3 = (\mathcal{V}_{\frac{t+1}{2};\bar{a}_1,b_1}, \mathcal{V}_{\frac{t+3}{2};\bar{a}_1,b_1}; \mathcal{E}_3) \quad (13)$$

$$\mathbf{G}_4 = (\mathcal{V}_{\frac{t-1}{2};\bar{a}_1,\bar{b}_1}, \mathcal{V}_{\frac{t+3}{2};\bar{a}_1,\bar{b}_1}; \mathcal{E}_4) \quad \mathbf{G}_5 = (\mathcal{V}_{\frac{t-1}{2};a_1,b_1}, \mathcal{V}_{\frac{t+3}{2};a_1,b_1}; \mathcal{E}_5)$$

From Table 2, similar to the discussion in Example 2 the following statement holds.

Lemma 2. Each of the bipartite graphs in (11), (12) and (13) has a saturating matching.

Now let us consider the bipartite graphes in (11) first. From Lemma 2 and Table 1, the number of unpaired messages is

$$n_1 = \left| \mathcal{V}_{\frac{t+1}{2};a_1,b_1} \right| + \left| \left| \mathcal{V}_{\frac{t+1}{2};\overline{a}_1,\overline{b}_1} \right| - \left| \mathcal{V}_{\frac{t-1}{2};\overline{a}_1,b_1} \bigcup \mathcal{V}_{\frac{t+3}{2};a_1,\overline{b}_1} \right| \right|$$

$$+ \left| \left| \mathcal{V}_{\frac{t+1}{2};\overline{a}_1,b_1} \right| - \left| \mathcal{V}_{\frac{t+3}{2};\overline{a}_1,b_1} \right| \right| + \left| \left| \mathcal{V}_{\frac{t+1}{2};a_1,\overline{b}_1} \right| - \left| \mathcal{V}_{\frac{t-1}{2};a_1,\overline{b}_1} \right| \right|$$

$$+ \left| \left| \mathcal{V}_{\frac{t-1}{2};\overline{a}_1,\overline{b}_1} \right| - \left| \mathcal{V}_{\frac{t+3}{2};\overline{a}_1,\overline{b}_1} \right| \right| + \left| \left| \mathcal{V}_{\frac{t-1}{2};a_1,b_1} \right| - \left| \mathcal{V}_{\frac{t+3}{2};a_1,b_1} \right| \right| \tag{14}$$

$$= \left[\left(\frac{t+1}{K-t-1} \right)^2 + \left| 1 - 2\frac{t+1}{K-t-1} \right| + 2\left| \frac{t+1}{K-t-1} - \frac{(t+1)(t-1)(K-t-3)}{(t+3)(K-t+1)(K-t-1)} \right| \right] \left(\frac{K/2-1}{(t+1)/2} \right)^2$$

$$= \left[\frac{|K-3t-3|}{K-t-1} + \frac{(t+1)^2(K-t+1)(t+3)+8K(t+1)(K-t-1)}{(K-t-1)^2(t+3)(K-t+1)} \right] \left(\frac{K/2-1}{(t+1)/2} \right)^2.$$

The ratio of unpaired messages is

$$\Delta_1 = \frac{n_1}{\binom{K}{t+1}} < \frac{n_1}{\left| \mathcal{V}_{\frac{t+1}{2}} \right| + \left| \mathcal{V}_{\frac{t-1}{2}} \bigcup \mathcal{V}_{\frac{t+3}{2}} \right|}$$

$$= \left[\frac{|K-3t-3|}{K-t-1} + \frac{(t+1)^2(K-t+1)(t+3)+8K(t+1)(K-t+1)}{(K-t-1)^2(t+3)(K-t+1)} \right] \frac{\left(\frac{K/2-1}{(t+1)/2} \right)^2}{2\binom{K/2}{(t-1)/2}\binom{K/2}{(t+3)/2}+\binom{K/2}{(t+1)/2}\binom{K/2}{(t+1)/2}} \tag{15}$$

$$= \left[\frac{|K-3t-3|}{K-t-1} + \frac{(t+1)^2(K-t+1)(t+3)+8K(t+1)(K-t-1)}{(K-t-1)^2(t+3)(K-t+1)} \right] \frac{\frac{(K-t-1)^2}{K^2}}{2\frac{(t+1)(K-t-1)}{(K-t+1)(t+3)}+1}$$

$$\approx \frac{|1-3\lambda|(1-\lambda)+\lambda^2}{3}.$$

From Table 1 and similar to the calculations in (14), (15), the number of unpaired messages and its ratio based on bipartite graphes in (12) are

$$n_2 = \left(\frac{K}{(K-t-1)^2}|2t+2-K| + \frac{t+1}{K-t-1}\frac{8K}{(t+3)(K-t+1)} \right) \left(\frac{K/2-1}{(t+1)/2} \right)^2,$$

$$\Delta_2 = \frac{n_2}{\binom{K}{t+1}} < \frac{n_2}{2\binom{K/2}{(t-1)/2}\binom{K/2}{(t+3)/2}+\binom{K/2}{(t+1)/2}\binom{K/2}{(t+1)/2}} \approx \frac{1}{3}|2\lambda-1|, \tag{16}$$

and based on bipartite graphes in (13) are

$$n_3 = \left(1 + \frac{K}{(K-t-1)^2}|3t+3-2K| + \frac{t+1}{K-t-1}\frac{8K}{(t+3)(K-t+1)} \right) \left(\frac{K/2-1}{(t+1)/2} \right)^2$$

$$\Delta_3 = \frac{n_3}{\binom{K}{t+1}} < \frac{n_3}{2\binom{K/2}{(t-1)/2}\binom{K/2}{(t+3)/2}+\binom{K/2}{(t+1)/2}\binom{K/2}{(t+1)/2}} \approx \frac{(1-\lambda)^2+\lambda|3\lambda-2|}{3} \tag{17}$$

T he detailed calculations in (16) and (17) can be found in Subsection III-B and Subsection III-C [2] respectively. By (7), (15), (16) and (17), Theorem 2 can be obtained.

5   More Refined Methods

We should point out that the rate in Theorem 2 can be further improved when t is odd. First let us generalize the notations in (8), i.e., define

$$\mathcal{V}_{w;\overline{a}_1,\ldots,\overline{a}_{h_1-1},a_{h_1},\overline{b}_1,\ldots,\overline{b}_{h_2-1},b_{h_2}}$$
$$= \{ \mathcal{S} \in \mathcal{V}_w \mid a_{h_1}, b_{h_2} \in \mathcal{S}, a_i, b_j \notin \mathcal{S}, i \in [1,h_1), j \in [1,h_2) \} \tag{18}$$

where $w = \frac{t-1}{2}, \frac{t+1}{2}, \frac{t+3}{2}$ and $h_1 \in [1, \frac{K}{2} - w + 1]$, $h_2 \in [1, \frac{K}{2} - t + w]$. It is easy to check that

$$|\mathcal{V}_{w;\bar{a}_1,\ldots,\bar{a}_{h_1-1},a_{h_1},\bar{b}_1,\ldots,\bar{b}_{h_2-1},b_{h_2}}| = \binom{K/2-h_1}{w-1}\binom{K/2-h_2}{t-w}$$

and

$$\mathcal{V}_{w;\bar{a}_1,\ldots,\bar{a}_{h_1-1},a_{h_1},\bar{b}_1,\ldots,\bar{b}_{h_2-1},b_{h_2}} \bigcap \mathcal{V}_{w;\bar{a}_1,\ldots,\bar{a}_{h'_1-1},a_{h'_1},\bar{b}_1,\ldots,\bar{b}_{h'_2-1},b_{h'_2}} = \emptyset$$

for any distinct vectors $(h_1, h_2) \neq (h'_1, h'_2)$. In addition,

$$\binom{K/2}{w}\binom{K/2}{t+1-w} = \sum_{h_1=1}^{K/2-w+1}\sum_{h_2=1}^{K/2-t+w}\binom{K/2-h_1}{w-1}\binom{K/2-h_2}{t-w}$$

since it is well know that $\binom{n}{m} = \binom{n-1}{m-1} + \binom{n-2}{m-1} + \ldots + \binom{m-1}{m-1}$, $1 \leq m < n$ always holds. So we have

$$\mathcal{V}_w = \bigcup_{h_1=1}^{K/2-w+1}\bigcup_{h_2=1}^{K/2-t+w}\mathcal{V}_{w;\bar{a}_1,\ldots,\bar{a}_{h_1-1},a_{h_1},\bar{b}_1,\ldots,\bar{b}_{h_2-1},b_{h_2}}.$$

Then we can also compute the degree of each vertex in the bipartite graph generated by any subsets in (18). Similar to the discussions in Sects. 4, we can further reduce the value of Δ' in (2) by sacrificing run-time efficiency on constructing the most appropriate classes of bipartite graphs. In fact the sacrificing run-time is very small comparing with that of finding the maximal matching of graph $\mathbf{G} = (\mathcal{V}_{\frac{t-1}{2}} \bigcup \mathcal{V}_{\frac{t+1}{2}} \bigcup \mathcal{V}_{\frac{t+3}{2}}; \mathcal{E})$.

6 Conclusion

In this paper, we considered the coded caching scheme for multiple servers setting in [6]. By a refined method for pairing we reduced the transmission in the case $\frac{KM}{N}$ is odd for the system with three data servers. Consequently an obviously smaller rate was obtained. Especially when K is large, $R \approx \frac{1}{2}R_{MN}(K, \frac{M}{N})$ if $\frac{M}{N}$ nears $1/2$, and $R \approx \frac{41}{81}R_{MN}(K, \frac{M}{N})$ if $\frac{M}{N}$ nears $\frac{1}{3}$ or $\frac{2}{3}$.

In addition, our modification can be generalized to further reduce the rate. However, with an exhaustive computer search, it will cost more running times to search the bipartite graphs generated by the subsets in (18) such that the unpaired messages as small as possible. So it would be of interest if one can found an efficient construction for such bipartite graphs.

Acknowledgements. The authors express their sincere thanks to the Associate Editor and three anonymous reviewers for their helpful suggestions which improved this paper significantly. M. Cheng was supported by 2016GXNSFFA380011. Q. Zhang was supported by IPGGE XYCSZ2018074. J. Jiang was supported by NSFC 11601096. R. Wei was supported by NSERC RGPIN 16-05610.

References

1. Bondy, J.A., Murthy, U.: Graph Theory with Applications. Elsevier, New York (1976)
2. Cheng, M., Zhang, Q., Jiang, J., Wei, R.: Reduced Transmission in Multi-Server Coded Caching. arXiv:1802.07410v1 [cs.IT], February 2018
3. Ghasemi, H., Ramamoorthy, A.: Improved lower bounds for coded caching. IEEE Trans. Inf. Theory **63**, 4388–4413 (2017)
4. Ji, M., Caire, G., Molisch, A.F.: Fundamental limits of caching in wireless D2D networks. IEEE Trans. Inf. Theory **62**, 849–869 (2016)
5. Karamchandani, N., Niesen, U., Maddah-Ali, M.A., Diggavi, S.: Hierarchical coded caching. In: IEEE International Symposium on Information Theory, Honolulu, HI, pp. 2142–2146 (2014). June
6. Luo, T., Aggarwal, V., Peleato, B.: Coded caching with distributed storage. arXiv:1611.06591 [cs.IT], November 2016
7. Maddah-Ali, M.A., Niesen, U.: Fundamental limits of caching. IEEE Trans. Inf. Theory **60**, 2856–2867 (2014)
8. Mital, N., Gunduz, D., Ling, C.: Coded caching in a multi-server system with random topology. arXiv:1712.00649 [cs.IT], December 2017
9. Sengupta, A., Tandon, R., Clancy, T.C.: Fundamental limits of caching with secure delivery. IEEE Trans. Inf. Forensics Secur. **10**, 355–370 (2015)
10. Shariatpanahi, S.P., Motahari, S.A., Khalaj, B.H.: Multi-server coded caching. IEEE Trans. Inf. Theory **62**, 7253–7271 (2016)
11. Tian, C., Chen, J.: Caching and delivery via interference elimination. In: IEEE International Symposium on Information Theory, Barcelona, pp. 830–834, July 2016
12. Wan, K., Tuninetti, D., Piantanida, P.: On caching with more users than files. In: IEEE International Symposium on Information Theory, Barcelona, pp. 135–139, July 2016
13. Wan, K., Tuninetti, D., Piantanida, P.: On the optimality of uncoded cache placement. In: IEEE Information Theory Workshop, Cambridge, UK, September 2016
14. Wang, C.Y., Lim, S.H., Gastpar, M.: A new converse bound for coded caching. In: IEEE Information Theory Workshop, Robinson College, October 2016
15. Yan, Q., Cheng, M., Tang, X., Chen, Q.: On the placement delivery array design in centralized coded caching scheme. IEEE Trans. Inf. Theory **63**, 5821–5833 (2017)
16. Yu, Q., Maddah-Ali, M.A., Avestimehr, A.S.: The exact rate-memory tradeoff for caching with uncoded prefetching. arXiv:1609.07817v2 [cs.IT] December 2017

Distributed Sensor Fusion for Activity Detection in Smart Buildings

C. Papatsimpa[1(✉)] and J. P. M. G. Linnartz[1,2]

[1] Eindhoven University of Technology, 5600 MB Eindhoven, The Netherlands
C.Papatsimpa@tue.nl
[2] Signify (Former Phillips Lighting), Eindhoven, The Netherlands

Abstract. Modern building systems often utilize multiple, physically separated sensors (sometimes of different type) to better detect occupancy. Such systems typically rely on a central processor where global data fusion takes place. However, such centralized architectures give rise to problems with communication and computational bottlenecks and are susceptible to total system failure should the central facility fail. There are significant advantages in distributing operations over multiple processing nodes. In the wake of this need, this paper addresses the problem of presence detection in a building by employing a decentralized sensing architecture. We focus on a network of radar sensor nodes, each with its own processing facility. Each node runs a hidden Markov model algorithm to provide a local estimate of the occupancy state and share it via wireless links. We introduce a distributed fusion algorithm that optimally combines the information generated by local nodes, having access to their private information, and recovers exactly the global estimation. System performance is evaluated in real world conditions, where sensor errors and communication may not exactly follow idealized model assumptions.

Keywords: Internet of Things (IoT) · Smart buildings · Energy efficiency
Sensor fusion

1 Introduction

The smart building concept is now becoming a reality thanks to the availability of low-cost, easy to install Internet of Things (IoT) devices, like sensors and actuators. Yet, most smart building applications found in the literature still make use of a centralized architecture with IoT nodes exchanging or delivering their readings to a data sink (e.g., a base station). While such a centralized processing approach is theoretically optimal if communication is error free and not constrained by bandwidth or power, there are significant advantages in distributing system operations over multiple processing nodes:

- Computational effort is distributed within the sensor network, i.e., the number of sequential numerical operations at each node is less than if all the sensor data were centrally processed. This is particularly important when different types of sensor data are involved that have different processing requirements. For example, radar sensor data processing that entail computationally "hungry" FFTs, or camera

© Springer Nature Switzerland AG 2018
Y. Xiang et al. (Eds.): IDCS 2018, LNCS 11226, pp. 87–99, 2018.
https://doi.org/10.1007/978-3-030-02738-4_8

systems that require high computational complexity techniques like Viola-Jones [1]. Many sensing systems additionally require the implementation of Privacy Enabling Technologies (PET), often based on cryptographic techniques [2, 3] that tend to entail significant computations.

- The communication capabilities of a wireless sensor network are also limited. The power consumption of wireless radios transmitting unprocessed high complexity data to a central base station have a diverse effect in the sensor battery lifetime, in addition to congesting the network. In-node processing allows to compress sensor information and reduce the amount of data to be transmitted, not only in terms of the pay load per transmission, but also in terms of the number of transmissions.
- It is well known that a centralized system is vulnerable to a single point-of-failure. On the contrary, in a decentralized approach, there is no single point of failure, i.e., every node in the network acts as a fusion center, thus, even if a sensor (or group of sensors) fail, the system can still operate.

Motivated by the above advantages, a vast amount of research effort in many application domains is dedicated to the problem of distributed estimation in sensor networks. Examples include the health care systems domain, where distributed Kalman filter updates are applied [4], and surveillance systems, where various distributed estimation and association techniques have been presented [5]. Most of these approaches use covariance-based fusion approaches to model errors between local estimates [6, 7]. In smart building control, which is the focus of this paper, the number of previous publications is less. Authors in [3] suggest to use distributed smart cameras in an object position estimation system called SCOPES [8], to create predictive occupancy models. The project focuses on lightweight algorithms for in-node data processing with the aim to reduce the amount of data transmissions and processing latency.

Earlier, we addressed the underlying theoretical problem of distributed sensing of a random process (room occupation, in our case) via multiple unreliable observation channels and where the observers may [9] or may not [10] have constraints in their communication. This motivated us to further elaborate these insights to the design of an architecture that achieves not only optimum performance, if communication is perfect, but also adequate or even near-optimum performance if some random communication failures can occur. It has been proposed to approximate office occupancy as a Markov process that moves between a number of states, e.g. presence or absence [9, 10]. Our challenge is to determine the current state of that process from the sequence of noisy observations made by (imperfect) sensors. This concept is known as a Hidden Markov Model (HMM) and has been extensively explored for other applications, but we extend this it to allow distributed sensing. In this paper, we propose an architecture that involves the use of individual, spatially separated nodes that make local observations and effectively estimate the state of the underlying process based on an HMM activity detection algorithm. Raw sensor observations are processed locally, thus independently. Instead of exchanging the latest observations (as in [9]), we propose to exchange the state estimation. This reduces the amount of data to be transmitted. We derive and analyze a distributed processing algorithm, further-on referred to as Distributed Estimation Merging (DEM) algorithm, which reconstructs exactly the optimal estimate, equivalent to the centralized one, using only the communicated information. System performance is evaluated in real world conditions, with results being compiled from data of a real-life experimental setup of a radar sensor network system. The effect of an unreliable communication channel and packet loss is also studied.

2 Distributed Fusion Algorithm

The Distributed Estimation Merging (DEM) algorithm aims to achieve the detection performance of a centralized algorithm that can access all actual sensor observations. Yet, we aim at substantially fewer transmission load, ensuring that nodes always have the best possible estimate even if no data is available from other nodes (thus being resilient to even a complete communication failure). Consequently, we shift most of the calculation to local nodes. The philosophy of this approach is graphically illustrated in Fig. 1. In an extremely centralized architecture, nodes do not perform any processing on the data, but just communicate the raw sensor observations to the fusion node, which then generates the optimal state estimate given the model and the data. In contrast, in a fully distributed architecture each node processes the data and generates a local estimate given its local view of the process. Then it communicates this estimate to the rest of the network. This requires an algorithm to combine all the local estimates to obtain the optimal centralized one.

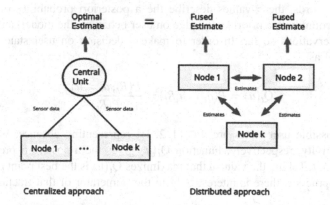

Fig. 1. Philosophy behind the distributed approach. Individual sensor nodes exchange state estimates instead of raw sensor observations. The fusion algorithm optimally reconstructs the centralized estimate based only on the communicated information.

2.1 Local HMM

For an office environment, we consider a Markov process q_t, evolving in discrete time, with three possible discrete user states, namely, $q_t = 1$ represents the state that the user is absent, $q_t = 2$ the state that the user is walking, whereas $q_t = 3$ the state that the user is present in his desk. These states represent a one-to-one correspondence to the NEMA

[11] recommended types of motion. The actual user state is unknown to the system (hidden), but can only be observed through another set of stochastic processes that produce the sequence of observations, i.e., the wireless sensor network.

An HMM can be fully described by the following set of parameters, namely, the state transition probabilities, an observation model (emission probabilities), and the initial state distribution [12]:

1. State transition probability matrix: $A = \{a_{ij}\}, a_{ij} = P(q_t = j|q_{t-1} = i)$. The transition probabilities describe how the occupancy of a space changes over time.
2. Emission probability matrix: $B = \{b_{ij}\}, b_i(j) = P(r_t = j|q_t = i)$, where, the sensor observation r_t, which of course depends on the current state q_t, corresponds to the physical output of the system being modelled. In essence, the emission probabilities are a metric that describes the quality of the sensor.
3. $\pi = \{\pi_i\}$: Initial state probability vector. The initial state distribution specifies the occupancy probability at the initial time step $t = 0$ prior to any observation.

For a given model $\lambda = \{A, B, \pi\}$, the forward-backward procedure allows to inductively calculate the forward variable $\alpha_t(j) = P(r_1 r_2 \ldots r_t, q_t = j|\lambda)$, i.e., the joint probability of the partial observation sequence $R_t = r_1, \ldots r_t$ (until time t) and state q_t at time t, as

$$\alpha_t(u) = P(q_t = u, R_t) = b_u(r_t) \sum_j a_{ju} \alpha_{t-1}(j) \tag{1}$$

In simple words, the α-values describe the a posteriori probability of user state taking into account both a priori knowledge on user behavior (the model) and the series of sensor observations so far. In order to make a decision on user state, we define function $Q_t(u)$ as

$$Q_t(u) = P(q_t = u|R_t) = \frac{P(R_t, q_t = u)}{P(R_t)} \tag{2}$$

where, the possible user states are $u \in \{1, 2, 3\}$, representing absence, walking and desk work activity, respectively. Function $Q_t(u)$ gives the a-posteriori probability of state at instance t. Taking the value u that maximizes $Q_t(u)$ is the best point estimate for user state. In practice, there is interest only in the numerator of that fraction, thus,

$$u = \text{argmax}\{\alpha_t(u)\}. \tag{3}$$

Thus, our best estimate on user state is the value u that maximizes the corresponding α-values. The well-known theory of how to handle sequences R_t coming from a single sensor into multiple sensor data has been covered in [9]. From our analysis in [10], it can be seen that in the case that communication is intermittent and long sequences of observations are missing, each sensor may have to resend its entire history in every transmission to optimally reconstruct the global state estimate. This, of course, is impractical and sending only a few recent observations does not affect the performance excessively. We rather send only a few bytes per node per unit of time. The next section reveals how α-values can be used for this. Intuitively one may think that the α-values collapse the history and contain an intertwined mixture of previous observations from one node that can no longer be separated to be used in recovering the appropriate forward backward trellis for a multi-sensor situation. We formally prove that α-values can nonetheless be used and experimentally confirm this.

3 Fusion Algorithm

Consider a sensor network with K nodes taking observations of the same state process. The observations of a single node i at time t are measurements r_t^i of q_t described by the emission probability

$$B^i = \{b_{kj}\}, b_k(j)^i = P(r_t^i = j | q_t = k) \tag{4}$$

The fusion problem at hand can be described as follows. At each t, each node i communicates the local estimation on user state in the form of the α-value $\alpha_t^i(u)$ for all possible states u. Each node uses only this communicated information to optimally reconstruct the global state estimate, equivalent to the centralized one. As we derive in the appendix, this is possible using the following new recursive fusion scheme

$$P(q_t = u, R_t) = \frac{\prod_{i=1}^{K} \alpha_t^i(u)}{c_u^{K-1}} \tag{5}$$

where, the correction term c_u is defined as $c_u = \sum_j a_{ju} \alpha_{t-1}(j)$. This term can be pre-calculated in every algorithmic step, using simply the previous α-values and the stored Markov model transition parameters a_{ju}.

The structure of the fusion term is interesting. Basically, nodes account for the presence of correlations between the local estimators, due to the fact that they all observe the same state process, by compensating the product of the local estimators with the times that the "best idea of being in state u now" was double counted by the single estimator.

According to our new fusion algorithm, each single node i in the network computes the local state estimate, in the form of the α-values, a single variable that encapsulates all the necessary information (the state and history of sensor observations). The node communicates the following information:

$$msg = \left(\alpha_t^i(u)\right)$$

The message consists of the local α-values. This communication scheme is fully compatible with packet-based broadcast mode communication in a real-world wireless sensor network. The message size is $O(Ub)$ with U being the number of states and b the desired precision (a typical choice would be 16-bit fixed point representation).

Of course, transmitted messages may be subject to communication failures that result in packet losses. However, we experienced that under mild connectivity conditions and medium network size, packet losses do not significantly affect the performance.

4 Performance Evaluation

The goal of our distributed architecture is to function as activity detection system for smart building environments, such as for example office buildings. In this section, we evaluate system performance using a network of radar sensing modalities in a real-life experimental setup, although the solution also supports other modalities, and even appeared well suited for mixtures of nodes. The effect of communication outages is also studied.

4.1 Choice of Sensing Modality

Most common presence sensors used for this function today, are PIR sensors (Passive Infrared). These PIR sensors are relatively large and need a direct line of sight (which hampers usage behind e.g. plastic covers inside a luminaire) and are limited in sensitivity. In addition, PIR can only detect (major) motion, not presence. Alternative, microwave (radar) sensors offer the significant advantage of a "richer" signal, in the sense that the radar signals contain more information than only the regular motion detection of people. Based on this richer information, and with smart algorithms, also classification of movements and activities can be achieved (e.g. movement direction, activity recognition). However, this comes at the cost of higher processing complexity and latency. Especially if the system needs to transmit uncompressed raw radar data and combine information from multiple sources, this may give rise to problems with computational and communication bottlenecks. In that sense, a wide adoption of radar sensing technology will be possible if distributed approaches are used in order to distribute the processing effort among the available nodes and compress the available information.

4.2 Experimental Deployment

A key step in our research methodology is the data collection phase. We deployed 4 nodes on the ceiling of a typical office environment in Signify (Philips Lighting) Turnout, Belgium. The office plan was divided into two groups as depicted in Fig. 2. In each group, two commercially available CW radar sensors[1], operating at 24 GHz, sense the same area at the same time. The radar sensors were used to collect Doppler signatures of human targets performing the following activities:

- Walking, at different speeds inside the area defined by group 1, at various distances from the sensors.

---

[1] https://www.innosent.de/en/sensors/smr-radar-serie/smr-313/.

- Desk work at a distance of 0.5 m from sensor F2. The placement of the desk is shown in Fig. 2. The participants were asked to perform typical desk work activities like typing, browsing the net etc.

The experiments were carried out over a 1-day period and sampling rate was set to 44.1 kHz. The data was then recorded by a data acquisition device with $f_s = 1.2$ kHz sampling frequency. Each target was measured for three sessions of ten minutes walking at various speeds, distances and angles according to a specific script to collect all possible combinations of location and direction, resulting in overall 3600 recordings of walking activity, each one second length. Three sessions of five minutes of the targets performing typical desk work were recorded, resulting in an overall of 1800 Doppler signature frames of desk work activity, each one second length. Additionally, the empty room was measured for a period of 20 min, to obtain the Doppler signature of class absence and to capture radio interference and potentially Doppler-shifted reflections from neighboring rooms.

In parallel to the radar sensor data collection, in order to collect information about typical occupancy profiles in an office, we implemented a baseline study in an office at Eindhoven University campus. Participants were asked to maintain their working style as usual. No activities were scripted in any form. In total, 10 participants were recorded for 15 days, resulting in a total of 150 daily 24-hour profiles of presence of occupants in their offices.

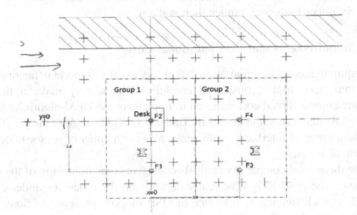

Fig. 2. Sketch of the experimental set-up. Sensors were placed in positions F1–F4, at height 2.7 m above the floor. The targets were asked to perform walking activity inside the area defined by group 1. Desk work activity was performed at a distance of 0.5 m from the sensor F2.

4.3   Simulation Methodology

Our simulations are based on measured target activity trajectories (absence, walking from/towards the sensor and desk work), thus, not necessarily matching any pre-assumed Markov process. Pre-recorded Doppler signatures of each activity were fed into the algorithm to simulate fine grain sensor samples matching real-life office occupancy profiles based on the baseline study we previously described. For computing the detection performance, we compare the processed ground truth data derived from the baseline study with the data collected from the simulation logs.

4.4 Feature Selection

The classification features used in this work are the commonly adopted, for radar sensing, filter-bank energy coefficients (FBEs). To implement this filter-bank, the signal is sliced into short-time frames. A Hann window function is applied on the sampled data to further reduce noise. The signal is then transformed using a Fast Fourier transform (FFT) and the magnitude is taken. The magnitude coefficients are mapped to a frequency bin using triangular overlapping windows, in a way that each frequency bin holds a weighted sum representing the spectral magnitude in that filter bank channel.

The design choices for this particular FBE implementation are given as follows: The length of FFT is 1024 samples, resulting in a frequency resolution of 1.17 Hz, given that the sampling rate is 1.2 kHz. The number of filter bank coefficients (number of frequency bins) is 30. The cut-off frequencies were set to 0 and 300 Hz, respectively. According to the International Labor Office, the average human walking pace is around 4.8 k/h [13]. Thus, for a transmission frequency of 24 GHz, it makes no sense to design the upper frequency limit as higher than 300 Hz, since this would correspond to speed of 6.8 km/h (pretty fast for office activity). Motions like typing or clicking typically lie in lower frequency ranges than walking.

4.5 Time Requirements and Computational Cost

The time requirements and computational cost are usually important factors in such processing thus need to be considered carefully. We initially make a theoretical analysis of the computational cost required to implement the DEM algorithm based on radar sensing. Results are summarized in Table 1. In Table 1, N is the length of the FFT, M is the number of filterbank coefficients, K is the number of sensor nodes and U is the number of states.

While the theoretical complexity analysis does give some indication of the required compute power, the processing time really depends on the processor under consideration: the CPU clock frequency, presence of DSP support, presence of floating point unit (if needed), etc. In order to get a meaningful estimate of the required processing time, we map the algorithm on a chosen platform and do the cycle count. We provide an example implementation that acts as a proof of concept for the DEM algorithm. We consider a 16-bit real 1024 FFT, $U = 3$ possible user states and $K = 2$ nodes. Signal processing was performed on STM32F412 microcontroller[2] featuring ARMCortex-M4 core operating at 100 MHz, and 512 kB Flash memory. The timings of the various operations (after code optimization) are summarized in Table 2.

---

[2] http://www.st.com/en/microcontrollers/stm32f412.html?querycriteria=productId=LN1916.

Table 1. Operations required for DEM algorithm

Operation	Computational power
FFT (Radix-2 method [14])	$O(N \ log_2 N)$
FBEs calculation	$O(MN/2 - 1)$ multiplications $O(MN/2)$ additions
α-values calculation (Eq. 1)	$O(UU + 1)$ multiplications $O(U^2)$ additions
Fusion algorithm (Eq. 5)	1 division 1 power $O(UU - 1)$ additions $O(K - 1 + U^2)$ multiplications

Table 2. Processing time for microcontroller operations (after code optimization).

Operation	Cycles	Processing time (ms)
Initialization	26725	0.26725
Data pre-processing	35421	0.35421
1024-point FFT	63664	0.63664
FBEs	40042	0.40042
State Estimation	230	0.0023

These timing estimations correspond to a particular implementation of the algorithm that may act as a reference. Of course, the processing time will vary depending on the processor architecture, flash memory and the size of the FFT. In the above timing estimation, we have to add the sampling time to acquire the 1024-FFT points (853.33 ms) and the time required to receive information from the neighboring nodes.

4.6 Activity Recognition

We performed experiments to evaluate the performance of the DEM algorithm. When no communication limitations are considered, our solution optimally reconstructs the global state estimate from the collapsed radar features. In fact, classification performance is exactly the same as the centralized approach, where all nodes send their observations to a central processing unit. The detection accuracy is presented in Table 3. Results are presented with 95% confidence interval using t-distribution. For comparison, the individual radar sensor accuracies, without any form of communication between sensors, are also given. As expected, combining information from both sensors improves overall detection. In fact, the fused estimate compensates for the limitations of each individual sensor. Detecting Walking activity exhibits a larger variability in reliability. This can be explained by the fact that we experimented with walking traces from various angles, which may result in different performance.

Table 3. Detection performance

Activity	Fused estimate	Sensor 1	Sensor 2
Absence	97.57 ± 0.6%	98.02 ± 1.5%	35.31 ± 2%
Walking	79.07 ± 2.6%	55.81 ± 1.1%	79.07 ± 0.7%
Desk work	97.25 ± 0.8%	84.7 ± 0.48%	96.17 ± 0.14%

Table 4. Detection performance under channel erasure

Activity	Ideal channel	20% Erasure probability	40% Erasure probability
Absence	97.57 ± 0.6%	97.16 ± 1.3%	96.29 ± 1.6%
Walking	79.07 ± 2.6%	77.3 ± 4%	76.74 ± 6%
Desk work	97.25 ± 0.8%	97.14 ± 0.9%	96.99 ± 0.9%

4.7 Effect of Channel Erasure

In many cases, sensor communication may be performed over an unreliable communication channel, with unpredictable "outages", or may not be frequently enough, limited by the available channel capacity. We evaluate the performance of the suggested distributed approach in the presence of channel erasures. Results are presented in Table 4.

A comparison between the classification accuracy should not be the only measure of performance. In a peer to peer estimation architecture, since no central node exists, every single node in the network is supposed to have the same state estimate, thus, the disagreement between node estimates is also important. For this analysis, we use the notion of disagreement as a measure. Considering a group of K sensor nodes that have to decide between mutually exclusive possible user states, the disagreement between any two pairs of sensors is one if they choose a different state, else, it is zero [15],

$$d_{ij} = 1 \ if \ i \neq j, else \ d_{ij} = 0. \tag{6}$$

Averaging over the whole day results in the percentage of time the nodes had a different estimate of user state. Having a consensus estimate can be rather important for such distributed architectures. Results are presented in Table 5 for 20% and 40% channel erasure, respectively.

Table 5. Disagreement between sensor nodes

	20% Erasure probability	40% Erasure probability
Percentage of in estimates	0.13%	0.42%

According to our experiments, packet losses (even up to 40%) do not significantly influence system performance. In fact is it equivalent to a few seconds per day, mainly during transitions of people entering or leaving, which can presumably be mitigated by a smooth transition between on an off involving dimming. This is a direct derivation of the HMM model formulation. In an HMM, the α-values hold information not only on the current observation, but incorporate the history of observations so far. Taking this into consideration, even if some messages fail to be communicated, the node still holds information on the global estimate resulting from previous updates. In that sense, a series of continuous packet losses is required in order for the α-values to completely deviate from the central estimate and contribute to the disagreement measure.

5 Conclusions

Most practical IoT applications implement centralized architectures with sensing nodes exchanging or delivering their readings to a central processing unit. Such centralized approaches, though easier to approach the optimal solution, in practice give rise to problems with computational and communication bottlenecks and are susceptible to total system failure should the central facility fail. Distributing processing among available resources offers significant advantages, and in this context we proposed and formalized a new Distributed Estimation Fusion (DEM) approach based on HMMs. The equivalence of the DEM algorithm and the optimum solution has been confirmed theoretically by a mathematical derivation. The proposed framework for decentralized sensor fusion is generic and may be applied to any service or application which uses multiple distributed sensors to monitor a process that is reasonably well described as Markovian. Yet, in this work we focus on smart buildings service as a particular example and evaluated system performance in real world conditions with results being compiled from data of a real-life experimental setup of a radar sensor network system. Our results demonstrate that the new algorithm is able to optimally reconstruct the global state estimate, equivalent to the centralized one, while ensuring low latency and long lifetimes. That is, it is not needed to exchange explicit observations to perform the DEM algorithm.

Acknowledgment. The authors would like to thank Abhinav Durani for his help in assessing the computation effort on typical processors, and the Signify (former Philips Lighting) research team in Eindhoven for their help in the office measurements.

Appendix

We show that optimal fusion can be performed for multiple spatially separated sensors, even if not the observations, but locally prepared α-values are exchanged. Starting from the expression that describes the global estimate (given that all observations $R_t = \{r_t^1, r_t^2, \ldots, r_t^K\}$ are known)

$$P(q_t = u, R_t) = b_u(R_t) \sum_i a_{iu} \alpha_{t-1}(i) \tag{7}$$

Assuming conditional independence of observations given the state

$$b_u(r_t) = P(r_t|q_t) = \prod_{i=1}^{K} P(r_t^i|q_t) = \prod_{i=1}^{K} b_u(r_t^i) \tag{8}$$

We reach

$$P(q_t = u|R_t) = \left[\prod_{i=1}^{K} b_u(r_t^i)\right] \sum_j a_{ju}\alpha_{t-1}(j) \tag{9}$$

$$= \frac{\prod_{i=1}^{K} \left[b_u(r_t^i) \sum_j a_{ju}\alpha_{t-1}(j)\right]}{\left[\sum_j a_{ju}\alpha_{t-1}(j)\right]^{K-1}} \tag{10}$$

$$= \frac{\prod_{i=1}^{K} P(q_t = u|R_t^i)}{\left[\sum_j a_{ju}\alpha_{t-1}(j)\right]^{K-1}} \tag{11}$$

$$= \frac{\prod_{i=1}^{K} \alpha_t^i(u)}{\left[\sum_j a_{ju}\alpha_{t-1}(j)\right]^{K-1}} \tag{12}$$

Thus, the fusion algorithm can reconstruct the centralized using the following recursive formula,

$$P(q_t = u, R_t) = \frac{\prod_{i=1}^{K} \alpha_t^i(u)}{c_u^{K-1}} \tag{13}$$

where, $c_u = \sum_j a_{ju}\alpha_{t-1}(j)$.

References

1. Viola, P., Jones, M.J.: Robust real-time face detection. Int. J. Comput. Vis. **57**(2), 137–154 (2004)
2. Boult, T.E.: PICO: privacy through invertible cryptographic obscuration. In: Computer Vision for Interactive and Intelligent Environment, CVIIE 2005, pp. 27–38 (2005)
3. Carrillo, P., Kalva, H., Magliveras, S.: Compression independent reversible encryption for privacy in video surveillance. EURASIP J. Inf. Secur. **2009**(1), 1–13 (2009)
4. Olfati-Saber, R.: Distributed Kalman filtering for sensor networks. In: 2007 46th IEEE Conference on Decision and Control, pp. 5492–5498 (2007)
5. Liggins, M.E., Chong, C.Y., Kadar, I., Alford, M.G., Vannicola, V., Thomopoulos, S.: Distributed fusion architectures and algorithms for target tracking. Proc. IEEE **85**(1), 95–107 (1997)
6. Chang, K.C., Tian, Z., Mori, S.: Performance evaluation for MAP state estimate fusion. IEEE Trans. Aerosp. Electron. Syst. **40**(2), 706–714 (2004)

7. Mori, S., Barker, W.H., Chong, C.Y., Chang, K.C.: Track association and track fusion with nondeterministic target dynamics. IEEE Trans. Aerosp. Electron. Syst. **38**(2), 659–668 (2002)
8. Kamthe, A., Jiang, L., Dudys, M., Cerpa, A.: SCOPES: smart cameras object position estimation system. In: Roedig, U., Sreenan, C.J. (eds.) EWSN 2009. LNCS, vol. 5432, pp. 279–295. Springer, Heidelberg (2009). https://doi.org/10.1007/978-3-642-00224-3_18
9. Papatsimpa, C., Linnartz, J.P.M.G.: Improved presence detection for occupancy control in multisensory environments. In: 2017 IEEE International Conference on Computer and Information Technology (CIT), pp. 75–80 (2017)
10. Papatsimpa, C., Linnartz, J.P.M.G.: Energy efficient communication in smart building WSN running distributed hidden Markov chain presence detection algorithm. In: 2018 IEEE 4th World Forum on Internet of Things (WF-IoT), pp. 112–117 (2018)
11. Occupancy Motion Sensors Standard. https://www.nema.org/Standards/Pages/Occupancy-Motion-Sensors-Standard.aspx
12. Rabiner, L.R.: A tutorial on hidden Markov models and selected applications in speech recognition. Proc. IEEE **77**(2), 257–286 (1989)
13. International Labour Standards on Working Time 2005 report
14. Cooley, J.W., Tukey, J.W.: An algorithm for the machine calculation of complex fourier series. Math. Comput. **19**(90), 297 (1965)
15. Whitworth, B.: Measuring disagreement (Chapter XIX) (1999)

Climbing Ranking Position
via Long-Distance Backlinks

V. Carchiolo, M. Grassia, A. Longheu(✉), M. Malgeri, and G. Mangioni

Dip. Ingegneria Elettrica, Elettronica e Informatica,
Università degli Studi di Catania, Catania, Italy
{vincenza.carchiolo,alessandro.longheu,michele.malgeri,
giuseppe.mangioni}@dieei.unict.it

Abstract. The *best attachment* consists in finding a good strategy that allows a node inside a network to achieve a high rank. This is an open issue due to its intrinsic computational complexity and to the giant dimension of the involved networks. The ranking of a node has an important impact both in economics and structural term e.g., a higher rank could leverage the number of contacts or the trusting of the node. This paper presents a heuristics aiming at finding a good solution whose complexity is $N \log N$. The results show that better rank improvement comes by acquiring long distance in-links whilst human intuition would suggest to select neighbours. The paper discusses the algorithm and simulation on random and scale-free networks.

Keywords: Online social network · Ranking · In-attachment
Link-building problem

1 Introduction

In the real world, having a lot of friends is amazing; sometimes though, having few *good* friends or even just one *best* friend is better, since our life is more comfortable when we can rely on (even just one) trusted person that does not leave us alone when we are in trouble.

Shifting this poetic methapor towards online networks, where more and more social relationships take places, the scenario still holds by adapting some elements, in particular *'having a friends'* becomes *'acquiring new backlinks'*, i.e. the new node is pointed by existing ones in the network, according to the widely adopted graph-based model, whereas 'good friend that makes us feel good' is actually dependent on what *feeling good* means in the network being considered.

Usually, being part of a network provides some advantage, such as gathering specific information, or achieving some relevant role (e.g., influencer); in this strictly utilitarian sense, a friend is as good as he/she endorses that advantage.

A well known metric used to quantify the usefulness in network participation is the *ranking*, usually a number that allows nodes ordering; therefore, a good friend is a node that increases our rank in that network.

© Springer Nature Switzerland AG 2018
Y. Xiang et al. (Eds.): IDCS 2018, LNCS 11226, pp. 100–108, 2018.
https://doi.org/10.1007/978-3-030-02738-4_9

The semantics of ranking changes accordingly to the specific context it is applied to, from recommendation networks [21,27], to webpages relevance in Search Engines Optimization (SEO) [17], data envelopment analysis [5], scientific journals prestige [16], e-commerce transactions [15] and many others.

Several algorithm for ranking assessment are also available as PageRank [23], HITS [19], SALSA [20]; a shared idea however is that a node's rank is proportional to its esteem in the network. Hence, increasing the ranking is a highly attractive goal, and consequently looking for new good friends is also desiderable.

In this paper we investigate on how to select nodes in order to achieve the best rank, in other (more poetic) words, how to choose good friends. In our previous works [11,12], we started to consider the impact of backlinks (a.k.a. in-links) in rank improvement and their distance from starting link, in particular we focused on a new node 'target' t that joins a network via an in-link with one existing node j.

To increase its rank (measured via PageRank), intuition suggests that t could collect new in-links from j's neighbourhood, as in real social networks, where t's new friend j introduces him to his/her acquaintances. Despite this consideration, results shown that a better rank improvement comes by acquiring *long distance* in-links (with respect to the first node j the target t connects to), and this occur for different networks both in type and size, therefore in this paper we exploit such evidence to build an heuristic that guarantees a target node t to achieve the best rank.

Specifically, after the newcomer t joins the network with a backlink from a (generic node) j, the second backlink is chosen from the farthest node in the network (with respect to t), and further backlinks are built with the same criteria, i.e. always choosing the longest distance link, until t reach the best rank, that is first position in ranking order (note that at each step distances require to be evaluated since network topology changes due to the new backlink). Several experiments aim to assess how many long-distance backlinks are required to get the best rank depending on the type and size of the network.

The rest of the paper is organized as follows. In Sect. 2 we briefly recall the scenario and the PageRank metric, whereas in Sect. 3 we propose an new heuristic and illustrate our simulations and discuss the results, presenting final remarks and future works in Sect. 4.

2   Scenario

2.1   Link Building

In the hypothesis of directed networks, that models better social relationships, whenever a newcomer joins a network this can occur either by out-links, where the new node tries to establish contacts with others, or with in-links, where the newcomer is pointed by existing nodes.

Clearly, the former is easier since it depends on the newcomer direct initiative, whereas in the latter case the newcomer has to convince others to establish a relationship with him and this is generally harder to achieve. As a result, although network links can actually have different semantics depending on what that network represents, the intrinsic value of an in-link is generally higher than out-links, therefore the question of being pointed by others is more relevant.

In literature, such a question is known as *best attachment* or *link building* problem, and it has been analyzed from various points of view, e.g., in [14] constrained Markov decision processes are used as a model for link building, while [2] shows the use of asymptotic analysis to establish how a page's rank depends on creating new links and [18] generalized the approach to multiple pages websites. Authors in [26] consider the impact that node out-links changes has on the resulting PageRank, whereas in [22] the demonstration that the best attachment problem is NP-hard and also show that there exist both upper and lower bounds for certain classes of heuristics is introduced.

In a broader context, the work presented here comes from our research on the same topic [6,8], but also other similar scenarios are involved as in [7,9,10,12,13], where EigenTrust based attachment process in trust networks has been addressed (EigenTrust [25] is actually a trust evaluation algorithm leveraging PageRank).

2.2 PageRank

PageRank algorithm [23], is based on the *random surfer* model.

The surfer is an abstraction of a person that visit network nodes (web pages) starting from a random node, and jumping to others through initial random node out-links (a uniform distribution probability leads the choice of which link is actually followed). Instead of selecting one of the out-links (hyperlinks from initial page), each time the surfer also has a not-null probability to jump towards a completely random node (a random website); this is to deal with situations when no outgoing links are available or when the surfer falls into a set of nodes pointing each other but isolated from the rest of network - *rank sink* in [23].

The mathematical formalization is as follows: say N is the number of nodes in the network and A the $N \times N$ *network adjacency matrix* or *link matrix*, where each a_{ij} is the weight of the arc going from node i to node j. S is the $N \times 1$ *sink vector*, defined as:

$$s_i = \begin{cases} 1 & \text{if } out_i = 0 \\ 0 & \text{otherwise} \end{cases} \quad \forall i \leq N$$

where out_i is the number of outlinks of node i. V is the *personalization vector* of size $1 \times N$, that is obtained using the transposed initial distribution probability vector in the Markov chain model P_0^T. This vector should be stochastic; usually each term is $1/N$. $T = 1_{N \times 1}$ is the *teleportation vector*, where the notation $1_{N \times M}$ stands for a $N \times M$ matrix where each element is 1.

As described in [23], the *transition matrix* M, used in the associated random walker problem, is derived from the link matrix, the sinks vector, the teleportation vector and the personalization vector defined above:

$$M = d(A + SV) + (1 - d)TV \tag{1}$$

where $d \in [0,1]$ is called *damping factor* (0.85 in [23]).

The random walk probability vector at step n can be calculated as:

$$P_n = M^\mathsf{T} P_{n-1} \tag{2}$$

the related random walker problem can be calculated as:

$$P = \left(\lim_{n \to \infty} M^n \right)^\mathsf{T} P_0 = \lim_{n \to \infty} (M^\mathsf{T})^n P_0 = M_\infty^\mathsf{T} P_0 \tag{3}$$

The meaning of each probability vector term is '*the probability for the random surfer of being at a page at any given point in time during the walk*', and this is defined as that page's Rank, or PageRank; high values will be assigned to pages visited more frequently, i.e. more popular.

3 Long-Distance In-link Based Heuristic

As discussed in the previous section, the link building problem is not feasible due to computability complexity, therefore an approximated solution must be studied to solve the problem in real cases. The main goal of the proposed heuristic is to select the minimum set of nodes that would give a new node t the best rank position.

In this section, we detail the algorithm and then we show some experiments that highlight the behavior of the proposed heuristic and its dependence on network topology. Specifically, the proposed algorithm works in the following way:

1. a random node j is selected;
2. the newcomer t joins the network with a backlink from j;
3. the farthest node k in the network, with respect to t, is computed;
4. a link from k to t is then added (long distance link);
5. steps 3 and 4 are then repeated until t reaches the best rank, i.e. the first position in the ranking order.

Calling m the number of steps required by t to get the best rank (i.e. the number of times the steps 3 and 4 are repeated) the computational complexity of the proposed algorithm is $O(m \times N \times log(N))$, where N is the number of nodes in the network. The term $N \times log(N)$ is the computational complexity of the step 3 used to find the node k for which t is the farthest node.

3.1   Results

To study the performance of the heuristic proposed above, we conduct a set of experiments on two well-known family of networks: Erdos-Renyi random networks (ER) and scale-free (SF) networks. A random ER network is generated by connecting nodes with a given probability p. The obtained network exhibit a normal degree distribution [1]. A scale-free network (SF) [3] is a network whose degree distribution follows a power law, i.e. the fraction $P(k)$ of nodes having degree k goes as $P(k) \sim k^\gamma$, where γ is typically in the range $2 < \gamma < 3$. A scale-free network is characterized by the presence of hub nodes, i.e. with a degree that is much higher than the average. The scale-free network employed in this work is generated by using the algorithm proposed in [24] as implemented in the Pajek [4] tool.

In Fig. 1 the degree distributions of 100 K nodes networks is shown. As expected, the ER network (Fig. 1(a)) exhibits a normal degree distribution, while the SF degree distribution (Fig. 1(b)) follows a power–law.

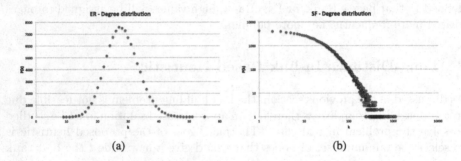

(a)   (b)

Fig. 1. Degree distribution for ER and SF networks

Simulations have been performed by using 100k nodes networks of both topologies. All simulations are repeated by using five different networks in order to avoid biasing connected to a single network realization. Results in the following are the average results of all the simulations performed.

Figures 2 and 3 reports the performance of the proposed algorithm for respectively ER and SF networks.

The figures highlight the expected dependence of the algorithm performance on the type of networks. In ER networks the algorithm exhibits a slower dynamics with respect to SF networks. With only 1 in-link, there is no rank gain in the ER networks, while in SF networks the target node t can gain more than 28500 positions! It means that selecting the right node k can give a great advantage in a short time to the node t in SF networks, while this is not the case in ER networks. Moreover, with 10 in-links, our algorithm is able to place the node t in the position 4070 in SF networks, while it ranks 18397 in ER networks. This results confirm the above considerations about the different dynamics displayed by SF and ER networks. On the other hand, in SF networks is very hard to

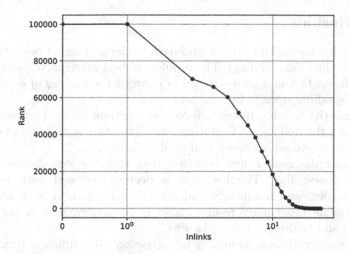

Fig. 2. Heuristics performance on ER network with 100 K nodes

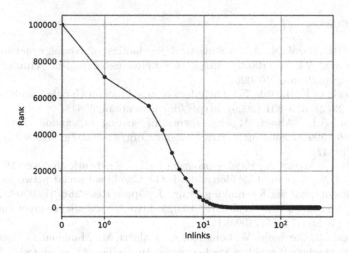

Fig. 3. Heuristics performance on SF network with 100 K nodes

obtain the rank 1. For example, in our experiments, position 1 requires more than 400 in-links in SF networks, while is it requires only 26 links ER networks. This results confirm the behaviour described in [6].

In [13] the authors present a study concerning the in-linking building problem. In that work the authors use a random selection strategy of the node k. While our results cannot be directly compared to those presented in [13], The results highlight that our selection strategy is much better if compared to a pure random approach. Of course, further investigation will be devoted to stress this point.

4   Conclusions

In this work we discuss an heuristic approach to the problem of best attachment (sometimes called link building). The problem of best attachment can be formulated as follows: *to find a good strategy to improve the ranking of a node inside a network by adding specific in-links arcs.*

Of course the selected metric affects the solutions so we have studied the problem using the well known PageRank since literature shows a lot of examples and it is currently used in several real applications.

This paper discusses a new heuristic that uses the long-distance in-links instead of closest link. The heuristic is deeply discussed with respect to both effectiveness and complexity and finally we compare it with some other approaches. The preliminary results shows good performance in both Erdös-Rényi (ER) and Scale-Free (SF) networks.

These considerations need further investigation using different topology and different size of the networks.

References

1. Albert, R., Barabasi, A.L.: Statistical mechanics of complex networks. Rev. Mod. Phys. **74**, 47 (2002). http://www.citebase.org/cgi-bin/citations?id=oai: arXiv.org:cond-mat/0106096
2. Avrachenkov, K., Litvak, N.: The effect of new links on Google PageRank. Stoch. Models **22**(2), 319–331 (2006). http://doc.utwente.nl/63648/
3. Barabasi, A.L., Albert, R.: Emergence of scaling in random networks. Science **286**, 509 (1999). http://www.citebase.org/abstract?id=oai:arXiv.org:cond-mat/9910332
4. Batagelj, V., Mrvar, A.: Pajek - program for large network analysis (1999)
5. de Blas, C.S., Martin, J.S., Gonzalez, D.G.: Combined social networks and data envelopment analysis for ranking. Eur. J. Oper. Res. **266**(3), 990–999 (2018). https://doi.org/10.1016/j.ejor.2017.10.025. http://www.sciencedirect.com/science/article/pii/S0377221717309384
6. Buzzanca, M., Carchiolo, V., Longheu, A., Malgeri, M., Mangioni, G.: Dealing with the best attachment problem via heuristics. In: Badica, C., et al. (eds.) IDC 2016. SCI, vol. 678, pp. 205–214. Springer, Cham (2017). https://doi.org/10.1007/978-3-319-48829-5_20
7. Buzzanca, M., Carchiolo, V., Longheu, A., Malgeri, M., Mangioni, G.: Direct trust assignment using social reputation and aging. J. Ambient. Intell. Humaniz. Comput. **8**(2), 167–175 (2017). https://doi.org/10.1007/s12652-016-0413-0
8. Carchiolo, V., Longheu, A., Malgeri, M., Mangioni, G.: Gain the best reputation in trust networks. In: Brazier, F., Nieuwenhuis, K., Pavlin, G., Warnier, M., Badica, C. (eds.) IDC 2011. SCI, vol. 382, pp. 213–218. Springer, Berlin (2012). https://doi.org/10.1007/978-3-642-24013-3_21
9. Carchiolo, V., Longheu, A., Malgeri, M., Mangioni, G.: Trust assessment: a personalized, distributed, and secure approach. Concurr. Comput.: Pract. Exp. **24**(6), 605–617 (2012). https://doi.org/10.1002/cpe.1856
10. Carchiolo, V., Longheu, A., Malgeri, M., Mangioni, G.: Users' attachment in trust networks: reputation vs. effort. Int. J. Bio-Inspired Comput. **5**(4), 199–209 (2013). https://doi.org/10.1504/IJBIC.2013.055450

11. Carchiolo, V., Longheu, A., Malgeri, M., Mangioni, G.: A heuristic to explore trust networks dynamics. In: Zavoral, F., Jung, J.J., Badica, C. (eds.) IDC 2013. SCI, vol. 511, pp. 67–76. Springer, Cham (2014). https://doi.org/10.1007/978-3-319-01571-2_9

12. Carchiolo, V., Longheu, A., Malgeri, M., Mangioni, G.: The cost of trust in the dynamics of best attachment. Comput. Inform. **34**, 167–184 (2015)

13. Carchiolo, V., Longheu, A., Malgeri, M., Mangioni, G.: Network size and topology impact on trust-based ranking. IJBIC **10**(2), 119–126 (2017). https://doi.org/10.1504/IJBIC.2017.10004323

14. Fercoq, O., Akian, M., Bouhtou, M., Gaubert, S.: Ergodic control and polyhedral approaches to PageRank optimization. IEEE Trans. Automat. Contr. **58**(1), 134–148 (2013). http://dblp.uni-trier.de/db/journals/tac/tac58.html#FercoqABG13

15. Fung, R., Lee, M.: EC-Trust (trust in electronic commerce): exploring the antecedent factors. In: Proceedings of the 5th Americas Conference on Information Systems, pp. 517–519 (1999). http://aisel.aisnet.org/amcis1999/179

16. Guerrero-Bote, V.P., Moya-Anegón, F.: A further step forward in measuring journals scientific prestige: the SJR2 indicator. J. Informetr. **6**(4), 674–688 (2012). https://doi.org/10.1016/j.joi.2012.07.001. http://www.sciencedirect.com/science/article/pii/S1751157712000521

17. Jiang, J.Y., Liu, J., Lin, C.Y., Cheng, P.J.: Improving ranking consistency for web search by leveraging a knowledge base and search logs. In: Proceedings of the 24th ACM International on Conference on Information and Knowledge Management, CIKM 2015, pp. 1441–1450. ACM, New York (2015). https://doi.org/10.1145/2806416.2806479

18. de Kerchove, C., Ninove, L., Dooren, P.V.: Maximizing PageRank via outlinks. CoRR abs/0711.2867 (2007)

19. Kleinberg, J.M.: Authoritative sources in a hyperlinked environment. J. ACM **46**(5), 604–632 (1999). https://doi.org/10.1145/324133.324140

20. Lempel, R., Moran, S.: SALSA: the stochastic approach for link-structure analysis. ACM Trans. Inf. Syst. **19**(2), 131–160 (2001). https://doi.org/10.1145/382979.383041

21. Liu, X.: Towards context-aware social recommendation via trust networks. In: Lin, X., Manolopoulos, Y., Srivastava, D., Huang, G. (eds.) WISE 2013. LNCS, vol. 8180, pp. 121–134. Springer, Heidelberg (2013). https://doi.org/10.1007/978-3-642-41230-1_11

22. Olsen, M., Viglas, A., Zvedeniouk, I.: An approximation algorithm for the link building problem. CoRR abs/1204.1369 (2012). http://arxiv.org/abs/1204.1369

23. Page, L., Brin, S., Motwani, R., Winograd, T.: The PageRank citation ranking: bringing order to the web (1998). https://citeseer.ist.psu.edu/article/page98pagerank.html

24. Pennock, D.M., Flake, G.W., Lawrence, S., Glover, E.J., Giles, C.L.: Winners don't take all: characterizing the competition for links on the web. Proc. Natl Acad. Sci. **99**(8), 5207–5211 (2002). https://doi.org/10.1073/pnas.032085699. http://www.pnas.org/content/99/8/5207.abstract

25. Kamvar, S.D., Schlosser, M.T., Garcia-Molina, H.: The EigenTrust algorithm for reputation management in P2P networks. In: 2003 Proceedings of the Twelfth International World Wide Web Conference (2003). https://citeseer.ist.psu.edu/article/kamvar03eigentrust.html

26. Sydow, M.: Can one out-link change your pagerank? In: Szczepaniak, P.S., Kacprzyk, J., Niewiadomski, A. (eds.) AWIC 2005. LNCS (LNAI), vol. 3528, pp. 408–414. Springer, Heidelberg (2005). https://doi.org/10.1007/11495772_63

27. Weng, J., Miao, C., Goh, A., Shen, Z., Gay, R.: Trust-based agent community for collaborative recommendation. In: AAMAS 2006: Proceedings of the Fifth International Joint Conference on Autonomous Agents and Multiagent Systems, pp. 1260–1262. ACM, New York (2006). https://doi.org/10.1145/1160633.1160860

Financial Application on an Openstack Based Private Cloud

Deepak Bajpai, Muskan Vinayak, Ruppa K. Thulasiram$^{(\boxtimes)}$,
and Parimala Thulasiraman

Department of Computer Science, University of Manitoba, Winnipeg, Canada
{bajpaid,vinayakm,tulsi,thulasir}@cs.umanitoba.ca

Abstract. We build a private Cloud using off-the-shelf servers and do extensive experiments for application and performance testing. We studied a real-world application of financial option pricing by implementing two algorithms (Monte-Carlo simulation and binomial lattice for option pricing) on this private Cloud and used this application for the purpose of accuracy testing in comparison to a well established closed-form solution available as Black-Scholes-Merton formula. Also, using these algorithms we analyze performance of Cloud VMs. We compare the performance with standalone servers and found that the performance of Cloud VM is better to standalone servers when (a) the number of vCPUs are limited to a single node and (b) load balancing issues are not considered.

Keywords: Cloud computing · Private cloud · Openstack
Financial option pricing · Performance

1 Introduction

Cloud computing is an established profit driven business technology for IT Infrastructure, software and others services, while still evolving technologically for various untapped industries such as military, medical and finance. It has provided financial freedom to clients by introducing a popular "pay-as-you-go" model. Integration of security has given an additional edge to this technology. However, providing an effective and cost beneficial solution in all application areas is still in progress [1]. For example, in finance, military, medical applications, public Clouds are not preferred due to inherent reasons for data security and privacy. Hence, many of these specialized industries and government organizations prefer private Cloud. In this work, we study a major problem (financial option pricing) from one of these industries, finance, on a private Cloud.

Major service models such as IaaS, PaaS and SaaS are available in public and private Clouds but security remains major point of concern for the organizations in public Clouds. Private Clouds have shown reliable solutions for security and privacy issues of businesses and hence many organizations have jumped into offering private Cloud systems [2]. A private Cloud is more secure as the organization builds its own infrastructure and uses their own data storage servers.

© Springer Nature Switzerland AG 2018
Y. Xiang et al. (Eds.): IDCS 2018, LNCS 11226, pp. 109–121, 2018.
https://doi.org/10.1007/978-3-030-02738-4_10

Private Cloud owners may also outsource their requirements like application to a third party but underlying resources such as servers, storage and network remain non-shared.

Among various problems in the market of Cloud service, significant one is the implementation and performance evaluation for the user critical data. IT infrastructure organizations typically have a central data repository that contains all the important data required for the proper functioning of the organization. Data allocation and then replication are essential part of IT infrastructure. In a public Cloud environment data remains at different locations; VMs at different locations hold that data which can be migrated from one host to another host to meet the requirement of load balancing [3] and cost efficiency [4]. To create a replication environment in Cloud infrastructure, these VMs need to be replicated and their state needs to be stored as well.

The introduction of open-source software platforms has provided advancements in Cloud service deployment. Now, small businesses are using private Clouds [5] based on these open source platforms to satisfy their needs of elastic demand for resources and high-end computing business requirements. Elastic demand is the term used by Cloud vendors for dynamic provisioning of Cloud resources using workload sharing and VMs migration to other physical machines [6].

1.1 Problem Description

Implementing a private Cloud is a complex and cumbersome process for system analyst and administrators. Association of various components to make it service oriented architecture adds to design complexity. The primary objective of our work is to test the performance with respect to various parameters such as access to data on a data-critical and time constrained application in addition to execution time. We selected Openstack in this study as the Cloud computing software to build a private Cloud and the application we study on our private Cloud is financial option pricing problem. We set the following important tasks in building a private Cloud that would satisfy the above objectives:

- implement Openstack on (Dell) servers to create a prototype of private Cloud to get VM on demand as a service;
- deploy financial option pricing algorithm(s) on private Cloud for application testing;
- analyze performance of VMs in this private Cloud on the basis of execution time on the VMs using financial application. Compare performance with standalone servers as well.

While building a private Cloud using off-the-shelf infrastructure could be achieved with some efforts, using this platform for data-critical applications such as financial options is a concentrated effort that requires highly specialized background knowledge on the application domain area. In this perspective, this work is a novel contribution to study a financial application on a private Cloud.

1.2   Infrastructure

To build a private Cloud, we have used Dell R420 servers with multiple Ethernet ports. All servers have 4 GB RAM and 12 Intel Xeon processors on each of them. Ubuntu 14.04 server was used as the operating system running on each of them. We have used Openstack to create a private Cloud environment for these machines. Openstack is a better Cloud software in comparison to OpenNebula and Eucalyptus due to its properties such as load balancing, scalability, market spread and security as explained later in Fig. 1 (see for example, [7]). Stratus clouds are groups of small clouds that collectively give a spectacular sight in the sky. The private Cloud we have built uses multiple small modules to achieve the stated goal and hence the name "Stratus" for our private Cloud.

Rest of the paper is organized as follows: A brief discussion on related work focusing on open source software to build private Cloud is presented in the next section. A primer on option pricing problem is presented in Sect. 3. One of the financial option pricing techniques used in this study, Monte-Carlo simulation, for performance testing is described in Sect. 4. Application and performance evaluation is done and described in Sect. 5. We conclude this study in Sect. 6 and suggest directions for further possible exploration.

2   Related Work

Any of the Open source software platforms such as Openstack [8], Cloudstack [9,10] and Eucalyptus [11] can be used to build a private Cloud.

Figure 1 compares Cloudstack, Openstack and Eucalyptus [8,9,11] on the basis of Cloud characteristics. On the basis of security and scalability Openstack is found to be is better in comparison to other two and hence used in this study.

Characterstics	Cloudstack	Openstack	Eucalyptus
Architecture	Monolithic	Fragmented, Distributed	Five parts
GUI	Strong EC2 like	Multiple CLI based	Limited
Security	Low	Strong token based	High
Load Balancing	Low	High	Medium
Scalability	Low	Very high	Medium
Market spread	Good	Very Good	Fair
Hybrid Support	Not supported	Supported	Best integrated with EC2
Installation	Medium expertise	Difficult	Medium level

Fig. 1. Open Source cloud software comparison

Saha et al. [12] described how a Eucalyptus based private Cloud can be used as service portal where various pricing algorithms are used and compared to get best results for Cloud provider. Service portal application acts as a finance service for Cloud provider, which can help to generate a pricing model for public Cloud instances. They also described how image and storage nodes can be integrated in the Cloud environment for scalability and reliability.

However, what makes Openstack advantageous compared to the other options is that Openstack supports small scale deployment. Openstack supports deployment onto a single, local machine for rapid application development and testing with minimal required effort in setting up. Openstack is a Cloud software platform with three node architecture [8]. In an earlier study [13], we built a private Cloud using Openstack Cloud based open-source software solution and generated a disaster recovery solution using Openstack component Cinder and Swift. We presented an experimental analysis of two strategies, block storage and object storage, to derive the best solution for an organization using private Cloud. From the set of experiments considered Cinder proved preferable over Swift. In the current work, we are using this private Cloud to deploy a financial application. Other than these two financial application studies, to the best of our knowledge there are no other financial benchmark studies on a Cloud system.

3   Finance Background

This section is intended to present (a) concepts from financial option application and (b) a couple of common approaches used in finance literature to price an option contract, since there are no related financial benchmarks on a private Cloud environment.

A financial derivative contract is an agreement between two individuals, groups, or organizations to buy or sell any underlying financial asset. There are many financial derivatives such as options, futures, swaps, etc. For expedited solution(s) advanced algorithms and architectures are used on these problems in finance. Private Cloud is one of the most suitable platforms that can be used for financial applications to deploy and compute results.

In our work, we have studied one of the most commonly used financial contracts called Option. A financial option is a contract where the option seller (writer) writes an agreement on an underlying asset (for example, a stock) with an option buyer (holder of the option). In an option contract, the holder has the right, but is not obligated to buy/sell the underlying asset during the contract period. An option contract is set for a certain period of time as per the agreement. Finding the worth of an option contract is known as the option pricing problem. Option pricing is one of the computationally intensive problems, which could use high performance computing.

Types of Options: There are two types of options: Call and Put. Call/Put option gives the holder the right to buy/sell an underlying asset at predetermined price, without any obligation to exercise that contract on or before expiration. There are multiple styles in which these two types of options can be exercised. For example, with an European style, the underlying asset could be exercised only on the expiration date and with an American style, it could be exercised anytime prior to the expiration date.

4   Monte-Carlo Simulation

Boyle [14] proposed a numerical method in option pricing using Monte-Carlo (MC) simulation in 1977. Many researchers have contributed to the literature on MC simulation such as Hull and White [15–18] who used MC approach to obtain more accurate option values than the Black-Scholes-Merton model. MC simulation [16] is divided into three steps: Simulation of the sample path for underlying asset prices, evaluation of option value on each path using discounting and averaging the calculated discounted option value over sample paths (Algorithm 1). After simulation of the sample path, payoff for each path is calculated. Each payoff value is evaluated using discounting factor to calculate the option value for each path. Averaging is done for all the sample paths to calculate final option value.

Algorithm 1. Monte Carlo Algorithm

---
1. Initialize the parameters such as S, r, K, T, σ,
2. for $i = 1$ to M do /*M = number of simulations. i.e., for each simulation*/
3.   for $j = 1$ to n
4.   simulate sample paths of the stock prices.
5.   next j
6.   for each simulated path, compute the pay-off of the option.
7. next i
8. Compute the discounted average of above simulated pay-offs.

MC simulation experiment is used for performance testing of the Cloud VM and compared with standalone servers running the same application. As we mentioned earlier, the performance comparison is not very thorough. On the private Cloud, the performance rely on Openstack's nova-compute feature for load balancing and task distribution among processors. However, we have not taken care of load balancing while implementing the code using MPI. It might amount to unfair comparison, however, this is a first step and expect to effective comparison in future.

5   Experiments and Evaluation

In this study, we have focused on two aspects of testing: application and performance. We make sure that the financial application implemented on the private Cloud yields accurate results to an academically acceptable level compared to real market data before we could discuss the performance of the private Cloud itself in achieving these acceptable results. In the following two subsections we present the application testing and performance testing of the private Cloud that we have done with this application.

5.1   Application Testing

In the application testing experiments, we checked if the VMs created in the private Cloud are able to withstand application load and generate results on user request so it can be used as SaaS. For the financial application that we are focusing on, option pricing, amount of data we need to handle is really large. Depending on the number of simulation paths (more simulation is expected to lead to better results) and number of steps in each path, there could be large number of points to handle. For a 6 months contract with n = 500 steps it would mean the step is about every 8 hours. For this, the data size we need to work with $10^6 * 500 * 8 * 5 = 2 * 10^{10}$ bytes, where each variable requiring 8 bytes, 5 variables each node and 500 steps for each path and a million paths would require easily terabytes of data. This is a huge amount of data, if we have to keep the data in memory, which is the case for some complex option pricing problem.

To implement this, there were five VMs deployed in the private Cloud. Four VMs (EuropeanCall, EuropeanPut, AmericanCall and AmericanPut) were used for the binomial lattice problem where binomial put and call options were used for European and American styles. One of the VM (Server) was used to deploy main code from where all the classes were called. Connection between VMs were done using the server VM. After the systems were deployed, a simple RMI application was developed and deployed on the instances to ensure they could communicate and transfer data between each other similar to replication testing process. All the implementation is done on the Cloud VM level and application is created using Java platform.

The configuration used to create the Cloud VMs are same for all five VMs. The Ubuntu Cloud image is used as the operating system, 512 MB RAM and 2 virtual CPUs are set as a configuration parameter. IP association is done to provide internet access and intercommunication on all the VMs.

Java code created for this problem was deployed on the server machine and each VM is responsible for its assigned problem. EuropeanCall VM was deployed for Java code of European call and likewise for EuropeanPut, AmericanCall and AmericanPut. Server has the main class which will revoke the user defined choice menu among the four VMs. On the selection of each one of the input parameters from above mentioned VM choices, activate the respective VM, which in response generates a user input values for stock price, strike price, rate of interest, time (no. of years) and number of steps. After the values are entered by the user, VM generates the output in the form of option value.

For each experiment, we have used several iterations to get multiple values for different set of inputs. Table 1 shows (for lack of space, results from other styles of options are not shown) the results for the European call where the option value is computed on the basis of set of values given by user for stock price, strike price, rate of interest, volatility, time (no. of years). To test the accuracy of the option value results, we computed the option value using only closed-form solution given by Black-Scholes-Merton (BSM) [19] formula for European Call. For example, the option value obtained (11.087) from the BSM formula

Table 1. Results for European call

Experiment	Stock price	Strike price	Interest	Volatility	Time (years)	Steps	Option value	BSM
I-1	50	40	5%	20	0.5	11	11.091	11.087
I-2	50	50	5%	20	0.5	11	3.374	3.444
I-3	50	60	5%	20	0.5	11	0.447	0.511
I-4	400	350	12%	30	1	22	101.536	101.227
I-5	600	600	12%	30	1	22	107.314	106.701
I-6	600	650	12%	30	1	22	82.130	82.507

for European call with the same parameters as in experiment I-1 in Table 1 is close to the option value that We computed on our private Cloud (11.091) using binomial lattice model for European call. Therefore, we can say that the binomial lattice implementation on Cloud VM is successful as it produces accurate results when compared to BSM model.

Application deployment is a complex process for a financial investment organizations that would like to keep their data secure and more agile. By using private Cloud features they can keep their data secure and at the same time process (internal data movement within organization) could be made easier and agile for the internal IT staff. This prototype implementation could be used in financial organization to secure their data privacy. Financial institutions prefer the traditional data-center architecture for their internal use. Application testing implemented for this work can be similarly deployed within an on-premise private Cloud in any financial institution.

These results show that private Cloud can be used to deploy application requiring data privacy/security with intercommunication among the Cloud VMs. This application test also helps to understand the mechanics of a private Cloud for a real-world application. We may also use this feature as a service for the investor (who may not be aware of advanced algorithm of option pricing) in the form of software-as-a-service (SaaS). Saha et al. [20] used the Eucalyptus Cloud to create the SaaS based financial application. The current work is different as it uses Openstack based private Cloud and explores the system level features of private Cloud in comparison to application level features. Also, as already explained in Fig. 1, Openstack has various advantages over Eucalyptus.

Figure 2 depicts a possible SaaS model for financial institutions. If the investors access secure webpage of the financial institution and provide parameters such as stock price, strike price, rate of interest, volatility, time and number of steps then that web page will respond with the option value using the secure channel on the on-premise based private Cloud. The parameters are transferred from secure web page to the Cloud server which can invoke the Cloud VM corresponding to option style (European or American) choice entered by the investor. Hence, the option value can be computed. The same process is triggered multiple times to get an average value with the help of the optimizer for accuracy of the computed option value. Finally, the option value is stored in the database and sent to the investor using the same web page. By using this model, financial institutions can make their data more secure and agile.

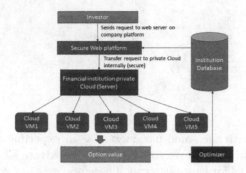

Fig. 2. SaaS model for application in private cloud

5.2   Performance Testing

With the application testing using the binomial lattice model of option pricing, we have shown that the private Cloud can be used to serve a commercial application of option pricing.

To check the performance of both the systems, we have used Monte-Carlo (MC) simulations for option pricing. MC is preferable to binomial lattice because of its inherent parallel nature, where set of simulation paths can be assigned to specific processors. It is easier to implement as well in comparison to binomial lattice, where computing requires many synchronization steps. MC can test the performance of the system as huge number of simulations are run to obtain value for the option price. To perform this experiment, we have used a Dell R420 standalone server with 12 CPU, 4 GB RAM and Ubuntu operating system. For the Cloud VM, the operating system is Ubuntu, RAM is 4 GB and the virtual CPUs (vCPU) will be gradually increased with each iteration of the experiment.

For the performance comparison, we have executed MC simulation in a parallel computing environment using MPI (message passing interface) where we can run the parallel tasks for each CPU in the server. We have used Mpich [21] to create a Cluster of 3 standalone servers to run the MPI code. We created multiple VMs simultaneously with different number of vCPUs. This can produce maximum utilization of CPUs as they will run the parallel task simultaneously. For the initial test purpose, the standalone server and Cloud VM had 2 CPUs and 2 vCPUs respectively. Operations for MC simulation will run on those 2 CPUs and 2 vCPUs. In the next set of experiments, we gradually increased the number of CPUs and vCPUs in standalone server and Cloud VM to measure the performance with respect to execution time to compute results for option value.

We deployed MC code on the VM similar to binomial lattice application. After the deployment, we ran the experiments on Openstack based Cloud VMs and standalone servers. Performance metrics for this experiment is measured by the execution time to get the final value of option price from a system. There is a limitation to this performance comparison. On the private Cloud, the performance rely on Openstack's nova-compute feature for load balancing and task distribution among processors. However, we have not taken care of load balancing while implementing the code using MPI. Due to virtualization overhead, it might be hard for Clouds to beat standalone machines. Clouds do provide generalized load balancing strategies. However, if the standalone servers support customized load balancing schemes, it's very likely to achieve better performance, which we leave as future work. Therefore, our current effort might amount to unfair comparison, however, this is a first step and we expect to do effective comparison in near future.

We did the experiments multiple times using one set of configuration for Cloud VM. After averaging out the result from multiple experiments, we changed the configuration of VM gradually for each set of experiments. As Cloud VMs can use the resources of multiple machines, we suspected how it will perform in case of cluster configuration because of the use of hypervisor. Cluster configuration for this case is when single VM is using resources such as vCPUs of three physical machines. Note that MPI code enables us to use all the CPUs of three physical standalone machines to test the performance of standalone servers.

The option parameters for the MC simulation for all the experiments are described in Table 2. The input parameters are stock price, strike price, rate of interest, time, volatility, number of steps (in one random walk) and number of simulations. To utilize the capability of CPUs and vCPUs the number of simulations are kept in the order of 100,000. The input values are kept the same for all the experiments in each iterations.

Table 2. Monte-Carlo input parameters for experiment

Input	Values
Stock price	50
Strike price	40
Rate of interest	5%
Time	0.5 year
Volatility	20%
Number of steps	500
Number of simulation	100000

Table 3 shows the execution time (ET) generated after running MC code on the cluster of standalone servers and Cloud VMs. Cloud VMs RAM is kept 4 GB for all the iterations.

As we can see in Table 3 and Fig. 3, as we increased the number of vCPUs for Cloud VM from 2 to 12 it takes less time than standalone servers cluster. Cloud VMs are more efficient in comparison to standalone server cluster as the

Table 3. Performance analysis using execution time

Experiments	CPU	vCPUs	VM RAM	Server ET	VM ET
I-1	2	2	4	11799 ms	9846 ms
I-2	4	4	4	10539 ms	8533 ms
I-3	8	8	4	9155 ms	7914 ms
I-4	12	12	4	7717 ms	7388 ms

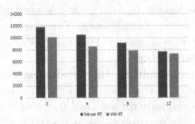

Fig. 3. Execution time (milliseconds) analysis

time standalone server consumes to distribute processes using MPI on cluster is relatively significant. The overhead of distributing processes is not there in Cloud VM, hence the Cloud VM performance is better. Openstack based Cloud VMs use nova-compute feature for load balancing and task distribution among processors, which makes it faster in comparison to MPI.

We also evaluated the performance for a large number of MC simulations and compared the option value results with the BSM option value to check the accuracy of results. Table 4 shows the results for these simulations. We have used the option parameters from Table 2 except the simulation numbers and number of steps. We have increased the number of steps to 1000 expecting to get more accurate results. VM execution time in Table 4 shows that as number of simulations were increased corresponding execution time also increased. These large number of simulations show that Cloud VMs can be used compute intensive tasks in financial applications.

Table 4. Performance analysis using high number of simulations

Experiments	Simulations (millions)	Option value	VM ET (sec)
I-1	1	11.3668	144.28
I-2	2	11.3720	287.72
I-3	3	11.3731	430.21
I-4	4	11.3671	577.17
I-5	5	11.3652	721.15
I-6	6	11.3645	866.43

Option value results obtained from Table 4 were later compared with the option value obtained from the BSM model. We calculated the relative error, which was shown to be less than 2.6% as presented in Table 5. In other words, the Stratus Cloud VMs are capable of producing accurate results in the high demanding financial applications.

Table 5. Accuracy evaluation using BSM

Experiments	MC option value	BSM option value	Error percent
I-1	11.3668	11.087	2.523%
I-2	11.3720	11.087	2.570%
I-3	11.3731	11.087	2.580%
I-4	11.3671	11.087	2.526%
I-5	11.3652	11.087	2.509%
I-6	11.3645	11.087	2.502%

6   Conclusion and Future Work

We showed first that the option value computed are accurate compared to a closed-form solution given by Black-Scholes-Merton model. With the application testing, we distributed the European and American style options on various VMs to generate the value of option price using single server, which communicated with other VMs. This distributed system within Cloud helped to utilize Cloud VMs and test them for the application workload. We also evaluated the performance of the private Cloud using the execution time feature of Linux and MC simulation code with the limitation mentioned earlier. We also tested for a large number of simulations for MC code to obtain option price value and compared with the BSM model for accuracy. Cloud VM was able to withstand compute intensive application load and performed efficiently.

This Stratus private Cloud is now ready for deploying applications, and for providing VMs on-demand. While building a private Cloud using off-the-shelf infrastructure could be achieved with some efforts, using this platform for data critical applications such as financial instruments becomes a highly specialized effort that requires highly specialized background on the application itself. In this perspective, this work is a novel contribution to study a financial application on a private Cloud. Hypervisor limits the Cloud VM to remain in a single node. In order to make use of the Cloud VM from multiple nodes, we need to have a distributed file system. The Hadoop distributed file system is one such software system that can be implemented on our private Cloud, which we leave as one of our future works.

References

1. Ghahramani, M., Zhou, M., Hon, C.T.: Toward cloud computing QOS architectrure: analysis of cloud systems and cloud services. IEEE/CAA J. Autom. Sin. **4**(1), 5–17 (2017)
2. Suciu, G., Ularu, E.G., Craciunescu, R.: Public versus private cloud adoption a case study based on open source cloud platforms. In: 20th Telecommunications Forum (TELFOR), pp. 494–497. IEEE (2012)
3. Hu, J., Gu, J., Sun, G., Zhao, T.: A scheduling strategy on load balancing of virtual machine resources in cloud computing environment. In: 2010 Third International Symposium on Parallel Architectures, Algorithms and Programming (PAAP), pp. 89–96. IEEE (2010)
4. Yuan, H., Bi, J., Tan, W., Zhou, M., Li, B.H., Li, J.: TTSA: an effective scheduling approach for delay bounded tasks in hybrid clouds. IEEE Trans. Cybern. **47**(11), 3658–3668 (2017)
5. Goyal, S.: Public vs private vs hybrid vs community-cloud computing: a critical review. Int. J. Comput. Netw. Inf. Secur. (IJCNIS) **6**(3), 20 (2014)
6. Herbst, N.R., Kounev, S., Reussner, R.: Elasticity in cloud computing: what it is, and what it is not. In: ICAC, pp. 23–27 (2013)
7. Wen, X., Gu, G., Li, Q., Gao, Y., Zhang, X.: Comparison of open-source cloud management platforms: OpenStack and OpenNebula. In: 2012 9th International Conference on Fuzzy Systems and Knowledge Discovery (FSKD), pp. 2457–2461. IEEE (2012)
8. Pepple, K.: Deploying OpenStack. O'Reilly Media, Inc., Newton (2011)
9. Cai, B., Xu, F., Ye, F., Zhou, W.: Research and application of migrating legacy systems to the private cloud platform with cloudstack. In: 2012 IEEE International Conference on Automation and Logistics (ICAL), pp. 400–404. IEEE (2012)
10. Sotomayor, B., Montero, R.S., Llorente, I.M., Foster, I.: Virtual infrastructure management in private and hybrid clouds. IEEE Internet Comput. **13**(5), 14–22 (2009)
11. Nurmi, D., et al.: The eucalyptus open-source cloud-computing system. In: 9th IEEE/ACM International Symposium on Cluster Computing and the Grid, CCGRID 2009, pp. 124–131. IEEE (2009)
12. Saha, R., Sharma, B., Thulasiram, R.K., Thulasiraman, P.: A novel architecture for financial investment services on a private cloud. In: Kołodziej, J., Di Martino, B., Talia, D., Xiong, K. (eds.) ICA3PP 2013. LNCS, vol. 8285, pp. 370–379. Springer, Cham (2013). https://doi.org/10.1007/978-3-319-03859-9_32
13. Bajpai, D., Thulasiram, R.K.: Comparing replication strategies for financial data on OpenStack based private cloud. In: Proceedings of the IARI International Conference on Cloud Computing, Rome, Italy, pp. 139–144. IARIA (2016)
14. Boyle, P.P.: Options: a Monte Carlo approach. J. Financ. Econ. **4**(3), 323–338 (1977)
15. Hull, J., White, A.: The pricing of options on assets with stochastic volatilities. J. Financ. **42**(2), 281–300 (1987)
16. Boyle, P., Broadie, M., Glasserman, P.: Monte Carlo methods for security pricing. J. Econ. Dyn. Control. **21**(8), 1267–1321 (1997)
17. Glasserman, P., Yu, B.: Simulation for American options: regression now or regression later? In: Niederreiter, H. (ed.) Monte Carlo and Quasi-Monte Carlo Methods 2002, pp. 213–226. Springer, Heidelberg (2004). https://doi.org/10.1007/978-3-642-18743-8_12

18. Rakhmayil, S., Shiller, I., Thulasiram, R.: Different estimators of the underlying asset's volatility and option pricing errors: parallel Monte - Carlo simulation. In: Proceedings of the International Conference on Computational Finance and its Applications, Bologna, Italy, pp. 121–131. ICCFA (2004)
19. Hull, J.C.: Options, Futures, and Other Derivatives. Pearson Education India, Bengaluru (2006)
20. Ranjan, R., Buyya, R., Nepal, S., Georgakopulos, D.: A note on resource orchestration for cloud computing. Concurr. Comput.: Pract. Exp. **27**(9), 2370–2372 (2015)
21. Mercier, G., Aumage, O.: MPICH/MADIII: a cluster of clusters-enabled MPI implementation. In: Third IEEE International Symposium on Cluster Computing and the Grid, CCGRID 2003, pp. 26–35 (2003)

Towards Island Networks: SDN-Enabled Virtual Private Networks with Peer-to-Peer Overlay Links for Edge Computing

Kensworth Subratie$^{(\boxtimes)}$ (iD) and Renato Figueiredo$^{(\boxtimes)}$ (iD)

University of Florida, Gainesville, FL 32611, USA
kcratie@ufl.edu, renato@ece.ufl.edu

Abstract. While solutions to many challenges posed by IoT lie at the network's edge, they cannot forego services available in the cloud which has over a decade of research and engineering to be leveraged. To bridge this gap, hybrid approaches in networking that account for characteristics of both edge and cloud systems are necessary. On cloud data centers, significant progress has been made on applying Software Defined Networking (SDN) to address networking challenges such as scalability, addressing, virtualization, and traffic engineering; administrators are now well-versed at managing data center SDN deployments in enterprise systems. However, the applicability of SDN in edge networks has not yet been thoroughly investigated. We propose a hybrid system that incorporates SDN software switches and overlay networks to build dynamic layer 2 virtual networks connecting hosts across the edge (and in the cloud) with links that are peer-to-peer Internet tunnels. These tunnels are terminated as subordinate devices to SDN switches and seamlessly enable the traditional SDN functionalities such that cloud and edge resources can be aggregated.

Keywords: IoT · Island overlay networks · Edge networking
Software defined networks · Distributed computing

1 Introduction

The scale of emerging IoT device deployment is expected to reach hundreds of billions of devices within the next decade [1]. The services and functionality that are expected from the applications built around the sheer volume and variety of IoT devices will also grow more sophisticated and complex. Such applications will have to integrate numerous hardware and software components to directly interact with the end user's real world. Applications will sense, analyze and actuate; in doing so they will need to communicate across its distributed components and match performance demands.

This explosive growth of connected devices presents new challenges to both application models and the communication infrastructure they utilize. Research [2] shows that the existing IoT-to-cloud models fail to adequately meet performance requirements in several use cases. Not only are upcoming advances in communication technologies and standards necessary [3, 4], but also an evolution of existing approaches to networking architecture, deployment and management are needed. In

© Springer Nature Switzerland AG 2018
Y. Xiang et al. (Eds.): IDCS 2018, LNCS 11226, pp. 122–133, 2018.
https://doi.org/10.1007/978-3-030-02738-4_11

particular, many applications will require a shift in computation paradigm from the more centralized cloud model to a more widely distributed one where the computing occurs near IoT devices across the network's edge. Such a transformation is necessary to exploit the latency and throughput benefits of proximity to the data sinks and sources [1, 5]. A fundamental aspect of edge computing is the relocation of compute, storage and network resources as edge nodes from the data center to the network's edge.

However, building a network at the edge poses challenges not typically encountered in the data center: the considerably larger area for deployment, the time and effort to physically access these locations, the heterogeneous mix of components to interoperate, and numerous independent owners/networks that contribute to the pool of edge resources. Thus, while core techniques developed for data center clouds may be leveraged, it will not be feasible to manage IoT infrastructure and services as it is currently done in clouds. At the edge, there is no centralized or consolidated premise for hardware, so existing approaches for identifying, leasing, and configuration deployment become impractical. New ways are needed to solve these issues in a manner that can be orchestrated via software.

Software Defined Networking (SDN) [6–8] is a mature technology widely used by network administrators in cloud data centers to orchestrate and manage networks via software. However, its use within a data center (and on backbone connections across data centers) is predicated on the fact that a single or a few administrative entities own the data plane (switches, routers, links) and can manage it through a centralized control plane. In contrast, applying SDN techniques to connect a multitude of IoT and edge devices across the Internet brings a very different set of challenges [9]. Nonetheless, SDN exposes key primitives for packet handling that can provide a basis for software-defined edge networking. For instance, using network virtualization to create a familiar environment, such as a flattened layer-2 networking namespace, in which administrators can utilize standard and familiar tools. This allows IoT/edge applications to reuse a plethora of middleware that works atop TCP/IP networks.

In this paper, we consider the challenges associated with the use of SDN in IoT/edge computing and propose a novel approach that integrates both SDN switches and overlay networks to create software-defined virtual networks across edge and cloud resources. The contribution of our approach lies in a novel way to integrate control/data planes for both the overlay and SDN layers. At the overlay layer, the control plane is realized by a distributed set of software modules (overlay controllers) that coordinate and, in a peer-to-peer fashion, create and manage virtual links as TCP/UDP tunnels across the public Internet – even when devices are in different edge providers and constrained by middleboxes (NATs, firewalls).

In our approach, the overlay layer controllers not only manage virtual links, but also dynamically bind them to ports of SDN-controlled software switches. Overlay links thus become the data plane for the SDN fabric, allowing packets sent/received by IoT, edge and cloud resources that reach a switch to be forwarded across the overlay to other nodes. Combined with virtualization primitives implemented at the SDN layer (by a centralized, or distributed SDN controllers), the resulting system delivers a software abstraction of a layer 2 (Ethernet) network, thereby reducing the complexities associated with the deployment of middleware and applications across edge and cloud resources across the Internet. In addition to establishing the data plane, the overlay network layer controllers allow dynamic membership and grouping of resources, and enforce authentication and privacy in communication, addressing key management and security concerns for edge/IoT applications.

In summary, our proposed approach creates a flexible virtual private networking (VPN) system which can dynamically aggregate IoT, edge and cloud resources into managed communication groups, with links that are peer-to-peer Internet tunnels terminating in SDN-programmable switches. The approach is demonstrated with the development and experiments with a prototype that builds on open-source frameworks for both the SDN and overlay layers. In particular, Open vSwitch (OVS) [10], a widely-used software switch that supports the standard OpenFlow API and various SDN controller frameworks (e.g., Ryu [11]), and IPOP tunnels, an open-source overlay network with built-in support for NAT/firewall traversal using STUN/TURN/ICE standards [12–14] and the WebRTC framework [15].

The rest of the paper is organized as follows; first, we introduce overlay and island networks concepts and then proceed to describe the notable traits of next generation IoT applications and its implications on network structure and the division of application roles. Next, we present our novel hybrid overlay/SDN approach for building virtualized network infrastructure. Finally, the experimental evaluation of our reference implementation is presented along with the characterization data obtained from our testbed.

2   IoT Application Characteristics

Software applications have continuously evolved to address the increasingly sophisticated requirements of a modern society, and they tackle workloads and problem spaces that cannot be addressed within singular systems. The IoT era promises to continue this trend, as the abundance of connected devices will generate new uses cases for engaging consumers, both in the physical and virtual world.

2.1   An Example Scenario

It is already conceivable to anticipate our everyday commute using autonomous vehicles. However, there are significant barriers to making this concept safe and reliable for use. Autonomous vehicles (AVs) comprise 3 major technology categories, sensing and perception, localization and mapping and driving policy. Multimodal sensor streams are an important facet of successfully accomplishing the first two, but contemporary technology is still restricted in its temporal and spatial resolution and this impacts the quality of the decisions that are made in the third category. As such, it is expected that AVs will be connected to the surrounding roadway infrastructure via wireless networks to exchange sensor data that will assist with navigation [16]. While it is a prudent design approach to ensure that any autonomous system can continue to operate reliably, even with diminished capabilities, when disconnected from the communication network, there is considerable benefit from leveraging information available from it.

If a hazardous condition exists and fixed roadway infrastructure can be used to detect this, e.g., using cameras and machine vision, it can be intelligently transmitted to approaching vehicles. Vehicles can initiate defensive maneuvers ahead of the time they could start sensing such conditions.

2.2 Model Characteristics

The scenario presented exemplifies the role for detection using sensor devices and analytics to reach a decision which ultimately should be acted on. The hardware components will unlikely all reside within a single physical unit but rather be separated according to their functional roles. The sensors and actuators must be distributed over the area of interest and the data sent to the processing nodes for analytics. This underscores another important facet of the system, the communication path.

As the usefulness of the decisions expire over time, the workflow of sense-analyze-actuate must be timely. As the data generating events exhibit spatiotemporal correlations with the actors, one approach is to keep data close to where is produced and/or finally consumed and bring the compute operations close to data.

We have also seen that there are multiple roles and device types involved in a single solution which produce heterogeneous mix of operational resources. Additionally, due to the vast geographic areas that require hardware coverage, it is reasonable to assume that it will be provided by multiple independent SDN vendors.

IoT ecosystems and the associated sense-analyze-actuate model inherently respond to real-world events, implying a data producer/consumer abstraction. It can be generalized as a process chain which starts with a data generating event, followed by one or more consumers that apply a transformative process and subsequently produce new events and data. The processes applied at each stage are application specific but can include storage, analysis, generating derivative data and actuation.

2.3 Networking Implications

To support the execution of distributed applications as exemplified above, an interconnection network must be in place to enable communication among the IoT devices and the various compute/storage agents that participate in the workflow. While, in principle (as implied by their name) IoT devices are connected to the Internet, the reality of establishing interconnectivity among devices such that communication occurs seamlessly is more complex.

First, owing to the shortage of identifiers in the IPv4 address space, devices may be private and not have addresses on the public network. Even if IPv6 deployments fully address the identifier shortage issue, private networks are unlikely to go away – private networks provide a line of defense against malicious actors in the network, by concealing the device behind a NAT/firewall middlebox. Second, devices participating in such workflow are likely to be connected to different ISP providers/network domains – for instance, a 5G wireless provider for an in-vehicle sensor, a city networking provider for infrastructure cameras, and one or more commercial edge/cloud providers. As a result, no single entity will be able to control the configuration/setup of the networking infrastructure end-to-end. Third, such applications will require privacy guarantees at many layers of the stack – including privacy in communications. The public Internet does not provide such guarantees. Fourth, in applications where the devices participating in the distributed workflow can dynamically join and leave, the networking layer must be adaptive to accommodate dynamic group membership (Fig. 1).

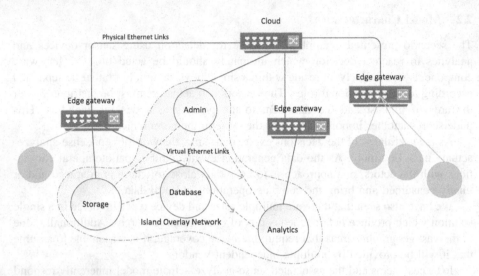

Fig. 1. An Overlay Network (ON). Four modules distributed across different resources on edge and cloud providers that are logically aggregated into an ON. While the physical devices are connected by Internet links, the ON encapsulates virtual network Ethernet frames and forwards across peer-to-peer tunnels.

2.4   Overlay and Island Networks Concepts

An overlay network is a network created atop another pre-existing network. The de facto approach to contemporary network design is to provide increasingly capable services within discrete layers. This provides the view of the Internet being constructed as a series of overlay networks. Additional overlays are created whenever a new network abstraction is presented, but which utilizes the services of another existing network. This is the case with network tunneling technologies and specifically IPOP [17]. IPOP creates a new layer 2 overlay network which is tunneled through layer 3 IP across the Internet.

There are several contemporary methodologies and technologies that are used in designing communication networks, and they impact how the hosts are connected and addressed. It is standard to use both physical and logical approaches which partition networks that interact through defined connection points. A single host can participate in multiple networks as it roles dictates; for instance, consider an application server that has a network dedicated for administration and another (or more) for its data path communication to other instances associated with the application. This paper refers to these as application networks, and its architecture as the attributes, protocols and structure of the networking infrastructure that is used to support complex distributed

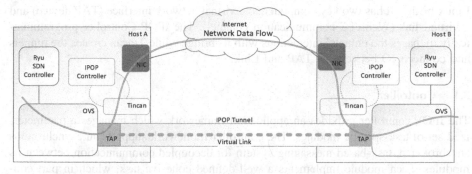

Fig. 2. IPOP Tunnel Architecture. Figure 2 illustrates the architecture of the IPOP Tunnel and its interaction with the rest of the system. The tunnel abstraction is composed of a TAP device which connected to the OVS bridge a and virtual link connecting two peers. The "Network Data Flow" indicates the actual transmission path contrasted to virtualized view of the tunnel.

applications. The network structure or its topology define the way the hosts are interrelated by means of the direct connections they establish among themselves, while the attributes and protocol specify how they are addressed and how they communicate.

Correctly done, partitioning a network into smaller individual components is a successful strategy for defining important functional, performance and security characteristics. As each component is its own private self-contained network that connects to and communicates with other component networks, this paper regards them as "island networks". Each island network can freely employ an architectural approach that best suits its internal needs, and by the encapsulation of its internal characteristics, these choices need not adversely impact other islands or the larger aggregate network.

3   An Architecture for Overlay Networks

IPOP provides flexible virtual networking infrastructure, using peer-to-peer tunneling techniques that can traverse NATs and firewalls, as well as peer/endpoint discovery and key exchange for private communication via online social network (OSN) based messaging. These features make IPOP a well-suited overlay substrate to build the Overlay Network for IoT/edge computing. Inspired by the SDN approach of separating the functional roles of a controller and data plane, the IPOP design consists of two modules: a controller, and a data-plane (referred to as Tincan, drawing an analogy to private peer-to-peer communication among friends). For ease of deployment on a variety of platforms (currently, it runs on Ubuntu and Windows desktops/servers, and on Raspberry Pi devices), IPOP is implemented as two user-mode processes – one implements the controller, one implements the tunneling data plane.

This paper extends the existing IPOP capability into the realm of SDN by proving integration with SDN and Open vSwitch. This is accomplished by creating a new abstraction called an IPOP Tunnel, which is programmatically connected to an OVS or

Linux bridge. It has two key components: a virtual network interface (TAP device) and a virtual link (WebRTC communication channel). The IPOP Controller programmatically manages the tunnels' interactions with its bridge while Tincan creates the tunnels and connects IO between its TAP and Link.

3.1 Controller

The IPOP controller provides an application framework which manages a parameterized set of task-specific modules. The controller framework supports an asynchronous and brokered, task-based messaging system for decoupled communication between its modules. Each module implements a well-defined cohesive task, which in part contributes to composite functionality of the controller model. Notable modules provided in the default model are not limited to signaling and link bootstrapping, tunnel creation and management, topology definition and enforcement.

Signaling for bootstrapping a link between peers is performed using instant messaging via the XMPP protocol, using software such as ejabberd. This mechanism also identifies the endpoints participating in the overlay network and provides the stage at which participants must authenticate credentials. By establishing an account on an ejabberd server and defining 'friend' relationships between other members, the user is implicitly defining who can participate in their private overlay network and to whom communication links may potentially be established.

Tunnel creation is a 9-way handshake between two peers, which exchanges the necessary data for establishing a virtual link. When a friend node is online, a presence notification is delivered via the Signal Module to both peers. This initiates the tunnel creation process, which involves allocating the local resources to be used for the tunnel and identifying each peer's role in the link setup process. Next, the set of candidate network addresses that can be used for local, reflection (STUN), and relay (TURN) connections – along with unique identifying fingerprints – is exchanged via signaling. With this information, the peers can negotiate keys and establish a private tunnel, which is then used as a virtual link for the overlay network.

The Topology module defines which peers will establish a virtual link, and the conditions that determine when the link is created (or removed). While any topology can be implemented, an all-to-all topology was used for this work.

3.2 Data Plane

The IPOP data plane (Tincan) implements the key abstraction of the IPOP-Tunnel. The IPOP-Tunnel, referred to simply as Tunnel throughout this article, is a construct of a virtual network interface (TAP device), and an associated virtual link. The virtual network interface is the approach used for creating separate network namespaces, i.e., network segments which can be switched or routed; this is as opposed to using IP rules, which are restricted to routing functionality.

Messages from the TAP device are sent on the associated link. While it is possible to apply an IP configuration to each TAP device, it is impractical for large networks. A more favorable approach is to create an in-memory bridge device, e.g., a Linux or OVS (Open Virtual Switch) bridge and connect the Tap devices as subordinate devices.

IPOP is then able to leverage the extensive switching functionality of these tools and further extend their reach and capabilities via its Tunnels.

Tincan links are built on top on of the WebRTC [15] C++ libraries and its transport and channel abstractions. Subsequently, IPOP links can perform NAT traversal and utilize TURN services around symmetric NAT and restrictive firewalls.

4 Experimental Evaluation

This section evaluates IPOP using our reference implementation. We describe the experimental setup and the scenarios tested, provide the corresponding results and finally discuss factors that influence them.

4.1 Experimental Testbed

To demonstrate the functionality of the hybrid SDN + IPOP Tunnel network we created an overlay with 5 peer nodes that are distributed geographically across the continental USA. 3 nodes were located at the University of Florida, another at Cloud Lab (Clemson), and 1 at Amazon AWS (Ohio). The hardware specification of the nodes was chosen to be representative of the heterogeneous mix of devices that would occur in an IoT deployment – an IoT type node, a virtual machine, edge processing nodes and server class cloud nodes. Each host is installed with the IPOP software, Open vSwitch, and IP Route2 network utilities. Iperf version 2 is also installed on hosts A, B and E for testing IP multicast (Table 1).

Table 1. Hardware specification for nodes used in experiment.

Host	CPU	RAM	NIC
A – AWS hosted VM	Intel Xeon E5-2676 v3, 1 core	990 MB	Low to moderate VIF
B – Bare metal desktop	Intel i7-6850, 6 cores	32 GB	1 GigE
C – Bare metal desktop	Intel i7-6700, 4 cores	16 GB	1 GigE
D – Compulab Fitlet2 IoT	Intel Celeron J3455, 4 cores	4 GB	1 GigE
E – Bare metal sever	2 x Intel Xeon E5-2660 v2, 28 cores	256 GB	1 GigE

The IPOP controller is configured for an all-to-all network topology, such that each node creates a tunnel with each peer. The tunnels are bridged locally and spanning tree protocol (STP) is enabled on the network bridge at all hosts. The bridge device has an internal interface and each one is configured with a unique IP v4 address in the 10.1.0.0/24 subnet. This interface is presented to the local host's operating system and is used for communication on the overlay network.

4.2 Scenarios and Results

The first demonstration is to establish basic end-to-end connectivity among all the peers. This is done using a combination of the console ping command and TCP

Dump. All the ping tests were successful between pairs of hosts. Table 2 indicates the round-trip times (RTT) between the IoT device and the AWS VM measured both on the systems native interface and the IPOP TAP interface. With TCP Dump output, the ARP and ICMP packets were verified.

Table 2. Ping latency test between hosts D and A showing round trip times. A total of 60 packets were transmitted and received.

RTT (ms)	Min	Avg	Max	MDev
Native Interface	42.047	42.229	42.758	0.226
IPOP Interface	42.731	42.990	43.375	0.170
Difference (%)	1.601	1.770	1.422	

The IPOP Controller code was also instrumented to record the time taken to create and connect each tunnel to its respective peer as well as the total time to establish a fully connected overlay. The latter includes the time from the first notification of a peer's presence to the final node's tunnel being connected. Measurements taken in host D are shown in Table 3.

Table 3. Time to create a fully writable link between the IoT class device and each peer in the overlay network.

Host D	Host A	Host B	Host C	Host E
Time to connect (s)	11.4309	10.6864	12.3229	10.7039
Total connection time (s)	42.1215			

The next demonstration verifies the overlay's correctness and functionality by performing an IP Multicast test. The iperf network performance measurement tool was used to create an IP multicast group as illustrated in Fig. 3. On hosts B and E iperf was invoked in its server role, with both hosts listening on the same IP v4 multicast address 239.252.0.1. This multicast address restricts communication to one site. On host A iperf was invoked as the client which sent packets to the same multicast address.

The first invocation of the test was done at the default UDP bandwidth rate of 1 Mbps and indicated a single packet lost in the first round of transmissions. Subsequent client invocations to the existing server processes did not show this loss but which was reproducible when the server process is restarted. We believe this to be associated with the initial address resolution process. Beyond this, there were no errors or failures reported and all remaining packets were received by both receiving hosts at the sending rate. We progressively increased the client transmissions rate and eventually observed packet loss at around the 35 Mbps rate at both server hosts.

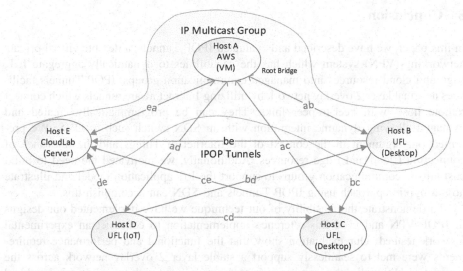

Fig. 3. Experiment Testbed Structure. IPOP Tunnels to create an all-to-all overlay topology. Host A is designated the root bridge for the spanning tree as indicated by incoming light arrowheads at Host A. Bold arrowheads at host indicate a forwarding link from the originating host.

4.3   Results Evaluation

Connection setup times are dominated by the connection bootstrap handshake which discovers and exchanges the peers' endpoint addresses and types and the WebRTC session establishment which may involve STUN and/or TURN. We observe an average connection time of 11.3 s per node. It is important to note that the total connection time for the overlay (42.12 s) is less that the sum of the individual connection times (45.14 s). This is due to the overlapping operations as multiple tunnels can bootstrap concurrently, however new operations must wait until the existing in-progress ones complete.

The latency between host D (IoT node) and host A (AWS VM) shows a smaller than 2% increased for RTT min/avg/max when using the IPOP overlay as compared to the host's native interface. Interestingly, the IPOP interface exhibits a lower standard deviation (mdev).

It is also important to understand the impact of STP on the overlay's available bandwidth and why this approach is undesirable. As the bridge must block certain tunnels from use, it results in packets being switched along longer paths. Additionally, when considering the underlying network, the increased routing cost and potential traversal of WAN links further exacerbates the problem. While blocking tunnels is necessary to eliminate cycles, it ignores lower cost paths to the destination. In Fig. 3, the resulting spanning tree of the overlay network requires a response from host C to B to be sent via the route bridge at host A. Within the underlying network, hosts B and A are connected to the same physical switch while host A is reached via a WAN link.

5 Conclusion

In this paper, we have described and evaluated IPOP Tunnels, a flexible virtual private networking (VPN) system which has the capabilities to dynamically aggregate IoT, edge and cloud resources into managed communication groups. IPOP Tunnels facilitates a virtual layer 2 overlay network by utilizing Internet aware tunnels which connect remote hosts with peer-to-peer links. They can be programmatically created and managed allowing dynamic integration with an SDN switch such as OVS. We presented our argument in the context of the Internet of Things and the relevance of connecting Cloud and Edge resources. Additionally, we motivated the need to build customized communication groups to support the IoT application model and illustrate how a hybrid approach using IPOP Tunnels and SDN can accomplish this.

To demonstrate the feasibility of our technique we have implemented our designs in IPOP-VPN and used this reference implementation to construct an experimental network testbed. Our evaluation show that the functional and performance requirements were met to seamlessly support a stable layer 2 overlay network across the Internet. Additionally, the increase in latencies associated with tunneling overhead and securing communication were within 2% increase of the native interface.

Our future work will continue to build on this abstraction to (i) improve system scalability through structured topology and multi-hop message routing, (ii) improve application perceive throughput and communication latency through improvements on the data plane, and (iii) introduce new information streaming functionality to better support application interactions.

Acknowledgments. This material is based upon work supported in part by the National Science Foundation under Grants No. 1527415, 1339737, 1234983 and 1550126. Any opinions, findings, and conclusions or recommendations expressed in this material are those of the author(s) and do not necessarily reflect the views of the National Science Foundation.

References

1. Bonomi, F., Milito, R., Zhu, J., Addepalli, S.: Fog computing and its role in the internet of things. In: Proceedings of the First Edition of the MCC Workshop on Mobile Cloud Computing, New York, NY, USA, pp. 13–16 (2012)
2. Zhang, B., et al.: The cloud is not enough: saving IoT from the cloud. In: Proceedings of the 7th USENIX Conference on Hot Topics in Cloud Computing, Berkeley, CA, USA, p. 21 (2015)
3. Standards - IEEE 5G. https://5g.ieee.org/standards. Accessed 29 June 2018
4. Dahmen-Lhuissier, S.: 5G, ETSI. https://www.etsi.org/technologies-clusters/technologies/5g. Accessed 29 June 2018
5. Satyanarayanan, M., Bahl, P., Caceres, R., Davies, N.: The case for VM-based cloudlets in mobile computing. IEEE Pervasive Comput. **8**(4), 14–23 (2009)
6. Feamster, N., Rexford, J., Zegura, E.: The road to SDN: an intellectual history of programmable networks. SIGCOMM Comput. Commun. Rev. **44**(2), 87–98 (2014)
7. SDN/OpenFlow | Flowgrammable. http://flowgrammable.org/sdn/openflow/. Accessed 29 June 2018

8. Software-Defined Networking (SDN) Definition: Open Networking Foundation. https://www.opennetworking.org/sdn-definition/. Accessed 29 June 2018
9. Qin, Z., Denker, G., Giannelli, C., Bellavista, P., Venkatasubramanian, N.: A software defined networking architecture for the internet-of-things. In: 2014 IEEE Network Operations and Management Symposium (NOMS), pp. 1–9 (2014)
10. Open vSwitch. https://www.openvswitch.org/. Accessed 19 June 2018
11. Ryu SDN Framework. https://osrg.github.io/ryu/. Accessed 29 June 2018
12. Matthews, P., Mahy, R., Rosenberg, J.: Traversal using relays around NAT (TURN): relay extensions to session traversal utilities for NAT (STUN). https://tools.ietf.org/html/rfc5766. Accessed 10 Aug 2018
13. Wing, D., Matthews, P., Mahy, R., Rosenberg, J.: Session traversal utilities for NAT (STUN). https://tools.ietf.org/html/rfc5389. Accessed 10 Aug 2018
14. Rosenberg, J.: Interactive connectivity establishment (ICE): a protocol for network address translator (NAT) traversal for offer/answer protocols. https://tools.ietf.org/html/rfc5245. Accessed 10 Aug 2018
15. WebRTC 1.0: Real-time Communication Between Browsers. https://w3c.github.io/webrtc-pc/. Accessed 29 Jun 2018
16. Pau, G.: Quickly home please: how connected vehicles are revolutionizing road transportation. IEEE Internet Comput. 17(1), 80–83 (2013)
17. Subratie, K., Aditya, S., Sabogal, S., Theegala, T., Figueiredo, R.J.: Towards dynamic, isolated work-groups for distributed IoT and cloud systems with peer-to-peer virtual private networks. In: Sensors to Cloud Architectures Workshop, SCAW 2017, Austin, Texas, USA (2017)
18. ejabberd | robust, massively scalable and extensible XMPP server. https://www.ejabberd.im/. Accessed 29 June 2018
19. Athreya, A.P., Tague, P.: Network self-organization in the Internet of Things. In: 2013 IEEE International Conference on Sensing, Communications and Networking (SECON), pp. 25–33 (2013)
20. Zinner, T., Jarschel, M., Blenk, A., Wamser, F., Kellerer, W.: Dynamic application-aware resource management using software-defined networking: implementation prospects and challenges. In: 2014 IEEE Network Operations and Management Symposium (NOMS), pp. 1–6 (2014)

Almost-Fully Secured Fully Dynamic Group Signatures with Efficient Verifier-Local Revocation and Time-Bound Keys

Maharage Nisansala Sevwandi Perera[1(✉)] and Takeshi Koshiba[2]

[1] Graduate School of Science and Engineering, Saitama University, Saitama, Japan
perera.m.n.s.119@ms.saitama-u.ac.jp
[2] Faculty of Education and Integrated Arts and Sciences,
Waseda University, Tokyo, Japan
tkoshiba@waseda.jp

Abstract. One of the prominent requirements in group signature schemes is revoking group members who are misbehaved or resigned. Among the revocation approaches Verifier-local revocation (VLR) is more convenient than others because VLR requires updating only the verifiers with revocation messages. Accordingly, at the signature verification, the verifiers check whether the signer is not in the given revocation detail list. However, the cost of the revocation check increases linearly with the size of the revocation details. Moreover, original VLR group signature schemes rely on a weaker security notion. Achieving both efficient member revocation and reliably strong security for a group signature scheme is technically a challenge. This paper suggests a fully dynamic group signature scheme that performs an efficient member revocation with VLR and which is much more secure than the original VLR schemes.

Keywords: Group signatures · Verifier-local revocation
Member registration · Almost-full anonymity
Dynamical-almost-full anonymity · Time-bound keys

1 Introduction

Group signatures, introduced by Chaum and van Heyst [4] grant group members to sign messages on behalf of the group such that the resulting signature will not reveal the identity of the signer (anonymity). However, anonymity may open paths to offenses. Thus in case of dispute, the tracing authority can identify the misbehaved members (traceability). These two key features of the group signatures attracted real-life applications such as e-commerce systems, digital right management, and key-card access.

© Springer Nature Switzerland AG 2018
Y. Xiang et al. (Eds.): IDCS 2018, LNCS 11226, pp. 134–147, 2018.
https://doi.org/10.1007/978-3-030-02738-4_12

In many settings, it is desirable to offer flexibility for members to join the group or leave the group as they wish. There are several models for revoking member's signing capability. When a member is removed, the group manager can issue a new group public key and give each member a new signing key, except to revoked member. This approach does not suit in practice well because it requires generating new keys and updating each member and verifier for each member revocation. Another method is when a member is revoked, distributing a message to all the existing signers. Thus signers have to prove his validity at the time of signing. However, this approach also cannot count as a suitable revocation method in real-life applications since each existing members have to keep track of revocation messages. Verifier-local revocation (VLR) suggested by Brickell [3] and formalized by Boneh et al. [2], also used in the schemes [1], [5], [6], and [8] seems to be the most flexible revocation approach because VLR requires to update only the verifiers when a member is revoked. Since the number of the verifiers is less than the number of members in a group, VLR is convenient than any other revocation approach.

In VLR group signature schemes, an additional argument called the revocation list (RL) is given to the algorithm Verify. Each member has another secret key called 'revocation token' other than the secret signing key. When a member is revoked, his revocation token is added to RL. At the verification stage, the verifier authenticates the signer against the latest RL. Thus, the algorithm Verfiy in the group signatures with VLR consists of two steps; Signature-check and Revocation-check. The signature-check verifies the signature is generated by a group member and the signature is generated on the given message. The revocation-check verifies whether the signer has not been revoked.

In some applications of group signatures with VLR, like roaming authenticity of a telecommunication company and visitors authentication in a hotel the size of the revocation list (RL) may increase in a short time. Moreover, any system that provides members to join the group for a short period leads to increase the size of RL, and this may decrease the efficiency of the revocation-check in Verify. In 2012, Chu et al. [5] suggested time-bound keys to group signature schemes with VLR to obtain more efficient group signature schemes. In their scheme, they have categorized the member revocation into two, namely, "natural-revocation" and "premature-revocation". If a member is revoking because of his expiration date (retirement/leaving date) is passed, then it is a natural revocation. If any member is revoking before the expiration date, then it is a premature-revocation. For instance, members who are retiring because their contract period is finished are natural-revoking members, and members who are eliminating because of their misbehavior are premature-revoking members. The technique in [5] is to get rid of the natural-revocation members to shorten the size of RL. Even though the scheme in [5] provides techniques to reduce the size of RL and speed up the revocation-check in signature verification, still it relies on a weaker security notion as most of the VLR group signature schemes.

The original VLR group signature schemes rely on *selfless-anonymity* which is a weaker security notion. Scheme in [8] suggested a security notion called, *almost-full anonymity* for VLR group signature schemes, which is much more stronger than the selfless-anonymity. Again another strong security notion called, *dynamical-almost-full anonymity* was proposed with a lattice-based fully dynamic group signature scheme with VLR [7]. While the almost-full anonymity is for group signature schemes only with member revocation with VLR, the dynamical-almost-full anonymity is for fully dynamic group signature schemes which satisfy both member registration and member revocation with VLR. However, cost of the verification checks in both of the schemes increases when we apply them to rapidly changing groups, where the members are joining the group for a short time.

Since all the schemes discussed above failed to provide a solution to minimize the verification cost of VLR fully dynamic group signature schemes while relying on strong security, this paper focuses on delivering a scheme with solutions for that matter.

Our Contribution

In this paper, we address two weaknesses of VLR group signature schemes. One problem is that the most of the existing VLR schemes are relying on the weak security notion, the selfless-anonymity. The next issue is when members are joining a group for a short time, the size of the revoked member detail list (RL) increases fast. Even some solutions are suggested separately for these problems in previous schemes they have not discussed the outcome when those results are added together. Thus, in this work, we improve the scheme given in [8] by proposing time-bound keys to reduce the size of RL, and we apply the security notion, the dynamical-almost-full anonymity to make our new scheme's security strong. We modify the methods of the scheme given in [8] to deliver a much more efficient fully dynamic VLR group signature scheme which supports both member registration and revocation and which relies on stronger security than original VLR schemes.

2   Preliminaries

In this section, we provide some notations that we use in this paper and the primitives with which we use in our scheme. Thus, we describe the time-bound keys and dynamical-almost-full anonymity. Then we define the three building blocks that used in [1] and [8] and which we use to construct the scheme.

2.1   Notations

We denote by λ the security parameter of the scheme and let $\mathbb{N} = \{1, 2, 3, ...\}$ be the set of *positive integers*. For any $k \geq 1 \in \mathbb{N}$, we denote by $[k]$ the set of integers $\{1, ..., k\}$. An empty string is denoted by ε. If s is a string, then $|s|$ indicates the length of the string and if $\mathcal{S}$ is a set, then $|\mathcal{S}|$ denotes the size of the set. If $\mathcal{S}$ is a finite set, $b \xleftarrow{\$} \mathcal{S}$ denotes that b is chosen uniformly at random from $\mathcal{S}$. We denote experiments by **Exp**.

2.2 Time-Bound Keys

Chu et al. [5] proposed time-bound keys as a solution for reducing the cost of revocation check. In their scheme, the group member's key has an expiration date. When a new user joins the group, the group manager selects an expiration date for the new user. Thus only the members having non-expired keys can create signatures. It leads to cut down the cost of checking the naturally revoked members (members with expired keys) at the signature verification. Since naturally revoked members cannot sign messages, the group manager does not need to add their details to the revocation list RL. Thus, the verifiers check whether the signers are being revoked prematurely. The technique used in [5] shows significant reduction of the revocation check because the number of naturally revoked members is higher than the number of prematurely revoked members in most of the real settings. However, the group member keys have an additional attribute, the expiration date. Thus, other than the signature generation, the signers should prove that their keys are not expired.

To efficiently compare two dates, Chu et al. [5] have used the date format as "YYMMDD" in integer form. For instance, the date 2018 June 20th is indicated as "180620". Accordingly, $t_1 > t_2$ represents that t_1 date is later than the date t_2. According to their scheme, the group manager selects the key expiration date t_r. Moreover, at the time of signing the signer can select a signature expiration date t_s which should satisfy $t_r > t_s$ and $t_s > t_v$, where t_v is the verification date. The requirement of the valid signature is satisfying $t_r > t_s > t_v$.

A VLR group signature scheme with time-bound keys is as follows.

- KeyGen($1^\lambda, \ell$): This key generation algorithm takes as inputs the security parameter λ and the maximum length ℓ of the defined date format, and it outputs a group public key **gpk** and a group master key **gmsk**.
- Join: This is the interactive protocol between the group manager GM and the new users who want to join the group. The user i takes as inputs **gpk** while GM takes as inputs **gpk**, **gmsk**, and t_{r_i}, where t_{r_i} is the key expiration date for the user i. Finally, GM outputs a revocation token **grt**[i] for the user i, and the user i outputs a secret signing key **gsk**[i].
- Sign(**gpk**, t_s, **gsk**[i], M): This algorithm takes as inputs the group public key **gpk**, the signature expiration date t_s, the secret signing key **gsk**[i] of the user i, and a message M. It creates and outputs a signature Σ on M if $t_s < t_r$ (t_r is included in **gsk**[i]). It outputs $\perp$ if this condition fails.
- Verify(**gpk**, t_v, RL, M, Σ): This algorithm takes as inputs **gpk**, the current date t_v, the revocation list RL, and a message-signature pair (M, Σ). It outputs valid if Σ is a valid signature on M and the signer is not a revoked member. It outputs invalid otherwise.
- Open(**gpk**, Σ, M, $\{\mathbf{grt}_i\}$): This algorithm takes as inputs the group public key **gpk**, a signature Σ, a message M, and the revocation tokens $\{\mathbf{grt}_i\}$ for all users, and it outputs the signer's index of Σ or $\perp$.

2.3 Dynamical-Almost-Full Anonymity

The security notion, the dynamical-almost-full anonymity is for fully dynamic VLR group signature schemes that serves both member registration and revocation. In an anonymity game between an adversary A and a challenger C, the dynamical-almost-full anonymity allows the adversary to add new members to the group. If the new user details are valid, then the challenger stores new user's index in a list called, **HUL**. **HUL** consists of indices of the members that A added. Even the revocation token is generated for the new user, the revocation token is not given to A at the time of member registering. The adversary can request revocation tokens of any member using the revocation query. If the indices used for requesting revocation tokens are not used for generating the challenging signature, then C returns revocation tokens. At the challenging phase, the signature is only generated for the indices that are in **HUL** and that are not used to request revocation tokens. Moreover, A can access opening oracle with any message-signature pair except one used in the challenging phase.

The dynamical-almost-full anonymity game between a challenger and an adversary is as follow.

- **Initial Phase:** The challenger C executes the key generation algorithm Key-Gen to obtain a group public key **gpk**, authorities' secret keys (**ik,ok**). Then C gives **gpk** and existing group members' secret signing keys **gsk** to the adversary A, and creates a new list **HUL**.
- **Query Phase:** The adversary A can add new users, request revocation tokens of the user, and he can ask to open signatures. If A adds new valid users to the group, then the challenger C adds the new user index to **HUL** and responses with a success message without delivering the revocation tokens. If A requests to reveal revocation tokens of a user, then C returns the revocation tokens. If C accesses the opening oracle with a valid message-signature pair, then A returns the index of the signer of the signature.
- **Challenge Phase:** The adversary A outputs a message M^* and two distinct identities i_0, i_1. If i_0, i_1 are added by the adversary ($i_0, i_1 \in$ **HUL**) and if i_0, i_1 are not used to request revocation tokens, then the challenger C selects a bit $b \xleftarrow{\$} \{0,1\}$, generates $\Sigma^* = \mathsf{Sign}(\mathbf{gpk}, [\mathbf{gsk}[i_b], M^*)$, and sends Σ^* to A. A still can query the opening oracle except for Σ^*, and A can query revocation tokens except using i_0, i_1. However, A can add new users to the group without any restrictions.
- **Guessing Phase:** Finally, A outputs a bit b', the guess of b. If $b' = b$, then A wins.

2.4 Digital Signature Schemes

A digital signature scheme $\mathsf{DS} = (\mathsf{K}_s, \mathsf{Sig}, \mathsf{Vf})$ consists of key generation K_s, signing Sig, and verification Vf algorithms. DS should satisfy the standard notion of unforgeability under chosen message attack. For an adversary A, consider an experiment $\mathbf{Exp}_{\mathsf{DS},A}^{unforg\text{-}cma}(\lambda)$. First obtain a pair of a public key and a corresponding secret key as $(\mathbf{pk}, \mathbf{sk}) \xleftarrow{\$} \mathsf{K}_s(1^\lambda)$. Then give $\mathbf{pk}$ to A and A can access $\mathsf{Sig}(\mathbf{sk}, \cdot)$ for any number of messages. Finally, A outputs a forgery message-signature pair (M, Σ). He wins if Σ is a valid signature on M and M is not queried so far. We let $\mathbf{Adv}_{\mathsf{DS},\mathcal{A}}^{unforg\text{-}cma}(\lambda) = \Pr[\mathbf{Exp}_{\mathsf{DS},\mathcal{A}}^{unforg\text{-}cma}(\lambda) = 1]$.

A digital signature scheme DS is secure against forgeries under chose message attack if $\mathbf{Adv}_{\mathsf{DS},\mathcal{A}}^{unforg\text{-}cma}(\lambda)$ is negligible in λ for any polynomial-time A.

2.5   Encryption Scheme

An encryption scheme $\mathsf{E} = (\mathsf{K}_e, \mathsf{Enc}, \mathsf{Dec})$ consists of key generation K_e, encryption Enc, and decryption Dec algorithms. E should satisfy the standard notion of indistinguishability under adaptive chosen-ciphertext attack. For an adversary A, consider an experiment $\mathbf{Exp}_{\mathsf{E},A}^{ind\text{-}cca\text{-}b}(\lambda)$. First obtain a pair of a public key and a corresponding secret key as $(\mathbf{pk}, \mathbf{sk}) \xleftarrow{\$} \mathsf{K}_e(1^\lambda, r_e)$ where r_e is a randomness string (the length of r_e is bounded by some fixed polynomial $r(\lambda)$). Let $\mathsf{LR}(M_0, M_1, b)$ a function which returns M_b for a bit b and messages M_0, M_1. We assume A never queries $\mathsf{Dec}(\mathbf{sk}, \cdot)$ on a ciphertext previously returned by $\mathsf{Enc}(\mathbf{pk}, \mathsf{LR}(\cdot, \cdot, b))$. We let $\mathbf{Adv}_{\mathsf{E},A}^{ind\text{-}cca}(\lambda) = |\Pr[\mathbf{Exp}_{\mathsf{E},A}^{ind\text{-}cca\text{-}1}(\lambda) = 1] - \Pr[\mathbf{Exp}_{\mathsf{E},A}^{ind\text{-}cca\text{-}0}(\lambda) = 1]|$.

An encryption scheme E is IND-CCA secure if $\mathbf{Adv}_{E,\mathcal{A}}^{ind\text{-}cca}(\lambda)$ is negligible in λ for any polynomial-time adversary $\mathcal{A}$.

2.6   Simulation-Sound Non-interactive Zero Knowledge Proof System

An NP-*relation over domain* $\mathsf{Dom} \subseteq \{0,1\}^*$ is a subset ρ of $\{0,1\}^* \times \{0,1\}^*$ and x is a *theorem* and w is a *proof* of x if $(x, w) \in \rho$. The membership of $(x, w) \in \rho$ is decidable in polynomial time in the length of the first argument for all x in Dom. Fix an NP relation ρ over Dom and take a pair of polynomial time algorithms (P, V), where P is randomized, and V is deterministic. Both P and V have access to a *common reference string* R and (P, V) is a non-interactive proof system for ρ over Dom if the following two conditions are satisfied for polynomials p and ℓ.

- *Completeness:* $\forall \lambda \in \mathbb{N}, \forall (x, w) \in \rho$ with $|x| \le \ell(\lambda)$ and $x \in \mathsf{Dom}$:
  $\Pr[R \xleftarrow{\$} \{0,1\}^{p(\lambda)}; \pi \xleftarrow{\$} P(1^\lambda, x, w, R) : V(1^\lambda, x, \pi, R) = 1] = 1$.
- *Soundness:* $\forall \lambda \in \mathbb{N}, \forall \hat{P}$ and $x \in \mathsf{Dom}$ such that $x \notin L_\rho$:
  $\Pr[R \xleftarrow{\$} \{0,1\}^{p(\lambda)}; \pi \xleftarrow{\$} \hat{P}(1^\lambda, x, R) : V(1^\lambda, x, \pi, R) = 1] \le 2^{-\lambda}$.

3 Our Scheme

We use the scheme given in [8] as the underlying scheme and change the techniques given in [8] to manage time-bound keys and to secure in the dynamical-almost-full anonymity. Using time-bound keys is not given in the scheme in [8]. Thus we change the joining-protocol, Sign, Verify, Open, and Judge algorithms given in [8] to suits with the time-bound keys in our scheme. At the joining-protocol, if a new user shows up with valid keys and if the keys are not being used before by previous members, then the group manager selects and sends a revocation token and a key expiration date. For instance, in a real-life application, the contract ending date is the key expiration date. Thus, after the contract period, the user cannot use those keys. At the end of the joining-protocol, the joining user (new member) creates his secret signing key with the key expiration date. At the time of signing, first, the signer should pass the key-expiration checking. A dishonest member can cheat on this validation step by giving a fake expiration date. To remove such kind of disputes, we allow the group manager to generate the member-certification with the key expiration date at the joining-protocol. Thus, at the time of signing, even the cheating member passes the key-expiration checking and produces the signature, his signature will not pass the validation process in signature verification. Moreover, the signer's signature includes the expiration date. This date should be later date than the time of validation. Otherwise, it will not pass the verification process. For instance, in the real-life application, within the contract period if a member issues a signature to a business certificate which should be validated within a certain period and should not be valid after that period, then the signature should have an expiration date. On the other hand, this ensures that the signature expires before the contract period.

3.1 Description of the Scheme

We denote the key expiration date as t_r, the signature expiration date as t_s, and the current time (verification time) as t_v. Our scheme uses date as "YYM-MDD". The new fully dynamic group signature scheme consists of two authorities, namely, the issuer (the group manager GM) and the opener (the tracing manager). The new scheme is a tuple $FDGS$=(GKg, UKg, Join, Issue, Revoke, Sign, Verify, Open, Judge), and we maintain a table called, registration table reg to track the registered member details. We depict *group joining protocol* of the scheme which executes Join and Issue in Fig. 1, and other algorithms in Fig. 2. Each algorithm function as described in below.

– GKg(1^λ): The trusted party executes *group-key generation* algorithm GKg at the setup stage on input 1^λ to produce a group public key **gpk** and authorities keys. Then passes authorities' secret keys, **ik** to the group manager and **ok** to the tracing manager.

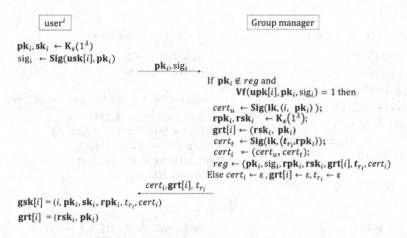

Fig. 1. Group joining protocol

- UKg(1^λ): Every new user before interacting with *group-joining protocol* executes *user-key generation* algorithm UKg. UKg takes as input 1^λ and outputs a long-term personal public and private key pair (**upk**[i], **usk**[i]) for user i. We assume that **upk**[i] is publicly available.
- Join, Issue: *Group-joining protocol* is an *interactive protocol* between the group manager and a new user. Any new user i who is expecting to be a new member and having a personal key pair (**upk**[i], **usk**[i]) can join the group via *group-joining protocol*. First, the new user generates his public and secret key pair **pk**$_i$ and **sk**$_i$. Then i produces a signature sig_i on **pk**$_i$ using **usk**[i] and interacts with the group manager by sending sig_i and **pk**$_i$. The group manager checks whether **pk**$_i$ is used by the previous members and whether sig_i is generated on **pk**$_i$. If those conditions are satisfied then GM produces a revocation token **grt**[i] and chooses a key expiration date t_{r_i}. Next GM creates member certification $cert_i$, saves the new member details in *reg* with the status (st) as 1 and sends $cert_i$, **grt**[i], and t_{r_i}. Finally, the new user i produces the secret signing key **gsk** = (i, **pk**$_i$, **rpk**$_i$, t_{r_i}, $cert_i$).
- Revoke(i, **grt**[i], **ik**, *RL*, *reg*): The group manager executes *member revoking* algorithm to remove disputed members from the group (premature revocation). Revoke takes, an index i of the revoking member, the group manager's secret key **ik**, *RL*, and *reg* as inputs. First, GM queries *reg* with the index i to obtain the details of the user stored and checks whether the user i is active and the queries are equal to the data collected by parsing **grt**[i]. If the data are identical to the queries and if the user i is active, then GM adds **grt**[i] = (**rsk**$_i$, **pk**$_i$) to *RL* and updates *reg* to inactive status 0.
- Sign(**gpk**, **gsk**[i], **grt**[i], M, t_s): This randomized *group signing* algorithm creates a signature Σ on a given message M. First, Sign confirms that the given signature expiration date t_s is not later than the key expiration date t_r included in the secret signing key **gsk**[i]. Then it generates Σ.

$\underline{\mathsf{GKg}(1^\lambda) \to (\mathbf{gpk}, \mathbf{ok}, \mathbf{ik})}$

$R_1 \xleftarrow{\$} \{0,1\}^{P1(\lambda)};$

$R_2 \xleftarrow{\$} \{0,1\}^{P2(\lambda)};$

$r_e \xleftarrow{\$} \{0,1\}^{r(\lambda)};$

$(opk, osk) \leftarrow K_e(1^\lambda; r_e);$

$(ipk, isk) \xleftarrow{\$} K_s(1^\lambda);$

$\mathbf{gpk} \leftarrow (1^\lambda, R_1, R_2, \mathbf{opk}, \mathbf{ipk});$

$\mathbf{ok} \leftarrow (osk, r_e);$

$\mathbf{ik} \leftarrow isk;$

Return $(\mathbf{gpk}, \mathbf{ok}, \mathbf{ik})$.

$\underline{\mathsf{UKg}(1^\lambda) \to (\mathbf{upk}, \mathbf{usk})}$

$(\mathbf{upk}, \mathbf{usk}) \xleftarrow{\$} K_s(1^\lambda);$

Return $(\mathbf{upk}, \mathbf{usk})$.

$\underline{\mathsf{Revoke}(i, \mathbf{grt}[i], \mathbf{ik}, RL, reg) \to (RL, reg)}$

Query $\mathbf{grt}[i] \to (i, \mathbf{grt}[i]', st);$

If $(st \neq 0$ and $\mathbf{grt}[i] = \mathbf{grt}[i]')$

then $RL \leftarrow RL \cup (\mathbf{grt}[i]);$

update $reg[i]$ to inactive;

Return RL, reg.

$\underline{\mathsf{Sign}(\mathbf{gpk}, \mathbf{gsk}[i], \mathbf{grt}[i], M, t_s) \to \Sigma}$

Parse $\mathbf{gpk}$ as $(1^\lambda, R_1, R_2, \mathbf{opk}, \mathbf{ipk});$

Parse $\mathbf{gsk}[i]$ as $(i, \mathbf{pk}_i, \mathbf{sk}_i, \mathbf{rpk}_i, t_{r_i}, cert_i);$

Parse $\mathbf{grt}[i]$ as $(\mathbf{rsk}_i, \mathbf{pk}_i);$

Parse $cert_i$ as $(cert_u, cert_t);$

If $t_s > t_{r_i}$ then return ε.

$s \leftarrow \mathsf{Sig}(\mathbf{sk}_i, M); r \xleftarrow{\$} \{0,1\}^\lambda;$

$C_{rt} \leftarrow \mathsf{Enc}(\mathbf{rpk}_i, s; r);$

$C \leftarrow \mathsf{Enc}(\mathbf{opk}, \langle i, \mathbf{pk}_i cert_u, s \rangle; r);$

$\pi_1 \xleftarrow{\$} P_1(1^\lambda, (\mathbf{opk}, \mathbf{ipk}, M, C),$
$(i, \mathbf{pk}_i, cert_u, t_{r_i}, \mathbf{rpk}_i, cert_t, s, r), R_1);$

$\Sigma \leftarrow (C, \pi_1, C_{rt}, cert_t, t_s, t_r, \mathbf{rpk}_i);$

Return Σ.

$\underline{\mathsf{Verify}(\mathbf{gpk}, M, \Sigma, RL, t_v) \to 1/0}$

Parse $\mathbf{gpk}$ as $(1^\lambda, R_1, R_2, \mathbf{opk}, \mathbf{ipk});$

Parse Σ as $(C, \pi_1, C_{rt}, cert_t, t_s, t_r, \mathbf{rpk}_i);$

If $t_v > t_s$ or $t_s > t_r$ then return ε.

If $\mathsf{Vf}(\mathbf{ipk}, \langle t_r, \mathbf{rpk}_i \rangle, cert_t) = 0$

then return ε.

If $V_1(1^\lambda, (\mathbf{opk}, \mathbf{ipk}, M, C), \pi_1, R_1) = 0$

then return 0

For $(\mathbf{grt} = (\mathbf{rsk}, \mathbf{pk})) \in RL:$

$\mathsf{Vf}(\mathbf{pk}, M, \mathsf{Dec}(\mathbf{rsk}, C_{rt})) = 1$

then return 0;

Return 1.

$\underline{\mathsf{Open}(\mathbf{gpk}, \mathbf{ok}, reg, M, \Sigma) \to (i, \tau, st)}$

Parse $\mathbf{gpk}$ as $(1^\lambda, R_1, R_2, \mathbf{opk}, \mathbf{ipk});$

Parse $\mathbf{ok}$ as $(osk, r_e);$

Parse Σ as $(C, \pi_1, C_{rt}, cert_t, t_s, t_r, \mathbf{rpk}_i);$

$M_s \leftarrow \mathsf{Dec}(osk, C);$

Parse M_s as $\langle i, \mathbf{pk}, cert_u, s \rangle;$

If $reg[i] \neq \varepsilon$ then Parse $reg[i]$ as
$(i, \mathbf{pk}_i, sig_i, cert_i, \mathbf{grt}[i], status);$

Else $\mathbf{pk}_i \leftarrow \varepsilon; sig_i \leftarrow \varepsilon; st \leftarrow \varepsilon;$

$\pi_2 \leftarrow P_2(1^\lambda, (\mathbf{opk}, C, i, \mathbf{pk}, cert_u, s),$
$(osk, r_e), R_2);$

If $V_1(1^\lambda, (\mathbf{opk}, \mathbf{ipk}, M, C), \pi_1, R_1) = 0$

then return $(0, \varepsilon, 0);$

If $\mathbf{pk} \neq \mathbf{pk}_i$ or $reg[i] = \varepsilon$ or $status = 0$

then return $(0, \varepsilon, 0);$

$\tau \leftarrow (\mathbf{pk}_i, sig_i, i, \mathbf{pk}, cert_u, s, \pi_2);$

Return (i, τ, st).

$\underline{\mathsf{Judge}(\mathbf{gpk}, i, \mathbf{upk}[i], M, \Sigma, \tau) \to 1/0}$

Parse $\mathbf{gpk}$ as $(1^\lambda, R_1, R_2, \mathbf{opk}, \mathbf{ipk});$

Parse Σ as $(C, \pi_1, C_{rt}, cert_t, t_s, t_r, \mathbf{rpk}_i);$

If $(i, \tau, st) = (0, \varepsilon, 0)$ then return
$V_1(1^\lambda, (\mathbf{opk}, \mathbf{ipk}, M, C), \pi_1, R_1) = 0.$

Parse τ as $(\overline{\mathbf{pk}}, \overline{sig}, i', \mathbf{pk}, cert_u, s, \pi_2);$

If $V_2(1^\lambda, (C, i', \mathbf{pk}, cert_u, s), \pi_2, R_2) = 0$

then return 0

If all of the followings are true then return
1 else return 0.

$\quad$ -$i = i'.$

$\quad$ -$\mathsf{Vf}(\mathbf{upk}[i], \overline{\mathbf{pk}}, \overline{sig}).$

$\quad$ -$\overline{\mathbf{pk}} = \mathbf{pk}.$

Fig. 2. Algorithms of the new scheme

- Verify(**gpk**, M, Σ, RL, t_v): This deterministic *group signature verification* algorithm allows the verifiers in possession of **gpk** to verify the given signature Σ is generated on the given message M. First, the algorithm verifies whether the signature expiration date t_s is later than the current date. Then it validates Σ and confirms the signer is not being revoked using RL. This algorithm outputs 1 if both the conditions are valid. Otherwise, it returns 0.
- Open(**gpk**, **ok**, *reg*, M, Σ): This deterministic verifiable *opening* algorithm traces the signers by taking **gpk**, the opener's secret key **ok**, *reg*, the message-signature pair (M, Σ) as inputs. It returns the index of the signer i, the proof of the claim τ and the status of the signer st in *reg*. If the algorithm fails to trace the signature to a particular group member, then it returns $(0, \varepsilon, 0)$.
- Judge(**gpk**, i, **upk**[i], M, Σ, τ): This deterministic *judge* algorithm outputs either 1 or 0 depending on the validity of the proof τ on Σ. This takes **gpk**, the member index i, the tracing proof τ, the member verification key **upk**[i], the message M and the signature Σ as inputs and outputs 1 if τ can prove that i produced Σ. Otherwise, it returns 0.

4   Security Analysis of the Scheme

To define the security requirements of the scheme we use a set of experiments as given in Fig. 3 and global variables, honest user list **HUL**, corrupted user list **CUL**, token revealed user list **TUL**, signing key revealed user list **SUL**, signatures queried users set SS, challenged signatures set CS, and revoked members set RS.

4.1   Applying Dynamical-Almost-Full Anonymity

When applying the security notion, the dynamical-almost-full anonymity to our scheme, we have to check whether the adversary can get advantage using the time bound keys to win the anonymity game.

Consider an anonymity game between an adversary and a challenger. The adversary may send two indices with one index having a later expiration date and another having a short expiration date which will expire before the validation. Then the adversary can identify the owner of the signature using that difference. For instance, if i_0 key expiration date is 180601, i_1 key expiration date is 180801, and the signature is generating with signature expiration date 180701, then the challenger generates the signature definitely using i_1. This is a very easy catch for the adversary. Thus, at the challenging phase the challenger should confirm both the challenging indices have later key expiration dates that satisfy $t_r > t_s$. This is already true because Sign generates signatures if only $t_r > t_s$. Next consider a scenario that the adversary changes the current date of Verify. For instance, consider a scenario that the key expiration dates of i_0 and i_1 are 180801 and 181001 respectively. The signature is generated with signature expiration date 180501. The real verification date is 180301. Thus, the challenging signature is a valid signature. Assume that the adversary changes the verification date to

$\mathbf{Exp}_{FDGS,A}^{corr}(\lambda)$

$(\mathbf{gpk}, \mathbf{ok}, \mathbf{ik}) \leftarrow \mathsf{GKg}(1^{\lambda}); \mathbf{HUL} \leftarrow \emptyset;$

$(i, M) \leftarrow A(\mathbf{gpk}; \mathsf{AddU}, \mathsf{ReadReg}, \mathsf{Revoke});$

If $i \notin \mathbf{HUL}$ or $\mathbf{gsk}[i] = \varepsilon$ or $\mathbf{grt}[i] = \varepsilon$ or $\mathbf{grt}[i] \in RS$ or
  $\mathsf{IsActive}(i, reg) = 0$ or $t_i = \varepsilon$ then return 0.

$\Sigma \leftarrow \mathsf{Sign}(\mathbf{gpk}, \mathbf{gsk}[i], \mathbf{grt}[i], M, t_s);$

If $\mathsf{Verify}(\mathbf{gpk}, M, \Sigma, RS, t_v) = 0$ then return 1.

$(i', \tau, st) \leftarrow \mathsf{Open}(\mathbf{gpk}, \mathbf{ok}, reg, M, \Sigma);$

If $i \neq i'$ then return 1.

If $\mathsf{Judge}(\mathbf{gpk}, i, \mathbf{upk}[i], M, \Sigma, \tau) = 0$ then return 1 else return 0.

$\mathbf{Exp}_{FDGS,A}^{anon-b}(\lambda);$

$(\mathbf{gpk}, \mathbf{ok}, \mathbf{ik}) \leftarrow \mathsf{GKg}(1^{\lambda})$

$\mathbf{HUL}, \mathbf{CUL}, \mathbf{TUL}, \mathbf{SUL}, SS, CS, RS \leftarrow \emptyset;$

$b^* \leftarrow A(\mathbf{gpk};$
  $\mathsf{AddU}, \mathsf{CrptU}, \mathsf{SendToUser}, \mathsf{RevealSk}, \mathsf{RevealRt}, \mathsf{Open}, \mathsf{ModifyReg}, \mathsf{Revoke}, \mathsf{Chal}_b);$

Return $b^*;$

$\mathbf{Exp}_{FDGS,A}^{trace}(\lambda)$

$(\mathbf{gpk}, \mathbf{ok}, \mathbf{ik}) \leftarrow \mathsf{GKg}(1^{\lambda})$

$\mathbf{HUL}, \mathbf{CUL}, \mathbf{TUL}, \mathbf{SUL}, SS, CS, RS \leftarrow \emptyset;$

$(M, \Sigma) \leftarrow A(\mathbf{gpk}, \mathbf{ok};$
  $\mathsf{AddU}, \mathsf{CrptU}, \mathsf{SendToIssuer}, \mathsf{RevealSk}, \mathsf{RevealRt}, \mathsf{Sign}, \mathsf{Revoke});$

If $\mathsf{Verify}(\mathbf{gpk}, M, \Sigma, RS) = 0$ then return 0.

$(i, \tau) \leftarrow \mathsf{Open}(\mathbf{gpk}, \mathbf{ok}, reg, M, \Sigma);$

$\mathsf{IsActive}(i, reg) = 0$ then return 0.

If $i = 0$ or $\mathsf{Judge}(\mathbf{gpk}, i, \mathbf{upk}[i], M, \Sigma, \tau) = 0$ then return 1 else return 0.

$\mathbf{Exp}_{FDGS,A}^{non-fram}(\lambda)$

$(\mathbf{gpk}, \mathbf{ok}, \mathbf{ik}) \leftarrow \mathsf{GKg}(1^{\lambda})$

$\mathbf{HUL}, \mathbf{CUL}, \mathbf{TUL}, \mathbf{SUL}, SS, CS, RS \leftarrow \emptyset;$

$(M, \Sigma, i, \tau) \leftarrow A(\mathbf{gpk}, \mathbf{ik}, \mathbf{ok};$
  $\mathsf{CrptU}, \mathsf{SendToUser}, \mathsf{RevealSk}, \mathsf{RevealRt}, \mathsf{Sign}, \mathsf{ModifyReg}, \mathsf{Revoke});$

If $i \notin \mathbf{HUL}$ then return 0.

If $\mathbf{gsk}[i] = \varepsilon$ then return 0.

If $\mathsf{Verify}(\mathbf{gpk}, M, \Sigma, RS) = 0$ then return 0.

If $\mathsf{Judge}(\mathbf{gpk}, i, \mathbf{upk}[i], M, \Sigma, \tau) = 0$ then return 0.

If $(i, M, \Sigma) \in \mathbf{SL}$ then return 0.

If $i \in \mathbf{BUL}$ or $i \in \mathbf{SUL}$ then return 0.

else 1.

Fig. 3. Security experiments for the scheme

180701 and tries to identify the signature is generated using i_0 or i_1. If the adversary executes Verify with current date (verification date) as 180701 then Verify returns invalid because $t_s < t_v$. Hence, the adversary cannot identify the signer. The adversary may try to generate a signature for i_0 or i_1 using the secret signing keys. But since the adversary does not know the revocation token of i_0 or i_1, he fails on generating signatures for i_0, i_1.

This proves that we can secure our scheme with time bound keys using dynamical-almost- full anonymity.

4.2 Correctness

A signature is verified as valid only if it is generated by a non-revoked member with a non-expired key.

Theorem 1. *For all* $t_r, t_s, t_v, RL, M \in \{0,1\}^*, (\textbf{gpk}, \textbf{ok}, \textbf{ik}) \leftarrow GKg(1^\lambda)$ *and* $(\textbf{gsk}[i], \textbf{grt}[i]) \leftarrow$ *Join,*
    Verify$(\textbf{gpk}, M, \text{Sign}(\textbf{gpk}, \textbf{gsk}[i], \textbf{grt}[i], M, t_s), RS, t_v) = valid \iff \textbf{grt}[i] \notin$
RL *and* $t_r > t_s \geq t_v$ *and*
    Open$(\textbf{gpk}, \textbf{ok}, reg, M, \text{Sign}(\textbf{gpk}, \textbf{gsk}[i], \textbf{grt}[i], M, t_s)) = i, \tau$ *and*
Judge$(\textbf{gpk}, i, \textbf{upk}[i], M, \text{Sign}(\textbf{gpk}, \textbf{gsk}[i], \textbf{grt}[i], M, t_s), \tau) = 1.$

4.3 Dynamical-Almost-Full Anonymity

Theorem 2 ([1]). *If E is an IND-CCA secure encryption scheme,* (P_1, V_1) *and* (P_2, V_2) *are simulation sound, computational zero-knowledge proof systems for* ρ_1 *over Dom$_1$ and* ρ_2 *over Dom$_2$ respectively, then fully dynamic group signature scheme FDGS is anonymous.*

As per the discussion in Sect. 4.1 and using the proof given in [1] the proposed scheme is dynamical-almost-full anonymous.

4.4 Traceability

Theorem 3 ([1]). *If D is secure against forgery under chosen-message attack,* (P_1, V_1) *and* (P_2, V_2) *are simulation sound, computational zero-knowledge proof systems for* ρ_1 *over Dom$_1$ and* ρ_2 *over Dom$_2$ respectively, then fully dynamic group signature scheme FDGS is traceable.*

If an adversary A can break the traceability of our scheme with non-negligible probability, then we construct another polynomial-time algorithm B that can break the unforgeability of the digital signature scheme D. According to the proof provided in [1], we claim that the proposed scheme is traceable.

4.5   Non-frameability

Theorem 4 ([1]). *If D is secure against forgery under chosen-message attack, (P_1, V_1) and (P_2, V_2) are simulation sound, computational zero-knowledge proof systems for ρ_1 over Dom_1 and ρ_2 over Dom_2 respectively, then fully dynamic group signature scheme FDGS is non-frameable.*

Similar to the proof of traceability, our scheme is non-frameable based on the non-frameability of the digital signature scheme D.

5   Evaluation of the Scheme and Conclusion

When generating signatures the signer has to proof that his secret key has not expired and he has to pass the expiration dates of the secret key and the signature. Thus, this makes additional work to the signer and it makes longer signature size comparing to the existing scheme. At the verification stage the verifier has to check the expiration dates. Even it is an additional work for verifiers, it is less than the cost of revocation check in previous schemes. At the time of joining, the group manager has to pick the expiration date for each new user. This is also not in the previous scheme [8]. However, all the additional cost in the proposed scheme is less when there are large number of revoked members. Thus, efficiency of the revocation check in our scheme is far better than the schemes like [1] and [8] when applying to a large group.

Since the proposed scheme intends to reduce the cost of revocation cost while being secured, we have achieved the goal with a reasonable solution. The proposed scheme can me improve to a system like a customer managing system where the customers are joining the group (system) for a short period.

Acknowledgments. This work is supported in part by JSPS Grant-in-Aids for Scientic Research (A) JP16H01705 and for Scientic Research (B) JP17H01695.

References

1. Bellare, M., Shi, H., Zhang, C.: Foundations of group signatures: the case of dynamic groups. In: Menezes, A. (ed.) CT-RSA 2005. LNCS, vol. 3376, pp. 136–153. Springer, Heidelberg (2005). https://doi.org/10.1007/978-3-540-30574-3_11
2. Boneh, D., Shacham, H.: Group signatures with verifier-local revocation. In: ACM-CCS 2004, pp. 168–177. ACM (2004)
3. Brickell, E.: An efficient protocol for anonymously providing assurance of the container of the private key. Submitted to the Trusted Comp. Group, April 2003
4. Chaum, D., van Heyst, E.: Group signatures. In: Davies, D.W. (ed.) EUROCRYPT 1991. LNCS, vol. 547, pp. 257–265. Springer, Heidelberg (1991). https://doi.org/10.1007/3-540-46416-6_22
5. Chu, C.K., Liu, J.K., Huang, X., Zhou, J.: Verifier-local revocation group signatures with time-bound keys. In: Proceedings of the 7th ACM Symposium on Information, Computer and Communications Security, pp. 26–27. ACM (2012)

6. Langlois, A., Ling, S., Nguyen, K., Wang, H.: Lattice-based group signature scheme with verifier-local revocation. In: Krawczyk, H. (ed.) PKC 2014. LNCS, vol. 8383, pp. 345–361. Springer, Heidelberg (2014). https://doi.org/10.1007/978-3-642-54631-0_20

7. Perera, M.N.S., Koshiba, T.: Achieving almost-full security for lattice-based fully dynamic group signatures with verifier-local revocation. In: Su, C., Kikuchi, H. (eds.) ISPEC 2018. LNCS, vol. 11125, pp. 229–247. Springer, Cham (2018). https://doi.org/10.1007/978-3-319-99807-7_14

8. Perera, M.N.S., Koshiba, T.: Fully dynamic group signature scheme with member registration and verifier-local revocation. In: Ghosh, D., Giri, D., Mohapatra, R., Sakurai, K., Savas, E., Som, T. (eds.) ICMC 2018, vol. 253, pp. 399–415. Springer, Heidelberg (2018). https://doi.org/10.1007/978-981-13-2095-8_31

Path Planning for Multi-robot Systems in Intelligent Warehouse

Hailong Chen[1], Qiang Wang[1(✉)], Meng Yu[1], Jingjing Cao[1], and Jingtao Sun[2]

[1] Wuhan University of Technology, Wuhan, China
812892887@qq.com, {wangqiang,bettycao}@whut.edu.cn,
ymmona@126.com
[2] National Institute of Informatics, Tokyo 101-8430, Japan
sun@nii.ac.jp

Abstract. In this work, the path planning problem of robotics group is surveyed in the context of multi-robot transportation tasks on an intelligent warehouse. The mainly researches focused on the a shortest path theory and algorithm for single robot system. To solve the path planning problem on multi-robot systems, a novel approach is presented for multi-robot systems in an intelligent warehouse by using the method of artificial potential function (APF) in this paper. The proposed improving method of APF that motioned the strategy of wall-following with priority and how to solve the unavoidable troubles in obstacle avoidance for multi-robot systems such as local minima, non-reachable target, collision and traffic jams. Finally, several numerical simulations were provided to show the effectiveness, and the performance of the proposed method with the theoretical results.

Keywords: Path planning · Multi-robot · Artificial potential
Intelligent warehouse

1 Introduction

Recently, the study of intelligent warehouse for multiple mobile robots has drawn significant interest among researchers in various fields, which is mainly due to the rapid development of industrial automation and the requirement of efficient automated logistics systems. Not only industrial such as Amazon proposed some approaches for achieving the problem of automated logistics system based on mobile manipulator [1, 2], but the academic also proposed some approaches for path planning of mobile robot [3, 4]. Both of them have simple and practical advantages in automatic system, however, all of them are trying to implement automatically systems with single robot, and adapt to its environment changes.

The coordinated path planning and obstacle avoidance are important to establish intelligent warehouse based on multi-mobile robots. During the last decade, there are a large number of researchers focusing their efforts on the algorithm and theory of path

© Springer Nature Switzerland AG 2018
Y. Xiang et al. (Eds.): IDCS 2018, LNCS 11226, pp. 148–159, 2018.
https://doi.org/10.1007/978-3-030-02738-4_13

planning and collision avoidance [3–9]. For instance, the wind driven optimization algorithm [3], the computational trajectory generation algorithm [4] and the routing optimization [5] are utilized for the autonomous mobile robot navigation and collision avoidance in static and dynamic environment. The characteristics of the obstacle border and fuzzy logical reasoning [6] and a learning-based motion modeling method [7] are utilized in the motion planning. The smoothing direction-first path planning algorithm [8] is proposed based on tree structure and the local obstacle avoidance path planning of apple harvesting robot in C-space is accomplished. However, these algorithms have been studying on the premise that system performance has not been optimized, computation time is long, or the environmental change of the system has already been detected. On the other hand, Asama et al. presented an effective artificial potential field-based regression search method that can obtain a better and shorter path efficiently without local minima and oscillations in a variety of complex environments [9]. But the research target is still single robot system. Recently, some new challenges are presented, such as the coordination and communication of the multi-robot systems. Pinkam et al. [10] and Muñoz et al. [11] had designed a multi-robot system for path-planning for mobile robotics applications. Dong et al. [12] proposed the sequencing rules for multiple destinations path planning in the smart home environment. However, those systems focus on specified environments, unlike us, the path planning problem is investigated in unknown complicated environments, therefore, and we need to solve the problem of obstacle avoidance between the robots.

This paper mainly investigates path planning and obstacle avoidance in multiple mobile robots for intelligent warehouse. The improved method is designed based on traditional APF to achieve the above problem. Our paper makes the following key contributions:

(1) Solving the local minima problem for multi-robot systems in path planning;
(2) Solving the non-reachable target problem for robots in intelligent warehouse;
(3) Solving the collision and traffic jams among multiple robots in warehouse.

The rest of the paper is organized as follows. In Sect. 2, the problem of path planning is formulated as well as preliminaries from graph theory. In Sect. 3, a motion strategy based on improved APF is proposed to escape the problems of local minima, non-reachable target, collision and traffic jams for multi-robot systems. To demonstrate proposed method, some simulations are validated in Sect. 4. Finally, conclusions are drawn in Sect. 5.

2 Statements and Preliminaries

2.1 Statements

In this paper, we proposed coordinate control method of path planning for multi-robot system in intelligent warehouse. The APF method is used for path planning and obstacle avoidance. However, there are some disadvantages with traditional APF method, such as local minima problem and non-reachable target problem. Furthermore, unlike those single robot systems, not only our research targets is different from them, but also we face to avoid to account of collision avoidance among multiple robots which works in complex environment, and dynamically adapt to changes of user's requirements immediately. Therefore, the improved APF and its algorithm are utilized to complete the path planning for multi-robot systems.

2.2 Preliminaries

In this paper, based on the above problem statements, we would like to optical path for the mobile robot in intelligent warehouse, and the APF[1] is used to implement our systems through our requirements as follows.

(1) The attractive potential U_{att} is produced by the goal;
(2) The repulsive potential U_{rep} is produced by different obstacles;

The total APF $U(q)$ is defined as shown below.

$$U(q) = U_{att}(q) + \sum_{i=1}^{n} U_{rep}(q) \tag{1}$$

where $i = 1, 2, \ldots, n$ (n is the number of obstacles), q is the position of robots. And the total artificial force field is shown as follow.

$$F(q) = F_{att}(q) + \sum_{i=1}^{n} F_{rep}(q) \tag{2}$$

For achieve the requirement 1, we designed the Definition 1 as following:

Definition 1. The goal attraction force to the robot i is defined as:

$$F_{att}(q_i) = \begin{cases} kd_{att}, & \|q_i - q_g\| > d_{att} \\ k\|q_i - q_g\|, & \|q_i - q_g\| \le d_{att} \end{cases} \tag{3}$$

where k is a positive scaling factor; d_{att} is the threshold defined artificially; q_i is the current position of the robot i and q_g is the goal position. Definition 1 means that the magnitude of attractive force is constant when the relative position between the robot i and the goal is larger than d_{att}, otherwise the attractive force is linearly related to the relative position between the robot i and the goal. This definition is more in line with the reality of life.

For achieve the requirement 2, we designed the Definitions 2 and 3 as following:

---

[1] The APF was first introduced by Khatib in 1985 [13], which is the assumption that a robot moves in an abstract artificial potential field, which is made up of an attractive potential and a series of repulsive potentials.

Definition 2. Suppose all robots have the same sensing radius R, and the interaction exist only the relative position between the robots or between robot and obstacle is less than R. Thus, the robot i is able to detect the obstacle when $\rho(q_i) = |q_i - q_o| \le R$, where q_o is a unique configuration in an obstacle (including other robots) closest to the robot i and $\rho(q_i)$ is the shortest distance between the robot i and the obstacle.

Definition 3. The obstacle repulsion force to the robot i is defined as:

$$F_{rep}(q_i) = \begin{cases} 0, & \rho(q_i) > \rho_0 \\ \eta(\frac{1}{\rho(q_i)} - \frac{1}{\rho_0})(\frac{1}{\rho^2(q_i)}), & \rho(q_i) \le \rho_0 \end{cases} \tag{4}$$

where η is a positive scaling factor; ρ_0 is the greatest impact distance of a single obstacle and $\rho_0 \le R$. Definition 3 indicates that the repulsion force exists only when the relative position between robot and obstacle (including other robots) is less than ρ_0. The advantage is that robot is able to move straight towards to the target point while obstacle is out of the sense range. Once obstacle is detected by robot, it will produce a repulsion force to slow down the robot. When the robot is going to knock into the obstacle, the repulsion force will increase rapidly until it is greater than the attraction force and push the robot away. In this way, robot is able to complete obstacle avoidance effectively.

Note that the existing APF methods had the following disadvantages: (1) local minima (2) non-reached target. However, our work would through control strategy to improve them and it is able to work in an unknown static and dynamic environment. Therefore, we improved traditional APF method and employed it to achieve path planning for multi-robot systems.

3   Solution for Troubles

As we have introduced in Sect. 2, multiple robots cooperation should take into consideration. Therefore, we proposed the wall-following with priority and how to solve the unavoidable troubles in obstacle avoidance for multi-robot systems such as local minima, non-reachable target, collision and traffic jams.

3.1   Local Minima

Firstly, the APF method might cause the local minima problem as shown in Fig. 1. When a robot moves from initial position to goal, the attractive force and the repulsive force is collinear reverse (or almost collinear reverse), then the total force of a robot is almost zero, a robot will be trapped in local minima and stop to move.

In order to guide a robot to escape from local minima, we proposed the wall-

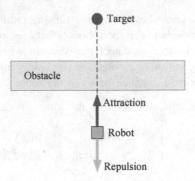

Fig. 1. A robot is trapped in local minima

following method to deal with it. Once a robot suffers from the local minima and oscillations problem, it should get location information about obstacle by sensors and select one side closed with itself (if both sides of obstacle are out of the sensing radius, select one side randomly) to move along with following the wall of obstacle until escaping from the local minima, as shown in Fig. 2.

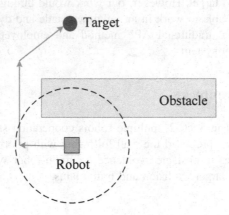

Fig. 2. Wall-following method

3.2 Non-reachable Target

When a target is extremely close to obstacle, the repulsive force may be much greater than the attractive force, and then the robot is unable to arrive at the position of target

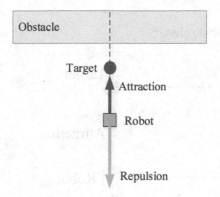

Fig. 3. A robot is unable to reach the target

forever, as shown in Fig. 3. This condition is named the non-reachable target problem, which is undesirable for the robot path planning.

To overcome the trouble of non-reachable target, we increased two factors to redefined APF. The factors are shown as below.

$$①. d_{ro} \leq D_{ro}$$
$$②. d_{rg} \leq D_{rg}$$

where d_{ro} and D_{ro} are current relative position and extreme relative position between robot and obstacle, respectively. d_{rg} and D_{rg} are actual distance and extreme distance between robot and goal, respectively. Thus, the potential function is redefined as below.

$$U(q) = \begin{cases} U_{att}(q), & d_{ro} \leq D_{ro} \quad \text{and} \quad d_{rg} \leq D_{rg} \\ U_{att}(q) + \sum_{i=1}^{n} U_{rep}(q), & \text{Otherwise} \end{cases} \tag{5}$$

The improved function means that if the target is greater close to obstacle, the robot will only move by effect of the attractive potential instant of the total APF when the robot is closed to target. Otherwise robot will move by the effect of total APF. By this way, robot is able to reach target which is too much closed to obstacle accurately, as shown in Fig. 4.

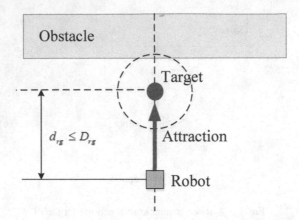

Fig. 4. A robot is only affected by attraction when it is greater closed to target.

3.3 Collision and Traffic Jams

The conditions of collision and traffic jams will occur inevitably for multiple robots in intelligent warehouse. To solve the problem, priority level strategy and collision avoidance algorithm are taken into consideration. Firstly, all robots are tagged with different priority level, which is related to the relative position between the robots and the goal. The longer the distance is, the higher priority will have. This strategy will make all robots complete the task at the same time. When the distance between two robots is less than the rated distance D_{rr}, robot with lower priority will reduce speed and stop, even reverse, meanwhile robot with higher priority will identify the former as an obstacle and carry on with the task. The procedure of the avoidance between two robots is shown as Fig. 5. Firstly, the robot R_m moves into the sensing radius of the robot R_n, the robot R_n obtains the priority information of the robot R_m through communication to each other. Furthermore, the speed of the robot R_n will not slow down and stop until the robot R_m move out of the sensing radius of the robot R_n.

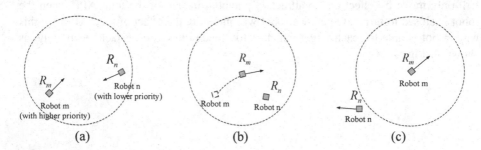

Fig. 5. Priority level strategy and collision avoidance algorithm

Furthermore, the situation will be more complex when three or more robots are closed to each other. For example, the collision avoidance algorithm of three robots is shown as Algorithm 1. It is defined that the actual distance between the robot 1 and the robot 2 is d_{12}. The parameter are same defined with d_{13} and d_{23}.

Algorithm 1: Collision avoidance algorithm of three robots

For $i \leftarrow 1\text{to}3$, $q(i) \leftarrow$ position of robot i, $q_g(i) \leftarrow$ position of goal i,

$P(i) \leftarrow \| q(i) - q_g(i) \|$ // Priority of robot i

$v(i) \leftarrow 0.6$ // Velocity of robot i (m/s)

$d_{12} \leftarrow \| q(1) - q(2) \|$, $d_{13} \leftarrow \| q(1) - q(3) \|$, $d_{23} \leftarrow \| q(2) - q(3) \|$

$D_{rr} \leftarrow 7$ // Safe distance of robots

If $d_{12} > D_{rr}$ & $d_{13} > D_{rr}$ & $d_{23} > D_{rr}$ Then

$v(1) \leftarrow 0.6$; $v(2) \leftarrow 0.6$; $v(3) \leftarrow 0.6$;

Else

Case 1 $d_{12} < D_{rr}$ & $d_{13} > D_{rr}$ & $d_{23} > D_{rr}$

    If $P(1) > P(2)$ **Then**

    $v(2) \leftarrow 0.1$

    Else

    $v(1) \leftarrow 0.1$

Case 2 $d_{12} > D_{rr}$ & $d_{13} < D_{rr}$ & $d_{23} > D_{rr}$

    If $P(1) > P(3)$ **Then**

    $v(3) \leftarrow 0.1$

    Else

    $v(1) \leftarrow 0.1$

Case 3 $d_{12} > D_{rr}$ & $d_{13} > D_{rr}$ & $d_{23} < D_{rr}$

    If $P(2) > P(3)$ **Then**

    $v(3) \leftarrow 0.1$

    Else

    $v(2) \leftarrow 0.1$

Case 4 $d_{12} > D_{rr}$ & $d_{13} < D_{rr}$ & $d_{23} < D_{rr}$

    $v(3) \leftarrow 0.1$

Case 5 $d_{12} < D_{rr}$ & $d_{13} > D_{rr}$ & $d_{23} < D_{rr}$

    $v(2) \leftarrow 0.1$

Case 6 $d_{12} < D_{rr}$ & $d_{13} < D_{rr}$ & $d_{23} > D_{rr}$

    $v(1) \leftarrow 0.1$

Case 7 $d_{12} < D_{rr}$ & $d_{13} < D_{rr}$ & $d_{23} < D_{rr}$

    If $P(2) > P(3)$ & $P(1) > P(3)$ **Then**

      $v(2) \leftarrow 0.1$; $v(3) \leftarrow 0.1$

    Else if $P(2) > P(1)$ & $P(2) > P(3)$ **Then**

        $v(1) \leftarrow 0.1$; $v(3) \leftarrow 0.1$

    Else

      $v(2) \leftarrow 0.1$; $v(3) \leftarrow 0.1$

---

4   Simulation

Combined with APF method, the path planning algorithm is proposed to solve the unavoidable troubles for multi-robot systems in intelligent warehouse. In this section, some experiments are shown to verify the effectiveness of the proposed method. Simulation is based on the development environment of MATLAB platform

It is assumed that three autonomous mobile robots execute transportation or sorting task in the intelligent warehouse. As shown in Fig. 6, the three colorized hollow squares represent the three robots. The robot 1 is marked with blue, the robot 2 is marked with red, and the robot 3 is marked with green. The rectangular black grids represent the shelves, and the black squares are goals to acquire objects. The right of map is conveyor belt and the bottom of map is aisle used to leads robots back to initial positions.

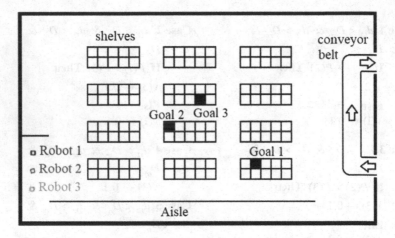

Fig. 6. Scenario of warehouse and three robots (Color figure online)

The routing system receives information about the transportation tasks from clients and sends instructions to robots to execute the tasks. After that, system sends target points to each robot and regularly verifies the progress of all tasks. And each robot starts to execute path planning to reach own goal and carries objects to the conveyor belt. Then the robot returns to the initial position and waits for a new task after unloading. The detailed parameters are shown as follow:

(1) The size of map is (160 m, 100 m) and the size of robot is (1.6 m, 1.6 m); the speed of robot is 0.6 m/s.
(2) The positive scaling factor of the attractive force k is 0.1. The threshold of attraction d_{att} is 4 m.

(3) The coefficient η for calculating the repulsive force is 1000. The radius of sensor R is 8 m and the positive coefficient ρ_0 for keeping the robot from obstacle is set as 7 m. And D_{rr} is 7 m as well for avoiding collision between robots. The extreme distance D_{og} is 4 m and D_{rg} is also 4 m, which are used to solve the target non-reachable problem.

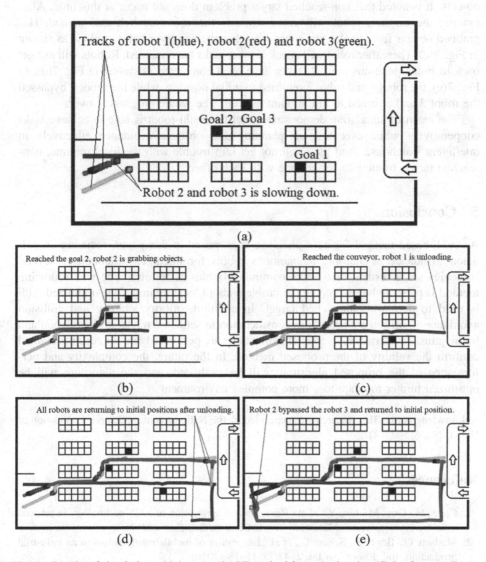

(a)

(b)   (c)

(d)   (e)

Fig. 7. Results of simulation with improved APF method for path planning (Color figure online)

The simulation displays the whole process of path planning based on improved APF method for multi-robot in intelligent warehouse. As shown in Fig. 7(a–e), the blue line is the track of the robot 1. Similarly, the red line is the track of the robot 2, and the green line is the track of the robot 3. In Fig. 7(a), three robots are much closed with each other. The robot 1, with the highest priority, is able to move on while other two robots have to slow down because of lower priority. The black rectangular border outside the colorized line means robot is slowing down at the position for collision avoidance. When the distance of them become long enough again, their velocities will recover. Figure 7(b) shows that the robot 2 reached the target point and stopped to grab objects. It is noted that non-reached target problem does not occur at this time. After loading the cargoes, robot will move towards the conveyor belt and unload. Has grabbed objects from goal 1, the robot 1 reaches the conveyor belt to unload as shown in Fig. 7(c). Thereafter robot will check if other tasks are remained. Robots will not get back to initial positions until all tasks have been completed as shown in Fig. 7(d). In Fig. 7(e), the robot 1 and robot 3 returned to initial position, while the robot 2 bypassed the robot 3 and returned to initial point as well. The whole progress is over.

The result of simulation demonstrates that the multi-robot is able to achieve tasks cooperatively while execute path planning and obstacle avoidance effectively in intelligent warehouse. And they will not get into trouble with the local minima, non-reached target, traffic jams or collude with each other.

5 Conclusion

An APF-based method for path planning is proposed in this paper, focusing on collision avoidance in multiple autonomous robots for intelligent warehouse. Several strategies are investigated to solve common troubles as follows. The wall-following method is presented to overcome the problem about local minima. The optimized APF is used to deal with unreached target. In addition, priority strategy and collision avoidance algorithm are taken into consideration to settle the matter with collision and traffic jams. Furthermore, a series of simulations are performed and the results obtained confirm the validity of the proposed method. In the future, the complexity and performance of the proposed algorithm will be evaluated, and the algorithm will be optimized further to adapt to a more complex environment.

Acknowledgment. This research was supported by the National Natural Science Foundation of China (No. 61503291).

References

1. Chen, M., Guo, M., Liu, Y., et al.: Research and application of AGV technology in tobacco industry logistics system. DEStech Trans. Comput. Sci. Eng. (2017)
2. Madsen, O., Bogh, S., Schou, C., et al.: Integration of mobile manipulators in an industrial production. Ind. Robot.-An Int. J. **42**(1), 11–18 (2015)
3. Pandey, A., Parhi, D.: Optimum path planning of mobile robot in unknown static and dynamic environments using fuzzy-wind driven optimization algorithm. Def. Technol. **13**(1), 47–58 (2017)
4. Hedjar, R., Bounkhel, M.: Real-time obstacle avoidance for a swarm of autonomous mobile robots. Int. J. Adv. Rob. Syst. **11**(1), 1 (2014)

5. Zhou, Y.C., Dong, Y.F., Xia, H.M., et al.: Routing optimization of intelligent vehicle in automated warehouse. Discret. Dyn. Nat. Soc. **2014**(1), 1–14 (2014)
6. Wang, T.-K., Dang, Q., et al.: Path planning approach in unknown environment. Int. J. Autom. Comput. **07**(3), 310–316 (2010)
7. Wei, Z., Chen, W., Wang, H., et al.: Manipulator motion planning using flexible obstacle avoidance based on model learning. Int. J. Adv. Robot. Syst. **14**(3), 172988141770393 (2017)
8. Zhao, D., Lv, J., Ji, W.: Smoothing obstacle avoidance path planning based on C-space for harvesting robot. In: Control Conference, pp. 5662–5666. IEEE (2013)
9. Li, G., Tamura, Y., Yamashita, A., et al.: Effective improved artificial potential field-based regression search method for autonomous mobile robot path planning. Int. J. Mechatron. Autom. **3**(3), 141–170 (2013)
10. Pinkam, N., Bonnet, F., Chong, N.Y.: Robot collaboration in warehouse. In: International Conference on Control, Automation and Systems, pp. 269–272. IEEE (2017)
11. Muñoz, P., R-Moreno, M.D., Barrero, D.F.: Unified framework for path-planning and task-planning for autonomous robots. Robot. Auton. Syst. **82**(C), 1–14 (2016)
12. Dong, Y.F., Xia, H.M., Zhou, Y.C.: Disordered and multiple destinations path planning methods for mobile robot in dynamic environment. J. Electr. Comput. Eng. **6**, 1–10 (2016)
13. Khatib, O.: Real-time obstacle avoidance for manipulators and mobile robots. In: Cox, I.J., Wilfong, G.T. (eds.) Autonomous Robot Vehicles. Springer, New York (1986). https://doi.org/10.1007/978-1-4613-8997-2_29

Dynamic Framework for Reconfiguring Computing Resources in the Inter-cloud and Its Application to Genome Analysis Workflows

Tomoya Tanjo[✉], Jingtao Sun, Kazushige Saga, Atsuko Takefusa, and Kento Aida

National Institute of Informatics, Tokyo 101-8430, Japan
{tanjo,sun,saga,takefusa,aida}@nii.ac.jp

Abstract. This paper proposes a framework that dynamically reconfigures an application environment by adding and removing computing resources during runtime. The main idea is that the conditions for the resources used for reconfiguration can be translated into constraints on specifications, such as the number of cores, memory size, and resource location. Our framework consists of two subsystems: an application scheduler, which determines the constraints on specifications for each application, and a resource allocator, which finds resources that satisfy the constraints established by the application scheduler. This structure enables us to apply various reconfiguration strategies by replacing the application scheduler, and also enables us to investigate new allocation strategies for the resource allocator.

As an example of the proposed framework, we developed a reconfiguration module for Galaxy, a workflow manager used in the bioinformatics field. Galaxy can act as an application scheduler by interacting with the reconfiguration module and Galaxy users can take advantage of our reconfiguration framework while using their own interface. The application scheduler applies an embedded strategy to decide when reconfiguration is invoked, whereas it can apply different reconfiguration algorithms to determine constraints on specifications by replacing algorithm modules for reconfiguration. We also describe a scheme for collecting resource metrics, such as CPU usage and memory usage, for use by the reconfiguration algorithms. Finally we conducted preliminary experiments to show the reconfiguration during runtime is necessary because the prediction of resource requirements may fail even if the algorithm uses previous execution records.

Keywords: Cloud computing · Virtual Cloud Provider
Runtime reconfiguration · Bioinformatics · Workflow analysis · Galaxy

1 Introduction

As a result of the improved performance of cloud computing platforms, there is a growing interest in the use of cloud computing for running big data anal-

© Springer Nature Switzerland AG 2018
Y. Xiang et al. (Eds.): IDCS 2018, LNCS 11226, pp. 160–172, 2018.
https://doi.org/10.1007/978-3-030-02738-4_14

ysis applications [5]. Especially, inter-cloud resources, where virtual machines and bare-metal servers (computing resources) from multiple cloud providers are federated [4], are expected to constitute the infrastructure for running big data applications that require distributed data and resources.

However, building and running such applications present several difficulties. First, it is not easy to build an application environment in the inter-cloud due to the difficulties of deploying software and configuring network connections between computing resources operated by different cloud providers. To reduce the difficulty of this problem, we have proposed Virtual Cloud Provider (VCP), which automatically builds an application environment by configuring a virtual network and deploying software over the inter-cloud [12,16]. We previously showed that our VCP could deploy a reproducible experimental environment in different cloud configurations [16].

Second, we have to maintain the application environment by adding or removing computing resources to optimize the environment as the application execution proceeds because the application state can change during runtime. There are many proposals and systems, such as Apache Mesos [13] and HTCondor [7], for selecting appropriate computing resources for an application. However, their reconfiguration strategies mainly aim to maximize the utilization of a given set of computing resources, and they do not consider the structure of the cloud environment, that is, they cannot dynamically add and remove resources. Some cluster managers, such as Kubernetes [14], can add and remove resources in a public cloud by using conventional reconfiguration strategies, such as auto-scaling and auto-healing. However, they only support the conventional reconfiguration strategies based on the state of the computing resources rather than the state of the application.

To solve these problems during runtime, we propose a framework that dynamically adds and removes computing resources for an application as it runs by considering application-specific metrics, such as progress of the workflow execution. The main idea is that we can translate the conditions of the computing resources for reconfiguration into constraints on the specifications of the resources, such as the number of CPU cores, memory size, and location of resources. We call such requirements *constraints on specifications*. In our implementation, the proposed framework consists of two subsystems: an application scheduler and a resource allocator. The application scheduler monitors the application state and defines the constraints on specifications. The resource allocator finds computing resources that satisfy the constraints established by the application scheduler. Our framework is applicable to various reconfiguration strategies for applications by replacing the application scheduler without changing the resource allocator. Furthermore, it can be a good basis for investigating new resource selection algorithms because their input is represented as constraints on specifications, which gives the resource allocator independence from application-specific metrics.

As an example of the proposed framework, we developed a reconfiguration module for Galaxy [3], which is a workflow manager that can be operated via web user interface (UI) and is used in the bioinformatics field. Galaxy can act as an application scheduler by interacting with the reconfiguration module and Galaxy users can take advantage of our reconfiguration framework while using the interface with which they are familiar. The application scheduler applies a reconfiguration strategy that can invoke reconfiguration before each step is executed, while it can apply different reconfiguration algorithms to determine constraints on specifications by replacing the reconfiguration algorithm module.

Finally, we discuss preliminary experiments that compare two reconfiguration algorithms. One is a simple algorithm that uses previous execution records and the other emulates human behavior by searching for the optimal resources for the workflow without knowledge about the workflow tools. The results show that using previous execution records can reduce the monetary costs and it is necessary to dynamically reconfigure the resources because the prediction of resource requirements may fail, even if the algorithm uses previous execution records.

The rest of this paper is organized as follows. Section 2 describes VCP that is the basis of our proposed framework. Section 3 provides an overview of our reconfiguration framework, and Sect. 4 describes an application scheduler for genome analysis workflow using Galaxy. We also describe a metrics collection schemes for the application scheduler. Section 5 describes our preliminary evaluation of several reconfiguration algorithms. Section 6 describes related work and Sect. 7 provides conclusions.

2   Virtual Cloud Provider

VCP is middleware that automatically configures an application environment in the inter-cloud [16]. VCP deploys software, including applications and system operating software, and creates a virtual network to connect computing resources over multiple cloud platforms. VCP achieves fast and easy deployment of software by using Linux container technologies, such as Docker [2]. Furthermore, VCP is able to utilize high-performance L2VPN services, such as SINET5 L2VPLS [15], to create a virtual network. Our proposed framework is designed to reconfigure an application environment configured by VCP.

3   Overview of Reconfiguration Framework

Figure 1 is an overview of our reconfiguration framework, which consists of two subsystems: an application scheduler and a resource allocator. The application scheduler, which is defined for each application, monitors the application state and resources. If the application scheduler detects the need for reconfiguration, then it translates the conditions that should be met by new resources into constraints on resource specifications. The application scheduler sends the constraints on specifications to the resource allocator, which finds the resources that satisfy the given constraints, obtains them from VCP, and sends them to the application scheduler. Finally, the application scheduler reconfigures the application environment using the newly allocated resources.

A resource reconfiguration strategy may highly depend on the target application. Our framework enables various reconfiguration strategies for applications by replacing the application scheduler without changing the resource allocator. Furthermore, we can develop resource selection algorithms for the resource allocator without information about a specific application.

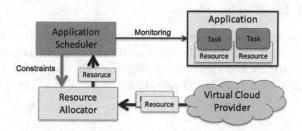

Fig. 1. Overview of dynamic framework for reconfiguring computing resources

3.1 Reconfiguration Mechanism

The application scheduler is defined for each application and reconfigures an application environment by using its embedded strategy. More precisely, the application scheduler:

- Monitors the state of the resources and the application environment they form,
- Detects the need for reconfiguration,
- Translates the conditions that should be met by new resources into constraints on specifications and transmit them to the resource allocator, and
- Takes the resources that satisfy the constraints from the resource allocator and reconfigures the application environment by using the newly allocated resources.

The resource allocator finds and allocates resources that satisfy the constraints provided by the application scheduler. The resource allocator:

- Takes constraints about specification and finds the resources that satisfy the given constraints, and
- Allocates resources obtained from VCP and sends them to the application scheduler.

Example 1. Let us consider a simple example of running the workflow (pipeline) for genome sequencing analysis shown in Fig. 2, where rectangles represent tools and rounded shaded rectangles represent data. Here, we assume that we have execution traces of the tools from previous runs. We may define a naive application scheduler with the following objective and reconfiguration strategy:

- **Objective:** prevent execution error due to memory/storage overflow.

- **Strategy:** collect execution traces for each tool and allocate resources that satisfy the resource demands.

For example, the application scheduler derives the following information about the tool bam2readcount from the previous execution traces:

- It will terminate abnormally due to memory overflow when it runs on a resource with 16 GB or less memory.

In that case, the application scheduler translates the objective of preventing abnormal terminations into the following constraint on specifications: "a resource should have over 16 GB memory." Accordingly, it asks the resource allocator to provide resources that satisfy the constraints.

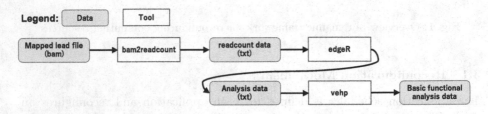

Fig. 2. RNA sequencing analysis workflow

3.2   Constraints on Specifications

As described in the previous section, we can translate the condition of the resources for reconfiguration into constraints on specifications. Now, we consider the following properties of the resources to construct constraints on specifications.

- **Performance specification:**
  This includes the number of CPU cores, memory size, storage size, and instance type.
- **Cost specification:**
  This consists of the monetary cost per hour for a resource for the specific region.
- **Location and provider of the cloud resources:**
  Sometimes we cannot transfer data to other countries or organizations due to the security or privacy issues. For those cases, this property allows us to restrict regions and cloud providers and prevent data transfers to them.

A constraint on specification consists of logical operators (i.e., logical and (∧) and logical or (∨)), arithmetic comparisons between the properties of the resources and immediate values, and objectives to be minimized or maximized.

Example 2. Here is an example of the constraints on specifications:

$$ncores(i1) \geq 3 \qquad \wedge$$
$$region(i2) = Japan \qquad \wedge$$
$$minimize(cost(i1) + cost(i2))$$

The variables $i1$ and $i2$ represent instances that are required by the application scheduler and $ncores(i)$, $region(i)$ and $cost(i)$ represent the number of CPU cores, the region and the cost for instance i respectively. The last expression $minimize(cost(i1) + cost(i2))$ specifies that the application scheduler requires instances that minimize the summation of the costs.

Note that the constraints on specifications can be easily mapped into a Constraint Satisfaction Problem or a Constraint Optimization Problem [11], which consists of a set of constraints on integer variables and floating-point variables. A resource allocator can find appropriate computing resources by using an external constraint solver that finds a solution (assignment to the variables) satisfying all given constraints.

4   Application Scheduler for Genome Analysis Workflows

In bioinformatics, users analyze genomic data by constructing a workflow that consists of existing tools executed with a workflow manager. Therefore, it is expected that performance of workflow execution can be improved by analyzing previous execution records and reconfiguring computing resources for each step to match the configurations using in previous executions.

This section describes an application scheduler for genome analysis workflows that uses the previous execution records. We implemented a reconfiguration module for Galaxy [3].

4.1   Overview

Figure 3 is an overview of the developed application scheduler. It applies an embedded reconfiguration strategy that decides when to invoke reconfiguration, while it can apply different reconfiguration algorithms for determining constraints on specifications by replacing the application scheduler (AS) core ("AS Core" in Fig. 3).

Here we provide the details of environment reconfiguration to execute workflow within our framework. The main idea is that it first determines an allocation plan for all workflow steps and then adjusts the plan before each step is executed by considering the application state.

- Before executing a workflow, the "Prepare Job" step makes allocation plans for all workflow steps to fit the requirements from the user (1 and 2 in Fig. 3).
- Before executing each step, a "Reconfigure Job" step asks the "AS module" whether the plan should be rescheduled to the "AS module" via a REST application interface (3 in Fig. 3).

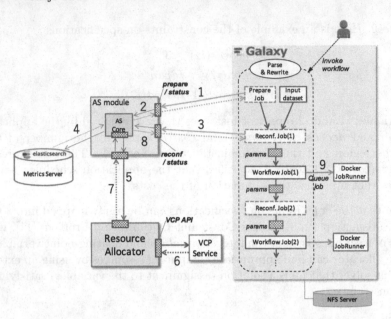

Fig. 3. Application scheduler for genome analysis workflow using Galaxy

- The "AS module" takes workflow information, input parameters, and user requirements from the Galaxy server and determines the constraints on specifications as needed using the "AS core." To determine a fine-grained reconfiguration, the "AS core" may send a query to the metrics server to search for previous execution records (4 in Fig. 3).
- The "AS module" sends constraints on specifications to the resource allocator and acquires computing resources for the next step (5, 6, and 7 in Fig. 3).
- Galaxy takes the allocated resource and uses it to execute the next step (8 and 9 in Fig. 3).

4.2   Metrics Collection Scheme

To achieve fine-grained reconfiguration strategies, it is important to monitor and record the application state periodically. We developed a prototype scheme to collect metrics, which are values that measure the state of application or resources, for containerized genome analysis applications.

Figure 4 is an overview of the metrics collection scheme we developed. It consists of Telegraf,[1] Fluentd,[2] and Elasticsearch[3]. The scheme works as follows:

- First, a Telegraf container collects the metrics of a containerized tool ("Application Container" in Fig. 4), such as CPU usage, memory usage, disk

---

[1] https://www.influxdata.com/time-series-platform/telegraf/.
[2] https://www.fluentd.org.
[3] https://www.elastic.co/products/elasticsearch.

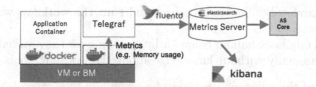

Fig. 4. Metrics collection scheme for dockerized tools

input/output, and network input/output.[4] In the current implementation, we collect all the metrics that can be collected using Telegraf to avoid developing a new AS core module.

- Second, Fluentd sends metrics from Telegraf to an external Elasticsearch server.
- Finally, the AS core examines previous execution records from Elasticsearch for fine-tuning the application environment. An AS core developer can also use a metrics server via Kibana[5] to investigate previous executions to improve their reconfiguration algorithms.

5 Evaluation

As preliminary experiments, we compared the following reconfiguration algorithms that determine constraints on specifications to show the effectiveness of using previous execution records for reconfiguration and to show an example execution that needs reconfiguration during runtime. We restricted the resource allocator to choose only computing resources from instances in the Amazon EC2 cloud [1] to simplify the discussion.

- Record using model (record model):
  The AS core searches for the latest execution record of the same tool (i.e. the same container image) with a similar input size and generates the following constraints on specifications to request a new resource i:

$$memory(i) \geq maximum\_consumption \wedge \quad (1)$$
$$minimize(cost(i)) \quad (2)$$

where $maximum\_consumption$ is the maximum memory consumption in the previous record. The resource allocator then allocates a resource from the instances in Amazon EC2 [1] that satisfies the constraints.
- Trial and error model (trial model):
  The AS core first allocates a resource with less memory and cheaper cost from "general purpose" instances in Amazon EC2. If the execution fails due to memory overflow for some steps, it allocates a resource with more memory

---

[4] For more details, see https://github.com/influxdata/telegraf/tree/master/plugins/inputs/docker.

[5] https://www.elastic.co/products/kibana.

than the previously allocated resource and runs the workflow with the allocated resource.

This model emulates human behavior by searching for the optimal computing resources manually without knowledge about the workflow tools.

We executed the following workflows for assembling the given RNA sequence with a 20-GB input file by applying the above reconfiguration algorithms. HISAT2 and STAR are mapping tools for RNA sequences and cufflinks and stringtie are assemblers for RNA sequences. Note that HISAT2 and STAR require more memory and time than other steps in the workflows.

– Workflow (HISAT2) consists of HISAT2, cufflinks and stringtie (Fig. 5).
– Workflow (STAR) consists of STAR, cufflinks and stringtie. It is almost the same as the workflow in Fig. 5 but it uses STAR instead of HISAT2.

We compared the total execution time of the three steps and the total monetary cost with the assumption of a per-minute charge to finish each workflow. As training data, we stored the metrics for both workflows in an input file with similar size.

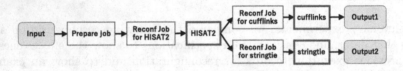

Fig. 5. Workflow for the evaluation consisting of HISAT2, cufflinks and stringtie (intermediate data omitted). Before executing each step, "reconf_job" allocates a computing resource for the next step.

Table 1. Instance types chosen from records and trial models

Instance	vCPU	Memory (GB)	cost ($/hour)
t2.small	1	2.0	0.03
t2.medium	2	4.0	0.06
m4.large	2	6.5	0.12
m4.4xlarge	16	64.0	0.98
r3.2xlarge	8	61	0.80
c3.large	2	3.75	0.12

Tables 2 and 3 show the results of workflow (STAR) for each model, and Tables 4 and 5 show the result of workflow (HISAT2) for each model. Each row shows the monetary cost of each step for the corresponding instance type in the first column. The bottom line shows the total monetary costs for each step and

Table 2. Monetary costs for executing workflow (STAR) with record model.

Instance	STAR	cufflinks	stringtie	Total ($)
r3.2xlarge	0.28	–	–	
c3.large	–	0.03	–	
c3.large	–	–	0.01	
	0.28	0.03	0.01	0.32

Table 3. Monetary costs for executing workflow (STAR) with trial model.

Instance	STAR	cufflinks	stringtie	Total ($)
t2.small	*0.01	–	–	
t2.medium	*0.01	–	–	
m4.large	*0.01	–	–	
m4.4xlarge	0.33	0.22	0.09	
	0.33	0.22	0.09	0.67

*: failure due to memory overflow

Table 4. Monetary costs for executing workflow (HISAT2) with record model.

Instance	HISAT2	cufflinks	stringtie	Total ($)
r3.2xlarge	0.76	–	–	
c3.large	–	0.03	–	
c3.large	–	–	0.01	
	0.76	0.03	0.01	0.80

Table 5. Monetary costs for executing workflow (HISAT2) with trial model.

Instance	HISAT2	cufflinks	stringtie	Total ($)
t2.small	*0.01	–	–	
t2.medium	*0.01	–	–	
m4.large	0.12	0.01	0.05	
	0.14	0.01	0.05	0.20

*: failure due to memory overflow

the total workflow completion. Table 1 shows the instances that were chosen for the record and trial models.

In the case of workflow (STAR), the record model (Table 2) has a lower cost than that of the trial model (Table 3) because it can choose cheaper resources for each step by using previous records while the trial model allocates inappropriate resources that cause memory overflows for STAR several times and it also uses more powerful but more expensive resources for other steps.

In contrast, in the case of workflow (HISAT2), the record model (Table 4) performed worse than the trial model (Table 5). The reason is that HISAT2 shows different memory usage characteristics when we execute it on resources with different memory sizes. For example, when we execute HISAT2 on a resource with small memory size, such as m4.large (with 6.5 GB of memory), it tries to save memory usage to prevent memory overflow. In contrast, when it is executed on a resource with larger memory size, such as r3.2xlarge (with 61 GB of memory), it uses as much memory as it requires. In the experiments, we stored execution records of HISAT2 on a resource with larger memory size. Therefore the record model allocated an expensive resource with too much memory, while the trial model could allocate a cheaper resource with smaller memory size. A similar situation will happen when we analyze unknown genomes or execute workflows that include tools with few metrics. In such a case, we have to reconfigure the rest of the workflow if the current situation may violate user requirements, such as time limits. Therefore it is important to adjust the plan periodically to provide an appropriate application environment.

6   Related Work

6.1   Resource Managers

Krauter *et al.* surveyed resource managers that allocate resources to applications [6]. As described in Sect. 1, their main objective was to maximize the utilization of resources. They did not use a cloud environment in which resources could be dynamically allocated and deallocated as needed. Therefore, a new allocation strategy is needed for the cloud environment, and our framework will be a good basis for investigating new strategies.

SlipStream, which is used in the CYCLONE project [4], can construct and manage an application environment with the inter-cloud. It constructs an application environment by using virtual machines and supports the deployment of software to different cloud platforms. However, it only supports conventional reconfiguration strategies such as auto-scaling that are based on the state of the computing resources.

6.2   Reconfiguration of Workflow Execution

Yu *et al.* [17] surveyed scheduling strategies for workflow execution and reconfiguration, such as failover. We can apply such techniques to our application scheduler by improving the embedded reconfiguration strategy.

Miura *et al.* [8,9] proposed a logic-based approach for a resource selection algorithm. They described specifications of the application using first-order logic and found the appropriate resources by reducing its expression via application of reduction rules defined for each application. We can apply this method to the AS core to make an allocation plan for all steps.

The metrics collection scheme described in Sect. 4.2 lacks application-specific metrics, such as connections between steps of a workflow and information about input genome data. Ohta *et al.* [10] proposed a framework named CWL-metrics to collect metrics of workflows written in the Common Workflow Language (CWL), as well as the runtime metrics of the containerized tools, which we can apply by extending our metrics collection scheme for containers. Metrics of the workflows collected by CWL-metrics can be applied to our reconfiguration algorithms but more work is needed to bridge the gap between CWL and the workflow description language used in Galaxy.

7   Conclusion

In this paper, we described a framework that dynamically reconfigures the application environment by adding and removing computing resources. The framework consists of an application scheduler, which determines the constraints on specifications for each application, and a resource allocator, which finds resources that satisfy the given constraints. We defined a set of constraints on specifications, such as the number of CPU cores, memory size, and resource location to encapsulate the differences between computing resources of various cloud providers.

We also provided an overview of an application scheduler for genome analysis workflow by adding a reconfiguration module to Galaxy. Although the embedded reconfiguration strategy is quite simple, Galaxy users can take advantage of our reconfiguration framework with their own interface (web UI). Sections 4.2 and 5 describes and show the importance of collecting metrics of various type of resources and datasets to investigate and develop fine-grained reconfiguration algorithms.

Currently we have been collecting metrics for various tools with various datasets by cooperating with the bioinformatics community. We will investigate reconfiguration algorithms that use these collected metrics, extend our reconfiguration module for genome analysis workflows to handle other reconfiguration strategies (such as failover), and improve the constraints on resources to handle resources with special devices such as GPU and FPGA. Also, we will investigate the specifications for networks between resources to make our framework applicable to network-intensive applications, such as web applications, and to network-intensive strategies, such as live migrations to other cloud providers.

Acknowledgments. This work was supported by the Japan Science Technology under CREST Grant JPMJCR1501.

References

1. Amazon Web Services Inc.: Amazon EC2. http://aws.amazon.com/ec2/
2. Docker Inc.: Docker. https://www.docker.com/
3. Galaxy: Data intensive biology for everyone. https://galaxyproject.org/
4. Gallico, D., et al.: Cyclone: a multi-cloud federation platform for complex bioinformatics and energy applications (short paper). In: Proceedings of the 2016 5th IEEE International Conference on Cloud Networking (CloudNet), pp. 146–149, October 2016. https://doi.org/10.1109/CloudNet.2016.44
5. Juve, G., et al.: Scientific workflow applications on Amazon EC2. In: Proceedings of the 2009 5th IEEE International Conference on e-Science Workshops, pp. 59–66, December 2009. https://doi.org/10.1109/ESCIW.2009.5408002
6. Krauter, K., Buyya, R., Maheswaran, M.: A taxonomy and survey of grid resource management systems for distributed computing. Softw.: Pract. Exp. **32**(2), 135–164 (2002). https://doi.org/10.1002/spe.432
7. Litzkow, M., Livny, M., Mutka, M.: Condor - a hunter of idle workstations. In: Proceedings of the 8th International Conference of Distributed Computing Systems, pp. 104–111, June 1988
8. Miura, K., Munetomo, M.: A predicate logic-defined specification method for systems deployed by intercloud brokerages. In: 2016 IEEE International Conference on Cloud Engineering Workshop (IC2EW), pp. 172–177, April 2016. https://doi.org/10.1109/IC2EW.2016.47
9. Miura, K., Ohta, T., Powell, C., Munetomo, M.: Intercloud brokerages based on PLS method for deploying infrastructures for big data analytics. In: Proceedings of the 2016 IEEE International Conference on Big Data, BigData 2016, pp. 2097–2102 (2016). https://doi.org/10.1109/BigData.2016.7840836

10. Ohta, T., Tanjo, T., Ogasawara, O.: Accumulating computational resource usage of data analysis workflow to select suitable cloud instance (poster). In: The 2018 Galaxy Community Conference (GCC2018) and Bioinformatics Open Source Conference 2018 (BOSC2018), June 2018
11. Rossi, F., Van Beek, P., Walsh, T.: Handbook of Constraint Programming (Foundations of Artificial Intelligence). Elsevier, New York (2006)
12. Takefusa, A., et al.: Virtual cloud service system for building effective inter-cloud applications. In: IEEE International Conference on Cloud Computing Technology and Science, CloudCom 2017, Hong Kong, 11–14 December 2017, pp. 296–303 (2017). https://doi.org/10.1109/CloudCom.2017.48
13. The Apache Software Foundation: Apache Mesos. http://mesos.apache.org/
14. The Linux Foundation: Kubernetes. https://kubernetes.io/
15. Urushidani, S., et al.: New directions for a Japanese academic backbone network. IEICE Trans. Inf. Syst. **E98.D**(3), 546–556 (2015)
16. Yokoyama, S., et al.: Reproducible scientific computing environment with overlay cloud architecture. In: Proceedings of the 9th IEEE International Conference on Cloud Computing (IEEE Cloud 2016), pp. 774–781, June 2016. https://doi.org/10.1109/CLOUD.2016.0107
17. Yu, J., Buyya, R.: A taxonomy of scientific workflow systems for grid computing. SIGMOD Rec. **34**(3), 44–49 (2005). https://doi.org/10.1145/1084805.1084814

Game-Theoretic Approach to Self-stabilizing Minimal Independent Dominating Sets

Li-Hsing Yen[✉] and Guang-Hong Sun

Department of Computer Science, National Chiao Tung University,
Hsinchu, Taiwan
lhyen@nctu.edu.tw, martian206@gmail.com

Abstract. An independent dominating set (IDS) is a set of vertices in a graph that ensures both independence and domination. The former property asserts that no vertices in the set are adjacent to each other while the latter demands that every vertex not in the set is adjacent to at least one vertex in the IDS. We extended two prior game designs, one for independent set and the other for dominating set, to three IDS game designs where players independently determine whether they should be in or out of the set based on their own interests. Regardless of the game play sequence, the result is a minimal IDS (i.e., no proper subset of the result is also an IDS). We turned the designs into three self-stabilizing distributed algorithms that always end up with an IDS regardless of the initial configurations. Simulation results show that all the game designs produce relatively small IDSs with reasonable convergence rate in representative network topologies.

Keywords: Independent dominating set · Self-stabilization
Distributed algorithm · Game theory

1 Introduction

Given an undirected graph $G = (V, E)$, where V is the vertex set and E is the edge set, $S \subseteq V$ is an *independent set* if no vertices in S are adjacent to one another. Vertex set $S \subseteq V$ is a *dominating set* if every vertex in $V \backslash S$ is adjacent to at least one vertex in S. Vertex set $S \subseteq V$ is an *independent dominating set* (IDS) if S is both independent and dominating. Figure 1 shows an example of IDS.

A dominating set (independent or not) is said to be *minimal* if it contains no proper subset that is also a dominating set. A dominating set (independent or not) is said to be *minimum* if it is of the minimum cardinality. Finding a minimum dominating set is NP-hard [6] for which many heuristics and approximations have been proposed. In this paper, we focus on minimal (rather than minimum) IDS identification in a distributed system. A distributed system consisting of multiple processes interconnected by communication links can

© Springer Nature Switzerland AG 2018
Y. Xiang et al. (Eds.): IDCS 2018, LNCS 11226, pp. 173–184, 2018.
https://doi.org/10.1007/978-3-030-02738-4_15

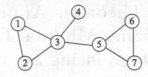

Fig. 1. Both vertex sets {3,6} and {3,7} are IDSs. Vertex set {3,5} is not an IDS because it is not independent.

be modeled as a connected undirected graph where vertices represent processes and edges represent communication links between processes. A dominating set in a distributed system may represent a collection of servers that provide some type of service or resource to adjacent non-server processes. An example is a set of cluster heads in a wireless sensor network that collect sensory data from nearby non-head sensor nodes and transmit the data to a remote base station. Here cluster heads should not hear each other's signal (i.e., independent to each other) to avoid potential transmission collisions and bandwidth contentions.

In this paper, we are interested in the design of self-stabilizing distributed algorithms for IDS identification. After a transient fault, a system is still alive but could be in an arbitrary, possibly illegitimate state. Starting from an arbitrary state, a *self-stabilizing* distributed algorithm takes actions step by step bringing the system back to legitimate states in finite time [3]. Self-stabilization provides a paradigm for designing distributed algorithm that autonomously resolves transient faults without external intervention. There have been some self-stabilizing distributed algorithms that identify minimal dominating sets [7,10,12,15,17] and maximal independent sets [8,11,14,15]. However, to the best knowledge of the authors, there has been no self-stabilizing algorithms for IDS in the literature.

We have designed self-stabilizing distributed algorithms under the framework of game theory [18,19]. Game theory helps us derive stability, correctness, and efficiency properties of the corresponding design. We follow the same thread to derive the solutions, which include three games and associated self-distributed algorithms. One of the games is a modification on the maximal independent set (MIS) game we proposed in [19] and the others are extensions to our previously-proposed minimal dominating set (MDS) game [18].

We conducted simulations to evaluate the proposed approach. Various types of network topologies were considered, including Erdös-Rényi (ER) [5], Watts-Strogatz (WS) [16], and Barabási-Albert (BA) [1] graphs. Simulation results indicate that the approach based on MIS game outperforms the other twos in the size of dominating sets and also the time to stabilization.

The rest of this paper is organized as follows. Section 2 presents background knowledge and related work. The proposed game-theoretic approaches to the minimal IDS are presented in Sect. 3. Section 4 compares the three proposed approaches in terms of the cardinality of IDS and the time to stabilization. Section 5 concludes this paper.

2   Background and Related Work

To clearly define self-stabilization for a system, we need a predicate over all states of the system [13] that differentiates correct or *legitimate* states from incorrect or *illegitimate* states. Concerning our problem, a system state is legitimate if all processes that claim themselves as dominators indeed form a minimal IDS. A distributed algorithm is self-stabilizing with respect to the predicate if, starting from *any* system state, *any* sequence of state transitions leads to a legitimate state and all states following it (if any) are also legitimate. The proposed approach corresponds to *silent* stabilizing [4], meaning that all legitimate states are quiescent states for which no further state transition is possible. Some approaches do not achieve self-stabilization but weak stabilization, which implies the existence of *at least one* sequence of state transitions that leads the system to a legitimate state. Weak stabilization implies stabilization under some reasonable conditions [9].

We assume an asynchronous system, where processes perform computations at arbitrary relative speeds and interleave one another in an arbitrary order. We also assume a *central daemon*, which is a conceptual scheduler that allows only one process to execute at a time. Note this scheduler is not needed at run time. We need this daemon only for analysis and verification purpose.

All the games considered here are dynamic non-cooperative games, where players make decisions by turns (asynchronously) only for their own good. This abstracts the asynchronous nature of process's execution and communication speeds. However, the game model assumes that a player knows the current decisions of all other's when making a decision. This assumption demands some state or communication synchronization facility among processes. Most self-stabilizing approaches assume *shared-variable* inter-process communication model, where a process can update its own variables but not other's. A process can only read variables of its own and all its neighbor's. Therefore, if a process need access some process's variable value to make its decision and that process is not its neighbor, it is possible that the value is not the latest. This limitation may cause problem, as we shall explain later.

Designing self-stabilizing approaches in the framework of game theory is still a new concept with a very few studies in the literature. In [2], selfish processes seeking their own payoffs will form a spanning tree. This approach is weakly stabilizing. We proposed a game-theoretical approach to minimal multi-dominating set in [18], which is a generalization of dominating set by allowing each vertex to demand a specific number of adjacent dominators. Though the game design itself guarantees stability (Nash equilibrium), the corresponding distributed algorithms are weakly stabilizing. The gap comes from the memory access constraint imposed by the shared-variable inter-process communication model.

We also proposed another game-theoretical approach to *maximal* weighted independent sets [19]. An independent set is maximal if there is no proper superset of it that is also an independent set. A weighted independent set aims to maximize the total vertex weight in an independent set. The game designs guarantee stability and are Pareto optimal. The distributed algorithms transformed from the game designs are self-stabilizing.

Theoretically speaking, there are two possible approaches to identifying a minimal IDS in a graph. One is to find a minimal dominating set that is also independent. However, no self-stabilizing dominating set approach ever considers the constraint of independence. The other is to identify a maximal independent set because maximal independent sets are also minimal dominating sets. However, existing approaches to maximal independent sets normally seek large cardinalities. In contrast, when finding a minimal IDS, we usually want to minimize the cardinality of the IDS as much as we can. Existing approaches to maximal independent set thus do not perform well.

3   IDS Games

This section presents three game designs and associated self-stabilizing algorithms as distributed approaches to the IDS problem. The game-theoretic approaches here are extensions to our previous work in [18,19]. We assume a distributed system consisting of n processes (vertices) interconnected by communication links. Each process is a player in the IDS game. Let $P = \{p_1, p_2, \ldots, p_n\}$ be the *player set* that represents all processes in the system. For each $p_i \in P$, p_i's *strategy set* S_i is the collection of all p_i's feasible decisions. Each player p_i has a strategy variable $c_i \in S_i = \{0, 1\}$, which indicates whether p_i is a member of IDS. The *strategy space* of the game $\Sigma = S_1 \times S_2 \times \cdots \times S_n$ is the Cartesian product of all strategy sets. A *strategy profile* $C = (c_1, c_2, \ldots, c_n) \in \Sigma$ is a tuple of n strategies, where $c_i \in S_i$. For a specific p_i, we may express C as $C = (c_i, c_{-i})$, where $c_{-i} = (c_1, c_2, \ldots, c_{i-1}, c_{i+1}, \ldots, c_n)$ denotes the set of all player's strategies excluding c_i. p_i's payoff with respect to a strategy profile C is given by p_i's utility function $u_i(C)$. We define *IDS game* as $\Gamma = [P; \{S_i\}_{i=1}^n; \{u_i(\cdot)\}_{i=1}^n]$. The objective of each player $p_i \in P$ in Γ is $\max_{c_i \in S_i} u_i(c_i, c_{-i})$.

We do not presume any action sequence among players to reflect the non-deterministic nature of process's executions in an asynchronous distributed system. Due to numerous potential state transition sequences, players do not perform backward induction but are rather myopic in the sense that a player chooses a *best response* that maximizes its utility with respect to the current strategy profile. Formally, the best response for player p_i is a function

$$r_i(c_{-i}) = \{c_i \in S_i | \forall c_i' \in S_i : u_i(c_i, c_{-i}) \geq u_i(c_i', c_{-i})\}. \tag{1}$$

Players can change their strategies whenever their current strategies are not their best responses. It is theoretically possible that such strategy changes never stop and the game does not end up with a stable solution. A strategy profile is said to be a *Nash equilibrium* if every player's current strategy is already his best response. A Nash equilibrium corresponds to silent stabilization of a self-stabilizing distributed algorithm. Our goal is to define $u_i(\cdot)$ for every $p_i \in P$ such that Γ always ends up with a Nash equilibrium regardless of game play sequence, which renders a self-stabilizing distributed approach to minimal IDS.

In all the game designs, N_i is the set of players adjacent to p_i. We assume no isolated vertices so $|N_i| \geq 1$ for all p_i.

3.1   MIS-Based IDS Game

The first game modifies the MIS game proposed in [19]. We define the utility of p_i associated with a strategy profile $C = (c_i, c_{-i})$ as

$$u_i(C) = c_i \left(1 - \alpha \sum_{p_j \in L_i} c_j \right), \tag{2}$$

where α is constant greater than 1 and $L_i = \{p_j | p_j \in N_i, \deg(p_j) \geq \deg(p_i)\}$. The game here differs from the prior MIS game in that this game aims to identify an MIS with *small* cardinality (rather than large cardinality as the prior MIS game does.) This can been seen from that fact that any neighboring vertex of p_i in L_i, which has equal or higher node degree than p_i, can prevent p_i from declaring itself as a member of the IDS. The stability of the game can be proved in a way analogous to that for the asymmetric weighted MIS game [19]. In fact, the MIS-based IDS game is a variant of the asymmetric weighted MIS game.

The best response of p_i is $c_i = 0$ if $c_j = 1$ for any $p_j \in L_i$. It would rather choose $c_i = 1$ if $c_j = 0$ for all $p_j \in L_i$. By the guidelines proposed in [19], the game design can be transformed into the following guarded commands:

R1 $c_i \neq 0 \wedge \exists p_j \in L_i, c_j = 1 \rightarrow$
     $c_i := 0$
R2 $c_i \neq 1 \wedge \not\exists p_j \in L_i, c_j = 1 \rightarrow$
     $c_i := 1$

A guarded command is a condition (i.e., a Boolean expression) followed by a statement. The condition and statement are separated by $\rightarrow$. The statement of a command can be executed only when the preceding condition is evaluated true.

Table 1 shows a possible game play sequence of the MIS-based IDS game for the network topology shown in Fig. 1. Observe that the game ends up with an IDS $\{3, 7\}$, at which time no player has the incentive to further change his strategy.

3.2   Symmetric MDS-Based IDS Game

The second game is a modification of the MDS game proposed in [18]. Formally, given $C = (c_1, c_2, \ldots, c_n)$, define

$$v_i(C) = \sum_{p_j \in M_i} c_j \tag{3}$$

Table 1. A possible game play sequence of the MIS-based IDS game

Step	c_1	c_2	c_3	c_4	c_5	c_6	c_7
0	1	1	0	0	0	1	0
1	1	1	0	0	1	1	0
2	1	1	1	0	1	1	0
3	1	0	1	0	1	1	0
4	1	0	1	0	1	0	0
5	1	0	1	0	0	0	0
6	1	0	1	0	0	0	1
7	0	0	1	0	0	0	1

for each player p_i, where $M_i = N_i \cup \{p_i\}$. Also define $g_i(C)$ as

$$g_i(C) = \begin{cases} \alpha & \text{if } v_i(C) = 1 \\ 0 & \text{otherwise,} \end{cases} \tag{4}$$

where $\alpha > 0$ is a constant. Define

$$w_i(C) = \sum_{p_j \in N_i} c_i c_j \gamma, \tag{5}$$

where $\gamma > n\alpha$ is a constant. The utility function of p_i is defined as

$$u_i(C) = \begin{cases} \left(\sum_{p_j \in M_i} g_j(C) \right) - \beta - w_i(C) & \text{if } c_i = 1 \\ 0 & \text{otherwise,} \end{cases} \tag{6}$$

where β is another constant such that $0 < \beta < \alpha$.

When two neighboring players are both in the set, both players will have negative utilities because $\gamma > n\alpha$. Any of them can get a positive gain by leaving the set. However, none of them has the priority over the other to stay in the set. Which one will stay is pure stochastic. This is why this game is referred to as symmetric game. Later we will present an asymmetric design.

The stability of the symmetric MDS-based IDS game can be proved by showing that this game is an exact potential game, i.e., there exists an exact potential function $\pi(C)$ such that $\pi(c_i^*, c_{-i}) - \pi(c_i, c_{-i}) = u_i(c_i^*, c_{-i}) - u_i(c_i, c_{-i})$ whenever an player p_i changes its strategy from c_i to c_i^*.

Theorem 1. *The symmetric MDS-based IDS game is an exact potential game.*

Proof. The function

$$\pi(C) = \left(\sum_{j=1}^{n} \sum_{k=0}^{v_j(C)} h_j(k) \right) - \eta(C), \tag{7}$$

where

$$h_i(k) = \begin{cases} \alpha & \text{if } k = 1 \\ 0 & \text{otherwise} \end{cases} \tag{8}$$

and

$$\eta(C) = \beta \sum_{j=1}^{n} c_j + \frac{1}{2} \sum_{j=1}^{n} w_j(C), \tag{9}$$

is an exact function. If $(c_i, c_i^*) = (0, 1)$,

$$\pi(C^*) - \pi(C) = \sum_{p_j \in M_i} g_j(C^*) - \beta$$

$$= u_i(C^*) - u_i(C). \tag{10}$$

If $(c_i, c_i^*) = (1, 0)$,

$$\pi(C^*) - \pi(C) = - \sum_{p_j \in M_i} g_j(C) + \beta + |\Omega_i|\gamma$$

$$= u_i(C^*) - u_i(C). \tag{11}$$

□

In an exact potential game, Nash equilibrium always exists and can be found by player's individual movements. In fact, exact potential games enjoy the *finite improvement property*, which means every game play sequence is finite.

Table 2. A possible game play sequence of the symmetric MDS-based IDS game

Step	c_1	c_2	c_3	c_4	c_5	c_6	c_7
0	1	1	0	0	0	1	0
1	1	1	0	<u>1</u>	0	1	0
2	<u>0</u>	1	0	1	0	1	0

Table 2 shows a possible game play sequence of the symmetric MDS-based IDS game running on the network topology shown in Fig. 1. Here no node has a priority other any others. Therefore, p_3 cannot become an MIDS member when some of its neighbors (i.e. p_4) is already in the set.

There are extra considerations when transforming the game design into guarded commands. When making decisions, p_i has to know the value of $v_j(C)$ for all $p_j \in M_i$. This involves the access of c_k for $p_k \in M_j$. However, with the shared-variable inter-process communication model, p_i cannot read the value of c_k for all $p_k \in M_j \backslash M_i$. To overcome this limitation, each process p_i maintains an auxiliary variable d_i to denote the current domination status of p_i. More explicitly,

$$d_i = \begin{cases} \text{UNDER} & \text{if } |\{p_j | p_j \in M_i, c_j = 1\}| < 1, \\ \text{EQUAL} & \text{if } |\{p_j | p_j \in M_i, c_j = 1\}| = 1, \\ \text{OVER} & \text{if } |\{p_j | p_j \in M_i, c_j = 1\}| > 1. \end{cases} \tag{12}$$

However, when $p_j \in M_i$ changes c_j, p_j cannot update d_i as a constraint imposed by the shared-variable inter-process communication model. It is p_i itself that should update d_i. The result is a distributed algorithm consisting of six rules (R1–R6) in each process p_i as shown below.

R1 $|\{p_j|p_j \in M_i, c_j = 1\}| < 1 \wedge d_i \neq \text{UNDER}$
    $\rightarrow d_i := \text{UNDER}$

R2 $|\{p_j|p_j \in M_i, c_j = 1\}| = 1 \wedge d_i \neq \text{EQUAL}$
    $\rightarrow d_i := \text{EQUAL}$

R3 $|\{p_j|p_j \in M_i, c_j = 1\}| > 1 \wedge d_i \neq \text{OVER}$
    $\rightarrow d_i := \text{OVER}$

R4 $\exists p_j \in N_i, c_j = 1 \wedge c_i \neq 0$
    $\rightarrow c_i := 0$

R5 $\not\exists p_j \in N_i, c_j = 1 \wedge \exists p_j \in M_i, d_j = \text{UNDER} \wedge c_i \neq 1$
    $\rightarrow c_i := 1$

R6 $\not\exists p_j \in N_i, c_j = 1 \wedge \forall p_j \in M_i, d_j = \text{OVER} \wedge c_i \neq 0$
    $\rightarrow c_i := 0$

The first three commands are for the maintenance of d_i. The last three commands implement player's best response. It is possible that the conditions of two commands are both true at the same time. In that case, we assume that any one of them and only one of them can be executed. As a consequence, the value of c_i and d_i may be inconsistent at some instant. An example is $c_i = 1$ but $d_i = \text{UNDER}$. Note that the problem remains even if p_i updates d_i whenever it updates c_i because the value of d_i also depends on c_j of another neighbor $p_j \in N_i$. Though the game design itself ensures stability, this memory access constraint makes the game implementation weakly-stabilizing [18].

3.3 Asymmetric MDS-Based IDS Game

The symmetric MDS-based IDS game does not give priority to any vertex to stay in the set when one of two neighboring vertices should leave the set to preserve independence. However, giving priority to the vertex with higher degree, which is also used in the design of the MIS-based IDS game, may hopefully yield fewer set members. For this reason, we modified the symmetric MDS-based IDS game to incorporate the degree-based priority scheme. The result is referred to as asymmetric MDS-based IDS game.

The only difference with the symmetric MDS-based game is the definition of $w_i(\cdot)$ function. When determining whether p_i should leave the set, p_i only cares those that has a degree higher than p_i. Therefore,

$$w_i(C) = \sum_{p_j \in L_i} c_i c_j \gamma. \tag{13}$$

Table 3 shows a possible game play sequence of the asymmetric MDS-based IDS game with the network topology shown in Fig. 1. Here high-degree vertices

Table 3. A possible game play sequence of the asymmetric MDS-based IDS game

Step	c_1	c_2	c_3	c_4	c_5	c_6	c_7
0	1	1	0	0	0	1	0
1	1	1	0	0	1	1	0
2	1	1	1	0	1	1	0
3	0	1	1	0	1	1	0
4	0	1	1	0	1	0	0
5	0	1	1	0	0	0	0
6	0	1	1	0	0	1	0
7	0	0	1	0	0	1	0

like p_5 and p_3 can join the set even if some of their neighbors is already in the set.

Concerning the corresponding distributed algorithm, R1 to R3 remain unchanged. R4 to R6 are changed to

R4 $\exists p_j \in L_i, c_j = 1 \wedge c_i \neq 0$
    $\rightarrow c_i := 0$
R5 $\nexists p_j \in L_i, c_j = 1 \wedge \exists p_j \in M_i, d_j = \text{UNDER} \wedge c_i \neq 1$
    $\rightarrow c_i := 1$
R6 $\nexists p_j \in L_i, c_j = 1 \wedge \forall p_j \in M_i, d_j = \text{OVER} \wedge c_i \neq 0$
    $\rightarrow c_i := 0$

To see the stability of the asymmetric MDS-based IDS game, observe that the degree-based priority together with some tie-breaking information such as node identifier is transitive and asymmetric. Therefore, it is impossible to find any game play sequence that contains cycles. Since the strategy space Σ is finite, the acyclic property ensures stability.

4   Simulation Results

We measured the quality of IDS by its size and the time efficiency of self-stabilizing algorithms by the number of moves they take to reach stability. We conducted simulations to study the performance of all the proposed game-theoretic approaches. The quality results are compared with the optimum that was found by brute force. We considered representative network topologies generated by three models in the simulations: ER, WS, and BA. We fixed the number of vertices to be 30. Since self-stabilizing algorithms are supposed to start from arbitrary states, we assigned randomly generated values to variables (c_i's were randomly assigned either 0 or 1 and d_i's were either UNDER, EQUAL, or OVER with equal probability). Each average was obtained over 1000 runs.

The ER model [5] generates random graphs. In a random graph, whether an edge exists between a pair of vertices is an independent event with probability

p_e. We varied the value of p_e from 0.1 to 0.5. The result is shown in Fig. 2. As p_e increases, the expected number of edge also increases and the graph become denser. As a result, smaller IDS can be found with larger p_e value.

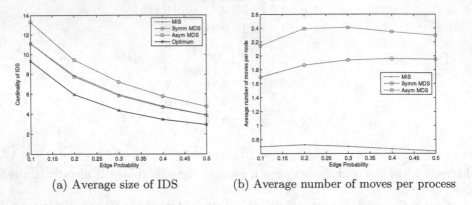

(a) Average size of IDS   (b) Average number of moves per process

Fig. 2. Performance in ER graphs (30 vertices)

The comparisons among the three proposed approaches reveal that the MIS-based IDS game (denoted by 'MIS') and the asymmetric MDS-based IDS game (denoted by 'Asym MDS') performed nearly the same. The symmetric MDS-based IDS game (denoted by 'Symm MDS') was inferior to the others. This is justifiable because Symm MDS does not favor vertices with higher node degree. In terms of convergence time, MIS performs the best, followed by Symm MDS and then Asym MDS. This is because the latter two need extra moves to update d_i's.

The WS model [16] builds a small-world network by first creating a regular network, where each vertex has exactly n_k links connecting to its n_k nearest neighbors. The regular network is then converted to a small-world network by rewiring each link with a probability p_r to a randomly chosen vertex. We varied the value of p_r from 0 to 0.8. The result is shown in Fig. 3.

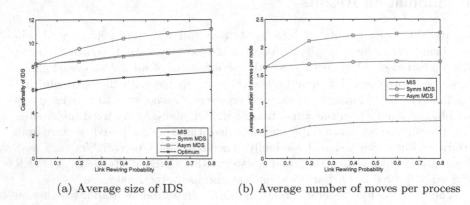

(a) Average size of IDS   (b) Average number of moves per process

Fig. 3. Performance in WS graphs (30 vertices)

When p_r increases, the variance of node degree increases. As a result, the size of IDS also increases. We found that Asym MDS performed slightly better than MIS while Symm MDS still performed the worst. In terms of convergence time, MIS performed the best, followed by Symm MDS and then Asym MDS.

The BA model [1] generates a scale-free network that exhibits a power-law distribution of node degrees. It starts with a small number (m_0) of connected vertices. At every round, a new vertex x with m ($m \leq m_0$) incident edges are added to the network. The probability of a new edge connecting x and an existing vertex y is proportional to the node degree of y.

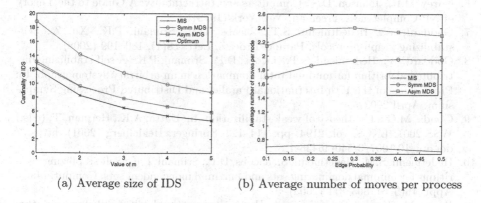

(a) Average size of IDS   (b) Average number of moves per process

Fig. 4. Performance in BA graphs (30 vertices)

Figure 4 shows the performance of the proposed approaches with respect to m. As m increases, the average node degree also increases. Consequently, smaller IDS can be identified. In general, the result here is similar to that in Fig. 3. MIS performed nearly the same as Asym MDS in terms of IDS cardinality, but outperformed the counterparts in terms of the time to convergence.

5   Conclusions

We have proposed three self-stabilizing distributed algorithms for minimal IDS in the framework of game theory. The first one based on MIS game is simple and guarantees self-stabilization. The second and the third ones based on MDS game are more complicated and can only guarantee weak stabilization. Simulation results show that the MIS-based approach is not inferior to any others in terms of the cardinality of IDS and outperforms all others in terms of the time to stabilization.

Possible extensions to the proposed approaches include (1) independent multi-dominating sets, where different nodes may demand different degrees of domination, and (2) weighted IDS, where nodes have weights and we want to minimize total weight of the IDS. Another way is to extend the self-stabilizing algorithms to run under distributed and synchronous daemons.

References

1. Barabási, A.L., Albert, R.: Emergence of scaling in random networks. Science **286**, 509–512 (1999)
2. Cohen, J., Dasgupta, A., Ghosh, S., Tixeuil, S.: An exercise in selfish stabilization. ACM Trans. Auton. Adapt. Syst. **3**(4), 15:1–15:12 (2008)
3. Dijkstra, E.W.: Self-stabilizing systems in spite of distributed control. Commun. ACM **17**(11), 643–644 (1974)
4. Dolev, S., Gouda, M.G., Schneider, M.: Memory requirements for silent stabilization. Acta Informatica **36**, 447–462 (1999)
5. Erdös, P., Rényi, A.: On random graphs I. Publ. Math. Debr. **6**, 290–297 (1959)
6. Garey, M.R., Johnson, D.S.: Computers and Intractability: A Guide to the Theory of NP-Completeness. Freeman, New York (1979)
7. Goddard, W., Hededtniemi, S.T., Jacobs, D.P., Srimani, P.K., Xu, Z.: Self-stabilizing graph protocols. Parallel Process. Lett. **18**(1), 189–199 (2008)
8. Goddard, W., Hedetniemi, S.T., Jacobs, D.P., Srimani, P.K.: A self-stabilizing distributed algorithm for minimal total domination in an arbitrary system graph. In: Proceedings of the 17th International Parallel and Distributed Processing Symposium, April 2003
9. Gouda, M.G.: The theory of weak stabilization. In: Datta, A.K., Herman, T. (eds.) WSS 2001. LNCS, vol. 2194, pp. 114–123. Springer, Heidelberg (2001). https://doi.org/10.1007/3-540-45438-1_8
10. Hedetniemi, S.M., Hedetniemi, S., Jacobs, D.P., Srimani, P.K.: Self-stabilizing algorithms for minimal dominating sets and maximal independent sets. Comput. Math. Appl. **46**(5–6), 805–811 (2003)
11. Ikeda, M., Kamei, S., Kakugawa, H.: A space-optimal self-stabilizing algorithm for the maximal independent set problem. In: Proceedings of the 3rd International Conference on Parallel and Distributed Computing, Applications and Technologies (2002)
12. Kakugawa, H., Masuzawa, T.: A self-stabilizing minimal dominating set algorithm with safe convergence. In: International Parallel and Distributed Processing Symposium, April 2006
13. Kshemkalyani, A.D., Singhal, M.: Distributed Computing: Principles, Algorithms, and Systems, p. 634. Cambridge University Press, Cambridge (2008)
14. Shukla, S.K., Rosenkrantz, D.J., Ravi, S.S.: Observations on self-stabilizing graph algorithms for anonymous networks. In: Proceedings of the 2nd Workshop on Self-Stabilizing Systems (1995)
15. Turau, V.: Linear self-stabilizing algorithms for the independent and dominating set problems using an unfair distributed scheduler. Inf. Process. Lett. **103**(3), 88–93 (2007)
16. Watts, D.J., Strogatz, S.H.: Collective dynamics of 'small-world' networks. Nature **393**, 440–442 (1998)
17. Xu, Z., Hedetniemi, S.T., Goddard, W., Srimani, P.K.: A synchronous self-stabilizing minimal domination protocol in an arbitrary network graph. In: Das, S.R., Das, S.K. (eds.) IWDC 2003. LNCS, vol. 2918, pp. 26–32. Springer, Heidelberg (2003). https://doi.org/10.1007/978-3-540-24604-6_3
18. Yen, L.H., Chen, Z.L.: Game-theoretic approach to self-stabilizing distributed formation of minimal multi-dominating sets. IEEE Trans. Parallel Distrib. Syst. **25**(12), 3201–3210 (2014)
19. Yen, L.H., Huang, J.Y., Turau, V.: Designing self-stabilizing systems using game theory. ACM Trans. Auton. Adapt. Syst. **11**(3), 18:1–18:27 (2016). Article no. 18

Towards Social Signal Separation Based on Reconstruction Independent Component Analysis

Hoang Long Nguyen[1], Khac-Hoai Nam Bui[1], Nayoung Jo[1],
Jason J. Jung[1(✉)], and David Camacho[2]

[1] Chung-Ang University, Seoul, Korea
longnh238@gmail.com, hoainam.bk2012@gmail.com,
joenayoung2@gmail.com, j2jung@gmail.com
[2] Universidad Autonoma de Madrid, Madrid, Spain
david.camacho@uam.es

Abstract. We all know that the ratio of social data noise is pretty significant. Therefore, tackling with noise problem is always obtained attention from data scientists. In this paper, we present a research of using reconstruction independent component analysis algorithm for blind separation social event signals from their mixtures (i.e., mixture is the combination of source signal and noise). This issue can be categorized as *cocktail party problem*. Despite *cocktail party problem* is a classical topic, however, dealing with social media data can be considered as a new research trend. From the case study with two events on Twitter, we demonstrate that our approach is quite promising. Further, our work can be applied for recommendation systems, or is used as a pre-processing step for other studies (e.g., focus search and event detection).

Keywords: Reconstruction independent component analysis
Signal separation · Social event · SocioScope framework

1 Introduction

Blind source separation (BSS) is the problem of discovering source signals from mixtures in which we do not have any information about sources and how they are mixed. There are various applications which are related to BSS. It can be applied for acoustics different sound sources [11], radio communications [4,6], image processing [7,16], and brain imaging data [1,13,21]. Nevertheless, making use of BSS idea to handle social media issue, particularly social event, is still a new subject matter.

In the era of big data, every human activity is tended to conduct on-line [10]. Especially, with the support of social networking service, this seems more convenient. Social networking services are web applications which support users to build social relations and share digital contents (e.g., text, image, audio, and video). Whenever our society has activities, users quickly respond by sharing it

© Springer Nature Switzerland AG 2018
Y. Xiang et al. (Eds.): IDCS 2018, LNCS 11226, pp. 185–196, 2018.
https://doi.org/10.1007/978-3-030-02738-4_16

to social networking services. Therefore, events on social networking services happens contemporaneously. With the development of smart devices, social events even occur real-time. Many researchers are interested in studying about discovering social events on social networking services [2,5,8,9,23] by applying diverse techniques (e.g., supervised approaches [19], unsupervised approaches [17,18], and hybrid approaches [3]). However, we find out that there are lack of studies about filtering noise from social events.

We realized that a practical issue of social event is very similar with famous cocktail-party problem in BSS. In social networking services, data is publicized by individuals, therefore, it is informal and contains lots of noise. One of the noise is created by the use of failure hashtags. Hashtag is a type of metadata which is used on social networking service to allow users to group data as specific content. Instead of using a particular hashtag for mentioning about an event, user may use general or ambiguous one. This causes many irrelevant data of an event because it may come from others.

Independent component analysis (ICA) is an effective algorithm to solve the aforementioned problems. However, original ICA also has some limitations: (i) depending on pre-processing step which is call as whitening, and (ii) requiring constrained optimizers to solve regularization problem. [12] overcomes above problem by providing reconstruction independent component analysis (RICA) which is the modification of ICA. By applying this method into a real case study, we prove that RICA can well support separating social event signals from noise.

In this section, we give short introduction about the research target of this study. The remainder of this paper is constructed as follows. In Sect. 2 we define our main problem and provide essential formula. Section 3 mentions about how to apply RICA algorithm to separate social events signals from noise. Further, we discuss about a case study in Sect. 4 about two summit events to demonstrate our research. Finally, we gine the conclusion and plan some future work in Sect. 5.

2   Problem Definition

Our goal is to separate noise from social event signals in this study. In order to simply explain about the algorithm in Sect. 3, we conducted the formulation to describe about crucial definitions in this section.

Definition 1 (Social Data). *Social data D is objective facts about events which happen in our society. It is contributed by individuals through social media activities. Social data can be formulated as:*

$$D_i = \langle E_i, S_i, P_i \rangle \tag{1}$$

$$P_i = \langle \tau_i, \varsigma_i, \lambda_i, \varepsilon_i \rangle \tag{2}$$

where E_i is used to denote for an entity who publishes social data D_i, S_i is the social networking services at where D_i is created and P_i is the social properties of this social data including topic τ_i, content ς_i, location λ_i, and time ε_i.

Social data is categorized as social tacit data and social explicit data [20]. Social tacit data is generated through experience and is stored in human mind (e.g., experience, and thinking). On the other hand, social explicit data is visible as printed and electronic materials (e.g., text, audio, and video). We limit social data which is used to define events in this paper as social explicit text data due to its ability to reflect social events through the use of words.

Definition 2 (Social text). *Social text is a type of social data in which its content D_{ς_i} is represented by a sequence of words W_i. The length of social text is diverse depending on particular social networking service.*

$$T_i = \langle D_i \mid D_{\varsigma_i} = W \rangle \tag{3}$$

$$W = \{w_i \mid w_i \in \mathscr{T}, \ w_i \in \mathscr{M} \text{ or } w_i \in \mathscr{H}\} \tag{4}$$

where w_i denotes for i-th word that belongs to social text T_i, types of w_i can be a term $\mathscr{T}$, a mention $\mathscr{M}$ or a hashtag $\mathscr{H}$.

Every time there is an activity occurs in our life, individuals respond by distributing social text to social networking services. Therefore, social networking services can mirror our life through their events.

Definition 3 (Event). *An event E_i is a specific activity which occurs in our society. It includes a set of social text T which mentions about same topic in a duration of time as follows:*

$$E = \langle T, O, I \rangle \tag{5}$$

$$T = \{T_i \mid T_{\tau_i} \in O, T_{\varepsilon_i} \in [I_s, I_e]\} \tag{6}$$

where O is topic of E, I is duration time of E, T_i is i-th social text that belongs to event E, I_s is the start time and I_e is the end time of this event E.

Hashtag is a technique to classify social text into a specific topic. They are supported by many social networking services such as Facebook, Twitter, Instagram. Hashtag is a word which starts by # (e.g., #TrumpKimSummit includes social text which discusses about the summit between American President Donald Trump meet with North Korean leader Kim Jong-un on 12th June 2018 in Singapore). A hashtag is considered as effective using if it is unique, related, and memorable. Making use of hashtag properties, social text topic is defined as follows:

Definition 4 (Social text topic). *Social text topic T_{τ_i} is determined by the set of hashtags in which social text T_i contains.*

$$T_{\tau_i} = \{w_i \mid w_i \in T_i \text{ and } w_i \in \mathscr{H}\} \tag{7}$$

Figure 1 represents a social text that we collected from Twitter. This social text is related to Trump Kim summit event in Singapore. Topic of this social text T_{τ_i} is the set of hashtag $\mathscr{H} = \{\#TrumpKimSummit, \#Cartoon, \#TrumpKimMeeting, \#DonaldTrump, \#KimJongUn, \#Trump \#Singapore, \#SingaporeSummit, \#Summit \#Haircut\}$. Based on this definition of social text topic, we define what is event topic as follows.

Fig. 1. A social text belongs to Trump-Kim summit event.

Definition 5 (Event Topic). *Event topic E_O is indicated by hashtags which are extracted from social text of this event.*

$$E_{o_i} = \{T_\tau \mid \forall i, j, \ T_{\tau_i} \neq T_{\tau_j}\} \tag{8}$$

However, event topic is often contains a lot of noise or counter-factual information as a result of they're self-generated by individuals. In Fig. 1, you may see some irrelevant hashtags (e.g., *#Cartoon* and *#Haircut*). Besides, some hashtags are ambiguous because they are not concentrated on a particular topic and may involved with other events (e.g., *#KimJongUn, #Trump #Singapore, #Summit*). For example, *#Trump* involved with other events that President Trump takes part in. Furthermore, people may use lots of hashtags in a social text to increase its ranking as shown in Fig. 1. For this reason, this social text is distributed to many events. In this study, we focus on filtering out overlap hashtags between two events E_a and E_b, especially two events have similar topic and occur at similar time. Because two events share similar topic, users may use hashtags that belongs to both events. In addition, they also have higher probability to create noise to each other.

Definition 6 (Event Noise). *Given a set of social text which belongs to both event E_a and event E_b, these social text is considered as event noise because it appears in both event signals.*

$$N_{E_a, E_b} = \{T_i \mid T_i \in E_a, T_i \in E_B, \exists w_i, w_i \in T_i, w_i \in E_{o_a} \cap E_{o_b}, w_i \in \mathcal{H}\} \tag{9}$$

where N_{E_a, E_b} denotes for the set of noise social text between event E_a and event E_b, T_i is a noise social text, w_i is a hashtag that belongs to social text T_i, E_{o_a} and E_{o_b} are used to denote for event topics of E_a and E_b respectively.

Our task in this paper is to separate event signals of event E_a and event E_b from the noise of by applying the reconstruction independent component analysis which will be explained in detail in Sect. 3.

3   Separating Social Event Signals from Noise with RICA

In this paper, we select RICA as the method to solve our problem. RICA is a computational method to solve the blind separation source problem. In this issue, the goal is to recover source signals from observed signals (i.e., observed signals is mixed from source signals and noise). It modified original ICA by lowering sensitiveness to whitening and removing orthogonality constrain optimizer to obtain better performance. This algorithm also can solve the overcomplete problem, however, we are not going to discuss about the overcomplete issue in this study.

Without lost of generality, we explain in detail how to separate two source signals from two observed signals. For the problem of n signals, all the process is conducted similarly. Giving two events E_a and E_b that require to filtered out noise from their temporal signals, our propose method is processed as follows: (i) generating temporal signals of two events by calculating its distribution by time, and (ii) ascertaining temporal signals from previous step is used as inputs for RICA algorithm for separating them from noise. Figure 2 represents the main work-flow of our procedure.

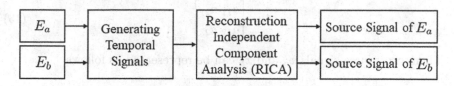

Fig. 2. The main work-flow.

At first, the duration time of two events E_{I_a} and E_{I_b} is divided into time windows. The number of time windows is also the number of dimension of temporal signal. In this research, we select 10,000 as the number of time windows. At each point, the value x_i is calculated as follows:

$$x_i = \sum_{j=t_s}^{t_e} \| T_j \| \tag{10}$$

where t_s is the start time of i-th time windows, t_e is the end time of this time windows, and $\| T_j \|$ is the number of social text at j-th time point.

Then, temporal signals of two events can be expressed as follows:

$$x_a = \{x_{a_1}, x_{a_2}, \ldots, x_{a_n}\} \tag{11}$$

$$x_b = \{x_{b_1}, x_{b_2}, \ldots, x_{b_n}\} \tag{12}$$

In order to apply RICA into two signals, they must have same length. There are two solutions for this problem: (i) selecting fixed number of time windows as we mentioned, and (ii) scaling signals to the same dimension by using interpolative functions as proposed by [14]. Figure 3 represents the principle of RICA algorithm.

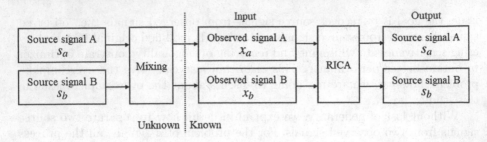

Unknown ⫶ Known

Fig. 3. RICA modeling.

Two observer signals consist of their sources signal and noise. Let's assume that matrix A is mixing coefficients. These coefficients are used to express how two sources signals are mixed together.

$$A = \begin{bmatrix} a_{11} & a_{21} \\ a_{12} & a_{22} \end{bmatrix} \tag{13}$$

Then, two source signals x_a and x_b can be represented as follows.

$$\begin{aligned} x_a &= a_{11}s_a + a_{12}s_b \\ x_b &= a_{21}s_a + a_{22}s_b \end{aligned} \tag{14}$$

where s_a and s_b are source signals, and a_{11}, a_{12}, a_{21}, a_{22} are mixing coefficients.

To solve RICA problem, our task is to estimate value of W which is the transformation matrix of A. From W, we can easily obtain source signals A as follows.

$$s = Wx \text{ with } W = A^T \tag{15}$$

This algorithm conducts the estimating by minimizing the cost function as follows.

$$minimize \ W, \ f = \frac{\lambda!}{2} \sum_{i=1}^{2} \| W^T W x_i - x_i \|_2^2 + \sum_{i=1}^{2} \sum_{j=1}^{k} g(W_j x_i) \tag{16}$$

where λ is the regularization coefficient parameter, we select $\lambda = 0.1$, and g is a contrast function, and k is the number of dimension.

There are various possible contrast functions which we can choose for the task of optimization:

$$g(u) = \frac{1}{2} log(cosh(2u)) \tag{17}$$

$$g(u) = -exp\frac{-u^2}{2} \tag{18}$$

$$g(u) = -exp\sqrt{x^2 + 10^{-8}} \tag{19}$$

where Eq. (17) is logcosh function, Eq. (18) is exponential function, and Eq. (19) is square root function.

The minimization is conducted by using Broyden-Fletcher-Goldfarb-Shanno quasi-Newton optimizer [22]. The optimization will iterate until the difference current value and previous value is smaller than a defined threshold, or the norm of the gradient at current point is less than τ, with τ is calculated as follows.

$$\tau = max(1, min(\| f \|, \| g(u)_0 \|)) \tag{20}$$

where $\| f \|$ is norm of cost function f, and $\| g(u)_0 \|$ is infinity norm of initial gradient.

Result is the minimal matrix W. From this matrix, we can recover source signals by applying it into Eq. (15).

4   Case Study with Social Events on Twitter

We use our SocioScope framework [15] for conducting the experiment. We select Twitter as the data source for this case study. Twitter is a popular social networking service that allows people to share their short messages (140 characters), which is called as tweets, from multiple devices (i.e., computer or smart devices) [14]. Because of this convenience, Twitter receives more than 8,000 tweets per second as a statistics from internetlivestats[1] in June 2018.

Table 1. Top hashtags of two summit events.

Event	Hashtags
G7 summit	#g7summit, #g7, #g72018, #g7charlevoix, #canada, #trudeau, #macron, #americafirst, #g7canada, #sundaymorning, #g6plusone, #cartoon, #theresistance, #bengarrison, #trump'ssummit, #trumpkimsummit, #trump, #summit, #presidenttrump, #maga
Trump-Kim summit	#trumpkimsummit, #kimjongun, #singaporesummit, #trumpkim, #peace, #trumpkimmeeting, #dennisrodman, #singapore, #interkoreansummit, #denuclearization, #kim, #tictocnews, #breaking, #northkorea, #worldpeace, #interkoreansummit, #trump, #summit, #presidenttrump, #maga

SocioScope supports crawling data from Twitter by passing the list of keywords. Besides, we can also filter data by geography or time constrain as shown in Fig. 4. As we mentioned before, two events must share similar topical, and

---

[1] http://www.internetlivestats.com/.

Fig. 4. Data collection by using SocioScope framework.

temporal property in order to create noise to each other. Due to this reason, we choose the G7 summit event (9th June 2018) and the Trump-Kim summit event (12th June 2018) as our case study. These two events are international meetings between heads of government.

For the G7 summit event, we first crawl data by using hashtag #g7summit. To identify the next hashtag, we split every tweet using unigram model. Then, we calculate the distribution of hashtag and select the highest distribution one as the next hashtag. The crawling process is stopped until we finish collecting data with top 20 hashtags. This task is conducted similarly with Trump-Kim

Fig. 5. The use of an ambiguous hashtag.

event. Table 1 shows top 20 hashtags of each event. Finally, we obtained 288,121 tweets for the G7 summit event and 1,191,536 tweets for the Trump-Kim summit event.

From Table 1, we recognize that there are some hashtags which belong to both events (e.g., #trumpkimsummit, #trump, #summit, #presidenttrump, #maga). This is reasonable because these two events share similar topic. If users do not use specific hashtags, they will be very easy to become failure one. Figure 5 shows an example of an ambiguous hashtag. Because the keyword #summit is not specific to an event, some users use it to mention about the G7 summit event while some other users use it to mention about the Trump-Kim summit event. These social text is consider as event noise.

From the set of tweets of two events, we generate their temporal signals which are used as input for RICA algorithm. The results is shown in Figs. 6 and 7. We use blue color to denote for observed signals and red color for source signals. We see that the algorithm discovered noise which happens at the time from 11th June 2018 to 12th June 2018. This is the duration time between two events. At this time, the G7 summit event has just finished and the Trump-Kim summit is going to happen. Hence, users tend to discuss about both events.

However, this result shows that RICA algorithm is not sensitive at low distribution time point. In Fig. 6, this method detects some noise at the time from 6th June to 7th June, however, it can not identify these noise in signals of Trump-Kim event as shown is Fig. 7. We plan to solve this limitation in our next study.

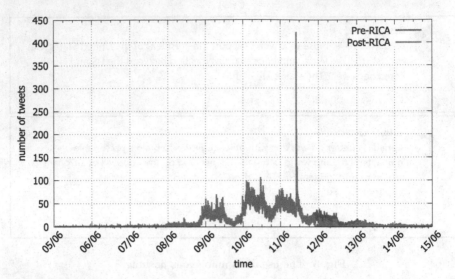

Fig. 6. Source signal of G7 summit event (red line). (Color figure online)

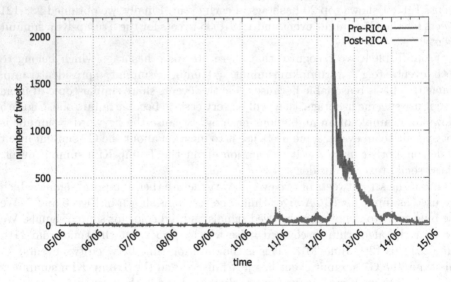

Fig. 7. Source signal of Trump-Kim summit event (red line). (Color figure online)

5   Conclusion and Future Work

In this paper, we focus on separating social event from noise by using reconstruction independent component analysis technique. We applied this idea to Twitter, as a popular social networking services, to prove the feasibility of our proposal. The output of our work can be applied for fraud detection, focusing search, or is used as pre-processing step for signal-based event discovering algorithms.

In the next study, we plan to research about applying RICA algorithm for overcomplete problem. We assumed that the number of source signals and observed signals are same in this paper, however, they are not always equal. Besides, RICA technique showed that they are not sensitive at time point with low distribution. We aim to modify RICA to overcome this problem. Finally, not only Twitter but also others social networking services will be selected for research in order to prove the adaptivity of this algorithm with various types of social data.

Acknowledgment. This research was supported by the MIST (Ministry of Science and ICT), Korea, under the National Program for Excellence in SW supervised by the IITP (Institute for Information & communications Technology Promotion) (20170001000021001). Also, this work was supported by the National Research Foundation of Korea (NRF) grant funded by the Korea government (MSIP) (NRF-2017R1A4A1015675, 2017R1A2B4010774).

References

1. Anemüller, J., Sejnowski, T.J., Makeig, S.: Complex independent component analysis of frequency-domain electroencephalographic data. Neural Netw. **16**(9), 1311–1323 (2003)
2. Becker, H., Naaman, M., Gravano, L.: Selecting quality twitter content for events. In: Proceedings of the 5th International Conference on Weblogs and Social Media (ICWSM 2011), Barcelona, Catalonia, Spain, 17–21 July 2011, pp. 442–445. AAAI Press (2011)
3. Benson, E., Haghighi, A., Barzilay, R.: Event discovery in social media feeds. In: Proceedings of the 49th Annual Meeting of the Association for Computational Linguistics: Human Language Technologies (ACL HLT 2011), Portland, Oregon, USA, 19–24 June 2011, pp. 389–398. ACL (2011)
4. Cruces-Alvarez, S., Cichocki, A., Castedo-Ribas, L.: An iterative inversion approach to blind source separation. IEEE Trans. Neural Netw. **11**(6), 1423–1437 (2000)
5. Cui, A., Zhang, M., Liu, Y., Ma, S., Zhang, K.: Discover breaking events with popular hashtags in Twitter. In: Proceedings of the 21st ACM International Conference on Information and Knowledge Management (CIKM 2012), Maui, HI, USA, 29 October–02 November 2012, pp. 1794–1798. ACM (2012)
6. Diamantaras, K.I., Papadimitriou, T.: MIMO blind deconvolution using subspace-based filter deflation. In: Proceedings of the 29th International Conference on Acoustics, Speech, and Signal Processing (ICASSP 2004), Montreal, Quebec, Canada, 17–21 May 2004, pp. 433–436. IEEE (2004)
7. Ding, W.: A new method for image noise removal using chaos-PSO and nonlinear ICA. Procedia Eng. **24**, 111–115 (2011)
8. Feng, W., et al.: STREAMCUBE: hierarchical spatio-temporal hashtag clustering for event exploration over the Twitter stream. In: Proceedings of the 31st IEEE International Conference on Data Engineering (ICDE 2015), Seoul, South Korea, 13–17 April 2015, pp. 1561–1572. IEEE (2015)

9. Fung, G.P.C., Yu, J.X., Yu, P.S., Lu, H.: Parameter free bursty events detection in text streams. In: Proceedings of the 31st International Conference on Very Large Data Bases (VLDB 2005), Trondheim, Norway, 30 August–02 September 2005, pp. 181–192. ACM (2005)

10. Hoang Long, N., Jung, J.J.: Privacy-aware framework for matching online social identities in multiple social networking services. Cybern. Syst. **46**(1–2), 69–83 (2015)

11. Kim, C.M., Park, H.M., Kim, T., Choi, Y.K., Lee, S.Y.: FPGA implementation of ICA algorithm for blind signal separation and adaptive noise canceling. IEEE Trans. Neural Netw. **14**(5), 1038–1046 (2003)

12. Le, Q.V., Karpenko, A., Ngiam, J., Ng, A.Y.: ICA with reconstruction cost for efficient overcomplete feature learning. In: Proceedings of the 24th Annual Conference on Advances in Neural Information Processing Systems (NIPS 2011), Granada, Spain, 12–14 December 2011, pp. 1017–1025. Curran Associates, Inc. (2011)

13. Li, Y., Ma, Z., Lu, W., Li, Y.: Automatic removal of the eye blink artifact from EEG using an ICA-based template matching approach. Physiol. Measur. **27**(4), 425 (2006)

14. Nguyen, H.L., Jung, J.E.: Statistical approach for figurative sentiment analysis on social networking services: a case study on Twitter. Multimed. Tools Appl. **76**(6), 8901–8914 (2017)

15. Nguyen, H.L., Jung, J.E.: SocioScope: a framework for understanding internet of social knowledge. Future Gener. Comput. Syst. **83**, 358–365 (2018)

16. Nuzillard, D., Bijaoui, A.: Blind source separation and analysis of multispectral astronomical images. Astron. Astrophys. Suppl. Ser. **147**(1), 129–138 (2000)

17. Petrović, S., Osborne, M., Lavrenko, V.: Streaming first story detection with application to Twitter. In: Proceedings of the 11th International Conference of the North American Chapter of the Association for Computational Linguistics (NAACL 2010), Los Angeles, California, USA, 2–4 June 2010, pp. 181–189. ACL (2010)

18. Phuvipadawat, S., Murata, T.: Breaking news detection and tracking in Twitter. In: Proceedings of the International Conference on Web Intelligence and International Conference on Intelligent Agent Technology (WI-IAT 2010), Toronto, Canada, 31 August–03 September 2010, pp. 120–123. IEEE (2010)

19. Sakaki, T., Okazaki, M., Matsuo, Y.: Earthquake shakes Twitter users: real-time event detection by social sensors. In: Proceedings of the 19th International Conference on World Wide Web (WWW 2010), Raleigh, North Carolina, USA, 26–30 April 2010, pp. 851–860. ACM (2010)

20. Smith, E.A.: The role of tacit and explicit knowledge in the workplace. J. Knowl. Manag. **5**(4), 311–321 (2001)

21. Vorobyov, S., Cichocki, A.: Blind noise reduction for multisensory signals using ICA and subspace filtering, with application to EEG analysis. Biol. Cybern. **86**(4), 293–303 (2002)

22. Wright, S., Nocedal, J.: Numerical optimization. Springer Sci. **35**(67–68), 7 (1999)

23. Yang, Y., Pierce, T., Carbonell, J.: A study of retrospective and on-line event detection. In: Proceedings of the 21st International Conference on Research and Development in Information Retrieval (SIGIR 1998), Melbourne, Australia, 24–28 August 1998, pp. 28–36. ACM (1998)

Performance, Resilience, and Security in Moving Data from the Fog to the Cloud: The DYNAMO Transfer Framework Approach

Raffaele Montella[1,2]($\boxtimes$)(iD), Diana Di Luccio[1,2](iD), Sokol Kosta[4](iD),
Giulio Giunta[1](iD), and Ian Foster[2,3](iD)

[1] Department of Science and Technology, University of Napoli "Parthenope",
Naples, Italy
{raffaele.montella,diana.diluccio,giulio.giunta}@uniparthenope.it
[2] Center for Robust Decisionmaking on Climate and Energy Policy,
Chicago, USA
[3] Department of Computer Science, The University of Chicago, Chicago, USA
foster@uchicago.edu
[4] CMI, Department of Electronic Systems, Aalborg University, Aalborg, Denmark
sok@cmi.aau.dk

Abstract. The data crowdsourcing paradigm applied in coastal and marine monitoring and management has been developed only recently due to the challenges of the marine environment. The pervasive internet of things technology is contributing to increase the number of connected instrumented devices available for data crowd-sourcing. A main issue in the fog/edge/cloud paradigm is that collected data need to be moved from tiny low power devices to cloud resources in order to be processed. This paper is about the DYNAMO data transfer framework enabling the data transfer feature in a internet of floating things scenario. The proposed framework is our solution to mitigate the effects of extreme and delay tolerant environments.

Keywords: Edge · Fog · Cloud computing
Internet of floating things · Data crowdsourcing

1 Introduction

Data crowdsourcing is the process of data gathering from heterogeneous and dislocated platforms [10]. Nowadays, this technique represents one of the most promising and uprising data gathering technique for data science and related business applications [19]. In our vision we consider the computation at the edge as a crucial architectural element joining a fog of sensors and actuators with their virtual counterpart on the cloud. We apply this fog/edge/cloud computing paradigm to the Internet of Things [1] where the fog side has in charge the direct

Y. Xiang et al. (Eds.): IDCS 2018, LNCS 11226, pp. 197–208, 2018.
https://doi.org/10.1007/978-3-030-02738-4_17

interaction with specific devices and the edge side act as a smart and active data logger as already depicted about similar industrial scenarios [17]. At the same time we have already experience about how the computation at the edge [15] could be strategically improved with a deep usage of CPU [12], GPU [2] and FPGA [5] offloading.

In the fog/edge/cloud computing paradigm applied to the Internet of Things, the fog located devices perform the interaction with sensors (and with actuator eventually) producing the main effort as a data logger [3]. Nevertheless, at the fog level, the lack of storage and computational resources implies the data aggregation, homogenization and pre-processing on devices located at the edge of the cloud [24].

We focus on marine data crowdsourcing applications, one of the most promising and, at the time of writing, still mostly unexploited [13]. The development of the framework described in this work has been driven by the requirement of coastal monitoring making this scenario remarkably peculiar: (i) Homogenization: data are gathered in a really heterogeneous fashion; (ii) Resiliency: the vessel to cloud connectivity is ephemeral, unstable, costly or simply not available for long time; (iii) Performance: when the vessel to cloud networking is available, it could be for a narrow time windows when as much as possible data must to be transferred; (iv) Security: gathered data involve sensible information about people (position, time), vessels (type, performance); because data will be used for coastal monitoring and modelling, the integrity has to be ensured. Both professional and leisure vessels are provided with a local network of sensors mostly compliant the fog computing paradigm (Fig. 1).

In this paper we describe how DYNAMO (Distributed leisure Yacht-carried sensor-Network for Atmosphere and Marine data crowdsourcing applications) [14] moves data from the boats to the cloud using a data transfer framework to define a protocol compliant with the environment requirements [16].

The rest of the paper is organized as follows: Sect. 2 gives an overview of the related work, comparing and contrasting our approach with the already existing IoT data transfer protocols, carrying out the motivations of our work; The design of the DYNAMO transfer framework is described in Sect. 3, while Sect. 4 is about its implementation. An evaluation in a controlled environment is provided in Sect. 5. The conclusions and the future directions of our research work are presented in Sect. 6.

2   Related Work

The design of Delay Tolerant Networks (DTNs) remains an open research topic in computer networking and no standard protocols are available in order to mitigate their drawbacks. An experimental application protocol called Bundle Protocol (BP) [20] has been proposed in 2007 by the Delay Tolerant Networking Research Group (DTNRG) of the Internet Research Task Force (IRTF). The idea of this protocol, as the name suggests, is to group data in bundles in order to store and forward them when the network is available. BP is not designed for

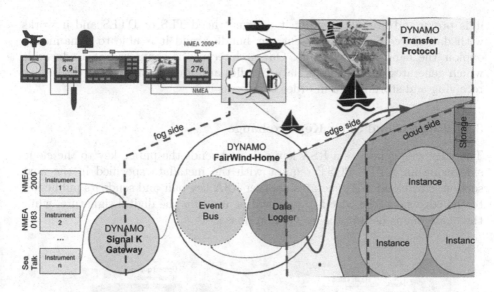

Fig. 1. The DYNAMO transfer framework for edge/cloud data movement in the marine application context.

IoT devices and for their communication with cloud infrastructures, but today is the only acknowledged data transfer protocol for DTNs and the best reference point for new proposals in this field.

The two widely used IoT application protocols which represent the current state of the art are Message Queuing Telemetry Transport (MQTT) [11] and Constrained Application Protocol (CoAP) [22]. MQTT is an internet application protocol for extreme environments. The first version dates back to 1999 and the last one has been made in 2014. MQTT today is an OASIS standard, widely used for every kind of IoT application, including cloud data transfer. CoAP is a modern standard specialized application protocol for constrained devices published by Internet Engineering Task Force (IETF) in 2014.

Both protocols are machine-to-machine protocols for IoT environments where devices have few computational resources and networking is discontinuous but today MQTT is more widespread because of its maturity and stability. Nevertheless, they don't implement any resilient feature mainly because the transmission rate cannot be dynamically adjusted in response to changes in available bandwidth [21]. The security is enforced by the transport layer affecting the interaction with the network infrastructure [23]. In order to ensure a lightweight footprint, MQTT and CoAP perform no payload compression [26].

3   Design

DYNAMO is an HTTP-based protocol, so it is stable and easy to integrate with existing technologies. Our protocol is endowed with a security layer so it is proxy and firewall friendly; it does not need TLS or DTLS and it works with data parcels which represent our bundles, and it is able to dynamically exploit the bandwidth available. Our architecture is composed of a edge side which generates and transmits data bundles and a cloud side which deals with receiving and storing data in order to process it.

3.1   Edge/Cloud Sides Key Exchange

The edge side generates a RSA key pair and sends the public key to the cloud side using an HTTP POST request with the metadata specified in the next section. The cloud side generates another RSA key pair and sends its public key to the edge side. The edge key pair will be used for the digital signature, while the cloud one is used in the encryption phase.

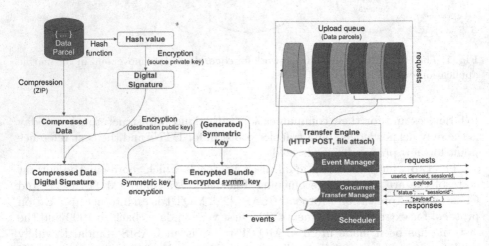

Fig. 2. Edge side (data producer) data pipeline. Each data parcel is signed using a hash function and the edge device's private key. On the other hand, data are compressed. The bundle composed of the compressed data parcel and the digital signature is encrypted using a symmetric key. The latter is encrypted using an asymmetric key and attached to the bundle in order to enqueue it in the upload queue. The CTM and scheduler handle the data transfer.

3.2   Edge Side Design

The edge side handles data segments as json encoded parcels in according to the application the framework is bonded with (Fig. 2):

(i) **Data parcel generation:** Data are collected into data parcels before the transfer phase. When a new update is generated on the edge, it is stored temporarily in a local cache until it is sent. (ii) **Bundle composition:** A digital signature is computed for each data parcel with SHA-2 and the edge device private key using the RSA with Optimal Asymmetric Encryption Padding (OAEP) [4]. (iii) **Bundle encryption:** The bundle is encrypted using the RSA-OAEP approch. In order to exceed the constraint limiting encrypted data size, the bundle is encrypted with AES using the Cipher Block Chaining (CBC) mode and PKCS5 padding [8] and the AES key is encrypted with RSA-OAEP. The encrypted bundle and the encrypted key are written into a file which is enqueued in the upload queue. (iv) **Bundle sending:** Files are transferred as file attachments, while the metadata are embedded in the HTTP headers as key/value pairs.

Concurrent Transfer Manager Plug-In. The heart of our protocol is the Concurrent Transfer Manager (CTM), which dynamically computes the number of concurrent transfer threads. Our approach is based on network speed analysis based on sending well-known data bundles and evaluating the network performance [8].

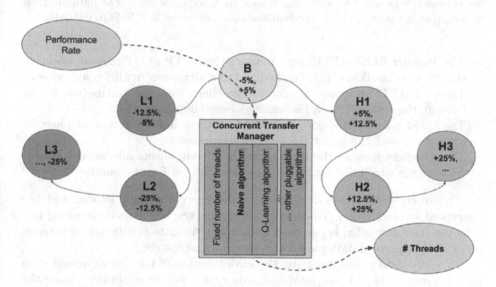

Fig. 3. The plug-in architecture of the CTM. The rules of the naive algorithm come from empirical measurements and have been tailored to yield satisfactory results.

The CTM makes its decisions based on the *performance rate*, the ratio between the instantaneous gross network speed and the average gross network speed over the previous N exchanged messages. We thus limit bandwidth utilization and mitigate data transfer overheads (Fig. 3).

3.3 Cloud Side Design

The cloud side is symmetric with respect to the edge side, as shown in Fig. 4.

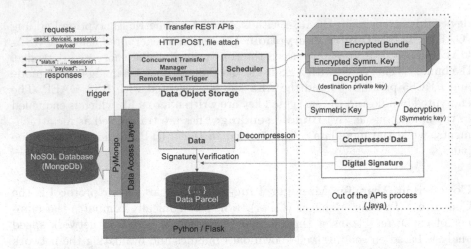

Fig. 4. *Cloud side* (consumer) data pipeline. The symmetric key is decrypted with the consumer's private key, and then is used to decrypt the data. The data are then uncompressed, the signature is verified, and data are stored in a NoSQL database.

- The Transfer REST API Engine analyzes the HTTP POST request, ensuring that there is an allowed file attached and that all mandatory fields are present. Then an HTTP response is sent to the client with the status (success or failure), the session ID, and a message describing the status.
- The CTM manages the computational resources in the decryption phase in order to respect the quality of services requirements;
- The scheduler handles the requests from different clients allocating a thread for each file which decrypts, decompresses, and verifies the bundle.

The received bundle is composed of the encrypted data bundle and the encrypted symmetric key. To decrypt, the symmetric key is used the cloud private key. The decrypted key is used to decipher the data bundle which is made up of the compressed data parcel and the digital signature.

To verify data parcel integrity, the hash function of the decompressed data parcel is computed and compared to the decrypted signature obtained using the edge device's public key. If these steps are successful, the data are stored into a NoSQL database through the Data Access Layer, which decouples the Transfer REST API Engine from the database.

4   Implementation

We next describe the languages and technologies used for the DYNAMO FairWind-Home App, showing the algorithms both for the edge and cloud side.

Edge Implementation. The edge side has been developed in Java, leveraging the SignalK (free and open source software) open data format for marine use.

Navigation instruments on boats typically use data protocols such as NMEA0183 or NMEA2000 to communicate their information. The data pipeline is simple: the edge side is composed of a SignalK gateway, a SignalK client and the Data Logger. The SignalK gateway retrieves data packets from the vessel instruments and presents them to the SignalK client via a web socket in JSON format. On the other side, the Data Logger gets data packets from the SignalK client thanks to a publish/subscribe event bus and collect them into data parcels that are transferred to the cloud side.

Figure 2 clarifies the data pipeline based on SignalK, while Algorithm 1 shows how the Data Logger generates data parcels as files. JSON data segments received by the Data Logger are stored in a memory cache. Every *updateMillis* milliseconds the cache is written into a logging file ad every *cutMillis* milliseconds the file is closed (the data parcel corresponds to the closed file) and the Uploader *moveToUpload()* method is called. This method takes all the files added to the Uploader and process each one according to the edge side data pipeline. The prepared file is moved into the upload folder, then a new file is generated with the timestamp as name and added to the Uploader. Another important parameter is *fullMillis* which represents the milliseconds after that a full dump of all the cache is periodically made in order to avoid data losses. The Uploader sends files generating HTTP asynchronous clients (a thread for each client) according to the CTM rules described in the "edge side design" subsection. The Algorithm 2 shows this phase: *getSpeed()* and *getAverageSpeed()* calculates the instantaneous and average gross speed respectively.

Cloud Implementation. We implemented the protocol cloud side with Flask[1], a micro-framework for Python based on Werkzeug and Jinja 2. We use the Infrastructure as a Service (IaS) like, but not limited to, Amazon Web Services getting an out of the box HTTP server scaling and load balancing thanks to the auto-scaling. The NoSQL database is MongoDB.

Algorithm 3 shows how the data parcel is handled at the cloud side. First, the server tries to get all the parameters values and checks if there is the attached file and its extension is allowed. If there are no problems, the file is saved and handled in a completely asynchronous way by a new thread, submitting concurrent jobs to a local queue manager. In every case, a response is returned to the edge side with the session ID, the status (success or fail) and an optional text message.

5   Evaluation

In order to evaluate our data transfer protocol we set *cutMillis* to 60000, *fullMillis* to 30000 and *updateMillis* to 15000.

Every 60 s, the Uploader tries to send a data parcel. The data protocol has been tested using our DYNAMO/FairWind-Home App for 19 min. Figure 5 shows the number of accumulated data parcels as a function of time. Each cross

---

[1] http://flask.pocoo.org.

Result: Encrypted file in the upload folder
updateMillis=update data frame in milliseconds;
cutMillis=data time frame in milliseconds;
fullMillis=full data frame in milliseconds;
millis=currentTimeMillis();
if *millis-lastCutMillis* ≥ *cutMillis* then
 if *the uploader is active* then
  | Uploader.moveToUpload();
 end
 currentFileName=YYYYMMDDZHHMMSS.json;
 lastCutMillis=millis;
 if *the uploader is active* then
  | Uploader.add(currentFileName);
 end
end
if *(millis-lastFullMillis* ≥ *fullMillis) or (lastCutMillis=millis)* then
 write full data on currentFileName;
 lastFullMillis=millis;
 Remove all events from the cache;
else
 add the event to the cache;
 if *millis-lastUpdateMillis* ≥ *updateMillis* then
  write update data on currentFileName;
  lastUpdateMillis=millis;
  Remove all events from the cache;
 end
end

Algorithm 1: Data Logger: the SignalK data collecting and local storing.

represents an upload attempt in presence of data parcels to send. From $t = 0$ to $t = 240$ and between $t = 600$ and $t = 850$ no data parcels are accumulated because network is stable and every time a parcel is available is immediately sent. From $t = 300$ to $t = 600$ the connection is not available and 6 data parcels are accumulated (Fig. 5, *Data parcels to be send*). When the connection is back, data parcels are sent quickly according to the number of available clients used (Fig. 5, *Current clients*). The same happens from $t = 900$ where 3 parcels are locally stored and then sent in parallel by the transfer threads.

Figure 5 shows the number of available clients (computed with the CTM) and the number of effective used clients as a function of time. From the beginning to the time $t = 240$ the networking is stable and the number of available clients is fixed to 6. Every time a data parcel is available, a client is generated in order to send it, in fact the number of current used clients is fixed to 1. At time $t = 300$ a connection lost is detected and the number of available clients decreases as the number of failures increases as shown in the Algorithm 2.

The number of current clients is 0 because data parcels cannot be sent. In the 5 min between $t = 300$ and $t = 600$, 6 data parcel are accumulated. From

Result: Transferred data
get the content of the upload directory;
while *files to be transferred are available* **do**
 if *at least one concurrent thread is available* **then**
  post the request;
  if *is Success* **then**
   rate=getSpeed()/getAverageSpeed();
   apply the rule described in Fig. 3;
  else
   increase the number of failures;
   if *number of failures=number of available threads* **then**
    decrease the number of available concurrent threads;
   end
   if *number of available concurrent threads = 0* **then**
    set the number of available concurrent threads to 1;
   end
  end
 end
end

Algorithm 2: Uploader: uploading based on CTM.

Result: Data parcels in a NoSQL database
initialization;
if *upload()* **then**
 if *is POST* **then**
  get the *sessionId*;
  get the *deviceId*;
  get the *userId*;
  if *the file is attached and its extension is allowed* **then**
   save the parcel in a local temporary storage;
   start a **new thread** for parcel management;
  end
  return the result (success or failure);
 end
end

Algorithm 3: Data handling at cloud side.

the time $t = 600$ network is available and the stored parcels are sent in this way: the first 3 parcels are sent every 5 s by a single client because the CTM is still updating the number of available threads, the next 3 parcels are sent in parallel using the available 3 clients computed by the CTM.

Now the network is stable and every 60 s a data parcel is created and sent to the cloud. At $t = 900$ another connection lost is detected and 3 data parcels are accumulated. When the network is back available the number of available clients is 6 so the protocol immediately use them in order to send the remaining parcels in parallel.

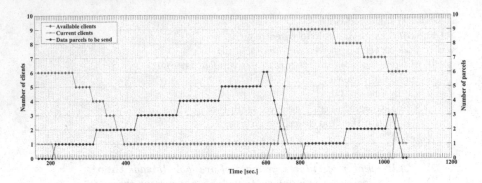

Fig. 5. Number of accumulated data parcels as a function of time in seconds. Number of available and current clients as functions of time in seconds. Comparison between the available data parcels and the concurrent working clients.

Figure 5 compares the number of accumulated data parcels and the number of clients used. It is interesting to see how from $t = 615$ to $t = 620$ the number of current clients steeply increases from 1 to 3 and at $t = 620$ the number of data parcels immediately go down from 3 to 0 because the transfer is made in parallel. The same happens after $t = 1000$.

6   Conclusion and Future Directions

We proposed a novel data transfer framework designed for use in the DYNAMO ecosystem but not limited to it. In particular, any data crowdsourcing application based on the paradigm of fog computing and its edge-located use of cloud resources could leverage this framework. The same technology, upon minor adaptations, could be applied to the automotive sector in order to provide data such as driving style, engine performance and vibrations, fuel or battery consumption, and pollutant emission. Once such data are ready to be processed in the cloud, the range of possible applications is limitless [6].

We strongly believe in the concept of *neogeography* [7], in which people, using their own instrumented devices for geographically referenced data collection, contribute to the creation of themed maps with features coming from different sources [25] and on cloud computing as a flywheel for science democratization [18].

The proposed framework enables the implementation of a data transfer protocol able to transfer data in delay tolerant environments using a store and forward approach. It is resilient thanks to the innovative CTM, which takes advantage of the bandwidth available. It is also secure without the need for an external security layer and lightweight thanks to payload compression.

The experiments shown in the last section are promising with encouraging evaluation results figuring out applications in different application fields than marine electronics [27]. We are aware that the current evaluation experiment are only a preliminary stage and more experimental results are necessary to verify the validity of this proposed approach.

Our main goal now is to design the CTM with a machine learning algorithm which is able to automatically compute the number of concurrent transfer threads according to the performance rate and other system and network parameters [9].

Acknowledgments. This work has been supported in part by U.S. National Science Foundation awards 0951576 and 1331782; and by the University of Napoli Parthenope, Italy (project DSTE333 "Modelling Mytilus Farming System with Enhanced Web Technologies" funded by Campania Region/Veterinary sector).

References

1. Aloi, G., et al.: Enabling IoT interoperability through opportunistic smartphone-based mobile gateways. J. Netw. Comput. Appl. **81**, 74–84 (2017)
2. Deyannis, D., Tsirbas, R., Vasiliadis, G., Montella, R., Kosta, S., Ioannidis, S.: Enabling GPU-assisted antivirus protection on android devices through edge offloading. In: Proceedings of the 1st International Workshop on Edge Systems, Analytics and Networking, pp. 13–18. ACM (2018)
3. Fortino, G., Trunfio, P. (eds.): Internet of Things Based on Smart Objects: Technology, Middleware and Applications. IT. Springer, Cham (2014). https://doi.org/10.1007/978-3-319-00491-4
4. Fujisaki, E., Okamoto, T., Pointcheval, D., Stern, J.: RSA-OAEP is secure under the RSA assumption. In: Kilian, J. (ed.) CRYPTO 2001. LNCS, vol. 2139, pp. 260–274. Springer, Heidelberg (2001). https://doi.org/10.1007/3-540-44647-8_16
5. Gomes, T., Pinto, S., Tavares, A., Cabral, J.: Towards an FPGA-based edge device for the Internet of Things. In: 2015 IEEE 20th Conference on Emerging Technologies & Factory Automation (ETFA), pp. 1–4. IEEE (2015)
6. Guo, H., Crossman, J.A., Murphey, Y.L., Coleman, M.: Automotive signal diagnostics using wavelets and machine learning. IEEE Trans. Veh. Technol. **49**(5), 1650–1662 (2000)
7. Heipke, C.: Crowdsourcing geospatial data. ISPRS J. Photogramm. Remote Sens. **65**(6), 550–557 (2010)
8. Kosta, S., Aucinas, A., Hui, P., Mortier, R., Zhang, X.: ThinkAir: dynamic resource allocation and parallel execution in the cloud for mobile code offloading. In: 2012 Proceedings of the IEEE INFOCOM, pp. 945–953. IEEE (2012)
9. Li, H.: Multi-agent Q-learning of channel selection in multi-user cognitive radio systems: a two by two case. In: 2009 IEEE International Conference on Systems, Man and Cybernetics, SMC 2009, pp. 1893–1898. IEEE (2009)
10. Lin, Y.W., Bates, J., Goodale, P.: Co-observing the weather, co-predicting the climate: human factors in building infrastructures for crowdsourced data. Sci. Technol. Stud. **29**(3), 10–27 (2016)
11. Locke, D.: MQ telemetry transport (MQTT) v3. 1 protocol specification. IBM developerWorks Technical Library, p. 15 (2010)
12. Mao, Y., Zhang, J., Letaief, K.B.: Dynamic computation offloading for mobile-edge computing with energy harvesting devices. IEEE J. Sel. Areas Commun. **34**(12), 3590–3605 (2016)

13. Marcellino, L., et al.: Using GPGPU accelerated interpolation algorithms for marine bathymetry processing with on-premises and cloud based computational resources. In: Wyrzykowski, R., Dongarra, J., Deelman, E., Karczewski, K. (eds.) PPAM 2017. LNCS, vol. 10778, pp. 14–24. Springer, Cham (2018). https://doi.org/10.1007/978-3-319-78054-2_2

14. Montella, R., Kosta, S., Foster, I.: DYNAMO: distributed leisure yacht-carried sensor-network for atmosphere and marine data crowdsourcing applications. In: 2018 IEEE International Conference on Cloud Engineering (IC2E), pp. 333–339. IEEE (2018)

15. Montella, R., et al.: Accelerating linux and android applications on low-power devices through remote GPGPU offloading. Concurr. Comput. Pract. Exp. **29**(24), e4286 (2017)

16. Montella, R., Ruggieri, M., Kosta, S.: A fast, secure, reliable, and resilient data transfer framework for pervasive IoT applications. In: IEEE INFOCOM 2018-IEEE Conference on Computer Communications Workshops (INFOCOM WKSHPS). IEEE (2018)

17. Pace, P., Aloi, G., Gravina, R., Caliciuri, G., Fortino, G., Liotta, A.: An edge-based architecture to support efficient applications for healthcare industry 4.0. IEEE Trans. Ind. Inf. (2018)

18. Pham, Q., Malik, T., Foster, I., Di Lauro, R., Montella, R.: SOLE: linking research papers with science objects. In: Groth, P., Frew, J. (eds.) IPAW 2012. LNCS, vol. 7525, pp. 203–208. Springer, Heidelberg (2012). https://doi.org/10.1007/978-3-642-34222-6_16

19. Salim, F., Haque, U.: Urban computing in the wild: a survey on large scale participation and citizen engagement with ubiquitous computing, cyber physical systems, and Internet of Things. Int. J. Hum.-Comput. Stud. **81**, 31–48 (2015)

20. Scott, K.L., Burleigh, S.: Bundle protocol specification. RFC 5050 (2007)

21. Sen, S., Balasubramanian, A.: A highly resilient and scalable broker architecture for IoT applications. In: 2018 10th International Conference on Communication Systems & Networks (COMSNETS), pp. 336–341. IEEE (2018)

22. Shelby, Z., Hartke, K., Bormann, C.: The constrained application protocol (CoAP). RFC 5272 (2014)

23. Singh, M., Rajan, M., Shivraj, V., Balamuralidhar, P.: Secure MQTT for Internet of Things (IoT). In: 2015 Fifth International Conference on Communication Systems and Network Technologies (CSNT), pp. 746–751. IEEE (2015)

24. Stojmenovic, I., Wen, S.: The Fog computing paradigm: scenarios and security issues. In: 2014 Federated Conference on Computer Science and Information Systems (FedCSIS), pp. 1–8. IEEE (2014)

25. Turner, A.: Introduction to Neogeography. O'Reilly Media Inc., Newton (2006)

26. Yokotani, T., Sasaki, Y.: Comparison with HTTP and MQTT on required network resources for IoT. In: 2016 International Conference on Control, Electronics, Renewable Energy and Communications (ICCEREC), pp. 1–6. IEEE (2016)

27. Zhou, J., Dong, X., Cao, Z., Vasilakos, A.V.: Secure and privacy preserving protocol for cloud-based vehicular DTNs. IEEE Trans. Inf. Forensics Secur. **10**(6), 1299–1314 (2015)

Development of a Support System
to Resolve Network Troubles by Mobile
Robots

Kohichi Ogawa and Noriaki Yoshiura[✉]

Department of Information and Computer Sciences, Saitama University,
255, Shimo-ookubo, Sakura-ku, Saitama, Japan
yoshiura@fmx.ics.saitama-u.ac.jp

Abstract. Universities have campus networks and different network administration policies. In some universities, network users can install network devices, which are printers, routers or Ethernet switches, in the networks of the rooms of users for themselves. All the users are not familiar with IT and cannot resolve the network troubles whose causes are the installed network devices. The users ask campus network operators of the universities to resolve the troubles instantaneously, but the operators do not know the network environment of the users or resolve the troubles. The network devices do not have management functions such SNMP because the users do not think that the functions are necessary. These network troubles are burdens of campus network operators and increase the cost of network administration. This paper proposes the support system which resolves the network troubles in the user network environments. This paper also implements and evaluates the support system.

1 Introduction

Universities have campus networks and different network administration policies. In some universities, network users can install network devices, which are printers, routers or Ethernet switches, in the networks of the rooms of the users for themselves. All the users are not familiar with IT and cannot resolve the network troubles whose causes are the installed network devices. If the troubles occur in the networks of the rooms of the users, the users ask network operators of the universities to resolve the troubles instantaneously. Resolving the troubles takes much cost for network administration in the universities or there is no network operator to resolve the troubles in the user networks. Conversely, in companies, users cannot install network devices for themselves. In the campus networks in the universities, resolving the troubles in the networks in the rooms of users is an important problem. On the other hand, the administration of company networks does not confront the problem.

In order to resolve the problem in the campus networks of universities, we have proposed a monitoring system [1] which monitors the LED indicators of the

© Springer Nature Switzerland AG 2018
Y. Xiang et al. (Eds.): IDCS 2018, LNCS 11226, pp. 209–220, 2018.
https://doi.org/10.1007/978-3-030-02738-4_18

network devices of users. We have also proposed a mobile robot which collects information that is obtained by monitoring network devices. Although the monitoring system and the mobile robot can detect the troubles of network devices, they cannot resolve the troubles yet. Therefore, after the monitoring system and the mobile robot detect a network trouble in a room of a user, network operators need to go to the room of the user, identify the causes of the trouble and resolve the trouble. In order to reduce the cost of network administration, we require a new method to identify causes of network troubles and resolve them.

This paper proposes a method to support identification of the causes of network troubles in the rooms of users. The method interacts with the users in the network troubles to identify the causes of the troubles. This paper implements a prototype system of the proposed method and evaluates it by an experiment at the campus network of Saitama University, where we are administrating the campus network.

The paper is organized as follows; Sect. 2 explains the previous research that is a basis of this paper. Section 3 proposes the new method. Section 4 explains the implementation of the proposed method. Section 5 explains the experiments of the prototype system. Section 6 discusses the proposed method. Section 7 explains related researches. Section 8 summarizes the paper.

2   Monitoring System of Network Devices by Robots

This section explains the researches that are the basis of this paper.

2.1   Monitoring System of Network Devices

Almost all network devices in the rooms of users have minimal functions and do not have management functions such as SNMP (Simple Network Management Protocol) [2] because users tend to buy cheap network devices, which do not have management functions. Therefore, we have proposed a monitoring system which constantly monitors the blinking state of the LED indicators of a network device by using a small computer and a USB camera [1]. Almost all network devices have LEDs to show their states even if they do not have SNMP.

There are two kinds of methods of collecting the information of the states of network devices according to the functions of the LEDs. One method is to compare the LED states by still images; the method records the still images of LEDs by camera and checks whether the still images show the normal states of network devices. The other method is to analyze videos of LEDs. For example, the LEDs blink intensely when forming the loop of Ethernet switches. In order to detect forming the loop, we check whether the LEDs blink intensely by using videos. The method uses optical flow and video of 60 frames at wide angle.

We have implemented the monitoring systems by using a Raspberry Pi and a USB camera to record still images and by using Intel NUC and a USB camera to analyze videos. Analyzing video requires CPU power and we use Intel NUC instead of a Raspberry Pi. Figure 1 shows the implemented monitoring systems.

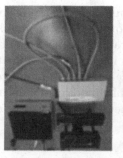

Fig. 1. Monitoring system (left: network switch monitoring system, right: media converter monitoring system)

The right system in Fig. 1 analyzes still images and the left system in Fig. 1 analyzes videos. The systems are prototypes and will be downsized for practical use. In order to notify troubles to network operators, the systems use 3G/LTE mobile communication. because the monitoring systems must work even if campus networks do not work. We evaluated the prototype systems by using them in the campus network monitoring in Saitama University.

2.2 Collecting Information by Robots

The monitoring systems use 3G/LTE mobile communication to notify the troubles in network devices, but communication cost is high if all monitoring systems have the mobile communications. In order to reduce the cost, we have implemented a robot which collects information from the monitoring systems. The left in Fig. 2 shows the robot. Each monitoring system has only a WiFi interface and communicates with the robot. The robot collects information from monitor systems via WiFi network and sends the information to network operators via 3G/LTE. The right in Fig. 2 shows the behavior of the robot when collecting information from monitoring systems; the mobile robot cannot open doors. The mobile robot only moves along a corridor, stops near each monitoring system and communicates with each monitoring system.

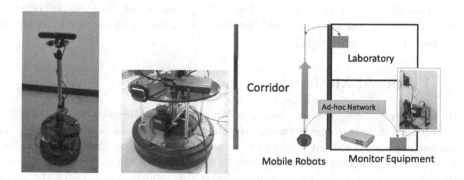

Fig. 2. Robots for collection of information

Figure 3 shows the overview of the monitoring system for network devices. The monitoring system consists of monitoring devices, a mobile robot, a monitoring information server and an administrator terminal (monitoring data display, robot control). The monitoring device is installed for each network device which needs monitoring. The monitoring device has a WiFi interface and forms ad hoc network with the mobile robot. The mobile robot communicates with the server via 3G/LTE. The control program of the mobile robot runs on the terminal.

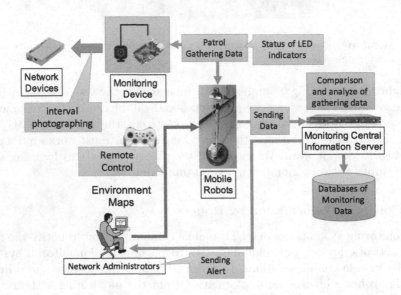

Fig. 3. Overview of monitoring system for network devices

The operation of the monitoring system is as follows; the mobile robot moves around an area where monitoring devices are installed. The mobile robot collects the data in monitoring devices when the mobile robot goes near the monitoring devices. The mobile robot sends the data to the server the via mobile communications. The network administrators know the latest states of network devices by the data from monitoring devices. The robot is controlled manually by network administrators, but moves around the area automatically by setting a way-point for each monitoring device [3].

3   Proposed Method

By our previous researches [3] which is described in the previous section, network operators can detect the network troubles in the room of users; however, the network operators cannot identify the causes of the troubles. This paper develops a method of supporting identification of the causes of network troubles in the rooms of users. The method is as follows; the mobile robot visits the room where the network troubles occur, and interacts with the users in the room to identify the causes of the network troubles. The mobile robot supports the users to operate PCs or network devices and to identify the causes of the troubles.

As shown in Fig. 2, the mobile robot only moves along corridor. Since there are many things in the rooms of users, the robot cannot move in the rooms. Therefore, we use a tablet PC as user support system. The tablet PC is on the mobile robot and removable from the mobile robot. We suppose that users pick up the tablet PC from the mobile robot and interact with the tablet PC to identify the causes of the troubles.

The previous researches developed the monitoring system that detects the troubles in a room of a user and goes to the room. This paper develops and adds the support system on the tablet PC. Figure 4 shows the overall of behavior of the monitoring system with the proposed support system and the following is a behavior of the support system.

(1) The support system retrieves the measures for the trouble from the database, which stores measures for troubles.
(2) The user uses the terminal, inputs commands and checks the state of the network devices according to the voice guidance or display guidance of the support system.
(3) The user photographs the display images of the outputs of the commands and the states of network devices by the camera of the tablet PC. The tablet PC sends the images to the server.
(4) The server processes the images that are sent from the tablet PC. The server knows the states of the network devices and sends the new measure to the support system (go to (2)).
(5) If the problem is not resolved by repeating (2) to (4), the network operators find a new measure by using the data obtained by repeating (2) to (4) and send it to the support system.
(6) The server saves the data of resolving the troubles in the database as new data for the trouble.

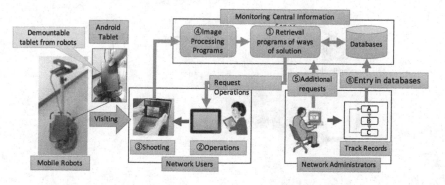

Fig. 4. Overview of proposed method

This paper focuses on the behavior from (1) to (4), which is an interaction with users. Concretely, the interaction part is implemented by an Android application. We also develop an image processing program which obtains the OS of the network device from the display images which are captured by the tablet PC. The image processing program also recognizes characters on the display images of the outputs of the commands to identify the causes of network troubles. The information, which is acquired from the image processing, is analyzed by morphological analysis of natural language processing and classification method of machine learning. The result of the analysis provides necessary measures from the database.

4   Implementation

4.1   Overview of System

Networks which have troubles are supposed to be unusable. The tablet PC uses mobile communication line of the robot in order to communicate with the server and network operators. The robot works as WiFi access point, the tablet PC and the robot construct ad hoc network. The tablet PC uses the mobile communication line in the robot via WiFi.

The tablet PC or the robot does not execute a heavy processing such as image processing and image recognition, but the server executes the processing. The tablet PC or the robot sends only the data or the images to the server and receives the results of the processing from the server. The network between the robot and the server is encrypted by VPN [4]. Figure 5 shows the network among the tablet PC, the robot and the server. As the tablet PC, we use Asus's Nexus 7 (2013) that has 7 in. display and a camera on the front side. We set a tablet PC folder on the mobile robot. The tablet PC is on the tablet folder

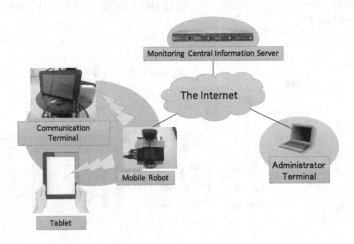

Fig. 5. Overview of system

and users can take the tablet PC from the tablet folder when the users use the tablet PC. This paper uses communication terminal for voice guidance and the tablet PC for display guidance and taking images. Communication terminal is a 7-inch touch panel terminal that is based on Raspberry Pi 3 [5]. Voice guidance is implemented by the voice libraries of Linux OS.

4.2 Additional Functions to Robots

This paper uses the mobile robot that is developed in the previous researches [3]. We use iRobot's Rumba as the mobile robot. In order to realize automatic driving by SLAM (Simultaneous Localization and Mapping) [7,14], this paper uses sensors such as laser range finder as the previous research uses. ROS [6] is used as framework of mobile robot.

In order to resolve network troubles, we install a communication terminal in the mobile robot. The communication terminal is a type of touch panel, and output sounds from a speaker that is connected by Bluetooth. The role of the communication terminal is dialogue with the users. The GUI of the communication terminal uses Tkinter [8], which is a standard library for Python GUI.

When the mobile robot arrives at the room of a user, the mobile robot needs to inform the users of the arrival. The mobile robot cannot knock on the door. This paper uses a method of calling the user by voice in the front of the room; we use Open JTalk [9], which is a voice engine to inform the user of arrival. We also use Raspberry Pi 3 Touch for communication terminal and ANKER SoundCore nano A3104 for Bluetooth speaker.

4.3 Checking Terminal and Supporting Taking a Photo of Display

In Saitama University, when users cannot use network, network operators ask users about IP address and MAC address in order to check the network connectivity. The inquiry is via telephone and some users cannot answer IP address and MAC address because the users are not familiar with IT. Even if the network operators tell the users the method of finding IP address and MAC address, the users cannot find IP address and MAC address. Many users have not launched terminal software, command prompt or system configuration tools; the users hesitate to launch this kind of software. Therefore, the support system that is proposed in this paper helps users to launch and use the software and obtain the output of the software. In order to obtain the output of the software, we use the display images that are photographed by the tablet PC.

4.4 Confirming Whether Tablet PC Is Returned to Robot

The tablet PC is on the tablet folder on the mobile robot. A user picks up the tablet PC from the tablet folder and uses it in order to resolve the troubles. The tablet folder must check whether the tablet PC is returned. The tablet folder has the microswitch in order to confirm whether the tablet PC is returned.

If the microswitch is not turned on within a certain time after pressing the FINISH button of the communication terminal, the robot judged that the tablet PC is not on the tablet folder and a warning message is issued from the speaker. This paper uses Omron Amusement Co. D3M-01L1 for microswitches. The microswitch is connected to the communication terminal (Raspberry Pi) by a GPIO (General Purpose Input/Output) pin.

4.5   Operation of Tablet PC

The operation on the tablet PC is as follows.

(1) The user taps the icon on the tablet PC.
(2) The title screen (Fig. 6 left) starts up and the user taps "START button".
(3) The tablet PC explains how to use it. The user activates the camera and photographs the display images of the terminal.
(4) The user selects an image of the display on Image Selection Screen (Fig. 6 right) and sends the image to the server with "UPLOAD IMAGE button".

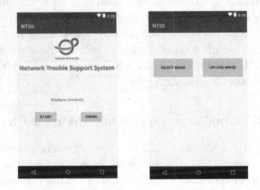

Fig. 6. Example of application in tablet

The Android tablet PC sends the image, which is selected by the user, to the server via HTTP. The server runs the Web server program and acquires the image by POST with Apache and PHP. After receiving the image, the server analyzes the image and sends the result of analysis to the communication terminal.

4.6   Obtaining Characters from Image

From the images that are sent from the robot, the server finds the information that may be a hint of resolving troubles. In order to obtain characters from the image, the server uses OCR (Optical Character Recognition). This paper uses Tesseract-OCR [10] for OCR. In order to use Tesseract-OCR from Python, we used pyacr [11] which is Wrapper of Tesseract-OCR.

During implementing the system, Tesseract-OCR does not recognize characters correctly from the images that are sent from the robot. In order to improve recognition, we binarize the images by OpenCV and eliminates noise before using OCR. As a result, the characters on the images can be recognized correctly. After recognizing the characters on the image, the support system checks whether IP address is correct in the network device. The support system analyzes the output of ipconfig in Windows OS as follows:

(1) 133.38.xxx.xxx: You are connected to the university network.
(2) 0.0.0.0: LAN cable is not connected.
(3) 169.254.xxx.xxx: IP is not acquired.
(4) 192.168.xxx.xxx: The network device is in private network.
(5) 10. xxx.xxx.xxx: You are connected to the authentication network.
(6) No display: LAN interface is not recognized.
(7) Otherwise: New measures are required.

When the output of OCR is (1) to (5), the support system provides an appropriate measure to the users from the database. When the output of OCR is (6) or (7), there is no measure in the current database and the network operators contact users in order to resolve the troubles.

5 Experiment

This section explains an experiment which evaluates the effectiveness of the support system. The experiment uses three rooms in a lecture building of the Faculty of Engineering, Saitama University.

We set up Windows 10 terminals in each room. In advance, the mobile robot creates an environmental map with SLAM. The mobile robot visits each room by way-point. Figure 7 shows the outline of the experiment. The experiment is carried out by deliberately generating fault conditions of (1) to (5) of Sect. 4.6. The experiment evaluates how much processing time in the whole system is required, and whether IP address can be correctly recognized. For each room, we execute generating fault conditions five times.

The times in the following four items are measured in the experiment.

(1) Time to press the START button from the robot's call
(2) After (1), the time to operate the tablet PC, to take the image of the terminal, and to send the image to the server
(3) After (2), the time at which measures can be provided by voice
(4) Time to press FINISH button (including operation time)

The size of one image that is taken with the tablet PC is about 2 MB. Time for processing is measured from the log files of each device in the system. Table 1 shows the durations for all rooms. The processing of (1) to (4) totally takes about 80 s on average for each room. The time from (1) to (3) is within one minute and users obtain the measure from the support system without irritation or stress.

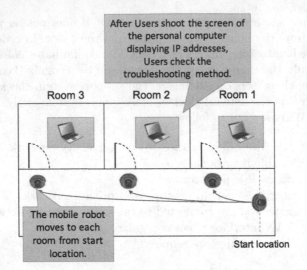

Fig. 7. Overview of experiment

When the robot visits the user in troubles after going through many rooms, the user must wait for the robot and the waiting time may be indefinite. There are several methods of resolving this problem; one is to estimate the waiting time and inform the users of the waiting time. Another is to use several robots.

6   Discussion

Some PCs have glossy displays. The reflections of interior lights must be considered when OCR processes the images of glossy displays. During implementing the system, OCR could not recognize some characters because of the reflections. In order to resolve this problem, the support system should detect the glossy display and instruct the user to obtain the images of the display with decreasing the reflections.

Table 1. Processing time

	Room 1				Room 2				Room 3			
	(1) [s]	(2) [s]	(3) [s]	(4) [s]	(1) [s]	(2) [s]	(3) [s]	(4) [s]	(1) [s]	(2) [s]	(3) [s]	(4) [s]
1	1.08	25.53	4.51	36.01	2.07	35.56	4.53	36.75	1.58	35.65	5.68	46.42
2	1.03	35.38	4.61	35.58	1.38	34.45	5.46	36.54	1.56	25.45	5.64	36.87
3	1.26	35.49	5.48	47.84	1.93	35.58	4.68	45.79	1.64	35.40	5.49	35.89
4	1.30	45.68	6.54	36.78	1.47	35.26	4.87	35.46	1.46	24.46	6.45	35.21
5	1.45	35.78	5.18	55.78	1.75	36.05	5.51	44.66	1.85	35.46	5.87	35.46
Avg	1.22	35.57	5.26	42.40	1.72	35.38	5.01	39.84	1.62	31.28	5.83	37.97

Currently, we must improve the method of notification of arrival of the room in network troubles. In the experiment, the robot called at the door of the room 1, but the user did not hear the sound well. Rooms 2 and 3 are glass-faced rooms and we can notice the arrival of the mobile robot before the robot calls. We also need to consider the possibility that the calling sound of robots may be a noise. One of the method of resolving this problem is to make a phone call before the robot visits or to notify the visiting time in advance by e-mail.

When photographing the images of displays, there is a possibility that the images include information that is not related with troubleshooting. In some cases, images may violate the privacy of users. In order to resolve this problem, the support system should narrow the ranges of images for necessary information and automatically remove unnecessary information or parts of images.

7   Related Studies

For dialogue, smart speakers such as Amazon Echo [12] and Google Home [13] have been released. These speakers recognize user's voice and provide services. By customizing the smart speakers, we may improve the support system, but these speakers cannot work in the environments where the Internet is unavailable.

The calling method which is used in this paper is based on utterances from speakers. However, there is a possibility that voice of the robot is noisy for other users. A method of using mobile phone to invite users has also been studied [15]. We must consider the case that the users are absent.

In the user environment, a robot that operates by interacting with users has been developed [16]. The purpose of this research is not to resolve the problem such as network troubles, but to promote communication. The purpose of the robot in [16] is different from that of this paper.

Since the robot in this paper interacts with users to solve problems, the research in this paper is considered to be one of human robot interactions [17]. The method proposed in this paper is effective not only for network troubles but also for user support.

8   Conclusion

This paper proposed a user support system to identify the cause of network troubles in the rooms of users. The user support system is on the mobile robot that is developed to detect network troubles. The system aims at reducing the burden on network administrators or operators of university networks. This paper implemented a prototype system of the proposed method and evaluated it by an experiment at the campus network. The future work is to improve the support system and to complete the whole system of mobile robots for network troubles.

References

1. Ogawa, K., Yoshiura, N.: Development of monitoring equipment for network devices by using small computers and image-processing technology. J. Inf. Process. **59**(3), 1026–1037 (2018)
2. Coexistence between Version 1, Version 2, and Version 3 of the Internet-standard Network Management Framework. The Internet Society (2003)
3. Ogawa, K., Yoshiura, N.: A method of automatically collection for monitoring information of network devices by environment maps of mobile robots, SIG Technical rports, 2017-IOT-39(1). Information Processing Society of Japan, pp. 1–7 (2017)
4. OpenVPN. https://openvpn.net/. Accessed 13 May 2018
5. Raspberry Pi3 Touch-Screen Kit. https://www.raspberrypi.org/products/raspberry-pi-touch-display/. Accessed 13 May 2018
6. Quigley, M., et al.: ROS: an open-source robot operating system. In: ICRA Workshop on Open Source Software (2009)
7. Menegatti, E., Zanella, A., Zilli, S., Zorzi, F., Pagello, E.: Range-only SLAM with a mobile robot and a wireless sensor networks. In: International Conference on Robotics and Automation (ICRA), pp. 1699–1705 (2009)
8. Tkinter. https://docs.python.org/ja/3/library/tkinter.html/. Accessed 13 May 2018
9. OpenJTalk. http://open-jtalk.sp.nitech.ac.jp/. Accessed 13 May 2018
10. Tesseract. https://github.com/tesseract-ocr/tesseract/wiki. Accessed 13 May 2018
11. pyocr. https://github.com/openpaperwork/pyocr/. Accessed 13 May 2018
12. Amazon Echo. https://www.amazon.co.jp/gp/product/B071ZF5KCM/ref=sv_dev icesubnav_0/. Accessed 13 May 2018
13. Google Home. https://store.google.com/product/google_home/. Accessed 13 May 2018
14. Grisetti, G., Stachniss, C., Burgard, W.: Improved techniques for grid mapping with Rao-Blackwellized particle filters. IEEE Trans. Robot. **23**(1), 34–46 (2007)
15. Saito, Y., Choi, Y., Iyota, T., Watanabe, K., Kubota, Y.: A self-position recoginition method for mobile robots based on robot calling by a user using cellular phone. IEEJ Trans. Electron. Inf. Syst. **127**(5), 778–786 (2007)
16. Fujie, S., Matsuyama, Y., Taniyama, H., Kobayashi, T.: Conversation robot participating in and activating a group communication. In: Proceedings of INTER-SPEECH 2009 (2009)
17. Goodrich, M.A., Schultz, A.C.: Human-robot interaction: a survey. Found. Trends Hum.-Comput. Interact. **1**(3), 203–275 (2007)

A Benchmark Model for the Creation of Compute Instance Performance Footprints

Markus Ullrich[1]([⊠]), Jörg Lässig[1], Jingtao Sun[2], Martin Gaedke[3], and Kento Aida[2]

[1] University of Applied Sciences Zittau/Görlitz, Brückenstr. 1, Görlitz, Germany
{mullrich,jlaessig}@hszg.de
[2] National Institute of Informatics, 2-1-2 Hitotsubashi, Chiyoda-ku, Tokyo, Japan
sun@nii.ac.jp
[3] Technische Universität Chemnitz, Str. der Nationen 62, Chemnitz, Germany
martin.gaedke@informatik.tu-chemnitz.de

Abstract. Cloud benchmarking has become a hot topic in cloud computing research. The idea to attach performance footprints to compute resources in order to select an appropriate setup for any application is very appealing. Especially in the scientific cloud, a lot of resources can be preserved by using just the right setup instead of needlessly over-provisioned instances. In this paper, we briefly list existing efforts that have been made in this area and explain the need for a generic benchmark model to combine the results found in previous work to reduce the benchmarking effort for new resources and applications. We propose such a model which is build on our previously presented resource and application model and highlight its advantages. We show how the model can be used to store benchmarking data and how the data is linked to the application and the resources. Also, we explain how the data, in combination with an infrastructure as code tool, can be utilized to automatically create and execute any application and any micro benchmark in the cloud with low manual effort. Finally, we present some of the observations we made while benchmarking compute instances at two major cloud providers.

Keywords: Cloud computing · Performance footprints
Cloud benchmarking · Compute instances

1 Introduction

Several research papers have highlighted various advantages of the cloud [12] already [2,13,21]. Especially relevant is the access to a seemingly unlimited pool of resources that can be provisioned and scaled on demand in combination with the pay-per-use cost model. On the other hand, the scientific community is also rapidly adapting the academic cloud to outsource expensive workloads [8,13,

© Springer Nature Switzerland AG 2018
Y. Xiang et al. (Eds.): IDCS 2018, LNCS 11226, pp. 221–234, 2018.
https://doi.org/10.1007/978-3-030-02738-4_19

17, 22]. However, one major issue in that regard is cloud provider and resource selection which is also related to the performance differences that have been observed for major IaaS providers [10, 11]. While higher performance is definitely an important goal for the execution of scientific or high-performance-compute applications, using resources optimally or close to optimal can also be a goal of researchers to save cost on cloud instances. Many research teams have performed analyses of different cloud resources and their efficiency for deploying certain applications [3, 7, 8, 10, 11, 13, 14, 16–18, 22]. All these results can help to select a cloud provider and, furthermore, the ideal infrastructure for an application. In this work, we are adding the following contributions to this area:

1. The introduction of a model to capture and combine the aforementioned benchmark results in a single database to create re-usable performance footprints of cloud compute instances and applications,
2. Automating cloud benchmarking for different providers by using the structured data from this database and
3. Providing example results for benchmarking a variety of instances in the AWS and GCP cloud.

The rest of this paper is organized as follows. In Sect. 2 we provide a more detailed formulation of the main idea behind our research. In Sect. 3 we discuss existing approaches in this research area. We briefly recap our previously published application and resource meta-model and introduce an extension for capturing benchmark results in Sect. 4. Our approach to automate the benchmarking process including example results are presented in Sect. 5. Finally, Sect. 6 concludes this work and we discuss the planned future applications of the presented meta-model.

2   Problem Formulation

Compute instances provide a simple solution to execute any type of application in the cloud. In the context of this work, a compute instance is a set of resources made available as a virtual machine with root access to a cloud user. It includes one or multiple CPU cores, memory, storage and network access. The cost for an instance are dependent on the provided resources. However, the pricing models as well as the provided resources vary between providers and a common standard for accurately describing the performance of an instance, which requires a standardized method for benchmarking, has not been established yet.

In recent years, a lot of methodologies, e.g. Cloud Spectator[1] which offers strategic cloud planning for enterprises, and benchmark suites, like the SPEC Cloud IaaS benchmark[2], have been created specifically for that purpose. Various research papers have been published as well in this area [4, 6, 9, 14–16]. Additionally, some also support the automatic benchmarking of applications. Selecting

---

[1] https://cloudspectator.com/.
[2] https://www.spec.org/cloud_iaas2016/.

an appropriate cloud provider along with the right compute instance type is still a difficult process, especially for new cloud adopters. Specifically, applications that have not been executed in the cloud before, need to be benchmarked at least a few times before an accurate prediction for the instance selection can be made to account for performance variations of the cloud instance, changes of the input data of an application or general failures during the execution [1, 20].

A standard methodology can drastically reduce the necessary benchmark effort as less benchmarks have to be repeated and similar instances as well as applications could be detected more easily. We envision the creation of compute instance and application performance footprints that can not only be used to calculate the similarity between resources and applications, but also to find the perfect set of instances for a given application.

3   Related Work

Cloud benchmarking and the idea to standardize the performance evaluation of compute instances has been an important research topic for nearly a decade. Regarding application benchmarks, the Cloudstone benchmark was one of the earliest attempts on creating representative workloads for the cloud [16]. Other benchmarks that have been created specifically for the cloud include Cloud-Suite [9], WPress [6], the SPEC Cloud^{TM} IaaS 2016 [4] and Cloud Work-Bench [15]. Further, benchmarks that are not specifically designed for the cloud, such as the TCP-W, have been used as well in a few studies [3, 18]. However, as stated by Binnig et al. the TCP-W is in fact not representative of actual workloads in the cloud [5].

Additionally, hardware or micro benchmarks have also been utilized in a number publications in an attempt to compare cloud instances. Li et al. compared public cloud providers using conventional computational benchmark metrics and noticed large differences in performance and cost across cloud providers [11]. In a later study, Leitner and Cito conducted a large literature review in which the authors confirmed these differences and other hypotheses based on the observations in existing research [10]. Very recently, Scheuner and Leitner created a benchmark suite that can be used to automatically measure the performance of compute instance by combining micro and application benchmarks [14]. Their findings include a significant reduction of network performance variations in the AWS cloud and cost-effective instance types for the Wordpress based web serving benchmark WPBench that offer more performance for fewer cost.

Similar experiments have been conducted by Sadooghi et al., however, instead of a synthetic application benchmark the authors evaluated the performance of a real scientific application along with the raw performance of the cloud instances on which it has been executed on [13]. Further, the results were compared with the performance of a private cloud setup. We believe that this approach is closest to our work as not only hardware but also application benchmarks have been conducted to enable scientists a better understanding the performance of cloud resources and how these can be used to support their work.

4   Benchmark Model

Despite the amount of research in cloud benchmarking we noticed that, to the best of our knowledge, no extensive effort has been made yet to utilize the combination of the individual results that have been created. The findings have been summarized in extensive surveys but due to the differences in the approach including, the cloud instances, applications and micro benchmarks that have been utilized it is not a simple task to make use of them in combination.

We developed a generic meta-model to store application and instance data and extended this model to capture performance benchmark results and to link these results to the application and resource infrastructure. The model has been created specifically with regard to the different approaches we have observed in the existing research so far. Our goal is to provide a single, structured approach for storing benchmark data linked to resources and application deployments in the cloud with enough additional information to automate the process of executing benchmarks in the cloud and collecting the results.

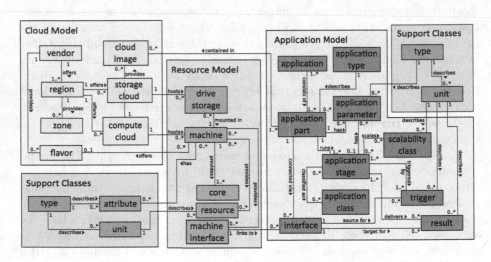

Fig. 1. Our previously published resource and application meta-model [19]

Figure 1 shows our previously published resource and application model [19]. Starting at the center, a *machine* usually represents a compute instance in the cloud, however, it can also refer to a containerized instance or even a physical machine. Machines can be linked to a *compute cloud* in which they are deployed. As machines in different regions will behave differently, especially regarding network response times, compute clouds are linked to a specific *region* in which a *vendor* operates one or multiple data centers represented as *zones*.

Basic information about a machine can be stored as a so called *flavor* which is the information provided by the cloud service provider about the resources of a compute instance and is also known as instance- or machine type. If more detailed information about machine *resources* and *attributes* like location or IP address is available it can be stored in two separate tables linked to machine. Exceptions to this are CPU cores and network interfaces which are stored in separate tables to enable linking benchmark results to a specific *core* and application interfaces, which we will explain shortly, to the corresponding *machine interface*. Further, block storage devices that can be attached to a machine are represented by the *drive storage* table which is managed by a *storage cloud*.

As for the application model, first, we would like to note that an *application* consists of at least one *application part*, to allow modeling distributed or multi-tier applications as well. The parameters which are part of the configuration of an application can be stored in the *application parameter* table. Next, if there is any data exchange between application parts, the corresponding *interfaces* can also be defined. Additionally, we added the *cloud image* table to the resource model, which is specific to a compute cloud and thus a region, and contains the identifier for this image as well as the provided application parts. This information can be used to automate the execution of these applications.

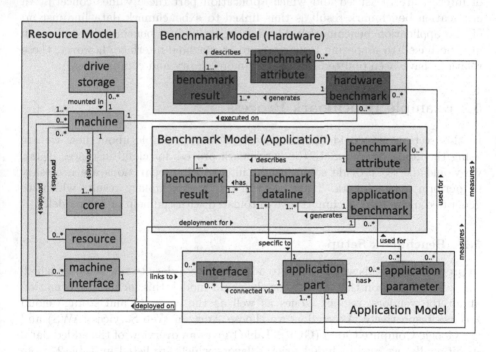

Fig. 2. The core of our proposed benchmarking meta-model

Figure 2 shows the additions to the existing model as it did not allow to store benchmark data for machines and applications in an efficient manner yet. Every benchmark is performed with at least one application part which we already model in our database. This includes the parameter values that can be set for a benchmark in case the default values are not used.

Whereas a *hardware benchmark* is assumed to run on a single machine only, with the exception of a network benchmark application like iperf for which a remote machine can be set, the setup for an *application benchmark* is defined in a separate link table between *machine, application part* and *application benchmark* to account for a distributed setup with multiple application parts. Another way to connect a benchmark with the application part that has been used is the respective *benchmark attribute* table which also links to the application part. A benchmark attribute describes a possible result of a benchmark execution, e.g. the average read and write rate for IO operations. The actual value that has been determined for an attribute during the benchmark is stored in the *benchmark result* table.

For applications the model is slightly different as usually continuous values are collected, like CPU or memory utilization every second, and not a single value determining the *value* of a resource, like a score that is generated by applications such as Geekbench[3]. Therefore, the table *benchmark data line* is introduced. One entry in this table represents a point in time in which all values of interest are measured and which application part these values concern. An application benchmark result is thus linked to a benchmark data line instead of the application benchmark table. Lastly, individual benchmark results can also be linked to a specific resource, core or machine interface, however, these relations have been omitted in Fig. 2 for more clarity and compactness.

5   Example Benchmark Process

In this section we would like to provide a short example about how we are using the model to automate the benchmark process for cloud instances. First, we would like to provide some insight into which preparations are necessary to perform a benchmark. Then, we will provide exemplary results which we generated using the benchmarks we automated with the help of our model.

5.1   Benchmark Setup

In preparation of this work we had to add some meta-data to the database which we created based on this model. For the cloud model, this includes information about the vendors, regions, zones as well as the compute and storage cloud services respectively. As vendors we choose Amazon Web Services (AWS) and the Google Compute Cloud (GCP). Table 1 gives an overview of the added data. Additionally, we also included several flavors which are listed in Table 2. Note that there are no comments about the network speed of GCP machine types.

We decided to use sysbench for the micro benchmarks as it already includes CPU, memory, thread and IO performance benchmarks and can be installed and executed with minimal effort. Therefore, we added sysbench as an *application* to the database and modeled it as a multi-part application. In this specific case we

---

[3] https://www.geekbench.com/.

Table 1. Meta-data for the cloud model used in our example.

Vendor	Regions	Compute cloud services	Storage cloud services
AWS	us-east-1	EC2 on demand	EBS gp2 S3
	eu-central-1		
	ap-northeast-1		
GCP	us-east4	Google compute engine	Persistent disk cloud storage
	europe-west3		
	asia-northeast1		

Table 2. The different flavors we used for our benchmarks.

Vendor	Flavor	Cores	Memory	Network
AWS	m4.large	2	8 GB	Moderate
AWS	r4.large	2	15.25 GB	Up to 10 Gigabit
AWS	i3.large	2	15.25 GB	Up to 10 Gigabit
AWS	c4.large	2	3.75 GB	Moderate
AWS	c5.large	2	4	Moderate
GCP	n1-standard-2	2	7.5 GB	–
GCP	n1-highcpu-2	2	1.8 GB	–

added every possible benchmark run that we want to use as an application part using the command line call as its distinctive feature, e.g. *'sysbench [params] cpu run'*. The *[params]* symbolizes that other parameters from the *application parameter* table can be inserted with their respective values set in the *hardware benchmark parameter* table. This allows us to automate the creation of scripts for every individual benchmark run. The only part that has to be provided manually for every benchmark application is a converter that extracts the relevant results from the output of the benchmark. Next, all results that can be extracted in this way, have to be added to the *hardware benchmark attributes* table.

Table 3 shows a non-exclusive list of parameters and attributes that we added to the database. Note that all values are stored as string. For every type we add a converter class which is also referenced in the database. We also added a special type to the database called 'param int' which should be used for integer values that are suffixed by one or multiple characters for further description of the type, e.g. a unit like 'G'. The column *'BM Value'* contains the values we used in the experiments which we talk about later.

Last, we prepared a benchmark image in every region of the respective cloud providers based on Ubuntu 16.04 LTS in which we installed sysbench and other benchmarking software. We also choose to include the AWS specific Amazon Linux operating system (OS) to measure the influence of the OS on the performance.

Table 3. Parameters and attributes of the various sysbench benchmarks we use

Parameters				
Benchmark	Parameter	Default value	BM value	Type
cpu	--cpu-max-prime	10000	20000	int
threads	--thread-locks	8	10	int
memory	--memory-total-size	100G	100G	param int
fileio	--file-total-size	2G	40G	param int
fileio	--file-test-mode	"	rndrw	string
all	--time	0	0	int
all	--events	10000	300 (fileio)	int
all	--threads	1	1	int
Attributes				
Benchmark	Attribute			Type
cpu	events_per_second			float
memory	memory_transferred_per_second			float
fileio	fileio_read_rate_mbs			float
fileio	fileio_write_rate_mbs			float

For the automation of the benchmarks we choose the infrastructure as code (IoC) tool Terraform[4]. Therefore, we have to prepare a template file for every cloud provider in which we add the provider and a resource, i.e. a compute instance. Terraform allows the utilization of variables which we use to add place-holders for information such as the id or name of the image, region, flavor, access information, ssh keys and the variables for the benchmark script. Most of this information still has to be provided manually, but, due to the use of placeholders, they can be easily provided to Terraform with a *variable* file.

We also utilize variables when we create the benchmark script which is added as a 'remote-exec' provisioner to the Terraform configuration. Parameters that differ from the default value are also added as placeholders to the script which allows the repetition of a benchmark using different parameters without the need to change the entire template. We also add a counter variable called *bm_run*. If a benchmark script is executed multiple times, the results of each individual benchmark will be uploaded to a separate folder in the persistent storage with the structure '/<*region*>/<*flavor*>/<*bm_run*>'.

Furthermore, we add commands to the configuration to store the starting and completion time of the script in a local file as well as the starting time of the benchmark in a remote file which will be executed as soon as the instance is running and accessible. This allows us to measure the provisioning delay of an instance. Lastly, every command in the remote script is also enveloped in the *time* command to measure the real, user and sys time which we also added as parameters to the database.

---

[4] https://www.terraform.io/.

After the termination of the remote script the destroy command from Terraform is used to terminate the instance. Then, we download the results from the persistent storage service. We also wrote a Java application which uses the conversion classes that have to be manually provided for every benchmark application to convert the results and insert them into the database.

We only talked about executing micro benchmarks for evaluating the performance of the hardware so far. To also capture application performance information in a generic fashion we choose *atop* as tool to collect continuous values about the system performance every second. To measure the effect of the concurrent execution of atop on the application performance, we executed the same sysbench benchmarks, except with atop as a background process. We made some minor modifications to the remote script executed by Terraform in which we added the commands for installing atop, starting it as background process and killing it after the completion of the benchmarks. Furthermore, the results are converted to CSV using atopsar for a simple way to interpret them. These results are uploaded to the persistent cloud storage after the benchmark completion as well.

Overall we ran the same experiment on 828 instances, created 13716 files and imported 127926 result values in our database so far, thus, generating an extensive collection of values to specify the performance footprint of an instance already. Furthermore, since we are using a generic model to store the benchmark results, we can, with the proper permissions, include results from other research papers as well to enhance the data without the necessity to perform more benchmarks.

5.2 Benchmark Results

First, we would like to focus on the provisioning delay for the instances based on the provider, region and operating system.

Table 4. Average delay for provisioning an instance in different regions of the AWS and GCP cloud using instances based on Ubuntu and the Amazon Linux OS

Region		Average provisioning delay	Standard deviation
ap-northeast-1	Amazon Linux:	54.60 s	11.20 s
	Ubuntu:	19.72 s	3.85 s
eu-central-1	Amazon Linux:	113.98 s	19.25 s
	Ubuntu:	27.36 s	3.07 s
us-east-1	Amazon Linux:	89.97 s	20.72 s
	Ubuntu:	22.57 s	19.23 s
asia-northeast1	Ubuntu:	27.04 s	3.07 s
europe-west3	Ubuntu:	22.54 s	2.87 s
us-east4	Ubuntu:	23.52 s	2.46 s

During our evaluation of the Amazon Linux OS, we noticed a significant difference in the provisioning delay between the three AWS regions. The results in Table 4 show that the Tokyo region has not only the shortest delay when starting an instance until it becomes available the variation in the delay is also significantly lower. Further investigations did not reveal a correlation with other data that has been collected so far, including the actual performance of the instance and the start time of the benchmark. It appears that instances with less memory like compute optimized instances such as c4.large and c5.large take less time to start, as one would expect, however, this conclusion is not backed up by enough data in our opinion to be completely justified.

Another observation we made is the difference in the provisioning delay based on the operating system. Whereas the AWS and GCP instances based on Ubuntu 16.04 are provided in about the same time, the instances using the Amazon Linux require significantly more time to start. This is a useful observation, especially for load balancing algorithms in which the time until an instance becomes operational is vital. We also would like to point out the large standard deviation for the Ubuntu instances in the AWS us-east-1 region. We observed a sometimes significantly larger provisioning delay during the evening between 6pm and midnight EST. For the GCP instances no large variations have been detected.

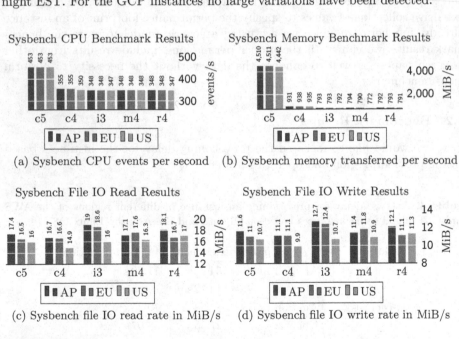

(a) Sysbench CPU events per second   (b) Sysbench memory transferred per second

(c) Sysbench file IO read rate in MiB/s   (d) Sysbench file IO write rate in MiB/s

Fig. 3. Sysbench performance comparison results for the ap-northeast-1 (AP), eu-central-1 (EU) and us-east-1 (US) regions using the Amazon Linux OS

Figure 3 shows the results of CPU, memory and fileio benchmarks for the Amazon Linux instances. While the CPU and memory performance appear to be similar in different regions, the fileio benchmarks reveal slightly less IO performance for instances in the us-east-1 region, except for instances of the r4.large type. Notably, the new c5.large generation of instance types show a significant performance boost compared to the previous generation of instances, especially regarding the memory benchmark. Further, no impact of the start time of the benchmark on the performance of the instances has been observed.

We repeated the same experiments with instances of the t2 family which use burst resources and noticed that their performance varies significantly by up to 10% regarding the attributes presented in Table 3, which is to be expected. The variations seem to be not only caused by the start time of the instance however. In fact we could not find a reliable correlation at all. Therefore, we suggest that instances that rely on burst resources require further attention or should be excluded from such benchmarks entirely, as their performance is not stable enough to be accurately predicted. For brevity, we did not include the overall t2 results in this paper.

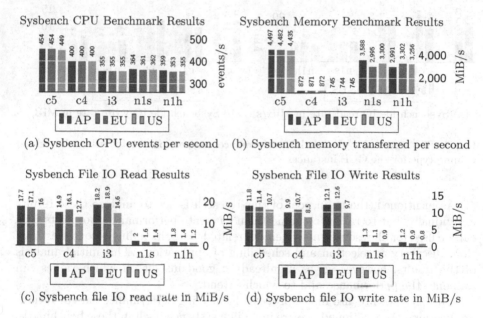

(a) Sysbench CPU events per second   (b) Sysbench memory transferred per second

(c) Sysbench file IO read rate in MiB/s   (d) Sysbench file IO write rate in MiB/s

Fig. 4. Sysbench performance comparison results for the respective regions N. Virginia (US), Tokyo (AP) and Frankfurt (EU) of the AWS and GCP cloud using the Ubuntu 16.04. operating system. The c5, c4 and i3 instance types are AWS specific, n1s (n1-standard-2) and n1h (n1-highcpu-2) are GCP specific.

Next, in Fig. 4 we provide the most notable results of the micro benchmarks for the Ubuntu instances. We excluded the AWS m4 and r4 instance types due to space limitations and since they performed very similar to the c4 and i3 instances respectively. One notable observation we made is that the c4 Ubuntu instances seem to achieve better results regarding their CPU performance and slightly worse results for the memory benchmarks compared to the Amazon Linux instances. Also, according to our evaluation, the GCP instances seem to operate with a similar level of CPU performance as the i3 AWS instances but are superior in terms of memory performance.

However, it also seems that the IO performance of the GCP instances is significantly worse compared to AWS. That is because the volume type for AWS instances defaults to SSD whereas on GCP it defaults to basic storage which is not preferable for many random IO operations, which we used for our evaluation. Therefore, we repeated the GCP benchmarks using the platform specific pd-ssd volume type. While the results are still slightly worse compared to the AWS instance types, as shown in Fig. 5, the SSD volumes outperform the basic types by a huge margin, which is to be expected.

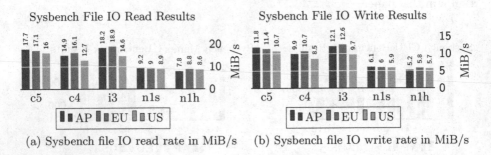

(a) Sysbench file IO read rate in MiB/s   (b) Sysbench file IO write rate in MiB/s

Fig. 5. The updated sysbench IO performance comparison results using the pd-ssd volume type for the GCP instances.

As mentioned, the main goal of this research is not to analyze these results individually, but to rather combine them to create performance footprints that can be used for all resource management related tasks, including resource estimation, discovery & selection and scheduling of applications. This initial analysis of the results, however, gives us already a good insight on which values can influence the performance and to which extend.

Currently, we are also in the process of collecting performance data of various applications. As mentioned, we are including sysbench itself in these benchmarks as it provides a unique application footprint for every benchmark run already. Concurrently, we are also benchmarking scientific workflow applications based on the Common Workflow Language (CWL) which are used in genome analysis using this process. The only necessary addition to the benchmark script is the installation of this application and, if necessary, to upload input data for it. Meta-data about the in- and output of an application can also be stored in the database and thus can be used as additional variable for the performance footprint creation.

6   Conclusion

We presented an extension for our application and resource meta-model to add the ability to include hardware and application benchmark results. With this addition the benchmark results can easily be related to the respective machine, application or individual resource which has been benchmarked. We further described a simple process to automate the benchmarking of machines in the AWS and GCP cloud which can also be adapted for other cloud providers quite easily. Naturally, there is still some work ahead to fully automate this process. Our next actions include the creation of scripts for other cloud providers, the addition of results from other research papers to enhance the model for the benchmarked *machines* and *applications* as well as the automatic creation of performance footprints for the benchmarked entity. Our current focus, besides generating more results as well as adding existing results to our database, lies on generating classification schemes that use all or part of the results linked to a resource and/or application for creating these footprints.

References

1. Alejandra, R.M., Rajkumar, B.: A taxonomy and survey on scheduling algorithms for scientific workflows in IaaS cloud computing environments. Concurr. Comput.: Pract. Exp. **29**(8), e4041 (2016). https://doi.org/10.1002/cpe.4041
2. Armbrust, M., et al.: A view of cloud computing. Commun. ACM **53**(4), 50–58 (2010). https://doi.org/10.1145/1721654.1721672
3. Bankole, A., Ajila, S.: Cloud client prediction models for cloud resource provisioning in a multitier web application environment. In: 2013 IEEE 7th International Symposium on Service Oriented System Engineering (SOSE), pp. 156–161, March 2013
4. Baset, S., Silva, M., Wakou, N.: Spec cloud^{TM}IaaS 2016 benchmark. In: Proceedings of the 8th ACM/SPEC on International Conference on Performance Engineering, ICPE 2017, p. 423. ACM, New York (2017). https://doi.org/10.1145/3030207.3053675
5. Binnig, C., Kossmann, D., Kraska, T., Loesing, S.: How is the weather tomorrow? Towards a benchmark for the cloud. In: Proceedings of the Second International Workshop on Testing Database Systems, pp. 1–6 (2009). https://doi.org/10.1145/1594156.1594168
6. Borhani, A., Leitner, P., Lee, B.S., Li, X., Hung, T.: Wpress: an application-driven performance benchmark for cloud-based virtual machines. In: 2014 IEEE 18th International on Enterprise Distributed Object Computing Conference (EDOC), pp. 101–109, September 2014
7. Chhetri, M., Chichin, S., Vo, Q.B., Kowalczyk, R.: Smart CloudBench - automated performance benchmarking of the cloud. In: 2013 IEEE Sixth International Conference on Cloud Computing (CLOUD), pp. 414–421, June 2013
8. Coutinho, R., Frota, Y., Ocaña, K., de Oliveira, D., Drummond, L.M.A.: A dynamic cloud dimensioning approach for parallel scientific workflows: a case study in the comparative genomics domain. J. Grid Comput. **14**(3), 443–461 (2016). https://doi.org/10.1007/s10723-016-9367-x

9. Ferdman, M., et al.: Clearing the clouds: a study of emerging scale-out workloads on modern hardware. SIGPLAN Not. **47**(4), 37–48 (2012). https://doi.org/10.1145/2248487.2150982

10. Leitner, P., Cito, J.: Patterns in the chaos–a study of performance variation and predictability in public IaaS clouds. ACM Trans. Internet Technol. **16**(3), 15:1–15:23 (2016). https://doi.org/10.1145/2885497

11. Li, A., Yang, X., Kandula, S., Zhang, M.: CloudCmp: comparing public cloud providers. In: ACM SIGCOMM, vol. 10, pp. 1–14 (2010). https://doi.org/10.1145/1879141.1879143

12. Mell, P., Grance, T.: The NIST definition of cloud computing, January 2011

13. Sadooghi, I., et al.: Understanding the performance and potential of cloud computing for scientific applications. IEEE Trans. Cloud Comput. **PP**(99), 1 (2015)

14. Scheuner, J., Leitner, P.: A cloud benchmark suite combining micro and applications benchmarks. In: Companion of the 2018 ACM/SPEC International Conference on Performance Engineering, ICPE 2018, pp. 161–166. ACM, New York (2018). https://doi.org/10.1145/3185768.3186286

15. Scheuner, J., Leitner, P., Cito, J., Gall, H.: Cloud WorkBench - infrastructure-as-code based cloud benchmarking. CoRR abs/1408.4565 (2014)

16. Sobel, W., et al.: Cloudstone: multi-platform, multi-language benchmark and measurement tools for web 2.0. Technical report, UC Berkeley and Sun Microsystems (2008)

17. Stockton, D.B., Santamaria, F.: Automating neuron simulation deployment in cloud resources. Neuroinformatics **15**(1), 51–70 (2017). https://doi.org/10.1007/s12021-016-9315-8

18. Tak, B.C., Tang, C., Huang, H., Wang, L.: PseudoApp: performance prediction for application migration to cloud. In: 2013 IFIP/IEEE International Symposium on Integrated Network Management (IM 2013), pp. 303–310, May 2013

19. Ullrich, M., Laessig, J., Gaedke, M., Aida, K., Sun, J., Tanjo, T.: An application meta-model to support the execution and benchmarking of scientific applications in multi-cloud environments. In: 3rd IEEE Conference on Cloud and Big Data Computing (CBDCom 2017) (2017)

20. Ullrich, M., Lässig, J., Gaedke, M.: Towards efficient resource management in cloud computing: a survey. In: The IEEE 4th International Conference on Future Internet of Things and Cloud (FiCloud 2016) (2016)

21. Varghese, B., Buyya, R.: Next generation cloud computing: new trends and research directions. Future Gener. Comput. Syst. **79**, 849–861 (2018). https://doi.org/10.1016/j.future.2017.09.020

22. Volkov, S., Sukhoroslov, O.: Simplifying the use of clouds for scientific computing with everest. Procedia Comput. Sci. **119**, 112–120 (2017). https://doi.org/10.1016/j.procs.2017.11.167. 6th International Young Scientist Conference on Computational Science, YSC 2017, Kotka, Finland, 01–03 November 2017

Developing Agent-Based Smart Objects for IoT Edge Computing: Mobile Crowdsensing Use Case

Teemu Leppänen[1], Claudio Savaglio[2(✉)], Lauri Lovén[1], Wilma Russo[2],
Giuseppe Di Fatta[3], Jukka Riekki[1], and Giancarlo Fortino[2]

[1] Center for Ubiquitous Computing, University of Oulu, Oulu, Finland
{teemu.leppanen,lauri.loven,jukka.riekki}@oulu.fi
[2] Department of Informatics, Modelling, Electronics and Systems,
University of Calabria, Rende, Italy
csavaglio@dimes.unical.it, {w.russo,g.fortino}@unical.it
[3] Department of Computer Science, University of Reading, Reading, UK
g.difatta@reading.ac.uk

Abstract. Software agents have been exploited to handle the inherent dynamicity in the Internet of Things (IoT) systems, as agents are capable of autonomous, reactive and proactive operation in response to changes in their local environment. Agents, operating at the network edge, enable leveraging cloud resources into the proximity of the user devices. However, poor interoperability with the existing IoT systems and the lack of a systematic methodology for IoT system development with the agent paradigm have hindered the utilization of software agent technologies in IoT. In this paper, we describe the development process and the system architecture of a mobile crowdsensing service, provided by an agent-based smart object that comprises agents in both edge and user devices. Mobile crowdsensing is an example of such an application that relies on large-scale participatory sensor networks, where participants have active roles in producing information about their environment with their smartphones. This scheme introduces challenges in handling dynamic opportunistic resource availability, due to mobility and unpredicted actions of the participants. We present how ACOSO-Meth (Agent-oriented Cooperative Smart Object-Methodology) guidelines the development process systematically from the analysis to the actual agent-based implementation of a crowdsensing service. The implementation is done with the ROAgent framework that utilizes resource-oriented architecture and REST principles to integrate agent-based smart objects seamlessly with the programmable Web.

Keywords: Smart object · Edge computing · Internet of Things
Agent-based computing · Programmable web

© Springer Nature Switzerland AG 2018
Y. Xiang et al. (Eds.): IDCS 2018, LNCS 11226, pp. 235–247, 2018.
https://doi.org/10.1007/978-3-030-02738-4_20

1   Introduction

The Internet of Things (IoT) vision of a seamless integration of the cyber and physical worlds can be realized with Smart Objects (SO) as the fundamental building blocks [1]. These are common objects of any context (industry, entertainment, healthcare, etc.) able to interact with conventional computer systems, human users and the physical environment, thanks to their embedded sensing, processing, communication and actuation units. Moreover, SOs exhibit intelligence, autonomy, reactivity, proactivity and social skills in their operation, thus enabling, in theory, straightforward provision of advanced, decentralized, and cyberphysical services. In practice, however, the development of SO's requires established, effective and flexible metaphors, techniques, methods and tools for systematically conceptualizing, designing and implementing complex, autonomous and interactive SOs. In addition, interoperability is required between the SOs and the existing IoT systems.

The SO features listed above can be achieved with the agent-based computing paradigm [2]. Agents are natively autonomous, reactive, proactive, social and, in some cases, mobile, being able to relocate themselves at runtime. With agents' capabilities, SOs can observe their operational environment, react to changes and interact with other components and with each other as a multiagent system (MAS). In such a way, agent-based SOs are enabled to concretely bring smartness, autonomy and interactivity into the operation of IoT systems [3].

Recently, edge computing [4] brings computational power and data storage into the proximity of user devices. The aim is to improve IoT application execution by reducing latencies and providing more bandwidth locally. Benefits are seen in robustness and security, and also, data traffic on the backbone network is reduced. However, such a decentralized model requires capabilities for autonomy, interoperability and smartness in application execution that takes the local circumstances into account. Here, agent-based SO's can be exploited in the development and implementation of such distributed applications. Mobile crowdsensing [5] is an example of a distributed IoT application, which is beneficial to leverage into the edge and where agent-based SO enables context-aware operation between the edge and user devices. Application components in the edge perform computationally heavy tasks and interact with resource-constrained user devices, i.e., smartphones, that perform data collection in dynamic and opportunistic settings as guided by agents.

In this paper, we analyze, design and implement a mobile crowdsensing SO as an IoT edge application. We tackle the methodology and interoperability challenges by following the guidelines provided by the agent-oriented IoT development methodology ACOSO-Meth [6] and the resource-oriented architecture (ROA) [7] principles. We utilize the ROAgent framework [8–10] to develop the agent-based SO, where the functionality is distributed as a MAS across the edge devices and user devices. The SO exposes a service on the edge platform that, first, provides a set of smartphones that meet specific criteria for participation into crowdsensing campaigns and, second, interacts with mobile agents in the smartphones to execute the campaign, as in [11]. The analysis, design and implementation of such a multiagent-based SO leads to a real-world prototype.

The rest of the paper is organized as follows. In Sect. 2, we describe the operation of crowdsensing SO as a MAS. In Sect. 3, we present how the crowdsensing SO is developed accordingly exploiting both the ACOSO-Meth agent-oriented approach and ROA resource-oriented paradigm. Section 4 then discusses implications of the approach and concludes the paper.

2   Agent-Based Crowdsensing System

Crowdsensing frameworks are typically cloud-based and centrally-controlled [5]. However, by following such a model, it is difficult to react to changes in the opportunistic environment and to the participants' behavior, possibly resulting in a significant reduction of data quality. Conversely, as shown in previous works, e.g., [11–13], agents and MAS can be effectively exploited to address the dynamicity in crowdsensing applications. In fact, agent-based development also allows enhancing privacy and energy efficiency in context-aware way, particularly beneficial for resource-constrained devices, such as smartphones [11].

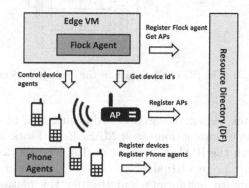

Fig. 1. System architecture of crowdsensing SO with the ROAgent framework.

Figures 1 and 2 present the agent-based crowdsensing SO system architecture within the ROAgent framework. The framework fully complies with ROA and the fundamental idea is to facilitate Representational state transfer (REST) principles [7] for agent-based applications in IoT in a standardized way [8–10]. As discussed in [10], the ROA approach can be optimized for resource-constrained IoT devices, while still enabling agent operations and interactions with other system components. The main abstraction is a resource that can be anything that has a value, e.g., an IoT device, its sensors and data, an edge device in the network infrastructure running VMs, an external data source (e.g., a Web service), or a software agent. The resources are accessed through a RESTful uniform interface that is based on the combined semantics of HTTP methods, resource

URLs and HTTP response codes. The ROAgent framework extends this uniform interface to agent operations and interactions. In addition, the framework follows FIPA specifications that enable a standardized way to integrate agents into a MAS. A set of FIPA components are implemented, i.e., Directory Facilitator (DF), Agent Management System (AMS) and Message Transport System (MTS). The DF is implemented as Distributed Resource Directory (DRD) [14]. The framework operation requires system devices to register their resources into the DRD, which enables runtime lookup for available resources in a given location. MTS is enabled through a Web server with HTTP as the communication and interaction protocol that implements the uniform interface.

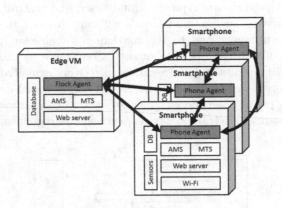

Fig. 2. The SO components in the system devices.

Figure 2 illustrates the agent-based crowdsensing SOs internal architecture and depicts the agents interactions as a MAS. Both Flock and Phone agents are implemented with the ROAgent platform [10]. The Flock agent platform is implemented within a Edge Virtual Machine (VM), which enables typical edge computing operations to instantiate and transfer the platform between edge devices. In the smartphones, the ROAgent platform runs an AMS to enable agent operations in the device and provides a database (DB) for data storage including agent knowledge base, i.e., SO data, and its interaction results. In detail, the agent's roles are the following. First, the Flock agent detects suitable participants, with the required sensor type, in a given area from the list its connected phones provided by the Wi-Fi access points (AP in Fig. 1) and the DRD. Flocks of participants, with similar behavior, can be detected from these data that meet the campaign requirements. For example, a set of participants moving into the same direction can be utilized to provide data with better quality than with a single participant. Moreover, movement patterns of participants can be detected, to get information about their performance and to control participation. Second, the Flock agent and Phone agents, in the participants smartphones, interact as a MAS to execute the campaign aiming to fulfill its goals and reacting to participants' behaviors.

3   Systematic Approach to Crowdsensing So Development

In this section, we apply the ACOSO-Meth [6] with ROA general guidelines
[7] for the development of ROAgent-based crowdsensing SO. Initially, ACOSO-
Meth and the ROAgent framework have been conceptually integrated in [15] by
re-engineering the ROAgent framework according to the methodology.

We provide an actual real-world development of an agent- and SO-based
crowdsensing service according to ACOSO-Meth and ROAgent framework guidelines. Regarding the service functionality, crowdsensing campaign participants
are recruited based on their reputation, that can be monitored by an agent [11].
However, integrating participation into the existing traveling routes improves
possibilities of participation [16], which justifies the presented crowdsensing service. In this paper, our focus is not on developing novel methods for agent-based
crowdsensing participant recruitment nor for flock detection, e.g., [17,18].

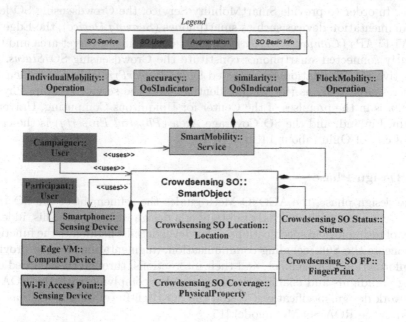

Fig. 3. Crowdsensing SO high-level metamodel of the analysis phase.

3.1   Analysis Phase

At the analysis phase, the ACOSO-Meth exploits of the SO High-Level meta-
model to specify SO basic features and information. This is a very general meta-
model, supporting the preliminary SO description regardless of any technological
or behavioral specification. Indeed, the SO High-Level metamodel outlines how
the SO can be identified, the provided services with related composing operations

and needed augmentation devices (e.g., sensors, actuators, processing units), and who are the SO users [19,20].

The SO High-Level metamodel instantiated on the *Crowdsensing SO* is shown in Fig. 3. The SO provides the SmartMobility *Service* for crowdsensing *Campaigners* as the users, who launch campaigns and need to recruit *Participants* meeting the campaign-specific requirements. For example, participants need to be in the target location in a specified timeframe. The SmartMobility Service is realized through two *Operations*: IndividualMobility to get the movement trace of an individual participant and FlockMobility to detect participant flocks in the specified area. As service content, the SO provides a list containing timeseries of movement traces of individual participants and detected flocks that meet the campaign parameters. This list provides the campaigners a selection of possible participants to recruit. The quality of SmartMobility Service is expressed in terms of two metrics or *Quality of Service (QoS) Indicators*: the detection accuracy of the individual trace and the similarity of participants' movements within a flock. In order to provide SmartMobility Service, the Crowdsensing SO leverages augmentation devices such as smartphones (*Sensing Device*), the Edge VM and Wi-Fi APs (*Computer Device*). The lists of APs in the target area and their currently connected smartphones constitute the Crowdsensing SO *Status*. The distinctive SO information are reported by its *FingerPrint*: the SO is identified by its resource URL as the unique identifier and the service creator. Physical *Location* is in the premises of the Center for Ubiquitous Computing, University of Oulu, Finland, and the SO Coverage Area (*Physical Property*) is the center zone of city of Oulu (about $1\,\text{Km} \times 1\,\text{km}$).

3.2 Design Phase

At the design phase, the ACOSO-Meth guides the refinement of the SO High-Level Metamodel with the goal of obtaining a design metamodel. This, independently of technological specifications or low level details, highlights the functional components the SO, including communication, augmentation, service provision and information management, and their interactions, through the adopted computing paradigms and enabling mechanisms. By complying with the ROAgent framework design specifications [8–10], the SO High-Level Metamodel has been refined in the ROA SO Metamodel [15].

The instantiated ROA SO Metamodel on the Crowdsensing SO is shown in Fig. 4. Following the ROAgent framework, the Crowdsensing SO is based on a lightweight and platform-neutral agent. The agent functionality is defined through resource abstractions, interactions realized via RESTful uniform interface and the agent operations are event-driven.

The Crowdsensing SO lifecycle is specified in terms of Behaviors. A *Behavior* consists of one or more *Tasks*, which are coordinated by the *Crowdsensing SO Manager*. The tasks refer either to internal system operations (*SystemTask*) or to SO application-specific functionalities (*ServiceTask*). The latter category contains IndividualTrace tasks that provide individual movement traces, and the FlockTrace task that provides flock movement traces. Both tasks acquire input through the uniform interface and resource URLs, which guarantees transparent access regardless of resource type and location, according to ROA.

Within the ROAgent framework, each *Resource* is identified with a URL that is registered to the DRD. Resources needed for the presented crowdsensing application are listed in Table 1. With respect to the Crowdsensing SO, the resources are: (i) *Internal Resources* which are logically located within the devices hosting the SO ROAgents and their internal components, i.e. Edge VMs host the Flock agent and the smartphones host the Phone agents, (ii) *External Resources* which are physically hosted in devices that are not part of the Crowdsensing SO, i.e., smartphones' sensors, or other devices co-located within the smart city infrastructure (i.e., DRD and Wi-Fi APs), and (iii) *Device Resources* which are SO sensors, actuators, and computing units, i.e., smartphones as agent platforms and their sensors. The SO ROAgentKB contains the current results of the agent programs, the agent's internal data, and the campaign parameters including required sensor data type, area, timeframe and the ending criteria.

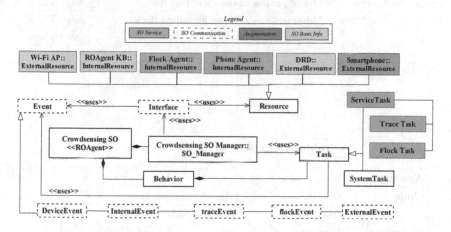

Fig. 4. Crowdsensing SO ROA Metamodel of the design phase.

The SO service resources in Table 1, including the resources provided by agents, are utilized as follows. The DRD, through the resource *drd*, allows retrieving a list of APs and information about individual devices connected to the framework. The WI-Fi APs, through the resource *wifi*, provide real-time information of smartphone availability, namely lists of their currently connected smartphones. The Flock Agent provides participant and flock movement traces, through the resource *flock*. The Phone Agents, through the resource *phone*, enable control the campaign execution. Smartphone sensors, through the resource *sensor_type*, provide requested sensor data for the campaigners.

As illustrated in Fig. 4, each resource request arriving to the SO through the uniform *Interface*, the Crowdsensing SO Manager executes the operation defined in the request URL and transports the obtained data through a specific *Event*.

Individual trace retrievals and flock detections are notified through the corresponding Trace and Flock *ServiceEvents*. The retrievals of Internal, External and Device resources (e.g., information about Crowdsensing SO status or smartphone availability) is performed through corresponding *InternalEvent*, *ExternalEvent* and *DeviceEvent* events.

Table 1. The resources for the crowdsensing SmartMobility cervice.

External resource		
/drd/{sensor_type}	Lookup for particular sensor in the DRD	*Infrastructure*
/wifi/devices	Connected devices (MAC addresses) in an AP	*Infrastructure*
Internal resource		
/trace/{MAC_addr}	Movement traces	*Edge VM*
/flock	List of detected flocks	*Edge VM*
/flock/map	Visualization of detected flocks in a map	*Edge VM*
/flock/{flock_id}	List of phones in the identified flock	*Edge VM*
/flock/{flock_id}/trace	Movement trace of the identified flock	*Edge VM*
/phone	Control phone operation	*Smartphone*
Device resource		
/{sensor_type}	Specific sensor and its data	*Smartphone*

Table 2. The flock agent architecture.

Agent name	flock		
Code	flock	*Agent program code*	
	trace	*Agent program code*	
Resource	**Remote**	wifi	*List of AP URLs*
		phone	*List of Phone agent URLs*
State	**Knowledge base**	campaign	*Campaign parameters*
	Service content	flock	*List of detected flocks*
		trace	*List of individual traces*

Internal Flock agent architecture follows ROAgent specifications [8–10] as illustrated in Table 2. The architecture comprises four elements. The agent name is derived from the resource listing (URL) to be *flock*. The agent programs, that implement the SO functionality, are defined as *flock* and *trace*. The resources that agent utilizes as data sources or to interact with are defined as local, i.e., in the hosting device, or remote, i.e., in other system component. Lastly, the agent state exposes the results of the agent program, e.g., flocks. The Phone agent architecture is similar as in [10], containing the agent program to process the sensor data for the particular campaign task, where the local resource is the utilized phone sensor.

3.3   Implementation Phase

At the implementation phase, ACOSO-Meth guides the exploitation of a meta-model that can elicit the programming paradigms and technology solutions which concretely realize the designed SO functionalities of communication, augmentation, service provision and information management. The ROA SO Metamodel of the design phase is implemented with regard to the heterogeneous ROAgent platforms, resulting in the ROAgent-based SO metamodel. Its instantiation on the Crowdsensing SO is shown in Fig. 5.

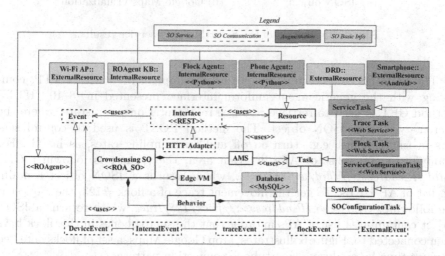

Fig. 5. Crowdsensing SO ROAgent Metamodel of the implementation phase.

The Edge VM hosting the Crowdsensing SO is implemented with Ubuntu 16.04 LTS, where MySQL database is installed for the ROAgentKB and Node.js provides the ROAgent platform and a Web server for interactions. The Flock agent program is implemented with Python, which is run in Node.js using the library Python-shell. The Phone agents also follow the ROAgent architecture and are implemented for the particular campaign task with Python for Android platform, as described in [11].

In addition to Fig. 4, the Fig. 5 reports the *ServiceConfigurationTask* that allows interacting with the ROAgents in the smartphones and Edge VM, for example, in order to set the campaign parameters. The *SOConfigurationTask* allows setting the Crowdsensing SO internal parameters, such as its resource URL as the identifier. The ROAgent platform *AMS* implements the uniform interface, presented in Table 1, for utilizing both internal and external resources in the service execution.

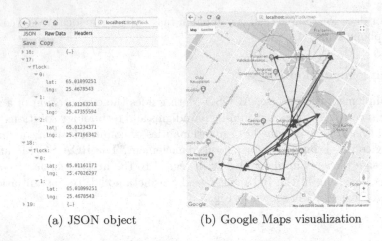

(a) JSON object   (b) Google Maps visualization

Fig. 6. Illustration of the SmartMobility service results.

The SO REST-based uniform interface is implemented with HTTP, complying with the generic agent uniform interface presented in [8–10]. HTTP method GET is used to retrieve resource representations, i.e., state, where the content-type is a JSON object. The method POST is used to control sensors in smartphones, e.g., turn on/off and set sampling rates, as in [11]. For example, to get a list of APs in given area, the request is following: *GET <drd_IP_address>://drd/wifi?area=...*, which returns a JSON object containing list of AP URLs. To get the movement trace of a flock #123, the request is the following: *GET <so_IP_address>://flock/123/trace*, which returns a JSON object containing a list of APs in order that the smartphones in this flock have been connected to. Figure 6 illustrates, atop Google Maps, a set of flocks detected at given time by analysing smartphone connection patterns.

In this paper, the SO service part is implemented, but the actual campaign execution with agents (studied in [11]) is not considered. To provide data for movement trace and flock detection, we utilized the existing smart city infrastructure [21] that includes a set of 1300 Wi-Fi APs and their data of connected devices during the years 2007–2015 in the city of Oulu. This dataset provides information about Wi-Fi connection data from the APs, containing a list of smartphone MAC addresses of connected devices for each AP as time series. A subset of 100 traces during one day (February 3rd, 2015) in the city centre area was imported for the Crowdsensing SO. The data was pre-filtered to remove outliers, i.e., APs with strong signal strength, which appeared in almost all traces across the city.

The Crowdsensing SO service provides the following content to campaigners to assist in campaign implementation: (i) the flocks, consisting in movement patterns of participants, i.e., individual smartphones, which behave similarly for a period in the target area. This data are dynamic, i.e., flocks appear and disappear and their participants may change any time, and (ii) the movement traces of individual participants retrieved from the APs data in the target area. To detect flocks, the algorithm presented in [18] was used. A strict threshold of 85% similarity was used between the individual traces to be considered a flock. Individual traces have low accuracy due to original data collected from APs that cover a large area. The flock detection and trace accuracy could be improved with Wi-Fi AP signal strength data from the smartphones, as in [18].

4   Discussion and Conclusion

Within the open and dynamic IoT edge computing scenario, the agent paradigm has been found useful [2]. Indeed, the paradigm allows exhibiting autonomous smart behavior in the collaborative execution of distributed IoT applications with both conventional computers and resource-constrained devices [10]. In mobile crowdsensing, data collection is a strictly coordinated effort in which the participants behaviors, such as unexpected actions or departures, can significantly affect the achievable results. The agent paradigm provides an approach to handle such situations in runtime, while aiming to save resources in the participating devices.

However, the lack of systematic methodology, that leads from initial analysis to actual agent-based implementation, has been an obstacle in agent-based IoT application development. Another obstacle has been poor interoperability, in general with the variety of existing system infrastructure, but also from the existing agent framework point-of-view. To address these both issues, we integrated the ROAgent framework with the development methodology ACOSO-Meth. As result, the ROAgent framework provides in a systematic way for interoperability through a programming language- and platform-independent agent architecture and exposing the agent as a Web service with standardized Web technologies.

Overall, this paper contributed to the full-fledged development of an agent-based SO under the form of a MAS. Jointly exploiting agent-oriented and resource-oriented paradigms, the ROAgent framework enabled heterogeneous, resource-constrained agent-based SOs interoperating in IoT systems in a standardized way. This made the agent-based SOs' resources and services browsable and searchable within the Internet as for any non-agent based service, integrating the agent-based SO's into the programmable Web for machines as well. The ACOSO-Meth approach drove the SO development across the phases of analysis, design and implementation through a set of metamodels, featured by different levels of abstraction and aimed at seamlessly supporting IoT developers in such a complex process.

Our future work aims at developing further the agent-based SO concepts for programmable Web under the umbrella of the integrated ACOSO-Meth and ROAgent framework.

Acknowledgments. This work has been carried out under the framework of INTER-IoT, Research and Innovation action - Horizon 2020 European Project, Grant Agreement #687283, financed by the European Union.

References

1. Kortuem, G., Kawsar, F., Sundramoorthy, V., Fitton, D.: Smart objects as building blocks for the Internet of Things. IEEE Internet Comput. **14**(1), 44–51 (2010)
2. Savaglio, C., Fortino, G., Ganzha, M., Paprzycki, M., Bădică, C., Ivanović, M.: Agent-based computing in the Internet of Things: a survey. In: Ivanović, M., Bădică, C., Dix, J., Jovanović, Z., Malgeri, M., Savić, M. (eds.) IDC 2017. SCI, vol. 737, pp. 307–320. Springer, Cham (2018). https://doi.org/10.1007/978-3-319-66379-1_27
3. Savaglio, C., Fortino, G.: Autonomic and cognitive architectures for the Internet of Things. In: Di Fatta, G., Fortino, G., Li, W., Pathan, M., Stahl, F., Guerrieri, A. (eds.) IDCS 2015. LNCS, vol. 9258, pp. 39–47. Springer, Cham (2015). https://doi.org/10.1007/978-3-319-23237-9_5
4. Shi, W., Cao, J., Zhang, Q., Li, Y., Xu, L.: Edge computing: vision and challenges. IEEE Internet Things J. **3**(5), 637–646 (2016)
5. Liu, J., Shen, H., Narman, H.S., Chung, W., Lin, Z.: A survey of mobile crowd-sensing techniques: a critical component for the Internet of Things. ACM Trans. Cyber-Phys. Syst. **2**(3), 18 (2018)
6. Fortino, G., Russo, W., Savaglio, C., Shen, W., Zhou, M.: Agent-oriented cooperative smart objects: from IoT system design to implementation. IEEE Trans. Syst. Man, and Cybern.: Syst. 1–18 (2017) https://doi.org/10.1109/TSMC.2017.2780618
7. Richardson, L., Ruby, S.: RESTful Web Services. O'Reilly, Newton (2008)
8. Leppänen, T., Liu, M., Harjula, E., Ramalingam, A., Ylioja, J., Närhi, P., et al.: Mobile agents for integration of Internet of Things and wireless sensor networks. In: IEEE International Conference on Systems, Man and Cybernetics, pp. 14–21 (2013). https://doi.org/10.1109/SMC.2013.10
9. Leppänen, T., Riekki, J., Liu, M., Harjula, E., Ojala, T.: Mobile agents-based smart objects for the Internet of Things. In: Fortino, G., Trunfio, P. (eds.) Internet of Things Based on Smart Objects. IT, pp. 29–48. Springer, Cham (2014). https://doi.org/10.1007/978-3-319-00491-4_2
10. Leppänen, T.: Resource-oriented mobile agent and software framework for the Internet of Things. Doctoral dissertation, University of Oulu, Finland, ISBN 978-952-62-1813-7 (2018)
11. Leppänen, T., Álvarez Lacasia, J., Tobe, Y., Sezaki, K., Riekki, J.: Mobile crowd-sensing with mobile agents. Auton. Agent Multi-Agent Syst. **31**(1), 1–35 (2017). https://doi.org/10.1007/s10458-015-9311-7
12. Bosse, S., Pournaras, E.: An ubiquitous multi-agent mobile platform for distributed crowd sensing and social mining. In: 5th IEEE International Conference on Future Internet of Things and Cloud, pp. 280–287 (2017)
13. Hu, X., Liu, Q., Zhu, C., Leung, V., Chu, T. H., Chan, H. C.: A mobile crowdsensing system enhanced by cloud-based social networking services. In: First International Workshop on Middleware for Cloud-enabled Sensing, no. 3 (2013)
14. Liu, M., Leppänen, T., Harjula, E., Ou, Z., Ramalingam, A., Ylianttila, M., et al.: Distributed resource directory architecture in Machine-to-Machine communications. In: IEEE 9th International Conference on Wireless and Mobile Computing, Networking and Communications, pp. 319–324 (2013). https://doi.org/10.1109/WiMOB.2013.6673379

15. Savaglio, C., Russo, W., Fortino, G., Leppänen, T., Riekki, J.: Re-engineering IoT systems through ACOSO-Meth: the IETF CoRE based agent framework case study, In: 19th Workshop from Objects to Agents (WOA 2018), Italy, 28–29 June 2018 (2018)
16. Chon, Y., Lane, N., Kim, Y., Zhao, F., Cha, H.: Understanding the coverage and scalability of place-centric crowdsensing. In: Proceedings of the 2013 ACM International Joint Conference on Pervasive and Ubiquitous Computing, pp. 3–12 (2013)
17. Kjaergaard, M., Wirz, M., Roggen, D., Tröster, G.: Mobile sensing of pedestrian flocks in indoor environments using WiFi signals. In: IEEE International Conference on Pervasive Computing and Communications, pp. 95–102 (2012)
18. Álvarez Lacasia, J., Leppänen, T., Iwai, M., Kobayashi, H., Sezaki, K.: A method for grouping smartphone users based on Wi-Fi signal strength. Forum Inf. Technol. 12(3), 449–452 (2013)
19. Fortino, G., Rovella, A., Russo, W., Savaglio, C.: Towards cyberphysical digital libraries: integrating iot smart objects into digital libraries. In: Guerrieri, A., Loscri, V., Rovella, A., Fortino, G. (eds.) Management of Cyber Physical Objects in the Future Internet of Things. IT, pp. 135–156. Springer, Cham (2016). https://doi.org/10.1007/978-3-319-26869-9_7
20. Fortino, G., Gravina, R., Russo, W., Savaglio, C.: Modeling and simulating Internet-of-Things systems: a hybrid agent-oriented approach. Comput. Sci. Eng. 19(5), 68–76 (2017)
21. Kostakos, V., Ojala, T., Juntunen, T.: Traffic in the smart city: exploring city-wide sensing for traffic control center augmentation. IEEE Internet Comput. 17(6), 22–29 (2013)

Path Planning of Robotic Fish in Unknown Environment with Improved Reinforcement Learning Algorithm

Jingbo Hu, Jie Mei[✉], Dingfang Chen, Lijie Li, and Zhengshu Cheng

Wuhan University of Technology, Wuhan 430063, Hubei, China
meijieben@foxmail.com

Abstract. Path planning is the primary task for robotic fish, especially when the environment under water of robotic fish is unknown. The conventional reinforcement learning algorithms usually exhibit a poor convergence property in unknown environment. In order to find the optimal path and increase the convergence speed in the unknown environment, an improved reinforcement learning method utilizing a simulated annealing approach is proposed in robotic fish navigation. The simulated annealing policy with a novel cooling method rather than a general ε-greedy policy is taken for action choice. The algorithm convergence speed is improved by a novel reward function with goal-oriented strategy. Then the stopping condition of the proposed reinforcement learning algorithm is rectified as well. In this work, the robotic fish is designed and the prototype is produced by 3D printing technology. Then the proposed algorithm is examined in the 2D unpredictable environment to obtain greedy actions. Experimental results show that the proposed algorithms can generate an optimal path in unknown environment for robotic fish and increase the convergence speed as well as balance the exploration and exploitation.

Keywords: Path planning · Robotic fish · Reinforcement learning
Simulated annealing

1 Introduction

Path planning problem is a very important field in robotics, especially in autonomous robotics, which is used to find a valid path from destination point to a target point while avoiding all obstacles on its way [1]. The optimization criteria for the path planning problem is short walking distance, low working cost and minimal walking time. Various planning methods have been proposed in global and local path planning in recent years. The most common methods in path planning include visibility graph method [2], grid method [3], topological method [4], potential field method [5], fuzzy logic method [6], genetic algorithm [7] and so on. Although these methods are all suit for robotic path planning, it needs prior knowledge in applications. In other words, robotics may move negatively instead of positively.

As a branch of machine learning, Reinforcement Learning (RL) has been obtained more and more focus and applied in path planning of robotic fish and some other mobile robots in recent years, since it can offer an effective method for autonomous

© Springer Nature Switzerland AG 2018
Y. Xiang et al. (Eds.): IDCS 2018, LNCS 11226, pp. 248–257, 2018.
https://doi.org/10.1007/978-3-030-02738-4_21

robots to make decisions from the surrounding unpredictable environment states. The algorithm gives robotic fish some rewards or punishments based on the reward function from the environment when robotic fish interact with its surroundings. In fact, reinforcement learning is a kind of learning method, which allows robotic fish to explore the unknown environments to learn what action it should choose in a certain state. In such a process, robotic fish is allowed to make mistakes and rectify its policy according to the rewards or punishments it receives.

The objective of the agent is to devise a strategy to choose the best action from the possible action set at the specific state to maximize the sum of the rewards from the initial state to target state over the state transition process [8]. In work [9], they present a novel deterministic Q-learning algorithm where the agent has a presumed knowledge about the distance from the current state to both the next state and the objective state, this knowledge will be used to update the Q-table. Reference [10] presents a reinforcement learning network based on an online sequential extreme learning machine to realize the path planning function of mobile robot in the indoor environment, which is used to improve the efficiency and speed of Q function approximation. The objective of work [11] is to make social robot move in an adaptive manner utilizing inverse reinforcement learning method that combines the feature extraction module and path planning module. As the classical method needs to store its Q-value for all actions, work [12] proposes a new methodology by using a hybridization of an improved Q-learning and improved particle swarm optimization to overcome storage problem. In work [13], the authors present an approach whose core idea is to set up a deep neural network (DNN) to learn the Q-function of reinforcement learning. The objective of work [14] is to overcome data deficiency of current data-driven algorithms, which proposes a parallel reinforcement learning system to improve complex learning system by self-guidance.

The performance of a reinforcement learning algorithm is greatly influenced by the convergence speed and the other two primary factors that is known as "exploration" and "exploitation" which are commonly used in the algorithm for control strategy. Exploration usually refers to selecting any action with nonzero probability in every encountered state to learn the environment by the agent. Exploitation, on the other hand, is targeted at employing the current knowledge to achieve good performance by selecting greedy actions [15]. In our research, we have integrated reinforcement learning techniques with simulated annealing to balance the exploration and exploitation and compute the optimal path of robotic fish from the specified initial state to the fixed goal state in the cluttered environment. Additionally, we propose a goal-oriented policy to improve the convergence speed of the proposed algorithm.

The remaining part of this paper is organized as follows. Classical Q learning, simulated annealing and the proposed improved reinforcement learning algorithm for robotic fish path planning is introduced in Sect. 2. The robotic fish and the 2D unknown environment for robotic fish used in the latter simulation is given in Sect. 3. Simulation results are shown in Sect. 4. Conclusions are listed in Sect. 5.

2 Improved Reinforcement Learning for Path Planning

2.1 Q Learning

In machine learning, there are supervised learning, unsupervised learning and rein-forcement learning. Q-learning [16, 17] is a model free algorithm, which is a kind of classical reinforcement learning. Specifically, Q-learning can be used to find an optimal action-selection policy for any given MDP (Markov decision process) [17]. For robotic fish, its model of reinforcement learning is a Markov decision process. Therefore, Q learning enables robotic fish to learn an action-value function responding to the current state according to the specific policy. The basic model between robotic fish and sur-roundings is shown as Fig. 1.

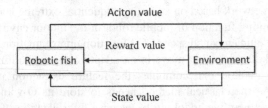

Fig. 1. The basic model between robotic fish and environment

Q learning algorithm consists of state S, action set A, reward function R and transfer probability function P. If robotic fish identifies its state s_t from the environment, it will select an action a according to the policy. A reward r will be received at the moment from the action and conducted to the next state s_{t+1}, which is stored in action-value function $Q(s_t, a)$.

$$\pi = arg\,max_a Q(s_t, a) \tag{1}$$

The target of robotic fish is to find actions a for each state s that can maximize aggregate rewards in the whole time. It is a kind of state-action pairs and can be called policy $\pi : S \to A$. Policy π makes robotic fish select the best actions which can get higher reward value at the current state. Then the state-action value action can be updated by Bellman formula.

$$Q(s, a) = Q(s, a) + \alpha[r + \gamma\,max_{a' \in A} Q(s', a') - Q(s, a)] \tag{2}$$

Where $\alpha \in (0, 1)$ is the learning rate, it indicates the extent to which the new value covers the old value. The discount factor $\gamma \in [0, 1]$, which indicates the importance of the future aggregate reward. The greater it is the more importance is given to future learning.

Q learning often makes robotic fish confuse if it just receives the latest best reward or obtain the future aggregate reward rather not considers whether the next step reward reaches the largest value. In such a process, robotic fish needs to ensure whether it should explore or just need to exploit, which is named the "exploration and exploitation dilemma". In some reinforcement learning algorithms especially in Q learning, one classical method used to balance exploration and exploitation is ε-greedy exploration [18], where the parameter ε denotes exploration probability that is used to control the ratio between exploration and greedy action selection.

2.2 Simulated Annealing

The simulated annealing algorithm is used to simulate the annealing process. It is a heuristic Monte Carlo method and a globally optimized probability algorithm. It converges to the optimal value with probability 1. Metropolis used the Monte Carlo method to study the properties of state equations for substances that composed of interacting single molecules, and proposed an important sampling criteria [19] in 1953, which was later called the Metropolis criteria. Metropolis criteria was applied into simulated annealing by Kirkpatrick [20] until 1983.

Metropolis criteria is crucial for simulated annealing process. In each step of this method, robotic fish can be offered with energy E of its current state. Then robotic fish obtains its next state according to the given policy π and correspondingly it is powered with energy E'. If $E' < E$, the next state is accepted and used as the starting point of the next step. Otherwise, the case $E' > E$ is treated probabilistically. Random number δ uniformly distributes in the interval $(0, 1)$ which is a convenient means to implement the random part of the algorithm [20]. In the algorithm, p is computed by formula $p = exp[-(E' - E)/kT]$, where the parameter T means temperature. Then the random number δ is selected to compare with p. If the value is less than that of p, then the next state is accepted and used as the starting point of the next step as mentioned above. Otherwise the current state is reserved and continue to be used as the starting point of the next step. The process will be repeated for several times until the objective is achieved.

The standard step of implement simulated annealing algorithm for minimizing the cost function $f(\cdot)$ is shown as follows:

(1). Initialize candidate solution s;
(2). Initialize temperature T;
(3). While $T > 0$
    (1). Repeat k times:
        (a). Rectify s into a next solution s';
        (b). If $f(s') < f(s)$ or $rand(0, 1) < exp[-(E' - E)/T]$: $s \leftarrow s'$;
    (2). $T \leftarrow \lambda.T$

(4). Output s;

2.3 Improved Reinforcement Learning

A simulated annealing algorithm is useful to solve combinatorial optimization problems. Its combination with Q learning can help improve its convergence speed and keep balance between exploration and exploitation, which can be called simulated annealing-Q (SA-Q) learning algorithm. In the SA-Q learning algorithm, Metropolis criteria is chosen as the action selection policy rather than some other classical methods. Besides, the setting of reward function and stopping condition are also considered as the influence factors on the convergence speed of the algorithm. Hence, we take further account for these two parts.

Reward Function
Reward function is one of components that may greatly impact on the optimal strategy. In order to distinguish the priority of the robot fish in different states, different reward and punishment values need to be set for different states. Here we have proposed a principle to determine the reward value, which is named goal-oriented principle. According to the goal-oriented principle, the reward function is mainly determined by the distance from the current state of the robot fish to the target point.

The reward value is set to be -10 when the robotic fish encounters an obstacle during the swimming. If the robotic fish reaches the target point, the reward value is set to be 10. And the linear distance between the current state s_t of the robotic fish and the target point is expressed as d_t. After it executed the action strategy, the robotic fish would reach the next state s_{t+1}, and let the linear distance between the state and the target point be expressed as d_{t+1}. If $d_{t+1} > d_t$, the next state of the robotic fish is worse than the current state, which means that the distance to the target point is further away. Then the reward value is set to be -5. If $d_{t+1} < d_t$, the next state of the robotic fish is closer to the target point, then the reward value is set to be 5. When the robotic fish selects the motion to move out of the boundary, the reward value is set to 0 at this time since the robotic fish does not perform the action.

In summary, the reward function can be expressed as:

$$R = \begin{cases} 10 & \text{if arrive goal} \\ 5 & \text{if } d_{t+1} < d_t \\ -5 & \text{if } d_{t+1} > d_t \\ -10 & \text{if meet obstacle} \\ 0 & \text{otherwise} \end{cases} \tag{3}$$

Stopping Condition
For the classical SA-Q learning algorithm, the stopping condition is single and only depends on the preset number of repeats——the algorithm can only stop when the program repeat numbers reach the preset episode value. However, in our actual simulation experiment, it is found that when the program is run up to a certain number of times, the robot fish will explore the surrounding environment. Through this process, the robot fish can keep reusing the existing superior strategy, which means that when the iteration for computing the swimming route reaches a certain number of times even the robotic fish does not explore of the whole environment, so it is no longer meaningful to continue running the algorithm.

For solving the problem, we propose a novel stopping condition. Firstly two sequential linked list are set up. The first sequential linked list is used to store the robotic fish swimming path in the previous cycle, represented by *last_route_state*. The second sequential linked list is used to store the robotic fish swimming path in current cycle, named as *now_route_state*. Then a variable named route is set to indicate the number of path repetitions and a variable N is set to indicate the maximum number of duplicate paths allowed. When the algorithm reaches the end condition in this cycle, the current robotic fish path is stored in the second list *now_route_state* and then compared with the path stored in the last list *last_route_state*. If the two linked lists are equal (that means the two paths are the same), the route repeat variable route is incremented by one. If the two linked lists are not equal with each other, the current list of the current path is assigned to the linked list *last_route_state*. When the foregoing process ends, if the route repetition number route is less than the maximum number N, the algorithm will process to the next cycle. Otherwise, the current cycle is ended and the current route is saved in the path list *now_route_state*. When the process is finished, the optimal or suboptimal path will be obtained.

Path Planning Based on SA-Q Learning
In the path planning application of robotic fish, the surroundings can be partitioned into non overlapped grids, which are called states. The states of the robotic fish are observed and referred to a station-action table (Q-table). There are four actions for robotic fish to select at every state. During the planning phase, the robotic fish will select the action that obtained max reward from the current state.

The pseudocode of SA-Q learning algorithm is given as follows:

(1). Initialize original temperature T_0, T, π, the maximum number N, α, γ
(2). For every episode, repeat:
(3). Initialize current state s_t, saved into the linked list *now_route_state*
(4). Initialize current temperature $T = T_0$
(5). For every step, execute:
(6). Select an action a_r from the action set A according to the current state s_t
(7). Select an action a_p according to the π, and let the current action $a_t = a_p$
(8). Generate a random number δ uniformly distributed in the interval $(0, 1)$
(9). Compute $p = exp\big[(Q(s, a_r) - Q(s, a_p))/T\big]$
(10). If $p > \delta, a_t = a_r$; else, $a_t = a_p$
(11). Execute a_t, the state of robotic fish $s_t = s_{t+1}$, saved into the linked list *now_route_state*, receives the Immediate reward value r_t
(12). Update the state-action value function $Q(s, a)$ by formula (2)
(13). If the state s_t is the goal state, next; else, let $t = t + 1$, and go to (5).
(14). Cooling down the temperature value T, this episode is ended. If *now_route_state = last_route_state*,   then   route = route + 1;   Else, *last_route_state = now_route_state*
(15). If route < N, then episode = episode + 1; else, the algorithm is ended.
(16). Until all the episodes is finished.

3   Robotic Fish and Environment Model

3.1   Robotic Fish

The developed robotic fish is inspired by natural carp fish. It is propelled by a servo that is located in the caudal fin. The original robotic fish model and its prototype are fabricated by 3D printer which are shown in Fig. 2 and the 3D model established by Solid works is shown in Fig. 3.

The robotic fish is equipped with 3 infrared sensors, the interval of each sensor is 90° and the detection distance is 5 m. Besides the infrared sensors, the robotic fish is also equipped with one humanity sensor, one buzzer and one infrared remote control function module. Robotic fish can swim by itself interfacing with its surroundings or be controlled by remote control.

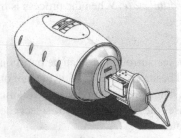   

(1) Inner layout of the robotic fish   (2) The prototype of the robotic fish

Fig. 2. The original robotic fish

   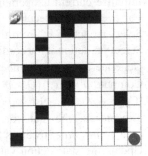

Fig. 3. The updated robotic fish   **Fig. 4.** The grid map of robotic fish

3.2   2D Environment Model

The 2D environment model is established by python, whose scale is 10□10. In the map, the environment is divided into grids one by one. The robot fish and the single obstacle occupy a grid respectively. Every obstacle is represented by a black grid and the robot fish is shown by its picture. The grid indicating the target point is represented by a grid placed with a blue circle, and the remaining white grids represent the safe position where the robotic fish can swim safely. The four boundaries of the map represent the boundary of the environment in which the robot fish is located. The grid map is shown as Fig. 4.

In this grid environment, the position of every obstacle remains changeless, which means that the environment is static. Each grid in which the robotic fish is located represents each state of the robotic fish. Before the robotic fish interacts with the environment, its information about the obstacles in the grid environment is completely unclear, which represents the environment is completely unknown for the robotic fish.

4   Experiment Results

Robotic fish starts exploring at a given location and attempts to explore for 1000 times. The initial temperature T is set to be 100 and the cooling parameter λ is set to be 0.9, the discount factor γ is 0.9. The learning rate α is set to be 0.01, the maximum allowable repetition number N of the path is set to be 50 and the Q value is initialized to be 0. The initial position of the robotic fish is in the upper left corner and the target position is located at the bottom right corner of the circular image. Six simulation experiments are performed on the robotic fish path planning problem. The time that the proposed algorithm spends in each simulation is shown in Table 1.

Table 1. The time spent in path planning simulations (s)

Number	1	2	3	4	5	6	Average
SA-Q	315.56	330.87	339.10	341.26	322.98	315.09	327.48

In the six simulation experiments, the algorithm has successfully achieved the convergence. Table 1 shows the time that the proposed algorithm has spent in every experiment. The paths learned by the robotic fish in these six experiments based on improved SA-Q learning algorithm are shown in Fig. 5.

The Fig. 5 shows that after a certain number of times with the improved SA-Q learning algorithm, the robotic fish can achieve the target point from a given starting point without collision and can find an optimal path. In this 10 × 10 grid environment, the robotic fish needs to perform 18 steps from the starting point to the target point.

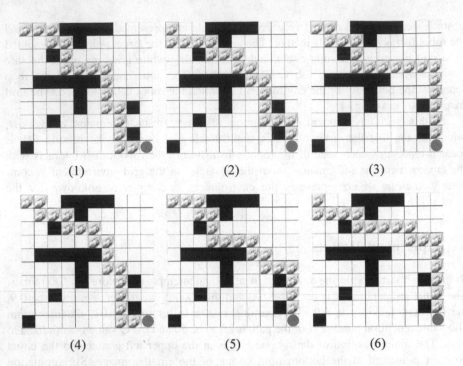

Fig. 5. The paths robotic fish learned

5 Conclusion

In this paper, we propose an improved reinforcement learning algorithm named improved simulated annealing-Q learning (SA-Q learning) algorithm to achieve desired convergence speed and keep balance between exploration and exploitation for robotic fish path planning in a completely unknown environment. The proposed method calculates an optimal policy for robotic fish to select the best action in different states of a 2D grid environment.

The simulation results show that the proposed algorithm present good performance without any prior knowledge of the obstacles and the environment, and robotic fish can obtain an optimal path in every simulation in the unknown environment. Besides, the results also show that the convergence speed of the proposed algorithm has been improved.

The proposed algorithm can be easily extended to the other robots path planning. Future work is to extend this method for robotic fish path planning in dynamic environment.

Acknowledgement. The author(s) disclosed receipt of the following financial support for the research, authorship, and/or publication of this article: This work was supported by the Natural Science Foundation of Hubei Province (20181j001: Interfacial Defects Initiation Mechanism of Flexible Laminated Thin Film Energy Harvester and its Fabrication Process).

References

1. Lamini, C., Fathi, Y., Benhlima, S.: Collaborative Q-learning path planning for autonomous robots based on holonic multi-agent system. In: 2015 10th International Conference on Intelligent Systems: Theories and Applications (SITA), pp. 1–6 (2015)
2. Kaluđer, H., Brezak, M., Petrović, I.: A visibility graph based method for path planning in dynamic environments. In: 2011 Proceedings of the 34th International Convention MIPRO, pp. 717–721 (2011)
3. Li, C., Lu, H., Cui, G.: The improved potential grid method in robot path planning. In: International Technology and Innovation Conference (ITIC 2009), pp. 1–5 (2009)
4. Chin, W.H., Saputra, A.A., Kubota, N.: A neuro-based network for on-line topological map building and dynamic path planning. In: 2017 International Joint Conference on Neural Networks (IJCNN), pp. 2805–2810 (2017)
5. Bounini, F., Gingras, D., Pollart, H., Gruyer, D.: Modified artificial potential field method for online path planning applications. In: 2017 IEEE Intelligent Vehicles Symposium (IV), pp. 180–185 (2017)
6. Lee, J., Park, W.: A probability-based path planning method using fuzzy logic. In: 2014 IEEE/RSJ International Conference on Intelligent Robots and Systems, pp. 2978–2984 (2014)
7. Cobano, J.A., Conde, R., Alejo, D., Ollero, A.: Path planning based on genetic algorithms and the Monte-Carlo method to avoid aerial vehicle collisions under uncertainties. In: 2011 IEEE International Conference on Robotics and Automation, pp. 4429–4434 (2011)
8. Lamini, C., Fathi, Y., Benhlima, S.: H-MAS architecture and reinforcement learning method for autonomous robot path planning. In: 2017 Intelligent Systems and Computer Vision (ISCV), pp. 1–7 (2017)
9. Konar, A., Chakraborty, I.G., Singh, S.J., Jain, L.C., Nagar, A.K.: A deterministic improved q-learning for path planning of a mobile robot. IEEE Trans. Syst. Man Cybern.: Syst. 43(5), 1141–1153 (2013)
10. Liu, Y., Liu, H., Wang, B.: Autonomous exploration for mobile robot using Q-learning. In: 2017 2nd International Conference on Advanced Robotics and Mechatronics (ICARM), pp. 614–619 (2017)
11. Kim, B., Pineau, J.: Socially Adaptive path planning in human environments using inverse reinforcement learning. Int. J. Soc. Robot. 8(1), 51–66 (2016)
12. Das, P.K., Behera, H.S., Panigrahi, B.K.: Intelligent-based multi-robot path planning inspired by improved classical Q-learning and improved particle swarm optimization with perturbed velocity. Eng. Sci. Technol. Int. J. 19(1), 651–669 (2016)
13. Li, L., Lv, Y., Wang, F.-Y.: Traffic signal timing via deep reinforcement learning. IEEE/CAA J. Autom. Sinica 3(3), 247–254 (2016)
14. Liu, T., Tian, B., Ai, Y., Li, L., Cao, D., Wang, F.-Y.: Parallel reinforcement learning: a framework and case study. IEEE/CAA J. Autom. Sinica 5(4), 827–835 (2018)
15. Busoniu, L., Babuska, R., Schutter, B.D., Ernst, D.: Reinforcement Learning and Dynamic Programming Using Function Approximators, p. 280. CRC Press, Inc., Boca Raton (2010)
16. Kaelbling, L.P., Littman, M.L., Moore, A.W.: Reinforcement learning: a survey. J. Artif. Intell. Res. 4(1), 237–285 (1996)
17. Watkins, C., Dayan, P.: Technical note Q-learning. Mach. Learn. 8, 279–292 (1992)
18. Sutton, R.S., Barto, A.G.: Reinforcement learning: an introduction. Trans. Neur. Netw. 9(5), 1054 (1998)
19. Metropolis, N., Rosenbluth, A.W., Rosenbluth, M.N., Teller, A.H., Teller, E.: Equation of state calculations by fast computing machines. J. Chem. Phys. 21(6), 1087–1092 (1953)
20. Kirkpatrick, S., Gelatt, C.D., Vecchi, M.P.: Optimization by simulated annealing. Science 220(4598), 671–680 (1983)

Review of Swarm Intelligence Algorithms for Multi-objective Flowshop Scheduling

Lijun He, Wenfeng Li$^{(\boxtimes)}$, Yu Zhang, and Jingjing Cao

School of Logistics Engineering, Wuhan University of Technology, Wuhan, People's Republic of China
523683829@qq.com, {liwf,sanli,bettycao}@whut.edu.cn

Abstract. Swarm intelligence algorithm (SIA) is an important artificial intelligence technology, which has been widely applied in various research fields. Recently, adopting various multi-objective SIAs (MOSIAs) to solve multi-objective flow shop scheduling problem (MOFSP) has attracted wide research attention. However, there are fewer review papers on the MOFSP. Many new MOSIAs have been proposed to solve MOFSP in the last decade. Therefore, in this study, MOSIAs of MOFSP over the past decade are briefly reviewed and analyzed. Based on the existing problems and new trend of Industry 4.0, several new promising future research directions are pointed out. These research directions are: (1) new hybrid MOSIA; (2) MOSIA with high computational efficiency; (3) MOSIA based on machine learning and big data; (4) multi-objective approach; (5) many-objective flowshop scheduling.

Keywords: Swarm intelligence algorithm
Multi-objective flow shop scheduling · Machine learning · Big data
Multi-objective approach

1 Introduction

Swarm intelligence algorithm (SIA) is an important research branch of artificial intelligence. The main idea of SIA is that it simulates various behaviors of swarm biology and uses the information interaction and cooperation among individuals in swarm to achieve the purpose of optimization. SIA is very suitable for solving discontinuous or non-convex large complicated problems. Recently, SIAs have been widely applied to various research fields and show excellent optimization performance [1–4]. Multi-objective flow shop scheduling problem (MOFSP) is an important industry production problem. It is a typical NP-hard problem, thus the traditional methods such as exact methods and heuristics are inefficient. Nevertheless, SIAs such as GA (genetic algorithm) and PSO (particle swarm optimization) can overcome the shortcomings of traditional methods, and tackling medium- and large-sized problems efficiently. Therefore, SIAs have been the most popular methods in solving MOFSP.

Figures 1, 2, 3 and 4 show the situation of papers published in the field of MOFSP over the past decade. Figure 1 is the annual publication trend. It is obvious that, many papers on the MOFSP have been published over the past decade, although the number fluctuates slightly. Figure 2 lists the active countries or regions in this field, of which

Y. Xiang et al. (Eds.): IDCS 2018, LNCS 11226, pp. 258–269, 2018.
https://doi.org/10.1007/978-3-030-02738-4_22

China, China Taiwan, Iran and Turkey are the four most active countries or regions. Figure 3 presents the proportion of various types of these papers published in the past decade. From Fig. 3, we can see that the number of papers using SIAs is the most, while the papers using other methods such as exact methods and heuristics are relatively fewer, and the review papers are the fewest. According to the literature statistics, only three review papers have been published in the past decade, they are [5–7]. Figure 4 shows the top five journals by the number of published papers over the past decade. It is revealed from Fig. 4 that the top five journals are the International Journal of Advanced Manufacturing Technology (IJAMT), Computers & Operations Research (COR), International Journal of Production Research (IJPR), Expert Systems with Applications (ESWA) and Control & Decision (CD).

It is obvious that many new papers on the MOFSP have been published and a large number of SIAs have been adopted to address the MOFSP in the past decade. To cover the latest research progress of SIAs of MOFSP, it is necessary to review the latest literature. In addition, industry manufacturing is undergoing the new situations of Industry 4.0 and intelligent manufacturing. This brings some new characteristics to flow shop scheduling production. Therefore, in this study, we firstly provide a brief review of SIAs for MOFSP in the last decade. Then, several new research trends different from the current reviews are proposed.

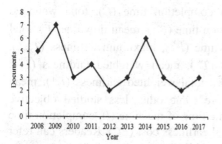

Fig. 1. The annual publication trends

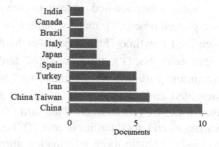

Fig. 2. The active countries or regions

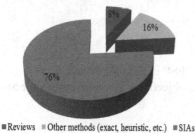

Fig. 3. The proportion of various types of papers

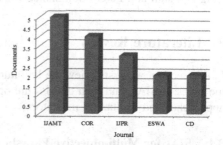

Fig. 4. The top five journals by the number of published papers

2 Multi-objective Flowshop Scheduling Problem

The MOFSP can be described as: n jobs with the same order are processed by m machines and the processing time of the job on the machine is given. The problem has the several assumptions: (1) each job can only be processed on one machine at any time; (2) each machine can only process one job at any time; (3) the processing of one job on a machine cannot be interrupted; (4) the machines are continuously available; (5) all jobs are independent and are available at time zero; (6) the set-up times of the jobs on machines are sequence independent and are included in processing times. The goal of MOFSP is to determine the processing sequence of jobs and optimize multiple objectives simultaneously.

Generalily, there are two groups of objectives commonly used for scheduling problems: (1) Objectives based on the completion time; (2) Objectives based on due date. In the first group of objectives, makespan (C_{max}) optimization guarantees good utilization and production line efficiency while the minimization of flowtime (F) provides a stable usage of resources and minimization of work-in-process [7]. According to [8], the combination of makespan and flowtime can improve production efficiency and decrease production cost. In addition, in the second group of objectives, objectives such as total tardiness (T) and total earliness (E) have been adopted to satisfy the customer demand.

Some other studied objectives are mean completion time ($\overline{C}$), total weighted completion time (C^w), mean weighted completion time ($\overline{C}^w$), mean flowtime ($\overline{F}$), total weighted flowtime (F^w), mean weighted flowtime ($\overline{F}^w$), maximum tardiness (T_{max}), mean tardiness ($\overline{T}$), total weighted tardiness (T^w), mean weighted tardiness ($\overline{T}^w$), maximum earliness (E_{max}), mean earliness ($\overline{E}$), total weighted earliness (E^w), mean weighted earliness ($\overline{E}^w$). In addition, there are some other less studied objective functions, such as number of job tardy (n_T), idle time of machine (I), completion time variance (ctv), total tardiness cost (TC) and total earliness cost (EC). Readers can refer to [5–7] to obtain more information about these objective functions.

To deal with the multiple objectives of MOFSP simultaneously, a multi-objective approach should be used. Generally, the mostly used multi-objective approaches are weighted sum and Pareto dominance [6, 7].

3 Literature Review

In this section, we first review the literature of MOFSP in the past decade according to the types of SIAs, and then discuss the optimized objectives, the used multi-objective approaches and evaluation indicators.

3.1 SIAs for Multi-objective Flowshop Scheduling

Genetic Algorithm. Genetic algorithm (GA) was firstly proposed by Holland [9]. It is a swarm evolution algorithm based on the survival-of-the fittest mechanism. GA works with a population of solution instead of just a single solution. Through three operators, that is selection, crossover and mutation, GA produces a new population that is more adaptable than the previous one. Later, Koza [10] developed the expanded genetic programming (GP) which is a technique whereby computer programs are encoded as a set of genes that are then modified using GA. It is an application of GA where the space of solutions consists of computer programs. GA has been widely used to address the MOFSP in the past decade. An artificial chromosome generating mechanism was proposed in [11]. The artificial chromosome generating mechanism was embedded in simple GA and NSGA-II (Non-dominated Sorting Genetic Algorithm II) to solve MOFSP. [12] presented two new weighting mechanisms. GA was integrated with the new weighting mechanisms to optimize the C_{max} and T_{max}. In [13], a solution strategy based on GA was proposed to minimize the C_{max}, F and T_{max}. In their work, the planner-specified weights were employed to handle the multi-objective optimization problem. A simple and efficient GA for MOFSP was presented in [14]. The proposed GA made use of Pareto archive to obtain the most repetitive solutions. In addition, variable neighborhood search was used to guide the search direction. A multi-population GA based on decomposition was presented in [15] to minimize the C_{max} and T_{max}. Experimental results showed that the proposed algorithm can achieve excellent performance. [16] proposed a bi-criteria improved GA for flowshop scheduling problem with the minimization of C_{max} and F of all jobs. NEH (Nawaz, Enscore and Ham) constructive heuristic. [17] studied the flowshop scheduling problem with a weighted sum of C_{max} and T_{max} subject to a T_{max} threshold value. A fast and effective GA was proposed and its performance was verified by computational and statistical experiments.

Particle Swarm Optimization. Particle swarm optimization (PSO) is a population-based stochastic optimization technique proposed by Eberhart and Kennedy [18]. PSO mimics the cluster behavior of birds swarm. Each individual of the swarm changes its search mode by learning its own experience and the experience of other individuals. PSO has shown excellent search performance for many optimization problems. In the past decade, the papers using PSO to address the MOFSP are as follows:

In [19], PSO and GA were applied to MOFSP. The variable neighborhood search was embedded in these two algorithms. With different weights, the C_{max} and T_{max} were optimized. A multi-objective PSO adopting different local search (LS) techniques was proposed in [20]. In their study, a random weighted linear sum function was used to aggregate multiple objectives to a single one. Similar to [20], a modified PSO for MOFSP was presented in [21]. The results showed that the proposed algorithm performed better than other traditional heuristics in terms of searching quality and efficiency. In [22], a hybrid PSO algorithm combining sliding level Taguchi method was proposed for solving the MOFSP. Additionally, the elitist preservation strategy was adopted in the new algorithm. In [23], a hybrid taguchi-based PSO was presented. Taguchi-based crossover was employed to avoid scheduling conflicts, and a fuzzy inference system was used to selecting weights. A new fitness assignment strategy based on relative entropy of fuzzy sets was proposed in [24]. This fitness assignment strategy was applied to PSO for solving MOFSP. Results revealed that the proposed algorithm was competitive.

Ant Colony Optimization. Ant colony optimization (ACO) was initially proposed by Dorigo [25]. The original idea of ACO was to search for an optimal path in a graph, based on the behavior of ants seeking a path between their colony and a source of food. Various ACO algorithms were used to solve a wider class of numerical problems. In the past decade, [26] presented a multi-objective ant colony optimization (ACO). Combined with local search technical, the new algorithm was used to solve MOFSP of minimizing the C_{max} and F. An effective multi-objective ACO algorithm was developed to optimize the two objectives of C_{max} and F in [27]. Compared with the results obtained by other algorithms, the proposed algorithm performed better.

Memetic Algorithm. Memetic algorithm (MA) was introduced by Moscato [28], it is an algorithm close to a form of population-based hybrid GA coupled with an individual learning procedure capable of performing local refinements. In MOFSP area, the minimization of C_{max} and F was studied in [29] by an effective memetic algorithm (MA) integrating the NSGA-II and the NEH. The performance of the proposed algorithm was compared with those of other 23 algorithms. [30] proposed a multi-objective MA. In this MA, the NEH heuristic was used to improve the quality of the initial solution, and a global search embedded with a perturbation operation was employed to improve the solutions of the entire population. The two objectives of C_{max} and F were optimized with this new algorithm.

Estimation of Distribution Algorithm. Estimation of distribution algorithm (EDA) is a stochastic optimization method that guides the search for the optimum by building and sampling explicit probabilistic models of promising candidate solutions [31]. In the latest decade, a Pareto optimal block-based EDA was presented in [32] to address the MOFSP. In their work, a bivariate probabilistic model was employed to generate block, and the non-dominated sorting technique was used to filter the solutions. The proposed algorithm was compared with NSGA-II to assess its performance. In [33], the authors proposed a novel EDA based on multi-objective decomposition using Kernels of Mallows models. The objectives of C_{max} and F were optimized by the proposed novel EDA.

Differential Evolution. Differential evolution (DE) is originally proposed by Storn and Price [34]. The basic DE is similar to GA, including mutation, cross operation and elimination mechanism. For MOFSP area, in the last decade, [35] presented a novel discrete DE algorithm. A simple and effective local search was adopted to balance the global exploration and the local exploitation. C_{max} and T_{max} are optimized in their study. In [36], a new fitness assignment strategy combining with the grey correlation analysis method and the information entropy was presented. This new fitness assignment strategy was integrated with DE and GA to solve MOFSP.

In addition to the SIAs mentioned above, some other SIAs are used to deal with the MOFSP. These SIAs are immune algorithm (IA) [37], shuffled frog-leaping algorithm (SFLA) [38], electromagnetism-like mechanism algorithm (EMA) [39], harmony search optimization (HSO) [40], food chain algorithm (FCA) [41], glowworm swarm optimization (GSO) [42], weed optimization algorithm (WOA) [43] and simulated annealing (SA) [8].

To make a further comparison of the literature of MOFSP, Table 1 lists more information including the optimized objectives, multi-objective approaches and evaluation indicators.

Table 1. Further comparison of the literature

References	Objectives	Multi-objective approaches	Evaluation indicators
[11]	C_{max}, T_{max}	Pareto dominance	DI_R metric, C metric
[12]	C_{max}, T_{max}	Weighted sum	DI_R metric, C metric
[13]	C_{max}, F, T	Weighted sum	/
[14]	C_{max}, T^w	Pareto dominance	NPS (Number of Pareto solutions)
[15]	C_{max}, T	Weighted sum	C metric, IGD (Inverse generational distance)
[16]	C_{max}, F	Weighted sum	/
[17]	C_{max}, T	Weighted sum	RPD (Relative percentage deviation), CPU time
[19]	C_{max}, T_{max}	Weighted sum	CPU time
[20]	C_{max}, $\overline{F}$, T_{max}	Weighted sum	C metric, SP (spacing metric), distance metric, quality metric
[21]	C_{max}, $\overline{F}$, I	Parceto dominance	RPD, maximum percentage deviation, CPU time
[22]	C_{max}, T_{max}	Weighted sum	C metric, SP, hypervolume
[23]	C_{max}, T_{max}	Weighted sum	/
[24]	C_{max}, T_{max}, EC, TC	Relative entropy of fuzzy sets	RPD, GD (Generational distance), SP
[26]	C_{max}, F	Weighted sum	RPD, CPU timc
[27]	C_{max}, F'	Weighted sum	CPU time
[29]	C_{max}, F	Pareto dominance	Epsilon, hypervolume
[30]	C_{max}, F	Weighted sum	Hypervolume, C metric
[32]	C_{max}, F	Pareto dominance	CPU time
[33]	C_{max}, F	Weighted sum	Hypervolume, C metric
[35]	C_{max}, T_{max}	Pareto dominance	DI_R metric, NPS
[36]	C_{max}, F, T_{max}	Grey and entropy relative analysis	/
[37]	$\overline{C}^w$, $\overline{T}^w$	Pareto dominance	NPS, error ratio, GD, SP, diversification metric
[38]	$\overline{T}^w$, $\overline{E}^w$	Pareto dominance	NPS, error ratio, GD, SP, CPU time
[39]	C_{max}, T^w	Weighted sum	RPD
[40]	C_{max}, T_{max}, F	Pareto dominance	NPS, CPU time
[41]	C_{max}, T	Pareto dominance	NPS, C metric, CPU time
[42]	C_{max}, T	Pareto dominance	GD, CPU time
[43]	C_{max}, F, T	Grey and entropy relative analysis	NPS, SP, C metric
[8]	C_{max}, F	Weighted sum	NPS

3.2 Discussion

In the literature, the objectives mostly optimized are the regular objectives, such as C_{max} and F. The number of objectives optimized is mostly two, three and more objectives are rarely studied. Additionally, multi-objective approach is an important factor affecting the performance of SIAs. It is revealed from Table 1 that weighted sum and Pareto dominance are still the most popular multi-objective methods for MOFSP in the latest decade. The reason behind this is that weighted sum method is simple and easy to implement, while Pareto dominance method has excellent search ability.

It is clear that the authors mostly adopt various evaluation indicators to compare the performance of different SIAs. For example, [11, 12] consider two evaluation indicators: DI_R metric and C metric. In [22], the authors consider three evaluation indicators: C metric, SP and hypervolume. According to [44], the performance of algorithms should be evaluated at least from the following three aspects: (1) the minimum distance to the Pareto-optimal front; (2) the goodness of the distribution; and (3) the maximum spread. Therefore, evaluation indicators should be chosen according to these three principles.

4 Future Research Directions

It is obvious that many innovative SIAs have been developed to address the MOFSP. Nevertheless, there are still many problems in the existing MOFSP research. Therefore, in this section we propose some new promising research directions for MOFSP.

4.1 New Hybrid MOSIA

Different SIAs have different advantages and disadvantages, thus various technologies such as NEH, LS and VNS have been integrated to enhance the performance of SIAs. Additionally, many new SIAs, such as WOA, EDA and FCA, are successively applied to solve the MOFSP. These new SIAs have shown better performances over the existing SIAs. It is obvious that more and more novel hybrid MOSIAs would be employed to address the MOFSP. Therefore, the study of novel hybrid MOSIAs would be an important research topic in the future. However, the following problems should be considered when constructing novel hybrid MOSIAs. First, most new SIAs are proposed for continuous optimization problems, thus how to discretize new SIAs is a challenge. Second, SIAs are population-based and stochastic algorithms, the value of parameters and the quality of initial population have a significant impact on the performance of SIAs. Third, the theoretical basis of new SIAs is usually very weak. Their convergence and stability have not yet been proven mathematically. Therefore, the study of the theoretical basis of new SIAs should be strengthened.

4.2 MOSIA with High Computational Efficiency

MOFSP takes more computation time to calculate multiple objective functions, thus MOSIAs with high computation time are not advisable. However, according to the literature of MOFSP, most researchers trend to construct complex SIAs with various techniques to pursue high-quality solutions. As a result, the quality of solutions improves and the computation time increases correspondingly. When addressing the MOFSP, the quality of solutions and the computational efficiency should be considered simultaneously. The design of novel SIAs of MOFSP which achieve a satisfactory balance between the quality of solutions and the computational efficiency is an interesting direction. Distributed computing and parallel computing are two computing modes to increase the speed of calculation. They are very suitable for solving large and complex problems. Accordingly, SIAs combining distributed computing and parallel computing would be a promising method to improve the computational efficiency.

4.3 MOSIA Based on Machine Learning and Big Data

Recently, inserting machine learning and big data into SIAs to improve their performance has received considerable attention [45–48]. The main idea is that in the optimization process, SIA can produce ample historical data such as population information, problem feature and search space. Machine learning and big data techniques, such as clustering, statistical learning, oppose-based learning, support vector machine, reinforcement learning [49], can be employed to analyze the useful information of historical data and predict the optimal search area for SIA. Consequently, the search performance of SIA can be significantly improved. At present, a variety of SIAs based on machine learning and big data have been proposed. However, these SIAs mainly focus on single objective continuous numerical optimization problems. For the discrete MOFSP, the research on the MOSIAs based on machine learning and big data is very rare. Nevertheless, the study of MOSIAs based on machine learning and big data is still a promising research topic. There are still many problems to be dealt with for MOFSP. For example, the machine learning technologies proposed for the continuous optimization problems cannot be directly applied to MOFSP. On the other hand, it is more difficult to analyze the useful information of discrete solutions, and small change in the solution may cause a significant effect on the objective value.

4.4 Multi-objective Approach

Note that multi-objective approach is an important factor affecting the performance of SIAs. According to the published literature for MOFSP in the latest decade, the mostly used multi-objective approaches are Pareto dominance and weighted sum. However, these two multi-objective approaches have several shortcomings. Pareto dominance method is widely adopted for multi-objective optimization problems due to its excellent search ability. Nevertheless, most SIAs based on Pareto dominance are time-consuming, which leads to the slow convergence and low efficiency. Weighted sum method assigns each objective a weight and these weighted objectives are finally aggregated into a single objective. The problem is that, objectives are dealt with different scales and it is difficult to map the weights into valid preferences of decision maker. Therefore, it is essential to develop more effective multi-objective approaches for MOFSP. In the future, the study of multi-objective approach would be an interesting issue.

Recently, some new multi-objective approaches have been proposed for MOFSP. For example, in [24] the relative entropy of fuzzy sets was developed as a new multi-objective approach. [36] and [43] use the grey and entropy relative analysis as multi-objective approach. MOSIAs based on these new multi-objective approaches have shown excellent performances. Some theories, such as grey theory and intuitionistic fuzzy set theory, would be promising methods to develop as new multi-objective approaches. By these methods, weights are not needed to assign to the multiple objectives. These methods can translate the multiple objective function values into a numerical sequence, which is in the range of 0 and 1. Thus, the influence of the magnitude and the unit of different objectives can be eliminated.

4.5   Many-objective Flowshop Scheduling

When MOFSP literature is reviewed, it is found that the objective functions mostly studied are makespan, flowtime and tardiness. These objectives are all regular objectives and there is few papers focus on three or more objectives. However, it should be noted that the real-word flow shop scheduling is affected by many production demands. Especially in Industry 4.0 and intelligent manufacturing environment, the manufacturing industry is transformed into highly intelligence with the help of cyber-physical system (CPS) [50, 51]. Some new production requirements, such as energy saving and high resource utilization, are usually sought. Thus, under the new trend of Industry 4.0 and intelligent manufacturing, except the regular objectives, more objectives functions (e.g. worker and machine utilization, material waste, carbon emission and energy consumption) are needed to be studied in flow shop scheduling production. In this case, the number of objectives that need to be optimized is more than three, and it is a many-objective flow shop scheduling problem. Therefore, many-objective flow shop scheduling problem would be a promising issues that deserve further study. Nevertheless, the existing multi-objective approaches may be invalid for many-objective flow shop scheduling problem. Many-objective flow shop scheduling brings some new challenges to the design of SIAs. Thus, some many-objective approaches should be developed. The results of MOFSP studies will form the basis for solving many-objective flow shop scheduling problem. Some similarity-based methods, such as the relative entropy of fuzzy sets [24], are the examples that can be referenced.

5   Conclusion

A brief review of MOSIAs for MOFSP over the past decade is presented in this study. The international publication situation of MOFSP is briefly analyzed. The definition of MOFSP and the regular objectives mostly studied are introduced. Then, a brief literature review of MOSIAs for MOFSP is presented and discussion is also carried out.

Based on the discussion and new industrial development trend, some promising future research directions are pointed out. The most important point is that in the future MOSIAs will still be a hot topic in MOFSP field.

Acknowledgement. This paper is supported by the National Natural Science Foundation of China (61571336 and 71874132).

References

1. Xing, Y., Chen, Y., Lv, C., et al.: Swarm intelligence-based power allocation and relay selection algorithm for wireless cooperative network. KSII Trans. Internet Inf. Syst. **10**(3), 1111–1130 (2016)
2. Lazzús, J.A., Rivera, M., López-Caraballo, C.H.: Parameter estimation of Lorenz chaotic system using a hybrid swarm intelligence algorithm. Phys. Lett. A **380**(11–12), 1164–1171 (2016)
3. Zhang, X., Zhang, X.: Shift based adaptive differential evolution for PID controller designs using swarm intelligence algorithm. Clust. Comput. **20**(1), 1–9 (2016)
4. De, D.H., Villarubia, G., DePaz, J.F., et al.: Multi-sensor information fusion for optimizing electric bicycle routes using a swarm intelligence algorithm. Sensors **17**(11), 2501 (2017)
5. Minella, G., Ruiz, R., Ciavotta, M.: A review and evaluation of multi-objective algorithms for the flowshop scheduling problem. Inf. J. Comput. **20**(3), 451–471 (2008)
6. Sun, Y., Zhang, C., Gao, L., Wang, X.: Multi-objective optimization algorithms for flow shop scheduling problem: a review and prospects. Int. J. Adv. Manuf. Technol. **55**(5–8), 723–739 (2011)
7. Yenisey, M.M., Yagmahan, B.: Multi-objective permutation flow shop scheduling problem: literature review, classification and current trends. Omega **45**(2), 119–135 (2014)
8. Lin, S.W., Ying, K.C.: Minimizing makespan and total flow time in permutation flow shops by a bi-objective multi-start simulated-annealing algorithm. Comput. Oper. Res. **40**(6), 1625–1647 (2013)
9. Holland, J.H.: Adaptation in Natural and Artificial Systems. University of Michigan Press, Michigan (1975)
10. Koza, J.R.: Genetic programming as a means for programming computers by natural selection. Stat. Comput. **4**(2), 87–112 (1994)
11. Chang, P.C., Chen, S.H., Fan, C.Y., et al.: Genetic algorithm integrated with artificial chromosomes for multi-objective flowshop scheduling problems. Appl. Math. Comput. **205** (2), 550–561 (2008)
12. Framinan, J.M.: A fitness-based weighting mechanism for multicriteria flowshop scheduling using genetic algorithms. Int. J. Adv. Manuf. Technol. **43**(9–10), 939–948 (2009)
13. Pour, N.S., Tavakkolimoghaddam, R., Asadi, H.: Optimizing a multi-objectives flow shop scheduling problem by a novel genetic algorithm. Int. J. Ind. Eng. Comput. **4**(3), 345–354 (2013)
14. Karimi, N., Davoudpour, H.: A high performing metaheuristic for multi-objective flowshop scheduling problem. Comput. Oper. Res. **52**, 149–156 (2014)
15. Fu, Y., Huang, M., Wang, H., et al.: Multipopulation multiobjective genetic algorithm for multiobjective permutation flow shop scheduling problem. Control Theor. Appl. **10**(33), 1281–1288 (2016)

16. Rajkumar, R., Shahabudeen, P.: Bi-criteria improved genetic algorithm for scheduling in flowshops to minimize makespan and total flowtime of jobs. Int. J. Comput. Integr. Manuf. **22**(10), 987–998 (2009)
17. Ruiz, R., Allahverdi, A.: Minimizing the bicriteria of makespan and maximum tardiness with an upper bound on maximum tardiness. Comput. Oper. Res. **36**(4), 1268–1283 (2009)
18. Kennedy, J., Eberhart, R.: Particle swarm optimization. In: Proceedings of IEEE International Conference on Neural Networks, pp. 1942–1948 (1995)
19. Uysal, O., Bulkan, S.: Comparison of genetic algorithm and particle swarm optimization for bicriteria permutation flowshop scheduling problem. Int. J. Comput. Intell. Res. **4**(2), 159–175 (2008)
20. Li, B.B., Wang, L., Liu, B.: An effective PSO-based hybrid algorithm for multiobjective permutation flow shop scheduling. IEEE Trans. Syst. Man, Cybern.-Part A: Syst. Humans **38**(4), 818–831 (2008)
21. Sha, D.Y., Lin, H.H.: A particle swarm optimization for multi-objective flowshop scheduling. Int. J. Adv. Manuf. Technol. **45**(7–8), 749–758 (2009)
22. Tsai, J.T., Yang, C.I., Chou, J.H.: Hybrid sliding level Taguchi-based particle swarm optimization for flowshop scheduling problems. Appl. Soft Comput. **15**(2), 177–192 (2014)
23. Yang, C.I., Chou, J.H., Chang, C.K.: Hybrid Taguchi-based particle swarm optimization for flowshop scheduling problem. Arab. J. Sci. Eng. **39**(3), 2393–2412 (2014)
24. He, L.J., Liu, C., Zhu, G.Y.: High-dimensional multi-objective flow shop scheduling optimization based on relative entropy of fuzzy sets. Comput. Integr. Manuf. Syst. **21**(10), 2704–2710 (2015)
25. Dorigo, M., Birattari, M., Stutzle, T.: Ant colony optimization. IEEE Comput. Intell. Mag. **1**(4), 28–39 (2007)
26. Yagmahan, B., Yenisey, M.M.: A multi-objective ant colony system algorithm for flow shop scheduling problem. Expert Syst. Appl. **37**(2), 1361–1368 (2010)
27. Rabanimotlagh, A.: An efficient ant colony optimization algorithm for multiobjective flow shop scheduling problem. World Acad. Sci. Eng. Technol. **5**(3), 598–604 (2011)
28. Moscato, P., Cotta, C.: A modern introduction to memetic algorithms. In: Gendreau, M., Potvin, J.Y. (eds.) Handbook of Metaheuristics. Springer, Boston (2010). https://doi.org/10. 1007/978-1-4419-1665-5_6
29. Chiang, T.C., Cheng, H.C., Fu, L.C.: NNMA: an effective memetic algorithm for solving multiobjective permutation flow shop scheduling problems. Expert Syst. Appl. **38**(5), 5986–5999 (2011)
30. Li, X.T., Ma, S.J.: Multi-objective memetic search algorithm for multi-objective permutation flow shop scheduling problem. IEEE Access **4**, 2154–2165 (2017)
31. Larranaga, P., Lozano, J.A.: Estimation of Distribution Algorithms: A New Tool for Evolutionary Computation. Kluwer Press, Boston (2002)
32. Chang, P.C.: A pareto block-based estimation and distribution algorithm for multi-objective permutation flow shop scheduling problem. Int. J. Prod. Res. **53**(3), 793–834 (2015)
33. Zangari, M., Mendiburu, A., Santana, R., Pozo, A.: Multiobjective decomposition-based mallows models estimation of distribution algorithm. A case of study for permutation flowshop scheduling problem. Inf. Sci. **397**(C), 137–154 (2017)
34. Storn, R., Price, K.: Differential evolution - a simple and efficient heuristic for global optimization over continuous spaces. J. Global Optim. **11**(C), 341–359 (1997)
35. Pan, Q.K., Wang, L., Qian, B.: A novel differential evolution algorithm for bi-criteria no-wait flow shop scheduling problems. Comput. Oper. Res. **36**(8), 2498–2511 (2009)
36. Zhu, G.Y., Chen, X.B., Liu, Y.L.: Flow shop multi-objective scheduling optimization research based on grey entropy relation analysis and the algorithm relation. Control Decis. **29**(1), 135–140 (2014)

37. Tavakkoli-Moghaddam, R., Rahimi-Vahed, A.R., Mirzaei, A.H.: Solving a multi-objective no-wait flow shop scheduling problem with an immune algorithm. Int. J. Adv. Manuf. Technol. **36**(9–10), 969–981 (2008)
38. Rahimi-Vahed, A., Dangchi, M., Rafiei, H., et al.: A novel hybrid multi-objective shuffled frog-leaping algorithm for a bi-criteria permutation flow shop scheduling problem. Int. J. Adv. Manuf. Technol. **41**(11–12), 1227–1239 (2009)
39. Naderi, B., Tavakkoli-Moghaddam, R., Khalili, M.: Electromagnetism-like mechanism and simulated annealing algorithms for flowshop scheduling problems minimizing the total weighted tardiness and makespan. Knowl.-Based Syst. **23**(2), 77–85 (2010)
40. Frosolini, M., Braglia, M., Zammori, F.A.: A modified harmony search algorithm for the multi-objective flow shop scheduling problem with due dates. Int. J. Prod. Res. **49**(20), 5957–5985 (2011)
41. Chen, K.J., Zhou, X.M.: Improved food chain algorithm for multi objective permutation flow shop scheduling. China Mech. Eng. **26**(3), 348–353 (2015)
42. Xu, Z.H., Li, J.M., Gu, X.S.: Multi-objective flow shop scheduling problem based on GMOGSO. Control Decis. **31**(10), 1772–1778 (2016)
43. Huang, X., Ye, C.M., Cao, L.: Chaos invasive weed optimization algorithm for multiobjective permutation flow shop scheduling problem. Syst. Eng.-Theory Pract. **37**(1), 253–262 (2017)
44. Zhu, G.Y., He, L.J., Ju, X.W., Zhang, W.B.: A fitness assignment strategy based on the grey and entropy parallel analysis and its application to MOEA. Eur. J. Oper. Res. **265**(3), 813–828 (2018)
45. Rahnamayan, S., Tizhoosh, H.R., Salama, M.M.A.: Opposition-based differential evolution. IEEE Trans. Evol. Comput. **12**(1), 64–79 (2008)
46. Chia, J.Y., Goh, C.K., Shim, V.A., et al.: A data mining approach to evolutionary optimisation of noisy multi-objective problems. Int. J. Syst. Sci. **43**(7), 1217–1247 (2012)
47. Wang, X.P., Tang, L.X.: An adaptive multi-population differential evolution algorithm for continuous multi-objective optimization. Inf. Sci. **348**(2), 124–141 (2016)
48. Zhang, H.X., Lu, J.: Adaptive evolutionary programming based on reinforcement learning. Inf. Sci. **178**(4), 971–984 (2008)
49. Zhang, J., Zhan, Z.H., Lin, Y., et al.: Evolutionary computation meets machine learning: a survey. IEEE Comput. Intell. Mag. **6**(4), 68–75 (2011)
50. Luo, Y., Duan, Y., Li, W.F., Pace, P., Fortino, G.: Workshop networks integration using mobile intelligence in smart factories. IEEE Commun. Mag. **56**(2), 68–75 (2018)
51. Luo, Y., Duan, Y., Li, F.W., Pace, P., Fortino, G.: A novel mobile and hierarchical data transmission architecture for smart factories. IEEE Trans. Industr. Inf. **14**(8), 3534–3546 (2018)

Exploiting Long Distance Connections
to Strengthen Network Robustness

V. Carchiolo, M. Grassia, A. Longheu$^{(\boxtimes)}$, M. Malgeri, and G. Mangioni

Dip. Ingegneria Elettrica, Elettronica e Informatica,
Università degli Studi di Catania, Catania, Italy
{vincenza.carchiolo,alessandro.longheu,michele.malgeri,
giuseppe.mangioni}@dieei.unict.it

Abstract. Network fault tolerance (also known as resilience or robustness) is becoming a highly relevant topic, expecially in real networks, where it is essential to know to what extent it is still working notwithstanding its failures. Different questions need attention to guarantee robustness, as how it can be effectively and efficiently (i.e. rapidly) assessed, and which factors it depends on, as network structure, network dynamics and failure mechanisms. All studies aim at finding a way to hold (or increase) resilience; in this work we propose a strategy to improve robustness for Scale-free networks by adding links between highly distant nodes in the network; results show that even adding few long-distance links leads to a significant improvement of resilience, therefore this can be assumed as an effective (and possibly with low cost) approach for increasing robustness in networks.

Keywords: Complex networks · Robustness · Resilience
Scale-free networks · Failure

1 Introduction

Complex networks differ not only their first eye-catching feature, i.e. the dimension, but also for a set of relevant properties that, together with the size, determine each network's behaviour [2,4,15]. Among them, the robustness is highly relevant, expecially in real networks, where it is essential to know to what extent it is still working notwithstanding failures in its structure [1,7,8,18]. Indeed, many real networks can be disrupted, either by malicious, as it occurs in case of Internet computer-based attacks [19] or by physical unpredictable events, as in the case of Japanese tsunami that lead to supply chain shortage [12], or the Icelandic volcano that affected European air traffic in April 2010 [16].

Due to the undeniable networks vulnerability as well as to large scale effects of their failure, the study of robustness in complex networks is more and more receiving a major attention, expecially in the case of networks of networks (NON), often used to model real scenarios but that exhibit a greater vulnerability since the disruption of nodes of one network can affect nodes of other

© Springer Nature Switzerland AG 2018
Y. Xiang et al. (Eds.): IDCS 2018, LNCS 11226, pp. 270–277, 2018.
https://doi.org/10.1007/978-3-030-02738-4_23

(interconnected) network, leading to a cascade of failures [5], e.g. the case of Italy black-out in 2003 [6].

A first question that has been addressed is how evaluate robustness; resilience is generally quantified measuring the impact of the removal of nodes (and corresponding links) on some of network's property. For instance, in [10] robustness is evaluated using the Largest Connected Component (LCC), while in [9] percolation thresholds is engaged; other amounts can be adopted, as the elasticity that capture throughput under node and link removal [20], or the spectrum of a graph [11], or via other more sophisticated approach [21].

Researchers also investigated on which factors robustness depends on; among these, the network structure is one of the most relevant [17], for instance it is well established that Scale-free networks are more robust than Erdos-Rnyi networks to random failures, but are particularly susceptible to intentional attacks directed to its hubs (nodes with very high degree that hold most of network connectedness) [1]. In addition, the network dynamics should also be considered [13], since the behavior of robustness of dynamic systems is not the same for static systems, where the breakdown only occurs in their structure (some real systems for example can spontaneously recover from failures after a while, as in brain seizures). Finally, a third factor to address is the failure mechanism [3,14], for instance the cascading failures between interdependent network in NON.

A main goal of all these studies is however the increase of robustness, hence some actions can be carried out to strengthen the network, for instance by properly manage nodes and links and/or by adding new ones whenever possible. In this paper we propose a strategy to improve robustness, in particular for Scale–free networks; specifically, we propose to add links between highly distant nodes in the network; results show that even adding few long-distance links leads to a significant improvement of resilience, therefore this can be assumed as an effective (and possibly with low cost) approach for increasing robustness in networks.

The rest of the paper is organized as follows. In Sect. 2 we introduce the Scale–free networks robustness enhancement strategy, whereas in Sect. 3 we illustrate our simulations and discuss the results, presenting final remarks and future works in Sect. 4.

2   Scale–Free Networks Robustness Enhancement

Scale–free (SF) networks are characterized by a nodes degree distribution that follows a power–law. In other words, the fraction $P(k)$ of nodes having degree k goes as $P(k) \sim k^{-\gamma}$, where γ is typically in the range $2 < \gamma < 3$. A SF network is characterized by the presence of hub nodes, i.e. nodes with a degree that is much higher than the average. Hubs play an important role in many structural and dynamical properties scale–free networks have. Among these, hubs are fundamental nodes in shaping SF networks resilience.

In the seminal work [1] the authors find that a SF networks exhibit a good robustness to errors (i.e. random nodes removal), while they are very vulnerable

with respect to attacks (i.e. hubs removal). In fact, by removing hubs a SF network rapidly becomes a collection of disconnected components with a topology
completely destroyed.

To enhance the robustness of a SF network, here we propose a rewiring
strategy based on the following idea. Let's consider a portion of a SF network
such as that reported in Fig. 1. It is composed by 6 nodes, where two of them
are hubs (nodes 3 and 4). It easy to understand that if we remove one of the two
hubs, e.g. node 3 it is likely that the network becomes splitted in two separate
components. Moreover, if we consider the distance (i.e. the shortest path) among
hubs, it is always very short, since hubs are generally connected (or are a few
steps far away) one each other. This effect is due to the combination of two
factors: (1) hubs are generally the core around which the network grown, and
(2) hubs have many links and thus they are connected among them with a high
probability. Therefore it is highly unlikely that two hubs are very distant one
each other. So our idea to enhance the network robustness is to connect farthest
nodes by adding a new (long–distance) link that can act as a sort of bridge
between the neighbourhood of two different hubs. Applying such a strategy to
the example reported in Fig. 1, we add a new link (dashed line) between nodes
1 and 6. In such a way the network remains connected even if hubs 3 and 4 are
removed.

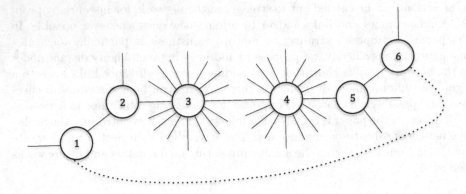

Fig. 1. SF network rewiring strategy

3   Results

In this section we present results obtained by applying our network robustness
enhancement strategy. All simulations are conducted on a scale–free network of
1000 nodes. As explained in the previous section, we compare our strategy with
a random one, where new links are added between two randomly selected nodes.

To visualize network robustness we report the size of the largest connected
component (LLC) as a function of the fraction of the removed nodes. All the

nodes are removed by using an attack strategy, i.e. nodes are removed in decreasing order of degree.

Figure 2 reports the robustness of the network obtained adding from 0 to 50 new links by using a random strategy. Note that the graph with label 0 corresponds to the original network. On the other hand, the graph with label 50 corresponds to the network where we added 50 new links, about 2.5% of total number of links. As highlighted in the inset in Fig. 2, there is a gain in the robustness the network. This is more evident in Fig. 3, where the gain (or delta) in the size of the LCC with respect to the original network is reported. By looking at this figure, we can see that the peak gain is about 7.5% obtained by adding 2.5% of new links.

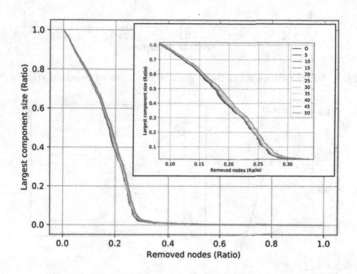

Fig. 2. SF networks robustness in the case of random strategy

The same simulations are then repeated by using the proposed robustness enhancement strategy, where long-distance links are added between farthest nodes.

As shown in Figs. 4 and 5 the network robustness increases as we introduce long–distance links. Specifically, we obtain a peak increment of about 17.5% of robustness by introducing only 2.5% of new links. This confirm our intuition that with just a small fraction of new links placed in the right way we can obtain a great improvement in the network resilience. Moreover, if we compare Figs. 3 and 5 we also note that in the last case there is always an increment in the robustness as we introduce new links. The same is not always true in the case of a random strategy. This fact is confirmed in Fig. 6, where the network robustness gain comparison between long-distance and random strategies is reported. Specifically, we report that the our proposed strategy performs better than a random strategy, with a peak difference of more than 13%.

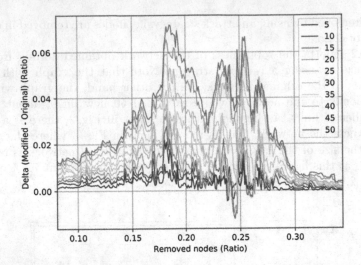

Fig. 3. SF networks robustness gain in the case of random strategy

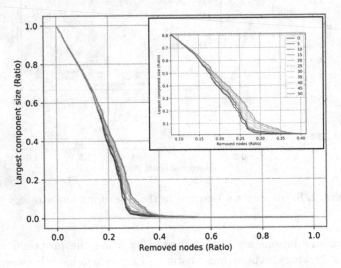

Fig. 4. SF networks robustness in the case of long-distance strategy

4   Conclusions

The study and the improvement of robustness in complex networks is becoming a major question to be addressed due to its importance. Here in particular, we introduced a re-wiring strategy for SF networks based on the addition of (possibly few) long-distance links; all the experiments presented above confirm our initial hypothesis about the role of long-distance links in an easily increasing of network resilience.

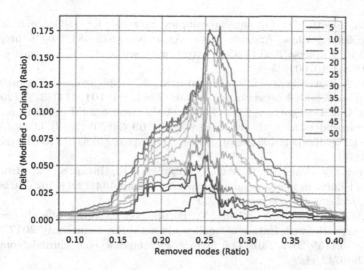

Fig. 5. SF networks robustness gain in the case of long-distance strategy

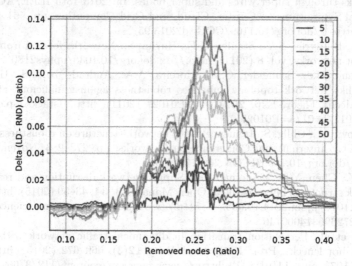

Fig. 6. SF networks robustness gain comparison between random and long-distance strategies

References

1. Albert, R., Jeong, H., Barabasi, A.: Error and attack tolerance of complex networks. Nature **406**(6794), 378–382 (2000)
2. Albert, R., Barabasi, A.L.: Statistical mechanics of complex networks. Rev. Mod. Phys. **74**, 47 (2002). http://www.citebase.org/cgi-bin/citations?id=oai:arXiv.org: cond-mat/0106096

3. Ash, J., Newth, D.: Optimizing complex networks for resilience against cascading failure. Phys. A: Stat. Mech. Appl. **380**, 673–683 (2007). https://doi.org/10.1016/j.physa.2006.12.058. http://www.sciencedirect.com/science/article/pii/S0378437107002543

4. Barrat, A., Barthélemy, M., Pastor-Satorras, R., Vespignani, A.: The architecture of complex weighted networks. Proc. Natl. Acad. Sci. **101**, 3747–3752 (2004)

5. Baxter, G.J., Dorogovtsev, S.N., Goltsev, A.V., Mendes, J.F.F.: Avalanche collapse of interdependent networks. Phys. Rev. Lett. **109**, 248701 (2012). https://doi.org/10.1103/PhysRevLett.109.248701. https://link.aps.org/doi/10.1103/PhysRevLett.109.248701

6. Buldyrev, S.V., Parshani, R., Paul, G., Stanley, H.E., Havlin, S.: Catastrophic cascade of failures in interdependent networks. Nature **464**(7291), 1025–1028 (2010). https://doi.org/10.1038/nature08932

7. Duan, Y., Fu, X., Li, W., Zhang, Y., Fortino, G.: Evolution of scale-freewireless sensor networks with feature of small-world networks. Complexity **2017**. https://doi.org/10.1155/2017/2516742. https://www.hindawi.com/journals/complexity/2017/2516742/cta/

8. Fu, X., Li, W., Fortino, G.: Empowering the invulnerability of wireless sensor networks through super wires and super nodes. In: 2013 13th IEEE/ACM International Symposium on Cluster, Cloud, and Grid Computing, pp. 561–568, May 2013. https://doi.org/10.1109/CCGrid.2013.95

9. Gao, J., Buldyrev, S.V., Stanley, H.E., Havlin, S.: Networks formed from interdependent networks, vol. 8 (2011). http://dx.doi.org/10.1038/nphys2180

10. Herrmann, H.J., Schneider, C.M., Moreira, A.A., Andrade Jr., J.S., Havlin, S.: Onion-like network topology enhances robustness against malicious attacks. J. Stat. Mech. Theor. Exp. **2011**(01), P01027 (2011). http://stacks.iop.org/1742-5468/2011/i=01/a=P01027

11. Jamakovic, A., Uhlig, S.: Influence of the network structure on robustness. In: 2007 15th IEEE International Conference on Networks, pp. 278–283, November 2007. https://doi.org/10.1109/ICON.2007.4444099

12. Kim, Y., Chen, Y.S., Linderman, K.: Supply network disruption and resilience: a network structural perspective. J. Oper. Manag. **33–34**, 43–59 (2015). https://doi.org/10.1016/j.jom.2014.10.006. http://www.sciencedirect.com/science/article/pii/S0272696314000746

13. Li, D., et al.: Percolation transition in dynamical traffic network with evolving critical bottlenecks. Proc. Natl. Acad. Sci. **112**(3), 669–672 (2015). https://doi.org/10.1073/pnas.1419185112. http://www.pnas.org/content/112/3/669

14. Majdandzic, A., Podobnik, B., Buldyrev, S.V., Kenett, D.Y., Havlin, S., Eugene Stanley, H.: Spontaneous recovery in dynamical networks. Nat. Phys. **10**, 34–38 (2014). https://doi.org/10.1038/nphys2819

15. Newman, M.: The structure and function of complex networks. SIAM Rev. **45**, 167–256 (2003). http://www.citebase.org/cgi-bin/citations?id=oai:arXiv.org:cond-mat/0303516

16. Peter, B.: Fear in a handful of dust: aviation and the icelandic volcano. Significance **7**(3), 112–115. https://doi.org/10.1111/j.1740-9713.2010.00436.x. https://rss.onlinelibrary.wiley.com/doi/abs/10.1111/j.1740-9713.2010.00436.x

17. Schneider, C.M., Moreira, A.A., Andrade Jr., J.S., Havlin, S., Herrmann, H.J.: Mitigation of malicious attacks on networks. Proc. Natl. Acad. Sci. **108**, 3838–3841 (2011). https://doi.org/10.1073/pnas.1009440108

18. Shao, J., Buldyrev, S.V., Havlin, S., Stanley, H.E.: Cascade of failures in coupled network systems with multiple support-dependence relations. Phys. Rev. E **83**, 036116 (2011). https://doi.org/10.1103/PhysRevE.83.036116
19. Strogatz, S.H.: Exploring complex networks. Nature **410**(6825), 268–276 (2001). https://doi.org/10.1038/35065725
20. Sydney, A., Scoglio, C., Youssef, M., Schumm, P.: Characterizing the robustness of complex networks. ArXiv e-prints, November 2008
21. Zhou, A., Maleti, S., Zhao, Y.: Robustness and percolation of holes in complex networks. Phys. A: Stat. Mech. Appl. **502**, 459–468 (2018). https://doi.org/10.1016/j.physa.2018.02.149. http://www.sciencedirect.com/science/article/pii/S0378437118302188

An Online Adaptive Sampling Rate Learning Framework for Sensor-Based Human Activity Recognition

Zeyi Jin[1], Jingjing Cao[1(✉)], Jingtao Sun[2], Wenfeng Li[1], and Qiang Wang[1]

[1] School of Logistics Engineering, Wuhan University of Technology,
Wuhan 430063, China
elevenjzy@126.com, {bettycao,liwf,wangqiang}@whut.edu.cn
[2] Information Systems Architecture Research Division,
National Institute of Informatics, Tokyo 101-8430, Japan
sun@nii.ac.jp

Abstract. In the field of sensor based human activity recognition, fixed sampling rate scheme is difficult to accommodate the dynamic characteristics of streaming data. It may directly leads to high energy consumption or activities detail missing problems. In this paper, an efficiency online activity recognition framework is proposed by integrating sampling rate optimization with novel class detection and recurring class detection algorithms. Based on the proposed framework, we believe that this system can effectively save battery life and computation capacity without decreasing the overall recognition performance.

Keywords: Human activity recognition · Sampling rate optimization
Novel class detection

1 Introduction

Sensor-based human activity data is composed of a great many of signals collected from various sensors. Most previous researches for machine learning and data mining have placed great emphasis on how to handle these obtained signals in an online environment, while the problem that how to appropriately determine the sampling rate before collecting these signals, has been overlooked. In real-world applications, appropriate sampling rate selection is of particular important for human activity recognition systems with regard to some factors. These factors include battery life of sensor, power of bandwidth if communication needed, storage and memory consumption and so on. As for system with fixed sampling rate, if sampling rate is high, reducing sampling rate can extend the system life by affecting these factors. In contract, increasing sampling rate can enhance the system classification behavior if sampling rate is low. Thus, it is necessary to analyse how to adaptively select optimized sampling rate in different situations.

© Springer Nature Switzerland AG 2018
Y. Xiang et al. (Eds.): IDCS 2018, LNCS 11226, pp. 278–281, 2018.
https://doi.org/10.1007/978-3-030-02738-4_24

Further, human activity recognition can be regarded as a typical data stream classification problem, i.e., data is collected over time in the form of stream instances or chunks. Learning under such condition intrigues new challenges which contain novel and recurring class detection[1][1,2] etc. To adaptively change sampling rate, these characteristics of stream data should be considered.

Existing sampling rate researches cover two directions:

- The first direction [3] is directly optimizing sampling rates by evaluating the similarity of two signals with respect to different sampling rate, and the iterations stop when similarity threshold condition holds.
- The assumption of another direction [4] is that if current activity has not been changed, the sampling rate can be set as low as possible.

Our work aims to take advantage of these two directions to design appropriate sampling rate generation mechanism regarding activity change detection, novel and recurring class detection problems.

The rest of the paper is organized as follows. Section 2 provides the proposed system architecture and Sect. 3 discusses some applied algorithms in detail. Finally, Sect. 4 give some conclusions.

2   Proposed Framework

By collecting T labeled data chunks, the system utilizes Learn++.NSE approach [5] to construct the initial ensemble of models[2], i.e., $L = \{L_1, \ldots, L_T\}$, where T is a time (chunk) index. With the arrival of new data chunk at time $T + 1$, the first step is to check whether there has been an activity change compared with activity label at time T. If there is, the data chunk is fed into the multi-activity classification module, otherwise the sampling rate is maintained for next time $T + 2$. Simultaneously, new chunk data has been divided into one class and the rest classes respectively, and extreme learning machine (ELM) algorithm [6] is adopted to general a basic binary model C_k for each class k.

Regarding multi-activity classification module, novel class detection algorithm firstly operates on obtained data chunk. Once the new data chunk is not a novel class, we label them as existing class; or else, we temporarily regard it as novel class. Due to the fact that recurring class normally appears to be a novel class, we present a detection to further distinguish between recurring class and true novel class according to per class model C_k. Then, we propose two buffers E and R with respect to sampling rate. Buffer E refers to optimal sampling rate for each current existing class c_i, while R contains optimal sampling rate for universal existing class u_j, namely at least one classifier has been trained with class u_j and these classifiers have been discard for a long time. Thus, the sampling

---

[1] b is a novel class if it never appears in stream data, while c is a recurring class if it appeared before but disappeared so long that c is discarded from current ensemble.

[2] Ensemble learning: A sort of machine learning algorithm by combining several weak learner to construct a strong learner.

rate can be determined for next time once the detection procedure completed, and the determined sampling rate will be updated to current existing class buffer E. The framework of our system is depicted in Fig. 1.

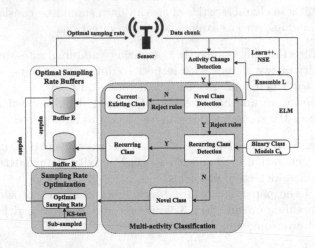

Fig. 1. Proposed online adaptive sampling rate learning framework

Based on the above brief description, the framework has the following advantages. On one hand, activity change detection avoids to update sampling rate frequently and sampling rate optimization module can always maintain an appropriate sampling rate. On the other hand, the buffer setting controls the times to call the sampling rate optimization module, which also reduces power consumption of the system.

3   Applied Algorithms

In this work, we have applied four algorithms respectively for ensemble construction and recognition, novel class detection, recurring class detection and sampling rate optimization. Some details of algorithms are described as follows:

Learn++.NSE Algorithm. Learn++.NSE algorithm is designed by employing a dynamic weighted majority voting scheme to ensemble multiple classifiers. The weight of the base classifier is determined by the error classification rate of each base classifier to the current training set, and the base classifier with less weight will be temporarily forgotten.

Novel Class Detection Based on Reject Rules. In our previous work [2], we have proposed a detection algorithm based on reject rule. This algorithm is designed based on Learn++.NSE and adding reject option with two parameters θ_1^T and θ_2^T with respect to time T. If the parameters satisfy the reject conditions, one can detect novel class. In this work, we also consider the rule to delete class.

Extreme Learning Machine Algorithm. With simple structure and low computational complexity advantages, ELM is employed to gain binary classifiers C_k for each class. Then C_k can be utilized to operate recurring class detection. And the assumption of this detection is that if recurring class exists, it should be close enough and show high confidence to one C_k.

K-S Test Algorithm. In this work, we adopt [3]'s work to optimize sampling rate with a two-sample Kolmogorov-Smirnov (KS) test. This test compares two signals without considering the underlying distribution of the data. This paper compared two signals at time T and $T + 1$, where $T + 1$ is current time.

Overall, all the algorithms are fast which is suitable for online learning. Learn++.NSE gives base classifier set, ELM and reject rule algorithms adapt to dynamic characteristics of steam data, and K-S test supports adaptive sampling rate that can save energy or reduce activity detail loss.

4   Conclusions

In this paper, we proposed a paradigm to embed adaptive sampling rate scheme into an online sensor-based human activity recognition system. It covers two dynamic characteristics of stream activity data, novel class detection and recurring class detection. It also present a activity change detection scheme to maintained optimal sampling rate as much as possible. Particularly, how to design adaptive sampling rate to suit more characteristics of stream data, such as concept drift, imbalance class, should be discussed in the future work.

Acknowledgment. The work was partially supported by National Natural Science Foundation of China under the Grant No. 61502360, No. 61571336 and No. 61503291.

References

1. Al-Khateeb, T., et al.: Recurring and novel class detection using class-based ensemble for evolving data stream. IEEE Trans. Knowl. Data Eng. **28**(10), 2752–2764 (2016)
2. Deng, C., Yuan, W., Tao, Z., Cao, J.: Detecting novel class for sensor-based activity recognition using reject rule. In: Li, W., et al. (eds.) IDCS 2016. LNCS, vol. 9864, pp. 34–44. Springer, Cham (2016). https://doi.org/10.1007/978-3-319-45940-0_4
3. Khan, A., Hammerla, N.Y., Mellor, S., Plötz, T.: Optimising sampling rates for accelerometer-based human activity recognition. Pattern Recognit. Lett. **73**, 33–40 (2016)
4. Qi, X., Keally, M., Zhou, G., Li, Y., Ren, Z.: AdaSense: adapting sampling rates for activity recognition in body sensor networks. In: 19th IEEE Real-Time and Embedded Technology and Applications Symposium, RTAS 2013, Philadelphia, PA, USA, 9–11 April 2013, pp. 163–172 (2013)
5. Elwell, R., Polikar, R.: Incremental learning of concept drift in nonstationary environments. IEEE Trans. Neural Netw. **22**(10), 1517–1531 (2011)
6. Ding, S., Zhao, H., Zhang, Y., Xu, X., Nie, R.: Extreme learning machine: algorithm, theory and applications. Artif. Intell. Rev. **44**(1), 103–115 (2015)

A Secure Video-Based Robust
and Aesthetic 2D Barcode

Changsheng Chen[1(✉)], Fengbo Lan[1], and Wai Ho Mow[2]

[1] The Guangdong Key Laboratory of Intelligent Information Processing and
Shenzhen Key Laboratory of Media Security, College of Information Engineering,
Shenzhen University, Shenzhen, China
cschen@szu.edu.cn, 2015130188@email.szu.edu.cn
[2] The HKUST Barcode Group, Department of Electronic and Computer
Engineering, Hong Kong University of Science and Technology (HKUST),
Clear Water Bay, Hong Kong S.A.R., China
eewhmow@ust.hk

Abstract. The conventional barcode is currently employed in some
mobile payment applications. The barcode serves as a token which represents the identity of a user. However, attacks on the payment process
can be initiated by intercepting the barcode images in various ways. In
this work, we proposed a ideo-based Robust and Aesthetic 2D barCode
(vRA Code) so that the security of the token is protected while the efficiency in the decoding process is guaranteed. Experiments with different
embedded video contents and capturing angles have been conducted to
show the practicality of the proposed system. Experimental results have
demonstrated that a vRA Code can be decoded in about 1.5 s.

Keywords: Security · Video · Aesthetic barcode

1 Introduction

As the rapid development on computational power and imaging capability of
mobile devices, there is a growing interest in applying two-dimensional (2D)
barcodes in the advertisement and mobile payment business in recent years. In
an advertisement, a 2D barcode is served as a storage media for some product
related information that can be retrieved through scanning the 2D barcode with
a camera and processing with an application on the mobile platform. In the
mobile payment application, a barcode can be employed as an offline media for
storing a token to represent the identity of each user. The barcode can be scanned

The work of C. Chen and F. Lan were supported by the NSFC Project under Grant
61702340, the Natural Science Foundation of Guangdong Province, China under
Grant 2017A030310382, and the Science and Technology Innovation Commission of
Shenzhen, China under Project 827/000213. The work of W. H. Mow was supported
by the General Research Fund from the Research Grants Council of the Hong Kong
Special Administrative Region, China (Project No. 16233816).

© Springer Nature Switzerland AG 2018
Y. Xiang et al. (Eds.): IDCS 2018, LNCS 11226, pp. 282–287, 2018.
https://doi.org/10.1007/978-3-030-02738-4_25

at the point of purchase during a transaction and the corresponding amount of currency is then deduced from one's digital wallet [6]. For security concerns, the token and the barcode are updated on a regular basis according to the framework proposed in [5]. Moreover, further security measures, such as proximity authentication and geometric models based physical security enhancement mechanism has been suggested in [8] and [7], respectively. However, some security loopholes are identified by the attackers. For examples, Bai *et al.* [2] propose an attack model for the barcode-based mobile payment system by introducing an over-the-counter payment frauds with a barcode image sniffing app. The sniffing app is able to eavesdrop the barcode from the glass reflection of the barcode scanner before the payment is successfully completed. The compromised barcode is then used for an unauthorized transaction. Moreover, news on mobile payment victims have been reported by other forms of QR code image eavesdropping. The People's Bank of China has strengthen the rule on barcode-based payment methods by setting a cap on individual payments [1]. However, the issue of image-based barcode eavesdropping remains to be addressed.

In this paper, we propose to use a video-based 2D barcode to solve this issue by taking the advantage that the difficulties in eavesdropping a sequence of video frames are much larger than that of an image. The resulting barcode is named Video-based Robust and Aesthetic (vRA) Code. It is a multi-frame barcode design based on our image-based barcode, RA Code proposed in [4]. The information, e.g., token of a payment transaction is stored in a multiframe-based vRA Code sequence. Obtaining partial information is useless. The attackers with image sniffing form of attacks will not be successful since they are able to get a complete sequence of barcode. Under such design, an eavesdropping attack will be more difficult since a much higher frame rate is required in video sniffing. Experimental results have demonstrated that the proposed solution has achieved a good balance in making the attack more difficult while preserving the decoding efficiency. The proposed vRA Code can be decoded in about 1.5 s.

2 The Proposed Video-Based Robust and Aesthetic 2D Barcode

As can be seen in Fig. 1, each vRA Code frame is of dimension 29×29 modules (excluding the finder pattern). The finder pattern of a vRA Code is featured with three 'L' shape corners at the top left, top right and bottom left positions, as well as a solid black module at the bottom right position. Enclosed by the finder pattern, the encoding region is designed as a module based structure. Each module is an image block modulated by the designed pattern.

In order to have a more decent quality of the vRA Code, the modulation amplitude proposed in our prior work, RA Code [4] is multiplied by a time-varying coefficient which produces a large modulation amplitude only once in a predetermined period T. That is

(a)   (b)   (c)

Fig. 1. Illustrations of the proposed video-based 2D barcode, vRA Code. Three video frames from a vRA Code with a moving WeChat logo are shown.

$$
P_k(x,y,i) = \begin{cases} (-1)^{B(k)} \sin\left[\frac{2\pi}{L}\left(x - \frac{1}{2}\right)\right] \sin\left[\frac{2\pi}{L}\left(y - \frac{1}{2}\right)\right] \\ \qquad\qquad\qquad\qquad\qquad \times \sin\left(\frac{\pi i}{T}\right), \text{for } x,y \leq L \\ 0, \qquad \text{otherwise} \end{cases} \tag{1}
$$

where $L = 2M/3$, M is the resolution for each module in the embedding image, $x,y \leq M$ are the image indices in each module, $B(k)$ is the k-th bit of the encoded message, i is the index of a given frame, and the range for a modulation pattern is $P_k(x,y,i) \in [-1,1]$. As is shown in Fig. 2, the modulation amplitude is time-varying. The modulation amplitude is varying with the term $|\sin\left(\frac{\pi i}{T}\right)|$ which achieves maximum at $i/T = 1/2 + n$ where n is an arbitrary positive integer. The value of T should be set properly by considering the transmission data rate and the obtrusiveness. A large value of T leads to less obtrusiveness with a slow varying modulation amplitude while a smaller data rate. In our implementation T is set to 0.5 s such that a two-frame vRA Code can be decoded in one second theoretically.

Furthermore, it is worth mentioning that the information is encoded with the Reed-Solomon (RS) channel coding scheme to yield multiple RS codewords. The data interleaving process is applied to the codewords across multiple frames such that each vRA Code contains a random partial information of the encoded message. To this end, a video-based robust and aesthetic 2D barcode system, vRA Code has been proposed to tackle the security threat induced by the image based sniffing attacks.

3   Implementation and Demo of the Proposed vRA Code

In order to demonstrate the practicality of the proposed vRA Code, the decoding algorithm has been implemented in C++ and ported to a mobile platform, i.e., the Android platform. The decoding algorithm runs smoothly in 720p preview resolution with a frame rate of 30 frames/second. Some demo videos of the vRA Codes and the associated decoding mobile App on Android platform have been uploaded to a shared Dropbox folder[1]. Some snapshots of the vRA Code samples have been shown in Fig. 3. Readers may install the app on ones' mobile devices and test the decoding performance. The recommended video player for the sample videos is the Window Media Player 12 available in Windows 10 operating system. It should also be noted that the physical size and display resolution are important factors which affects the decoding robustness. A display with HD resolution and a display size larger than $3 \times 3\,\text{cm}^2$ is recommended.

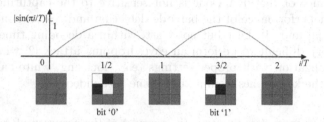

Fig. 2. Illustrations of the proposed time-varying modulation schemes in vRA Code.

(a) Avatar   (b) Happy Eastern   (c) Coby   (d) Big Buck Bunny

(e) Jingle Bells   (f) Love Home   (g) Take the Bus   (h) WeChat

Fig. 3. Some snapshots of the vRA Code samples with different embedded contents.

Some experimental results on the practicality of the proposed scheme have been shown in Table 1. A vRA Code video with 30 frames/second can be decoded in about 1.5 s with a typical off-the-shelf mobile device that is released in year

---

[1] https://www.dropbox.com/sh/z9m9jm8v41touo5/AADCQ64DoM_2GZa9nq9uG7 hTa.

2013 or later. More specifically, the experiments are conducted with a VAIO Z Laptop with display resolution of 2560×1440 pixels. The vRA Code is displayed with size about $5 \times 5 \, \text{cm}^2$. A handheld capturing device, the Google Nexus 5 with 720p preview resolution is employed. The average decoding time is calculated over 50 successful decoding trails under each condition. It should be noted that the decoding performances of vRA Code are consistent with those of the RA Code presented in [4]. The average decoding time is longer under the videos with rich texture, e.g., Big Buck Bunny and Jingle Bells. Moreover, the decoding performance of the vRA Code is not sensitive to the capturing angle due to the robust performance of the barcode detection and restoration algorithms proposed in [3] and [4]. Last but not least, within a decoding time window of 1.5 s, it is very difficult to perform an eavesdropping attack [2] which includes camera initialization with proper settings (e.g., focusing, white-balance, ISO) and sniffing the key frames from a high frame rate video.

Table 1. The average decoding time (in seconds) of the proposed vRA Code under different video contents and capturing angles.

Video contents	Avatar	Happy Eastern	Coby	Big Buck Bunny	Jingle Bells	Love Home	Take the Bus	WeChat
0°	1.30	1.24	1.18	1.50	1.64	1.22	1.30	1.26
20°	1.32	1.30	1.22	1.45	1.58	1.26	1.30	1.30

4   Conclusion

In this paper, a video-based Robust and Aesthetic 2D barCode, named vRA Code has been proposed to mitigate the security issue of the traditional image-based 2D barcode under an eavesdropping attack. Experimental results have demonstrated that the proposed vRA Code can be decoded in about 1.5 s. It has achieved a good balance in making the attack more difficult while preserving the decoding efficiency. There are several promising future directions based on the proposed vRA Code. First, the design of the proposed modulation scheme can be re-visited with a more sophisticated time-varying function such that the decoding time of an authentic user can be reduced while the same level of security against the eavesdropping attack can be maintained. Second, the robustness of the modulation pattern should be investigated to mitigate the performance degradation under texture-rich content.

References

1. The Verge, China begins regulating QR code payments, 28 December 2017. https://www.theverge.com/2017/12/28/16826698/china-qr-code-payment-regulation/
2. Bai, X., et al.: Picking up my tab: understanding and mitigating synchronized token lifting and spending in mobile payment. In: 26th USENIX Security Symposium (USENIX Security 17), pp. 593–608. USENIX Association (2017)

3. Chen, C., Huang, W., Zhou, B., Liu, C., Mow, W.H.: PiCode: a new picture-embedding 2D barcode. IEEE Trans. Image Process. **25**(8), 3444–3458 (2016)
4. Chen, C., Zhou, B., Mow, W.H.: RA Code: a robust and aesthetic code for resolution-constrained applications. IEEE Trans. Circuits Syst. Video Technol. (2017, early access). https://ieeexplore.ieee.org/document/8013082
5. Gao, J., Kulkarni, V., Ranavat, H., Chang, L., Mei, H.: A 2D barcode-based mobile payment system. In: 2009 Third International Conference on Multimedia and Ubiquitous Engineering. MUE 2009, pp. 320–329. IEEE (2009)
6. Lu, L.: Decoding Alipay: Mobile Payments, A Cashless Society and Regulatory Challenges (2018)
7. Zhang, B., Ren, K., Xing, G., Fu, X., Wang, C.: SBVLC: secure barcode-based visible light communication for smartphones. IEEE Trans. Mobile Comput. **15**(2), 432–446 (2016)
8. Zhuang, Y., Leung, A.C.M., Hughes, J.: Matching in proximity authentication and mobile payment ecosystem: what are we missing? In: Hancke, G.P., Markantonakis, K. (eds.) RFIDSec 2016. LNCS, vol. 10155, pp. 163–172. Springer, Cham (2017). https://doi.org/10.1007/978-3-319-62024-4_12

A Migratable Container-Based Replication Management for Inter-cloud

Mingkang Chen[1(✉)] and Jingtao Sun[2]

[1] Department of Electrical and Information Engineering,
China Central Normal University, Wuhan 430079, China
mingkang@mails.ccnu.edu.cn
[2] Information Systems Architecture Research Division,
National Institute of Informatics, Tokyo 101-8430, Japan
sun@nii.ac.jp

Abstract. This paper proposes a novel approach to rapidly deploy a migratable container-based replication management for inter-cloud. The key idea behind the proposed approach is to introduce the coordination of multiple autonomic managers in inter-cloud environments. Compared with existing researches, we can not only absorb features from heterogeneous clouds through the *Base Container*, but also we can periodically update the deployed container-based replication mechanism through asynchronous processes, in order to improve data consistency problem. In addition, this paper analyzes the feasibility through comparing between file reading and writing in same and different clouds in the proposed approach.

Keywords: Distributed storage · Replication · Container
Adaptability · Inter-cloud

1 Introduction

Cloud computing is rapidly gaining popularity in academia and industry. With its powerful computing resources, distributed computation, low-cost operation and maintenance, and the characteristics of high flexibility and high resistance to risk are very popular for now. In particular, with the development of Internet of Things (IoT) technology, a large amount of data collected through various sensors is often stored in the cloud. It's required that a dynamically adaptive absorption of different cloud-to-cloud changes and the implementation of a portable architecture without the need to reduce system availability, e.g., easier and faster recovery their systems, various replication mechanisms are proposed in related researches [1–7].

It is very common to deploy replication management in the same kind of cloud [3, 4, 7]. They proposed novel ways to maintain data consistency and demonstrate the effectiveness of their research methods by setting a number of evaluation methods. However, in dealing with some geographical differences, data security

© Springer Nature Switzerland AG 2018
Y. Xiang et al. (Eds.): IDCS 2018, LNCS 11226, pp. 288–292, 2018.
https://doi.org/10.1007/978-3-030-02738-4_26

protection, and mobile user's needs are constantly changed, those approaches are still difficult to achieve. Some new challenges, such as the replication management executed on heterogeneous clouds are proposed [1,5,6]. Most of them often provide replication services for specific applications through a number of algorithms and network protocol proposals, and through migration of virtual machine [2] to deploy its replication management. Unlike their approaches, in this paper, we proposed a novel approach to rapidly deploy a migratable container-based replication management for inter-cloud. The key idea behind the proposed approach is to introduce the coordination of multiple autonomic managers in inter-cloud environments. There are some advantages as follows for using the container technologies:

- Users don't need to need to set configuration files in the execution environment.
- Container technology is easier for migration and deploying among the platforms.
- Container technology is simpler for developers to deploy their services and applications.

The remainder of the paper is organized as follows. We proposed our system requirements in Sect. 2. Next, we describe our key ideas and the realization method in Sect. 3. Finally, we conclude our paper in Sect. 4.

2 Requirements

In this section, we propose our requirements for managing replication framework on inter-cloud as follows:

- **Adaptivity:** Replication between heterogeneous cloud needs adapting to different environment and architecture, for instance, in different geographically distributed clouds, the OS, physical devices, service providers may be different.
- **Portability:** Users located in different areas need connecting to different geographically distributed cloud servers to reduce latency, support localized services. Data and applications aimed at different services need replicating to other clouds in different areas to provide the portability of their services.
- **Fault Tolerance:** Cloud service needs providing services without interruption. If the cloud in a certain area is breakdown or area happens natural disaster, cloud needs recovering rapidly according to the backup system which implemented in different areas.

In order to achieve the above requirements, we design and implement a **container-in-container** mechanism. The next chapter describes this method in detail.

3   Approach

Our approach is based on the migration of containers, embedding replication management and its environment with **container-in-container** mechanism, for deploying replication management[1] and adopting asynchronous update between clouds in data consistency.

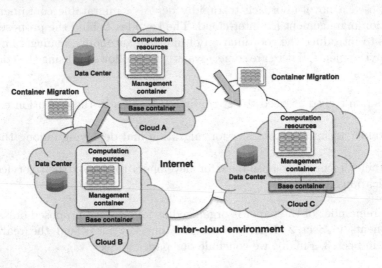

Fig. 1. Inter-cloud environment

As shown in Fig. 1, *Base Container* is composed of essential environments and dependencies for *Management Container* managing replication between clouds, making environment consistency of deploying applications. Developers can create predictable environments with *Base Container* defining running configurations for replication management, and help administrators to migrate to other clouds and deploy replication management according to their requirements. It enables replication management rapidly deploying and running on clouds anywhere, and introduce the cooperation of replication between clouds.

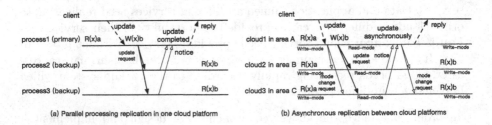

Fig. 2. Two situations of replication

---

[1] Currently, we designed our framework and now we are implementing it, we plan to evaluate the performance of our framework with other approaches in future.

In data consistency, we divide into two situations: parallel processing replication in one cloud platform of a certain area, and asynchronous replication among clouds platforms, i.e. geographically distributed cloud servers. We use Fig. 2(a) and (b) respectively depicting the two situations. We suppose the file x has the initial value a, at this moment, reading the file x will get the value a denoted by $R(x)a$, and similarly $W(x)b$ denotes writing the file x into the value b.

In one cloud platform, we suppose there are multiple processes. When a user writes the file x into the value b with process 1 in the cloud, parallel processing replication executes as follows:

- Process 1 simultaneously sends update requests to other two backups (process 2, 3).
- Process 1 copies the updated value of the file x, and sends to Process 2 and 3 for updating.
- Process 2, 3 complete updating and sends the notifications back to process 1.
- Process 1 received all notifications, and replies to the client that writing the file x is completed.

On the other hand, the geographically distributed cloud platforms, we adopt asynchronous update among clouds[2]. We suppose that there are three clouds platforms (cloud 1, 2, and 3) which were executed in three areas (area A, B, and C). The asynchronous update processing is shown as follows:

- Supposed the file x is the value a. When one user writes the file x in his local cloud (cloud 1) directly, which would not update it to other cloud platforms directly.
- Once periodically updates begin among clouds, cloud 1 will send mode change request to other all clouds.
- When the destination cloud 2, 3 received them, however, they change write-mode to read-mode and only support the file x read-only, which means that the users can't execute the write command. Then cloud 1 copies the file x and simultaneously sends to cloud 2, 3 for updating.
- After cloud 2, 3 completed update, they will send the notifications back to cloud 1.
- When cloud 1 received all notifications, it will send the mode change requests to these clouds for changing to write-mode.
- Finally, cloud 1 changes to write-mode and replies to the local user that writing the file x is complete updating. Up to now, all users served by other cloud platforms can read the file x with the same latest value b.

Therefore, it is asynchronous that users in a certain area read the replication from other cloud data centers in other areas. Especially, the above situation is that we design the file x is only written in cloud 1. During sequentially updating from cloud 2 to cloud 3, if a user writes the file x in cloud 2, after the whole

---

[2] Because of latency of data transmission between clouds in different areas, the whole processing of updating data between all clouds and matching local data in destination data centers for merging data is more complex than purely local replication.

update, the file x may be different from other clouds, which will destroy data consistency. Therefore, we adopt the RW locks to guarantee data consistency the whole processing of update among clouds.

Our proposal can be applied to more general-purpose applications deploying in geographically distributed clouds, for instance, helping edge computing more rapidly providing customized application services for users in different areas.

4 Conclusion

In this paper, we proposed an approach to rapidly deploy a migratable container-based replication management for inter-cloud. It introduces the coordination of multiple autonomic managers in inter-cloud environments. Currently, we are trying to implement our asynchronous update method, in particular, the implementation of simultaneous write operations on file copies in a heterogeneous cloud is still a topic for us in the future.

References

1. Abouzamazem, A., Ezhilchelvan, P.: Efficient inter-cloud replication for high-availability services. In: IEEE International Conference on Cloud Engineering (IC2E), pp. 132–139. IEEE (2013)
2. Nagin, K., et al.: Inter-cloud mobility of virtual machines. In: Proceedings of the 4th Annual International Conference on Systems and Storage, pp. 1–12. ACM (2011)
3. Wei, Q., Veeravalli, B., Gong, B., Zeng, L., Feng, D.: CDRM: a cost-effective dynamic replication management scheme for cloud storage cluster. In: IEEE International Conference on Cluster Computing (CLUSTER), pp. 188–196. IEEE (2010)
4. Bonvin, N., Papaioannou, T.G., Aberer, K.: A self-organized, fault-tolerant and scalable replication scheme for cloud storage. In: Proceedings of the 1st ACM Symposium on Cloud Computing, pp. 205–216. ACM (2010)
5. Smart, R., Jaramillo, D., Lu, C., Cook, T.: Implementing a cloud backed scalable note-taking application with encrypted offline storage and cross platform replication. In: Proceedings of the IEEE SoutheastCon, pp. 1–6. IEEE (2015)
6. Soares, J., Preguiça, N.: Combining mobile and cloud storage for providing ubiquitous data access. In: Jeannot, E., Namyst, R., Roman, J. (eds.) Euro-Par 2011. LNCS, vol. 6852, pp. 516–527. Springer, Heidelberg (2011). https://doi.org/10.1007/978-3-642-23400-2_48
7. Bowers, K.D., Juels, A., Oprea, A.: HAIL: a high-availability and integrity layer for cloud storage. In: Proceedings of the 16th ACM Conference on Computer and Communications Security, pp. 187–198. ACM (2009)

Dilated Deep Residual Network for Post-processing in TPG Based Image Coding

Yuan Yuan[1]([✉]), Jingtao Sun[2], and Miaohui Wang[1]

[1] Shenzhen University, Shenzhen 518060, China
{yuanyuan,mhwang}@szu.edu.cn
[2] National Institute of Informatics, Tokyo 101-8430, Japan
sun@nii.ac.jp

Abstract. Lossy image compression algorithms like JPEG usually introduce visually annoying artifacts on decoded images, such as blocking artifacts, blurring and ringing effects. The tiny portable graphics (TPG) based image/video compression technique is proposed to improve JPEG compression performance. However, the lossy compression artifacts cannot be fully removed, especially at low coding bit-rates. Recently, some shallow convolutional neural network (CNN) models have been proposed as post-processing techniques to reduce compression artifacts. Learning from the fact that deep CNNs have shown extraordinary ability in high-level vision problems, we propose to investigate how a deeper CNN can further enhance the quality of decoded images. Specifically, we adopt a network with 16 residual blocks. In order to increase the receptive field, we change the first convolution layer in the first five residual blocks to dilated convolution with size 2. The primary experimental results show that the proposed model can outperform existing CNN based post-processing methods.

Keywords: Post-processing · Artifacts reduction · TPG coding
Deep residual network

1 Introduction

Traditional image codecs like JPEG [1], H.264 [2] and HEVC [3] employ fixed block transforms like DCT and quantized transform coefficients for lossy compression. The uncorrelated block-based processing will result in blocking artifacts and the coarser quantization at low bit-rates will result in blurring and ringing effects in the decoded images. These complex artifacts not only severely reduce the perceptual visual quality, but also affect the subsequent image processing procedures which take the decoded images as input, such as segmentation [4] and super-resolution [5]. Recently, the Tencent company propose a new image

© Springer Nature Switzerland AG 2018
Y. Xiang et al. (Eds.): IDCS 2018, LNCS 11226, pp. 293–297, 2018.
https://doi.org/10.1007/978-3-030-02738-4_27

compression format—tiny portable graphics (TPG)[1], claiming that for the same image quality, the volume of TPG image is much smaller than that of other image formats (*e.g.* JPEG, PNG, GIF, WebP). However, the lossy compression artifacts cannot be fully removed, especially at low coding bit-rates. As a result, how to effectively reduce compression artifacts remains an important problem.

Some compressive sensing-based post-processing approaches are first proposed. The works in [6] perform filtering along block boundaries to reduce the blocking artifacts. Liew *et al.* [7] apply overcomplete wavelet representation to suppress block and ringing artifacts. Recently, convolution neural networks (CNN) have explosive popularity and powerful capability on both high-level and low-level image processing tasks. As to artifacts reduction problem, Dong *et al.* first propose a four-layer artifacts reduction CNN (ARCNN) [8] to improve the quality of JPEG compressed images. Later, Dai *et al.* [9] integrate varial filter size into ARCNN model to improve its performance for artifacts reduction in HEVC intra-coding images (known as VRCNN model). Both of these two methods using a shallow network with only four-layers. The limited number of parameters have imposed restrictions on the capability of CNN models.

Deep learning, as indicated by the name, a deeper network increases the network complexity, such that increases its learning ability. In addition, "deeper is better" is widely observed in high-level vision tasks. Recently, a deeper network also starts to reveal its superiority in low-level image processing task. For instance, in single image super-resolution problem, the EDSR model [10] (with 32 layers) shows higher PSNR value than VDSR model [11] (with 20 layers). Both of them outperform the 4-layer SRCNN [12] model (which is the predecessor of ARCNN model). As a result, we propose to investigate how a deeper CNN can enhance the quality of decoded images.

2   Methodology

Our proposed method is based on the current successful image super-resolution model—EDSR [10], which has won the first prize in the NTIRE 2017 challenge on single image super-resolution [13]. The EDSR model contains 16 ResNet blocks to learn the residual of input images. The two de-convolution layers at the end super-resolve input images by a factor of 4. Inspired by its extraordinary performance, we adopt the similar model for our post-processing work. Specifically, we also using 16 blocks and residual learning for artifacts removing. Since input and out images are of the same resolution in our case, we remove the two de-convolution layers. In order to increase the receptive field, we change the first convolution layer in the first five residual blocks to dilated convolution with size 2. We call our proposed model as DDResNet—dilated deep residual network.

The dataset we used for training is from the deep learning based image compression post-processing competition[2]. The competition aims at improving

---

[1] https://www.chinainternetwatch.com/20567/tencents-new-image-patent-challenging-googles-webp/.

[2] http://staff.ustc.edu.cn/~dongeliu/chinamm2018challenge/index.html.

the visual quality of compressed images by eliminating artifacts. They provide about 1500 high-quality image dataset and the TPG compression codec. We first randomly crop input images into 64 × 64 image blocks and then apply TPG to compress these blocks with proper quantization parameters (QP). Our proposed model is trained on decoded images in YUV domain. We conduct testing on the provided 50 validation images. Image blocks without compression are adopted as ground truth for supervised learning. We implement the proposed networks with PyTorch and train them on a Nvidia Tesla K80 GPU.

We next show some primary results. We set QP value as 52 for TPG. We compare the performance of our proposed work with previous VRCNN [9] model. Table 1 states the quantitative results in terms of PNSR and SSIM values. It shows that our proposed DDRestNet model can improve the quality of TPG compressed image with 0.5 dB on average, and outperform VRCNN with 0.2 dB. Subjective results of a cropped image patch are shown in Fig. 1. (a) is the TPG compressed image, we can see obvious block artifacts. The post-processed result with DDResNet is shown in (b), where the block artifacts have been removed. (c) is the ground truth. Results show that DDRestNet can effectively remove block artifacts.

Table 1. Quantitative evaluation of the proposed DDResNet model, in terms of PSNR (dB) and SSIM

Method	TPG	VRCNN	DDResNet (**proposed**)
PSNR (dB)	35.78	36.07	**36.27**
SSIM	0.8705	0.8782	**0.8814**

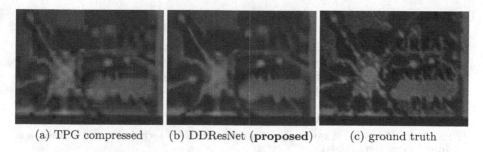

(a) TPG compressed   (b) DDResNet (**proposed**)   (c) ground truth

Fig. 1. Subjective results: (a) TPG compressed image with QP = 52; (b) result after our DDResNet post-processing model; (c) ground truth.

2.1   Discussing

Although our primary results demonstrate that a deeper network can result in better PSNR and SSIM values than a shallow VRCNN network, there are still some points require further investigation. First, as we can see in Fig. 1, although

DDResNet removed the block artifacts from the input image, the output becomes blurry. Moreover, some high-frequency details in ground truth images are not reconstructed in the output. Hence, is it possible we can add some demanding details during post-processing model? This is worth our further study.

The second concern is about running time. Real-time compression and transmission are important for a lot of image/video applications. Hence, we need to make sure the post-processing step run in a reasonable time. A deeper network always requires longer processing time. Our future work also needs to focus on how to further improve the quality of decoded images, but also cutting down the running time.

3   Conclusion

Lossy image compression algorithms usually induce annoying blocking artifacts, blurring and ringing effects on decoded images. To efficiently eliminate these artifacts is an important post-processing step. In this paper, inspired by the extraordinary performance of deeper network on single image super-resolution, we investigate how a deeper network can surpass a shallow network to further improve the quality of decoded images. We adopt a network with 16 residual blocks and change the first convolution layer in the first five residual blocks to dilated convolution with size 2. The primary experimental results show that the proposed model can outperform an existing CNN based post-processing method.

Acknowledgement. This work has been supported in part by the National Natural Science Foundation of China 61701310, and in part by the New Talent Start-up Foundation of Shenzhen University 2018080.

References

1. Wallace, G.K.: The JPEG still picture compression standard. Commun. ACM **34**(4), 30–44 (1991)
2. Wiegand, T.: Overview of the H. 264/AVC video coding standard. IEEE Trans. Circ. Syst. Video Technol. **13**(7), 560–576 (2003)
3. Sullivan, G.J.: Overview of the high efficiency video coding (HEVC) standard. IEEE Trans. Circ. Syst. Video Technol. **22**(12), 1649–1668 (2012)
4. Pal, N.R., Pal, S.K.: A review on image segmentation techniques. Pattern Recogn. **26**(9), 1277–1294 (1993)
5. Yuan, Y., et al.: Unsupervised image super-resolution using cycle-in-cycle generative adversarial networks. Methods **30**, 32 (2018)
6. Wang, C., Zhou, J., Liu, S.: Adaptive non-local means filter for image deblocking. Sig. Process. Image Commun. **28**(5), 522–530 (2013)
7. Liew, A.W.-C., Yan, H.: Blocking artifacts suppression in block-coded images using overcomplete wavelet representation. IEEE Trans. Circ. Syst. Video Technol. **14**(4), 450–461 (2004)
8. Dong, C., et al.: Compression artifacts reduction by a deep convolutional network. In: Proceedings of the IEEE International Conference on Computer Vision (2015)

9. Dai, Y., Liu, D., Wu, F.: A convolutional neural network approach for post-processing in HEVC intra coding. In: Amsaleg, L., Guðmundsson, G.Þ., Gurrin, C., Jónsson, B.Þ., Satoh, S. (eds.) MMM 2017. LNCS, vol. 10132, pp. 28–39. Springer, Cham (2017). https://doi.org/10.1007/978-3-319-51811-4_3

10. Lim, B., et al.: Enhanced deep residual networks for single image super-resolution. In: IEEE Conference on Computer Vision and Pattern Recognition (CVPR) Workshops, vol. 1, no. 2 (2017)

11. Kim, J., Kwon Lee, J., Mu Lee, K.: Accurate image super-resolution using very deep convolutional networks. In: Proceedings of the IEEE Conference on Computer Vision and Pattern Recognition (2016)

12. Chao, D.: Image super-resolution using deep convolutional networks. IEEE Trans. Pattern Anal. Mach. Intell. **38**(2), 295–307 (2016)

13. Agustsson, E., Timofte, R.: NTIRE 2017 challenge on single image super-resolution: dataset and study. In: IEEE Conference on Computer Vision and Pattern Recognition (CVPR) Workshops, vol. 3 (2017)

Underground Intelligent Logistic System Integrated with Internet of Things

Qiang Yang[1], Guohao Li[2], Ting Cai[3], and Qiang Wang[4(✉)]

[1] Huazhong University of Science and Technology, Wuhan, China
1056600872@qq.com
[2] Jilin University, Changchun, China
15171434275@163.com
[3] Sichuan University, Chengdu, China
1241568379@qq.com
[4] Wuhan University of Technology, Wuhan, China
wangqiang@whut.edu.cn

Abstract. In this paper, the urban underground intelligent logistic system is investigated to supply the demand of smart cities. The architecture, network layout, management and distribution are discussed in brief. Combined with Internet of Things (IoT) technology, smart monitoring, information integration, and intelligent decision-making will be built in the system to optimize the service efficiency and operational costs.

Keywords: Underground intelligent logistic · Internet of Things (IoT)
Smart cities

1 Introduction

Urban underground intelligent logistic system makes full use of city's three-dimensional space through converting freight into underground, and intensively dispatching resources to achieve low-carbon and high-efficiency transportation with optimal time and space costs. Its details are shown in Fig. 1.

With features such as high speed, full automation, low energy consumption and less pollution, integrating advanced theoretic methods such as IoT technology and artificial intelligence, and assisted with intelligent facilities and equipment, an intelligent and standardized logistic transportation system is constructed to guarantee the compatibility with smart cities in the future.

2 Architecture

According to the different functions, this system can be divided into physical part and control part. The physical part can be composed with underground operation facilities, ground connection and intelligent terminal, mainly including transportation network, delivery vehicles, power facilities, transportation terminals, etc. The control part mainly includes the information management, information control, navigation system, and

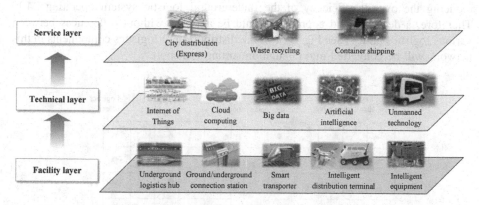

Fig. 1. Urban underground intelligent logistic system

maintenance management. Items are accepted or issued in the ground connection facilities, and automatic sorting and transportation are completed in the underground operation facilities. Finally, goods are delivered to the customer through intelligent terminals. The detail architecture is described as shown in Fig. 2.

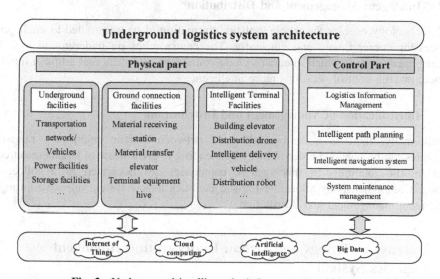

Fig. 2. Underground intelligent logistics system architecture

3 Conception

3.1 Decentralized Network Layout

The traditional logistics system usually adopts network layout with tree structured. However, traditional layout will cause nodes with different operational levels, thus reducing the overall efficiency of the underground logistic system operating 24 h. Therefore, a decentralized approach should be adopted without differences between various logistics nodes (See Fig. 3), and the distribution of logistics components in this network will be converted into circulation sorting transport.

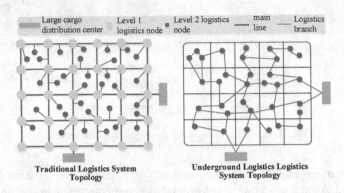

Fig. 3. Decentralized network layout

3.2 Intelligent Management and Distribution

IoT technology enables the whole logistic information to be transmitted to intelligent processing center timely and efficiently. The center relies on underground logistic management system which integrates cloud computing, big data, and artificial intelligence, making control decisions more intelligent.

3.3 Intensification of Management and Distribution

Traditionally, there is a "zero-sum" game between logistic enterprises. Logistic activities can be operated independently that leading to great waste of human resources and logistic facilities. In this system, companies are integrated as a collective group. Comprehensively allocating logistic facilities makes system intensive through intelligent management and distribution.

4 Internet of Things and Urban Underground Intelligent Logistics System

The application of the IoT technology in urban underground intelligent logistic system is divided into four levels, which are the perception layer, transport layer, support layer, and application layer. The detailed architecture can be seen in Figs. 4 and 5.

Internet of Things architecture

Application layer	Public logistics information platform	Intelligent temperature-controlled automatic guided vehicle	Embedded smart technology
			Blockchain technology
Support layer	Cloud computing	Database Technology	
Transport layer	Machine to Machine(M2M)	Digital trunking communication	
Perceptual layer	Wireless sensor networks (WSN)	Radio Frequency Identification(RFID)	Augmented Reality(AR)

Fig. 4. Internet of Things architecture

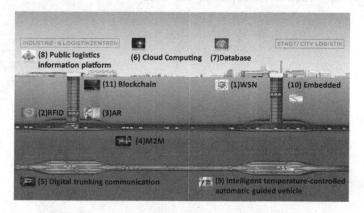

Fig. 5. Technology included in the Internet of Things

The perceptual layer uses sensor technology to fully sense and collect data information. The transport layer serves as a bridge between the perceptual layer and the support layer, and plays a decisive role in the transmission quality of information data. The support layer include cloud storage and cloud computing technologies, which can quickly process all kinds of information in the underground logistic system. The service layer is directly related to the final service quality of the logistic industry.

5 Summary

This paper puts forward a new concept of urban underground intelligent logistic system. It mainly elaborates on two parts of the overall design and technical analysis. In the overall design, a network structure of distributed logistics nodes is proposed, intelligent management, intensification of distribution and IoT technology are expected to build an underground smart logistic system to ensure quick and safe arrival of goods.

References

1. Yilmaz, A., Javed, O., Shah, M.: Object tracking: a survey. ACM Comput. Surv. (CSUR) **38** (4), 1–45 (2006)
2. Guerrero-Ibanez, J.A., Zeadally, S., Contreras-Castillo, J.: Integration challenges of intelligent transportation systems with connected vehicle, cloud computing, and internet of things technologies. IEEE Wirel. Commun. **22**(6), 122–128 (2015)
3. Ma, C.L., Mao, H.J., Yang, X.C., et al.: Study on the development mode of urban underground logistics system. Serv. Sci. Manag. Res. **3**(32), 7–12 (2014)
4. Yaqoob, I., Ahmed, E., Hashem, I.A.T., et al.: Internet of things architecture: recent advances, taxonomy, requirements, and open challenges. IEEE Wirel. Commun. **24**(3), 10–16 (2017)
5. Chen, Z., Dong, J., Ren, R., et al.: Urban underground logistics system in China: opportunities or challenges? Undergr. Space **2**(3), 195–208 (2017)
6. Li, T., Li, Q.Q., Su, W.L., et al.: Optimization layout of underground logistics network in big cities. Syst. Eng.-Theor. Pract. **33**(4), 971–980 (2012)

Author Index

Aida, Kento   1, 160, 221

Bajpai, Deepak   109
Bui, Khac-Hoai Nam   185

Cai, Ting   298
Camacho, David   185
Cao, Jingjing   148, 258, 278
Carchiolo, V.   100, 270
Chen, Changsheng   282
Chen, Dingfang   248
Chen, Hailong   148
Chen, Mingkang   288
Chen, Yen-Hao   52
Cheng, Minquan   75
Cheng, Zhengshu   248

Denzinger, Jörg   27
Di Fatta, Giuseppe   235
Di Luccio, Diana   197

Fan, Chun-I   52
Figueiredo, Renato   122
Fortino, Giancarlo   235
Foster, Ian   197

Gaedke, Martin   221
Giunta, Giulio   197
Grassia, M.   100, 270

He, Lijun   258
Hu, Jingbo   248
Huang, Jheng-Jia   52

Jiang, Jing   75
Jin, Zeyi   278
Jo, Nayoung   185
Jung, Jason J.   185

Koshiba, Takeshi   134
Kosta, Sokol   197
Kuo, Hsin-Nan   52
Kuo, Yuan-Han   40

Lan, Fengbo   282
Lässig, Jörg   221
Leppänen, Teemu   235
Li, Guohao   298
Li, Lijie   248
Li, Wenfeng   258, 278
Lin, Cho-Chin   40
Linnartz, J. P. M. G.   87
Longheu, A.   100, 270
Lovén, Lauri   235

Malgeri, M.   100, 270
Mangioni, G.   100, 270
Mei, Jie   248
Miyashita, Tomoyuki   16
Montella, Raffaele   197
Mow, Wai Ho   282

Nguyen, Hoang Long   185
Nygren, Nick   27

Ogawa, Kohichi   209

Papatsimpa, C.   87
Parque, Victor   16
Perera, Maharage Nisansala Sevwandi   134
Pistauer, Markus   64

Rech, Alexander   64
Riekki, Jukka   235
Russo, Wilma   235

Saga, Kazushige   160
Sage, Kazushige   1
Savaglio, Claudio   235
Steger, Christian   64
Subratie, Kensworth   122
Sun, Guang-Hong   173
Sun, Jingtao   1, 148, 160, 221, 278, 288, 293

Takefusa, Atsuko   160
Tanjo, Tomoya   1, 160
Thulasiram, Ruppa K.   109

Thulasiraman, Parimala   109
Tseng, Yi-Fan   52

Ullrich, Markus   221

Vinayak, Muskan   109

Wang, Miaohui   293
Wang, Qiang   148, 278, 298
Wei, Ruizhong   75

Yang, Cheng   1
Yang, Qiang   298
Yen, Li-Hsing   173
Yoshiura, Noriaki   209
Yu, Meng   148
Yuan, Yuan   293

Zhang, Qiaoling   75
Zhang, Yu   258

Printed in the United States
By Bookmasters